State housing in Britain

State housing in Britain

Stephen Merrett

Routledge & Kegan Paul
London, Boston and Henley

567724

First published in 1979
by Routledge & Kegan Paul
39 Store Street,
London, WC1E 7DD
Broadway House,
Newtown Road,
Henley-on-Thames,
Oxon RG9 1EN and
9 Park Street,
Boston, Mass.02108, USA
Set in IBM Press Roman
by Hope Services, Abingdon
and printed in Great Britain by
Lowe & Brydone Printers Ltd,
Thetford, Norfolk
© Stephen Merrett 1979

British Library Cataloguing in Publication Data

Merrett, Stephen

State housing in Britain.
1. Public housing – Great Britain – History
I. Title
363.5   HD7333.A3   79-40217

ISBN 0 7100 0264 5
ISBN 0 7100 0265 3 Pbk

Contents

Contents

Contents

Appendices 305

Figures and graphs

Figures and graphs

Tables

Preface

The subject matter of this book is the local authority housing sector in Britain. The importance of the subject derives from the fact that more than one-quarter of all British households live in a council house or flat.

The book is divided into three parts. Part I consists of two chapters and provides a historical introduction which reviews the origins and development of the local authority housing sector from the 1840s right through to the outbreak of World War II in 1939.

Part II covers the experience since 1945, in a series of six chapters which in turn deal with access to land, the housebuilding industry, the balance between rehabilitation and redevelopment, sources and costs of capital finance, determinants of rents and subsidies and, finally, the management of the municipal stock.

The third and last part of the book is concerned above all with the formation and implementation of policy. One chapter takes all the themes examined separately in Part II and integrates them in an analysis of the evolution of housing policy since the war within the context of broader political and economic change. A second chapter looks at the entire experience of the last 130 years and highlights its main features, linking them to an explicit view of the role of the state. The final chapter of the book puts forward proposals for the measures I believe to be necessary for the housing problem, as we at present understand it, to be be solved.

The appendices include some important and unique statistical series as well as a summary chronology from 1851 of all the parliamentary legislation on the building of local authority dwellings. There is also a select bibliography.

A few words seem justified about the academic discipline on which the analysis is based. I was trained as an economist and all my working life has been spent on applied economic research into subjects as diverse as education finance, manpower planning, the industrial economics of fertiliser production, international investment and trade, and the design of effective space rocket and satellite research programmes. Whilst *in principle* I believe in the need to create a single science of society, this work is marked heavily by my formal training in a single discipline. However, as the reader will see, at no point in this study are academic boundaries drawn from a fear of straying beyond the domain of the 'economics of housing'. In particular, in the investigation of the housing question in Britain, both past and present, I believe it is essential to explore the political dimension. Research which does not do this, particularly when one's concern is with housing provided by the state, is mutilated from the outset.

With respect to the discipline of economics, the school with which I most closely identify is that associated with the names of Joan Robinson and Piero Sraffa of the University of Cambridge, a paradigm sometimes referred to as the Anglo-Italian school. This brings together authors as distinct as David Ricardo, Karl Marx, Michal Kalecki and John Maynard Keynes. As a result I draw only marginally on neo-classical economic theory and do not employ at all the value analysis of Marxist political economy.

During the course of my work I have benefited enormously from the advice, comment and criticism of a great number of people. In particular I wish to thank the students and staff of the Bartlett School of Architecture and Planning at University College, London, where I teach, the members of the Political Economy of Housing Workshop where many of these ideas were first set out, and the staff of the Centre for Environmental Studies in London from which institution I received a one-year fellowship enabling me to complete the manuscript. I am especially indebted to Michael Edwards of University College, London, A.E. Holmans of the Department of the Environment and Richard Kirwan for their detailed comments on the draft of the book. I must stress that they bear no responsibility for its contents. I am also grateful to Andrew Laing, who drew the graphs and figures and Judy Harloe, who typed the manuscript. Finally a special vote of thanks goes to Fred Gray of the University of Sussex who wrote Chapter 8 of this book.

Stephen Merrett
University College, London

Abbreviations

ABCS	Annual Bulletin of Construction Statistics
AMC	Association of Municipal Corporations
BERU	Building Economics Research Unit
bph	bedspaces per hectare
CBA	Cost-Benefit Analysis
CDP	Community Development Project
CES	Centre for Environmental Studies
CHAC	Central Housing Advisory Committee
CIPFA	Chartered Institute of Public Finance and Accountancy
CIT	City Improvement Trust
CITB	Construction Industry Training Board
CLB	Central Land Board
CLF	Consolidated Loans Fund
CPO	Compulsory Purchase Order
CURS	Centre for Urban and Regional Studies
DCE	Domestic Credit Expansion
DLO	Direct Labour Organisation
DoE	Department of the Environment
EEDC	East End Dwellings Company
GB	Great Britain
GIA	General Improvement Area
GLC	Greater London Council
HAA	Housing Action Area
HCS	Housing and Construction Statistics
HIP	Housing Investment Programme
HMSO	His/Her Majesty's Stationery Office
HRA	Housing Revenue Account
HSGB	Housing Statistics Great Britain
IIDC	Improved Industrial Dwellings Company
IMF	International Monetary Fund
IMTA	Institute of Municipal Treasurers and Accountants
LCC	London County Council

Abbreviations

LGB   Local Government Board
MBW   Metropolitan Board of Works
MHLG   Ministry of Housing and Local Government
MLR   Minimum Lending Rate
MoH   Ministry of Health
MP   Member of Parliament
NBPI   National Board for Prices and Incomes
NEDC   National Economic Development Committee
NEDO   National Economic Development Office
NHBC   National House Building Committee
NIESR   National Institute of Economic and Social Research
OPEC   Organisation of Petroleum Exporting Countries
PSBR   Public Sector Borrowing Requirement
PWLB   Public Works Loan Board
PWLC   Public Works Loan Commissioners
SBC   Supplementary Benefits Commission
SSHA   Scottish Special Housing Association
SSRC   Social Science Research Council
TUC   Trades Union Congress
UK   United Kingdom
USA   United States of America
UTA   United Tenants Association

Part I

History

ONE

Before 1914: accumulation, contradiction and reform

1 Cities and slums

For reasons which continue to be a matter of controversy, the rate of growth of the population of Britain accelerated after the mid-eighteenth century to a level which was without historical precedent. Whilst the population of England and Wales rose from perhaps 5¼ million in 1700 to 6½ million fifty years later, by 1801 it exceeded 9 million, by 1841 it stood at some 16 million and by 1901 it was twice as large again.[1]

This absolute increase was accompanied during the course of the Industrial Revolution by a spatial concentration of people. The accumulation of productive capital, and thereby employment opportunities, took place predominantly in a relatively small number of urban areas because of the natural resource and climatic advantages of specific locations or because of the economies of proximity to existing suppliers and markets. As the great manufacturing towns grew, the labour supply generated by them itself then attracted new investment. For the first time in British history the working-class masses toiled together in industrial cities. In 1750 there were only two cities in Britain with more than 50,000 inhabitants; fifty years later the number stood at eight and then twenty-nine by 1851, when for the first time more people lived in the town than in the countryside. By 1881 two out of every five people in England and Wales lived in one of six conurbations: London, south-east Lancashire, the West Midlands, West Yorkshire, Merseyside and Tyneside.[2] The expansion of London was unmatched: one million inhabitants in 1801, 2 million in 1841, and 5 million by 1881.

The towns were abominable places in which to live. There was the excrement of the industrial process to endure—the sulphurous smoke of the furnace, the stench of the slaughterhouse, the poisonous effluent of the dye factory. There was the absence or inadequacy of those preconditions of a healthy urban environment, the disposal of sewage and refuse and the provision of unpolluted water. And there were the workers' dwellings themselves: by present standards the great majority were slums. De Tocqueville voiced the opinion of many contemporary commentators when, speaking of Manchester, he said:[3] 'Here humanity attains its most complete development and its most brutish; here civilisation works its miracles, and civilised man is turned back almost into a savage.'

The working class lived in slums because they could afford nothing better. Since 'slum' is most familiar as a moral, legal or physical term, it is worthwhile justifying briefly why its political economic dimension is stressed repeatedly in this chapter. In capitalist society the level of real wages is determined by the average level of labour productivity and by the proportion of the total product appropriated for consumption or reinvestment by the classes which own the land and the means of production. Labour productivity in nineteenth-century manufacturing and agriculture was extremely low, fundamentally because in comparison with the 1970s the stock of capital per worker was small, technical processes were primitive and the potential skills of the labour force were still undeveloped. The result was that real wages were low. Indeed, they were considered by the great authors of classical political economy, Malthus, Ricardo and Marx, to be barely sufficient for the subsistence of the working people. This was reflected in the quantity and quality of the entire range of commodities consumed by the workers, most palpably in the case of their dwellings.[4]

These were ill-lit, poorly ventilated, often without means of heating, bare of facilities such as water closets and sinks, with leaking roofs and bulging walls. Above all, they were overcrowded. Given the private ownership of the land and the structures thereon, it was necessary for the poor to pay a price 'for the permission to inhabit the earth'.[5] Low incomes imply weak effective demand for every commodity, and the most effective legal means for the indigent to assert their power in the housing market was by high-density living.[6] Cellars, back-to-backs, huddled courts and, towards the end of the century, soaring tenement blocks were the devices of design for increasing the number of rooms per acre. Overcrowding raised the number of persons per room. Landlords were often sufficiently moved by the plight of the multitude to push out their existing tenants, middle classes, tradesmen, and so forth, in order to pack in the poor 'in maggot numbers' and simultaneously raise the rate of return earned on their capital. This possibility was most evident when the houses in question were close to markets for casual labour. 'The crowding arises from the desire of the working population to be "near their bread", as they express it; and the high rental of the tenements, averaging four shillings a room per week, arises naturally from this rush upon a particular spot.'[7] In this case we have overcrowding not merely as a response to the inability of workers to pay the production costs of better homes but also to the spatial concentration of capitalist industry within the city driving up rents.

The sensation of these conditions at their worst can be conveyed to a degree by quoting the evidence of a city missionary on the public lodging houses:[8]

On my district is a house containing eight rooms, which are all let separately to individuals who furnish and relet them. The parlour measures 18 ft. by 10 ft. Beds are arranged on each side of the room, composed of straw, shavings, rags, etc. In this one room slept, on the night previous to my inquiry, 27 male and female adults, 31 children, and two or three dogs, making in all 58 human beings breathing the contaminated atmosphere of a close room. In the top room of the same house, measuring 12 ft. by 10 ft., there are six beds, and, on the same night, there slept in them 32 human beings, all breathing the pestiferous air of a hole not fit to keep swine in. The beds are so close together that, when let down on the floor, there is no room to pass between them; and they who sleep in the beds furthest from the door can, consequently, only get into them by crawling over the beds which are nearer the door. In one district alone there are 270 such rooms.

The slums consisted not only of existing structures in decay, although these were the worst. Slums were also built. Particularly in the first half of the century building was shoddy, foundations insecure and the materials used were unable to keep out the rain. 'In some cases new estates were built on sites still heaving with refuse, lightly cemented over to provide a surface which, if temporarily flat and dry, soon split to produce settlement cracks, rising damp, and unpleasant smells.'[9] The attempt to use every scrap of available land produced veritable warrens.

Thus developed the stinking labyrinths of our great cities with their narrow streets, their courts heaped with human excreta and rubbish, their decrepit buildings groaning with humanity. James Smith's account of Leeds—notorious Leeds—in the 1840s is worth repeating:[10]

But by far the most unhealthy localities of Leeds are close squares of houses, or yards, as they are called, which have been erected for the accommodation of working people. Some of these, though situated in comparatively high ground, are airless from the enclosed structure, and, being wholly unprovided with any form of under-drainage or convenience, or arrangements for cleansing, are one mass of damp and filth. In some instances I found cellars or under-rooms with from two to six inches of water standing over the floors, and putrid from its stagnation in one case, from receiving the soakage of the slop-water standing in pools in the street adjoining. The ashes, garbage, and filth of all kinds are thrown from the doors and windows of the houses upon the surface of the streets and courts; and in some cases, where a gallery of entrance has been erected for the inhabitants of the second floor, the whole of the slops and filth are thrown over the gallery in front of the houses beneath, and as the ground is often sloping towards the doors of the lower dwellings, they are inundated with water and filth, and the poor inhabitants placed in a miserable and unhealthy condition. The privies, as usual in such situations, are few, in proportion to the number of inhabitants; they are open to view both in front and rear, are invariably in a filthy condition, and often remain without the removal of any portion of the filth for six months.

2 Health, productivity and violence

These developments in capitalist urbanisation contained certain contra-dictions for capitalism itself, that is, they nurtured from within the social formation threats to its growth and even its stability. In the first place the towns were dangerous to live in because of the hazards to health. This was first brought to the notice of a horrified public with unchallengeable force in the 1830s through the work of Edwin Chadwick, the first Secretary to the Poor Law Commissioners and by a continuing flow thereafter of documented reports, official and private.

Medical science, and medical opinion even more so, was at this time a terrain of great ignorance. For example, before Snow's researches into cholera in 1848, the contagionists argued that it spread via contact with infected persons whilst the miasmatists argued that it had spontaneous origin in the putrescent gases thrown up by mounds of filth. Neither party understood that the disease was water-borne.[11] However, there soon developed a widespread acceptance of the view, whatever the scientific foundation, that polluted air, foul water supplies and high residential densities were together in large measure responsible for the appalling statistics on sickness and mortality. The resolution by the more prosperous members of society that something had to be done was probably stimulated most effectively by King Cholera, a malady without respect for social station. Unlike typhus, it struck in every residential quarter of the city. As if the misery of ill-health and untimely death were insufficient, Chadwick, a Benthamite, also expressed the argument against disease in the narrowest terms of cost and benefit to the middle-class ratepayer. Filth caused epidemics, epidemics brought the pauperisation of widows and orphans, and paupers meant increased taxation for poor relief.[12]

It is worth observing that it was in the middle decades of the nineteenth century that government policy on health and housing first became so entwined and examples without number could be cited to demonstrate this. For example, the first careful definition of the term 'overcrowding', drawn up by Dr John Simon, Chadwick's successor at the Poor Law Board, illustrates well the perceived relation between housing conditions, the stench of the slum and the threat to health. Overcrowding existed where people and space were in such proportion that:[13]

> no obtainable quantity of ventilation will keep the air of the
> dwelling-space free from hurtfully large accumulations of animal
> effluvium,—cases, where the dwelling-space at its best stinks more
> or less with decomposing human excretions, and where, at its worst,
> this filthy atmosphere may (and very often does) have, working
> and spreading within it, the taint of some contagious fever.

The second contradiction in the experience of urbanisation was that ill-health and poor housing reduced the productivity of labour and thereby profits. The direct relation, in principle, between the conditions of working-class existence and efficiency in employment was familiar. Productivity increases consequent upon higher real wages had been explained by Adam Smith in *The Wealth of Nations* as long before as 1776.[14] The argument was certainly accepted by the Royal Commission on Housing in its first report in 1885. Poor housing was said to be the major cause of poor performance at the work-place and absenteeism. Moreover, Gauldie has suggested that an important element in the material basis for the development of employer housing and company towns was the potential productivity gain:[15]

7

To some extent employers were feeling, indirectly, the effect of the workers' deteriorating living standards. The nagging ill health, the frequent absences, the apathy induced by poor diet and sleeplessness, the despair brought by constant infant deaths, the panic caused by rumours of fatal epidemics, the shiftlessness resulting from the impossibility of keeping clean or looking respectable, all these added up to make a poor, unresponsive labour force. The frequent early deaths of skilled and trained men meant the wastage of time spent in training and the need to teach processes and skills to a constantly replaced team of workers. The absence of the steadying effect of older men, when the average death of workers in towns was hardly into middle-age, left an unstable work force, easily roused to trouble-making, and, although fearful of openly expressed rebellion, often sullen with resentment.

The third contradiction was that 'the city destroyed society'. Hobsbawm has argued that the lack of human contact between classes brought about by the growth of manufacturing in the urban areas was far more explicit than it had been in agriculture and that 'The city was a volcano, to whose rumblings the rich and powerful listened with fear, and whose eruptions they dreaded.'[16] It was not by chance that in 1840 the first debate ever held in the House of Commons on the subject of health and housing went under the title 'Discontent among the Working Classes'. Edwin Chadwick himself was not slow to manipulate the prevailing fear of the violence of the mob among the well to do in order to consolidate support for the reform of public health. Social and political unrest was at its most turbulent between 1815 and 1848 but, in Gauldie's view, even after the suppression of organised protest the middle classes still feared that those whom economic circumstances forced to live in such squalor and misery might eventually rise up in revolution against the social order itself.[17]

3 The spectrum of reform

These problems of disease, low labour productivity and the real and potential violence of the urban multitude presented themselves with varying acuteness over time and place and with unequal impact on the fractions of the ruling classes. They were also conceptualised in many different ways. Nevertheless they did constitute the material basis from the 1840s onwards for the introduction of a spectrum of reforms. These reforms in aggregate and over many decades were to have the effect of resolving the contradictions of the urbanising process of the accumulation of capital. It was the very inconstancy in these determinants and in their perception by different social groups which gave reform a hesitant character: two steps forwards, one step back. This was particularly the case in that many governmental measures constituted breaches in the philosophy and policy of *laissez-faire* and it was untrammelled private enterprise which was credited with the technological triumph of the Industrial Revolution and the huge expansion of overseas trade, those foundations of British power and wealth in the nineteenth century. In retrospect, some of the rationalisations in defence of *laissez-faire* are stunning. Here, in opposition to the Public Health Bill of 1848, is *The Economist*, combining lugubriousness with pomposity:[18]

> In our condition suffering and evil are nature's admonitions;
> they cannot be got rid of; and the impatient attempts of
> benevolence to banish them from the world by legislation,
> before benevolence has learned their object and their end, have
> always been productive of more evil than good.

The measures taken to deal with slum housing and slum areas which I wish to consider here are public health legislation including the regulation of new building and the installation of social overhead capital; slum clearance; the 5 per cent philanthropy movement; and the growth of public housing. There were a number of other reformist activities which I shall not review at all, because in retrospect they made such little impact on the social life of the people as a whole. These were: employer housing and the company towns; the building societies; the freehold land societies; and the curious benevolence of the lady collectors.[19]

4 Legislating for the public health

It was the legislation on public health and the regulation of new building which constituted the strategic response to the self-destructive nature of *laissez-faire* urbanisation. Again it is necessary to emphasise that legislative progress was often faltering and that there was always a gap in the early years of an Act between what it laid down and what was practised.

What, then, were the main achievements in the decades before the First World War? First, the removal of existing accumulations of dung and muck and institution of regular street cleaning and garbage removal services. Second, the provision of pure supplies of water to most houses built in the last decade of the century, although not to every dwelling in the case of tenements. Third, the installation of enclosed sewerage systems and their connection to the majority of houses by means of drains. Fourth, the introduction of minimum requirements for the lighting and ventilation of houses and the banning of the building of back-to-backs. Fifth, legislative controls on the ventilation of rooms, on the structure of floors, hearths and staircases and on the height of rooms intended to be used for human habitation, and the abolition or regulation of the occupation of cellars. Sixth, a much more extensive provision of sinks, privies, water closets and wash-houses. Seventh, the creation of an administration at central and local government level to enforce the law. Eighth, the denomination of overcrowding as a statutory nuisance which laid the owner of a property open to prosecution.

The increasingly comprehensive legislation on housing and the regulation of building and its stricter enforcement over the six or seven decades before 1914 certainly helped to eradicate the worst manifestations of the existing slums and made the construction of new slums more and more difficult. But legislation did not at the same time raise the real wages of the proletariat, and thus there arose a conflict between the state's minimum requirements on the use-value of the workers' dwellings (in the broadest sense their quality), the higher construction costs which these implied and the exchange value of the workers' time in the labour market. We shall return to this question below; for the present the general relationships are set out in Fig. 1·1 whilst the concept of use-value is elaborated upon in note 20. It is worthy of note that the rise in average real wages in the second half of the nineteenth century did not solve the problem generated by this gap between the rental of adequate dwellings and what poorer tenants could pay.

5 Clearance and private improvement

The legislation referred to brought with it an amelioration in the condition of the existing slums. But it did not get rid of them altogether. The second dominant response to the problems associated with slum areas in the second half of the nineteenth century was clearance followed

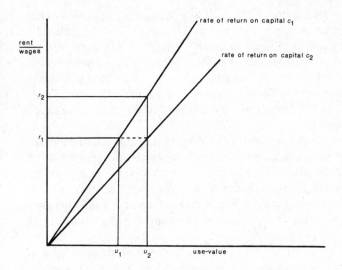

Figure 1·1   *The relation between private rent, dwelling use-value and the return on landlord's capital*
The vertical axis measures the family's rent payments as a percentage of household income. The horizontal axis measures the use-value of the dwelling which, given the organisation and labour productivity of the housebuilding industry, determines the capital cost of constructing the house and the current cost of maintaining it. Each of the two diagonal lines shows, for a given rate of return on landlord's capital (where $c_1 > c_2$), what the rent-wage ratio must be at any given use-value if wages are unchanged. We suppose that government legislation raises use-value from u_1 to u_2. If the required rate of return is c_1 the rent-wage ratio must rise from r_1 to r_2. If the ratio did not change, the rate of return would fall to c_2. Alternatively, if wages rose sufficiently, both the rent-wage ratio and the rate of return could remain unchanged. This figure demonstrates the economic tension between use-values (and therefore production costs), rent, wages, and the landlord's return. As use-values rise either the rent-wage ratio or money wages must also rise, or the rate of return must fall.

by 'improvement'. Enid Gauldie has argued in her invaluable history of working-class housing that the Victorian ruling class and middle class had conceived such a horror of those who lived in the slums that they wanted to be rid of them altogether. They settled, however, for the second best solution of demolishing their homes in a long-drawn-out

11

pacification programme. 'Clear away the filth, clear away disease, clear away the paupers. It was a simple and attractive logical progression.'[21] Dr John Simon employed an organic metaphor in his call for the amputation of diseased and congested areas. But the purging zeal of the reformers could also rise to a terrible lyricism. Octavia Hill, on a visit to the demolition of the Glasgow slums in 1874, said:[22] 'I felt as if some bright and purifying angel had laid a mighty finger on the squalid and neglected spot.'

These search and destroy tactics dovetailed neatly with the demand for cleared sites which the continuing progress of the economy thrust upon the cities. Land, land in huge quantities, was required in every part of our tangled urban areas in order to construct the newly invented railway, to provide grand new streets, to build law courts and the monumental architecture of our municipal administrations, to erect markets, warehouses and commercial offices.

I know of no statistics which show the scale of the demolition of working-class slum housing for the cause of improvement, but what is evident from the literature is how little new housing was built to rehouse those cleared. This is best documented in the case of the railway, likened by contemporaries to an invasion of the Huns. Dyos, for example, has calculated that in London alone 76,000 people were displaced by the advent of the steam train in the years 1853-1901. Where legislation existed, requiring the railway companies to provide alternative accommodation for those whose homes were destroyed, it was not effective. There appears to have been only one instance of a railway company actually carrying through its own rehousing scheme.[23]

With no new accommodation provided, the displaced poor moved into the existing stock of dwellings available in their area and consequently raised the degree of overcrowding there. '[Poor working men] rarely act till the men have come to pull the roof off their heads, and I have seen the people like people in a besieged town running to and fro, not knowing what on earth to do.'[24] Wohl informs us that in London in 1902-13, 70,000 working-class rooms were demolished to make way for improvements, of which only 15,000 were for new dwellings. 'The immediate result of this wholesale demolition and eviction was not the broad dispersion throughout London of the working-classes . . . but (due largely to the need to live near their work) increased crowding together in adjoining areas.'[25]

The legislation on which clearance with improvement was based consisted either of Acts specific to designated areas in particular cities or the two main measures which were countrywide: the 1868 Torrens Act and the 1875 Cross Act.[26] It was the local Acts which were most important in the total impact of improvement. In their case we see basically a transformation in land-use from workers' housing to commercial development and social infrastructure which rarely benefited the manual working class directly. In a sense these specific schemes appropriated the city for the bourgeoisie. The Cross Act was quite different. Torrens had given local authorities the power, but not the duty, to knock down individual insanitary houses. The purpose of the Cross Act was to permit area-wide clearance. However, it laid an obligation upon the local authority to rehouse on site those displaced during clearance. Admittedly an amendment to the Act in 1879 permitted rehousing on alternative sites and in 1882 the rehousing obligation was reduced to one-half of the original population.[27] Nevertheless, transformation in the type of land-use had clearly not been built into the Act.[28] Its purpose was essentially a transformation within a single land-use category, the tearing down of the slums and the erection of model dwellings in their place.

But by 1884–5 the Royal Commission on Housing reported that in the ten years since the passage of the Cross Act only nine towns had begun improvement schemes under it. Of these the only one of any size was in Birmingham where Joseph Chamberlain had raised a loan of £1·5 million to clear the central areas of the city for reletting to commercial developers.

How can we account for the ineffectiveness of the clearance legislation promoted by Torrens and Cross? This is best done by interpreting the process in terms of the interests of the social groups concerned.

The tenants. We know of no tenant opposition to the Acts, but this does not tell us very much. As Corrigan and Ginsburg have pointed out, working-class struggles on a local scale historically have been recorded only infrequently.[29] But it is worthwhile pointing out that the medical officers whose duty it was to report the existence of insanitary premises were often unwilling to act. For clearance meant eviction and eviction led to an increase in overcrowding in the remaining stock of low-rent property in the area. The Torrens Act contained no rehousing provision. Even the Cross Act, with its rehousing obligations, presented a threat to those who dwelt in the slum. The amendments of 1879 and 1882 meant that new housing sufficient for the needs of only half the original population would be rebuilt, possibly at a quite different site from that demolished. Furthermore, between eviction and resettlement there was a considerable time delay. There were even cases where there was no rehousing at all, as in Birmingham where Chamberlain had evaded the statutory obligations by using the argument that improvement was shifting factory employment to the suburbs and that therefore central city residence was no longer convenient to those displaced.[30] Above all, the central dilemma for the worker who lived in the slums was that he and his family simply would be unable to afford to pay the rents of the non-slums which replaced his existing home. Wohl writes:[31]

> The medical officer of health for St. Marylebone argued that to the working classes 'sanitary improvement is a very car of juggernaut, pretty to look at, but which crushes them. Not a house is rebuilt, not an area cleared, but their possibilities of existence are diminished, their livings made dearer and harder.' Had the Torrens and Cross Acts been used thoroughly, he continued, 'an appalling amount of misery, of overcrowding, and of poverty would have been the result', and voicing an opinion common to medical officers, he concluded that 'until tenements are built in proportion to those demolished at low rents, it is not humane to press on large schemes.'

The landlords. In general, they were opposed to the Act since these brought the destruction of income-bearing capital. Landlords knew well enough how profitable low-rent accommodation could be when conjoined with overcrowding: 'the exorbitant rentals obtained from certain classes of houses, create a powerful interest opposed to all sanitary reform, promote the maintenance of slums, and hinder the progress of public improvements . . .'[32] Torrens provided no compensation when unfit houses were closed and so some owners would choose to carry out minimal maintenance in order to avoid the demolition gang. The Cross Act did provide compensation, based on the rents generated by the property. The shrewder landlords stuffed in extra tenants before valuation to increase their claim and the cost of compensation also played a part in checking the widespread use of the Act.

The ratepayers. Their opposition rested on the fact that it was they who bore the burden of the financial losses incurred.

The councillors. Gauldie has suggested that the town councils attracted small tradesmen and shopkeepers, the same class to which the majority of investors in cheap housing belonged. Indeed, many slum landlords were councillors. Moreover, they might depend on the large ratepayers for patronage, employment, trade or social acceptance. These were the 'petty and sinister interests' against whom Chadwick raged. In these circumstances their opposition to Cross is not difficult to understand. Furthermore, the extraordinarily cumbersome character of the Act provided them with objective grounds for prevarication. The town councils represented the myopic interests of the local petit bourgeoisie. The Torrens and Cross Acts were a part, a small part, of those attempts by the state, representing the longer-term interests of the big financial and industrial bourgeoisie, to secure the health and safety of the capitalist city. The relative failure of the Acts was a victory for reaction. It was the same conflict of environmental interests which brought about the reform of local government in the second half of the nineteenth century so that the urban environment could be controlled more adequately by the state.

The developers.   A private developer who purchased or leased a cleared site had the statutory obligation to rehouse. There was little or no profit in this and it was another institution, the model dwelling association, which was found necessary to substitute for this lack of enterprise. It is to these bodies, the 5 per cent philanthropists, that we now turn.

6   Philanthropy at 5 per cent

The model dwellings associations intended to demonstrate in an exemplary manner that wage earners could be provided with dwellings containing a regular water supply, adequate sewage disposal and proper ventilation at a rent they could afford without overcrowding, and that simultaneously the investor in such dwellings could earn a modest return on his capital.

In terms of the scale of their construction efforts, the main institutions were the Peabody Trust, the Improved Industrial Dwellings Co., the East End Dwellings Co., the Guinness Trust and the 4% Industrial Dwellings Co. Of these five all but the EEDC were founded by extremely wealthy capitalists from the world of industry and finance: Peabody, Waterlow, Guinness, and Rothschild. It was in London that their efforts were concentrated.

The first point worth making about the associations is that to the

workers displaced from the sites cleared for these exemplary construc-
tions, they must have seemed a scourge rather than a case of capitalist
philanthropy. Those pushed out during clearance were not the ones
who moved in on the termination of building work. One woman told
an East-End clergyman:[33] 'I came to London 25 years ago and I have
never lived in any room more than two years yet: they always say they
want to pull the house down to build dwellings for poor people, but
I've never got into one yet.' Some were excluded because of their
unruly or immoral character. More effective still were the rent levels
charged, which exceeded what the poor were prepared to pay.

Who then did move in? At this point it is useful to recall that the
urban working class in the last century was not a homogeneous mass.
There were very wide variations in earnings, even within the manual
working class, reflecting differences in wage rates and the regularity of
employment. Hobsbawm writes:[34]

> R. Dudley Baxter, calculating the size of the various British classes
> in 1867, reckoned that over three quarters—seventy-seven per cent
> of the 24·1 million inhabitants of Great Britain belonged to the
> 'manual labour class'; and he included among the 'middle class'
> all office-workers, and shop assistants, all shopkeepers, however
> tiny, all foremen and supervisory workers, and the like. Not more
> than fifteen per cent of these belonged to a skilled or moderately
> well-paid aristocracy of labour—say, with wages of 28 shillings a
> week to £2—rather over half to the unskilled, agricultural, women
> and other underpaid—say with wages of 10–12 shillings a week—
> and the balance to intermediate ranges.

These data can be set alongside the declared objective of Sir Sydney
Waterlow of the IIDC:[35] 'the wisest plan is to meet the wants of that
portion of the working classes most worth working for, those earning
from £1.5s to £2 per week.' Waterlow's intention, then, was to house
the labour aristocracy. In practice the income levels of the tenants of
the model associations were scattered over a wider range. The average
wage of the head of household in Peabody flats in 1881–91 was 24
shillings and their rents were equal to 20 per cent of this wage.[36]

The inconsistency between philanthropic posture and the fact of
eviction without rehousing was ignored where possible. But this exclusiveness in practice of their lettings policy was defended in terms of
filtering, that recurrent rationalisation of inegalitarian housing policies
in modern times. The IIDC phrased it in this way:[37]

We must take the class as of various degrees; the upper, middle, and lower of the labouring classes; it would not have been right to build down to the lowest class, because you must have built a class of tenement which I hope none of them would be satisfied with at the end of 50 years; we have rather tried to build for the best class, and by lifting them up to leave more room for the second and third who are below them.

I have argued in Section 1 above that to compete successfully for the right to inhabit our cities, the poor were constrained to accept conditions of appalling overcrowding. Overcrowding was not permitted by the 5 per cent movement. By 1885 only 692 out of 9600 rooms in London's model tenements were in the form of one room flats and large families in any case were not permitted to pack into them.[38] Moreover, subletting was strictly prohibited in the multiroom flats.

If the rents of model dwellings were too high to make them accessible to the entire proletariat they were, at the same time, too low to generate more than a very modest return on capital, which meant the associations were unattractive investments. Prince Albert arrives at a sober assessment in a letter to Henry Roberts, the best known architect of the philanthropic movement:[39] 'Mr Roberts, unless we can get 7 to 8 per cent, we shall not succeed in inducing builders to invest their capital in such houses.' Nor were these rents sufficient to enable the associations to compete effectively against other users in the central city land market. The determination of their bid price for land was made crystal clear by Derbyshire, the Peabody Trustee's architect. Given the model standards in the flats provided, the construction cost per flat was known. The market rental for such a flat to the artisan class was also known as was the desired rate of return on capital. This left the bid price of the land set by the density of the scheme; that is, the number of flats per acre. The higher the density, the higher the bid price.[40] But in spite of the erection of five and six storey blocks, the model tenements still were unable to match the prices which commercial users could bid for central land.

It was these interrelated problems which led to the associations' metamorphosis from free enterprise institutions into quasi-public bodies, a term used of Peabody by the Select Committee of 1881-2. Their shortage of capital led some of them to turn to the state for funding. Indeed, the Labouring Classes Dwelling Houses Act of 1866 seems to have originated in a letter from Waterlow to the Treasury. The

Act permitted the Public Works Loan Commissioners to provide finance to the societies and trusts and it was used almost exclusively by them, particularly the IIDC. The experience of the EEDC was not dissimilar. Founded in 1884, its prospectus seeks to return to the first principles of the movement:[41]

> The main endeavour of the Company will be to provide for the poorest class of self-supporting labourers dwelling accommodation at the very cheapest rates compatible with realising a fair rate of interest upon the capital employed. Hitherto little or nothing of this kind has been done on a large scale, the buildings of the existing Companies and Associations being chiefly occupied by a class of industrial tenants more prosperous than those for whom this Company proposes to provide.
>
> They are convinced, however, that, unless the enterprise can be made to pay a reasonable dividend to the shareholders, there is little chance of attracting into this kind of investment a sufficient amount of capital to enable this Company—or any other Companies which may follow in its wake—to extend their operations, and make any substantial contribution towards evolving the great problem of housing decently the poor of London.

But Tarn, in his fascinating architectural and legislative history of the philanthropic movement, explodes this early rhetoric with the retrospective conclusion that most of their building work was funded by the PWLC.[42]

The movement's difficulties in acquiring sites had a similar outcome to the capital shortage already discussed. Peabody, the biggest of them all, relied entirely on the Metropolitan Board of Works for its sites in the last and most active phase of its building before the end of the century. This land had originally come into the MBW's possession through the exercise of its power under the Cross Act. Such sales by the metropolitan authority contained an important subsidy element, the cost of which was met by London's ratepayers. Under the Cross Act the board carried out in all sixteen schemes covering 42½ acres, displacing 23,000 people. Its compensation costs amounted to £1·57 million but the income from sales of the land to Peabody, Rothschild, the IIDC, and so on was only one-fifth of this outlay.[43]

The most vital achievement of the philanthropic movement was its failure. It demonstrated for those who had eyes to see that *laissez-faire* contradictions were not to be resolved by *laissez-faire* responses. More than forty years after the founding of the first model dwelling company in 1841[44] their contribution to the housing of the poor was brusquely dismissed by the Royal Commission on Housing.[45] In London, by 1914, they had provided less than 100,000 rooms, 'or little more than enough room to absorb two years' addition to the population'.[46]

In terms of the tension between rent, wage, use-value and return on capital to which I referred in Fig. 1·1, we can see that the objectives of the philanthropic movement were unattainable. The relatively high use-value of the new dwellings led to a situation in which the rent–wage ratio for the majority of the working class was unacceptably high yet the return on capital and the bid price for building sites were insufficiently competitive to permit large-scale model housebuilding independent of state aid.

7 The origins of municipal housebuilding

The argument this far points, I think, to a clear hypothesis on the origins of local authority housebuilding. Accumulation generated contradiction. Contradiction was met by a spectrum of reforms, one of which was clearance followed by replacement of the existing housing stock by model dwellings. This was not carried out by private capitalists because it was unremunerative. Neither had philanthropic capitalism been able to meet the challenge: the shortage of capital and the inability to compete in the city's land market had brought about the metamorphosis of the societies and trusts into quasi-public bodies. The failures of replacement were caused essentially by the low real wages of the proletariat which, in the absence of overcrowding, made them unwilling or unable to pay rents sufficient to generate a competitive rate of return on capital invested in model dwellings. Council housebuilding originates as a substitute for the failure of private enterprise and philanthropic capitalism.

With this hypothetical framework in mind, let me begin my review of the progress of council housebuilding before 1914 by referring the reader to Appendix 1, which lists all the Acts of Parliament of importance and of relevance since 1851.

The pre-war decades can be divided into three legislative periods, the first of which ran from 1851 to 1875. During these years it was possible for local authorities to build lodging houses within which the accommodation was communal, and this was done in towns such as Huddersfield, Dundee and Glasgow. The only exception to lodging house provision was the use in Liverpool of the 1866 Act to borrow £13,000 from the PWLC for the construction of St Martin's Cottages.[47]

The second period spans the years 1875 to 1890. With the passing of the Cross Act, Parliament had given the power to every populous town not only to clear and lease or sell land for new housebuilding, but also to carry out the building itself. However, the Act viewed municipal housing only as a measure of last resort and all dwellings so erected were to be sold off again within ten years. The general opposition of Sir Richard Cross himself to local authority housebuilding is unmistakable as the following quotation shows:[48]

> I take it as a starting-point that it is not the duty of the Government
> to provide any class of citizens with any of the necessaries of life,
> and among the necessaries of life we must of course include good
> and habitable dwellings. To provide such necessaries for any class
> is not the duty of the State, because, if it did so, it would inevitably
> tend to make that class depend, not on themselves, but upon what
> was done for them elsewhere, and it would not be possible to teach
> a worse lesson than this—'If you do not take care of yourselves, the
> State will take care of you'. Nor is it wise to encourage large bodies
> to provide the working classes with habitations at greatly lower
> rents than the market value paid elsewhere.

As far as I can discover the only council housing erected under this Act was in Devonport, Liverpool and Nottingham.[49] There was none in London. It was during this period, too, that Glasgow's municipal City Improvement Trust first began constructing workers' dwellings, using the 1866 Glasgow Improvement Act.[50]

The third legislative period can be assigned to the years 1890–1914. Area clearance continued under Part I of the 1890 Housing of the Working Classes Act. In addition, Part III of the same Act for the first time permitted council housebuilding quite separately from the clearance context.[51] It was through the 1890 Act that the great majority of municipal dwellings were built before the First World War.[52] The 1909 Housing and Town Planning Act was of some importance in terminating the requirement for local authorities to sell dwellings constructed under the Cross legislation after ten years. But its importance, in this context, seems to extend no further.

8 Subsidies and poverty

None of the Acts passed between 1851 and 1914 provided for a single penny of state subsidy towards municipal housing. There was no cash grant to councils from the Exchequer towards their housing stock. The rate of interest on PWLC loans for council housebuilding was never less than the rate at which central government had to raise these funds.[53] And there were no statutory instructions for some portion of the municipalities' rate income to be channelled into their dwellings accounts. Yet some subsidisation did take place in an indirect fashion, for where necessary an authority could 'write down' the accounting value of a municipal housing site below the cost paid in compulsory purchase, thereby lowering the cost rent at the expense of the rates. But this was done *faute de mieux*, so as not to drive away potential tenants and thereby leave an under-utilised block on the council's hands. Even in these cases the local authorities' official posture was that no subsidies were to be entertained.[54] But the main point stands: successive governments introduced no subsidisation policy whatsoever. This was no oversight.

Although local authority housebuilding began as early as 1864 it would be a mistake to believe that the ruling class accepted it with equanimity. Opinion was divided but even some of the most distinguished housing reformers were opposed to municipal housing except on a minimal scale. We have already quoted the views of Cross himself in the preceding section. The ubiquitous and indefatigable Octavia Hill attacked the provision of dwellings by the community since this would enable[55] 'the improvident to throw the burden of his support upon the provident'. Even *The Builder*, which had been a progressive force when Godwin was its editor, now opposed the state provision of housing.[56] If municipal housing was anathema to many, subsidisation of such housing was attacked by virtually all the housing reformers before the turn of the century. Here is Shaftesbury restating the self-help philosophy:[57]

Hitherto we have done too little; there is now a fear that in some respects we may do too much . . . if the State is to be summoned not only to provide houses for the labouring classes, but also to supply such dwellings at nominal rents, it will, while doing something on behalf of their physical condition, utterly destroy their moral energies.

In similar terms the architect John Honeyman, author of *Dwellings of the Poor*, fearful of 'the absolute supremacy of the lower grades of society' attacked subsidies because they would[58] 'compel the steady and sober to pay more than the unprincipled and dissipated, and to contribute to their support'.

The opposition to subsidisation was coupled in a curious way with a growing acceptance that the slums were, after all, a manifestation of poverty, an opinion often tempered with supplementary clauses on excessive drinking, gambling and frivolous expenditure amongst the working class. A spate of statements on the economic causes of slum life appeared in the 1880s. The Marquis of Salisbury wrote in 1883 in the *National Review* that[59] 'the difficulty in the case of the poorest class of town-workmen, as in that of the agricultural labourer, is their poverty. Until their wages rise they cannot pay for the bare cost of decent lodging.'

In 1884 *The Sanitary Record* concluded:[60]

1. That the poor of the labouring class, out of their limited resources, cannot afford to pay more than a rental of from 1s to 2s per week for their dwellings, of whatever size and construction, and wheresoever situate. 2. That no practical plan has yet been devised by which dwellings can be built, which . . . can be let at these low rentals, and prove remunerative to the builders.

My final example is the findings of the Royal Commission on Housing in 1885. Gauldie points out that:[61]

What the report did was to put into easily understood form the great body of causes which combined to prevent reform, and to put unequivocally at the top of the list, as prime cause of the terrible housing, the poverty of the people: the relationship borne by the wages they receive to the rents they have to pay.

If the slums were a manifestation of working-class poverty how was it imagined that local authority housing could alleviate the situation if it was carried out without subsidised rents? I suggest that the answer to this conundrum is similar to the defence of philanthropic capitalism. Municipal housebuilding would provide replacement dwellings during the course of slum clearance, supplying model dwellings for the artisan fraction of the working class because private enterprise failed to do so. There would be no rehousing because there was no rent subsidy and no overcrowding was permitted.[62] But the unemployed, the casual labourers and so forth could and would filter into the accommodation vacated by the artisans. Both Cross and the Marquis of Salisbury used the filtering argument to defend replacement without rehousing.[63]

9 Construction without clearance

Until now I have concerned myself almost entirely with council house-building within a clearance context. This was its origin. However, clearance is not the whole story as Part III of the 1890 Housing of the Working Classes Act makes plain. This permitted the erection of public housing quite separately from any clearance operations. Such a power and such activity is simply not explained by the hypothetical framework developed above in Section 7. In order to understand this second dominant mode of local authority activity I believe we have to return to the Report of the Royal Commission on Housing in 1884–5 and in particular to the situation in London.

The Royal Commission found that overcrowding was increasing in nearly all the towns it examined, in spite of the building societies, the philanthropists and the other segments of the housing movement. We know that in London, for example, the annual average addition to the size of the population was 85,000 persons in the last three decades of the nineteenth century.[64] Of course this growing population was not packing into a city of constant dimensions. The period 1851–91 witnessed the astounding growth of districts like Willesden, West Ham and Leyton. The development of suburban train services and, later, the tram was accompanied by a huge increase in London's size.[65] Nevertheless, this was no miracle cure for overcrowding as the following densities for London in terms of persons per dwelling show:[66] 1801 : 7·03; 1851 : 7·72; 1881 : 7·85; 1896 : 8·02. Wohl suggests London's overcrowding probably fell slightly after the 1890s but by 1911 it was still the case that more than 40 per cent of all London's one- and two-room tenements sheltered more than two persons per room.

I suggest that in the eyes of the Royal Commission the housing question was, in some senses at least, seen to be growing more critical. This explains their willingness to recommend a legislative concession which might assist in the relief of overcrowding and the prevention of slum formation by means of municipal housebuilding on a small scale in association with filtering—without clearance as a precondition for such activity. This concession took the form of defining lodging houses in the 1885 Act in a way that included family dwellings. This terminological innovation was embodied in Part III of the 1890 Act, which was written to amend and consolidate the Lodging Houses Acts dating from 1851.

It was the LCC which used Part III more extensively than any other authority in the country and the council itself gave a very clear statement of the need for local authority action in a situation where private enterprise housebuilding had failed to build save for the artisan fraction of the working class.[67]

> The most important question . . . is the extent to which municipal authorities should themselves undertake provision of house accommodation for the working classes . . . there is one serious danger in relying wholly upon private enterprise. The provision of the better rented accommodation suitable for the artisan with a regular income, is a more profitable enterprise than building for the poorer section of the working class . . . there is not much provision made for families which can only afford to pay for two or three rooms. The result is that several families have to make such common use as they can of the cooking, washing and sanitary convenience originally provided for one family only; and it is obvious that such accommodation is deficient in these cases, from the point of view of both health and decency.

This was the context within which before 1914 the council began to build its first four suburban estates at Tooting, Croydon, Tottenham and Acton. Almost two-thirds of the 2531 families accommodated there moved from within the boundaries of the County of London.[68]

10 The rise of working-class power

Up to this point in the narrative I have considered the development of policy entirely as the response of the ruling classes within the context of their own—often conflicting—perceptions of the housing question. I have tended to present the history of policy as the faltering development of a more enlightened rationality by those classes in their own long-term interests. This is to ignore the role of the workers themselves.

In the 1880s the organised power of the huge British working class began to assert itself, in the election of working people's representatives to councils and later to Parliament, in the growth of trade unions and in the shape of socialist societies and parties. In 1884 there had been a large extension in the number of workers permitted to vote in the national elections and after the Local Government Act of 1888 the workers were also given greater influence in the election of county representatives. Both the Fabian Society and the Social Democratic Federation were formed in the mid-1880s. In the early 1900s the trade unions and various independent groups converged to form the Labour Party and by 1914 there were forty Labour MPs.

A very early example of the working-class argument for municipal socialism in the housing field is the evidence given to the Royal Commission by George Shipton, representing the London Trades Council.[69]

> If the evils were all pointed out and the laws in every instance set in motion, the slums might be destroyed; but their inhabitants would be cast homeless into the streets. It is comparatively easy to obtain condemnation against overcrowded and unhealthy houses; but it is far more difficult to build and let out at cheap rents, suitable tenements. Private enterprise, aided by enlightened philanthropy, has done a great deal . . . nevertheless, it is totally impossible that private enterprise, philanthropy and charity can ever keep pace with the present demands . . . . Economic forces and population have outstepped their endeavours; hence evils accrue. But what the individual cannot do the State municipality must seek to accomplish . . . for it alone possesses the necessary power and wealth.

Later, an important voice in the formulation of working-class housing demands was that of the Workmen's National Housing Council. Without success the council sponsored legislation in Parliament from 1900 to 1914 to bring down the rate of interest on PWLC loans to 2 per cent, repayable over 100 years.[70] We know too, from the work of Enid Gauldie, that in places such as Sheffield, Bradford and Manchester the labour movement was agitating for municipal housebuilding from the 1880s onwards.[71] Unfortunately, too little research has been published on this aspect of the introduction and implementation of legislation to permit a final conclusion on the significance of pressure from below in stimulating the production of council houses.

11 The scale of municipal housebuilding

I now wish to provide an estimate of the scale of local authority house-building in Britain before the First World War. By the year 1914 the stock of such dwellings already completed must have been approximately 24,000 units, excluding 'cubicles' provided in municipally constructed lodging houses.[72] This was well under half of 1 per cent of the total stock of houses at the time. Of the total council sector stock about 10 per cent had been built in the period 1864-89 and the rest in 1890-1914. The number of municipal dwellings constructed per year was an infinitesimal proportion of total housebuilding output before 1890 and even thereafter it could only have averaged about 1 per cent.[73]

It hardly needs to be said that there are no national data for the annual number of starts or completions in the council sector before the war. Such a series could only be constructed by means of the aggregation of area-specific data, data which do not yet exist. However, one thing is quite certain: the rate of sanctioned starts was running at a very high comparative level immediately before the outbreak of the war. The average number of dwellings for which loan sanctions was approved in the three years 1912, 1913 and 1914 in England and Wales was as high as 3213 compared with an average of 870 completions per annum in the whole period after 1890.[74] The years preceding the war were a time of catastrophic slump in the housebuilding industry.[75]

With respect to their location we can say that probably less than 500 dwellings, or 2 per cent of the stock, were situated in rural districts. Urban building was dominated by the London County Council with 9746 units (excluding cubicles) completed after 1890.[76] The CIT in Glasgow had built 2199 units in the period 1866-1914. In all, 179 urban authorities received loan sanctions for municipal housebuilding after the passage of the 1890 Act.

The breakdown of the total between redevelopment schemes and those provided independent of rehousing obligation is impossible to estimate at present. What we do know is that in London of 11,972 dwellings provided by the municipal authorities between 1890 and 1914 as many as 46 per cent were independent of slum clearance provision.[77]

I have already argued that the 1890 Housing of the Working Classes Act marks a qualitative turning point in the history of British public housing. The data presented here demonstrates that it was also a quantitative watershed. The scale of building after 1890 was far, far greater in proportionate terms than it had been in the previous twenty-five years. But it must be emphasised again that municipal house-building in the quarter century before war broke out was still pitifully small in comparison with the housebuilding industry's total annual output. The petty and sinister interests were still blocking at the local level; the ideology of *laissez-faire* was still dominant; the direct provision of dwellings for the working class by the state was still regarded at all levels of entrenched political power as an exceptional measure; the working-class movement was still not strong in Parliament; and already some workers who had risen to positions of power, such as John Burns, had abandoned their socialism with their boots. They were not the last to do so.

In aggregate, then, the council housing sector was of minimal size before the First World War. However, I suspect future research will demonstrate that in specific cities and towns and at particular times municipal housebuilding formed a substantial part of total local construction for the working class. In such cases I believe that we shall find the enabling legislation of 1890 was used either by socialist and social democratic councillors, who looked on such building as part of the struggle to raise the standard of life of the workers, or by conservative local government administrations facing a local slump in private enterprise housebuilding.

12 The argument for a central subsidy

We have already seen that the provision of public housing by the local state—that is the municipal authority contained a significant ambiguity. In principle, the new accommodation was for the working class in general and for the displaced slum-dweller in the particular case of redevelopment. But the mass of workers were unable to afford even the 'cost rents' of model dwellings in the enforced absence of overcrowding. The filtering argument used by those who defended redevelopment without genuine rehousing was a threadbare rationalisation. Voluntary subsidies from the rates were out of the question with local government largely in the hands of local property owners. With no subsidy from the central state, and in the absence of higher real wages for the proletariat in general, council housing in model conditions could never be more than a minor palliative within the reformist spectrum. It was for this reason that in the years before 1914 some social reformers, quite apart

27

from representatives of the working class, argued for a central state subsidy for public housing.

Wilding suggests that the first official report calling for Exchequer aid for housing was that of the Parliamentary Committee considering the Bill which was later to be passed as the 1909 Housing and Town Planning Act.[78] Asquith, the Chancellor of the Exchequer, replied that the policy of doles was objectionable and dangerous.[79] The first Bill to propose state subsidies was introduced by a Conservative, Boscawen, in 1912 but never passed the committee stage.[80] The Conservative reformers' case cannot be better expressed than by this quotation from a party pamphlet of 1913.[81]

> If a certain number of houses are not built at a non-economic
> rent, the present housing evil is irremediable and the problem
> must be given up in despair. If on the other hand, those houses
> are to be built, it seems clear from experience that some state
> encouragement to Local Authorities will have to be given.

The authors asserted rather optimistically that the party was unanimous in accepting the need for Exchequer subsidies. Further Bills of a similar nature to Boscawen's were presented unsuccessfully in 1913 and 1914.

The Land Enquiry Committee set up by Lloyd George in 1912-13 to survey the housing situation recommended that it should be the statutory duty of local authorities[82] 'to see that adequate and sanitary housing accommodation is provided for the working-class population employed or reasonably likely to be permanently resident within their area' and that either Exchequer grants should be made available for that purpose or 'something' had to be 'done' to raise the wages of the lower-paid worker.

Finally, Wilding has traced a document which appears to indicate that in the months before the outbreak of war the Liberal Government was preparing legislation which included an Exchequer public health grant of £4 million per year to urban authorities which were satisfactorily tackling their local housing problem.[83]

If we take into account, then, the arguments of the Conservative and Liberal reformers, the pressure of the labour movement within Parliament and without, and the spurt in the loans sanctioned for the council sector in 1912-14, it does not seem unreasonable to suggest that a new qualitative turning point was drawing near. The First World War settled the question once and for all.

13 Synthesis

Rather than simply summarise events and list conclusions in this final section of the chapter, I wish to set out the structure of the argument in a more general and abstract fashion, at the same time introducing concepts which facilitate this theoretical overview. It is hoped that this higher-lever perspective will enable the reader more easily to locate in his or her mind those sections of the narrative which are most specific and empirical in their character.

The Industrial Revolution in Britain, which got seriously under way in the mid-eighteenth century, brought with it the triumph of a new pattern of economic relationships—the capitalist mode of production. Yet this system contained the seeds of its own destruction. The accumulation of productive capital and the unprecedented increase in the population together led to the concentration of the new proletarian class in our great cities and towns. The size of the class and the misery of its social conditions, in comparison with the opulence of the propertied classes, meant that it constituted a potentially revolutionary threat.

The capacity of the working class to reproduce itself, that is, to multiply and to present itself to the employers with the requisite capacities for labour, was at that time largely determined by the expenditures that their wages permitted them to make on food, clothing, shelter, transport to work, health care and education. The concern of this study is shelter. The use-value of the dwellings of the working class reflected the variation of wages between fractions of the class. For very great numbers their domestic situation was appalling. This became widely recognised in the second quarter of the nineteenth century. These conditions created specific contradictions for the existing social order for they reduced the productivity of labour, brought the ravages of disease to every social class, created impenetrable rookeries of criminal violence and gave strength to the voices of that subversive tradition which preached revolution.

In the nineteenth century the state at the central level was controlled by and represented the interests of the owners of landed property and the means of production. They recognised that government should fashion and implement policies which would serve to resolve these problems. As a result a wide variety of environmental reforms began to be introduced from about the 1850s. The pace of legislative reform was slowed, however, by the prevailing philosophy of *laissez-faire* whilst

implementation might be checked when this clashed with petty bourgeois and rentier interests which were more powerful at the local level.

One of the most interesting reform movements was that of the 5 per
cent philanthropists. Their evident failure to construct model dwellings
for the working class on a sufficient scale and their increasing reliance
on state assistance in one form or another served to stimulate an
increasingly wide acceptance of some direct state provision of accommodation. This had begun in 1851 with the Lodging Houses Act but
the national scale of building of family dwellings was negligible before
the 1890 Housing of the Working Classes Act, a consolidating measure
enacted five years after the report of the Royal Commission on Housing.

Much of the state activity which did take place in these early decades
was slum redevelopment. It is my view that much clearance was essentially repressive in nature, that it was done in order to physically destroy
nests of disease and crime. The building of new dwellings on the vacated
sites (or elsewhere) basically served to legitimise the destruction which
had preceded it. For the slum dwellers were only injured by redevelopment. They were rarely rehoused by the local authorities since they
were unable to afford the rents of the new accommodation and no state
subsidies, at least of an explicit kind, were made available before the
First World War.

Between 1890 and 1914 average completions of municipal dwellings
ran at little short of a thousand per annum, still only about 1 per cent
of the flow of total output. Much of it was in London and much of it
was independent of slum clearance. Public health legislation had imposed
increasingly stringent demands on the minimum use-values to which
housebuilders had to conform and this further discouraged dwelling
construction which would embrace all the fractions of the working
class. With the decline in average real wages after the first years of the
twentieth century, there was a remarkable slump in construction and in
the years immediately preceding the First World War there was a jump
in local authority activity as well as a series of legislative attempts to
introduce Exchequer subsidies for municipal housebuilding.

In a nutshell, the origins of local authority housing lie in the contradictions created for the social order by the failure of private enterprise
to finance and construct model dwellings for the working class.

TWO

1914-1939: housing policy and the balance of class forces

1 Homes fit for heroes

We have seen that by August 1914 local authorities had the power to build dwellings for the working class both as part of their slum clearance operations and in the attempt to check urban overcrowding. However, the scale of output had been less than 22,000 units in the preceding twenty-five years and no exchequer subsidy had ever been made available for the public housing effort.

The First World War marks a watershed in the history of British municipal housing. During the course of the years 1914–18 government economic policy was directed entirely to the defeat of Imperial Germany. One consequence was that the maintenance, repair and building of houses came to a virtual standstill. The flow of demand for these activities, and for the outputs of the construction industry in general, did not cease but accumulated like the waters behind a temporary dam. For example, in England and Wales between 1911 and 1918, the increase in the number of households needing separate dwellings amounted to 848,000 units whilst only 238,000 dwellings were added to the existing stock, a deficit of 610,000 houses. In Scotland the shortage of houses attributable to the war was 95,000 units.[1]

If the state itself destroyed the dam at the war's end by the abolition of controls on building, it was widely foreseen that one result of the release of the floodwaters of demand would be sharp rises in unit prices. In such a case the supply of working-class housing by private enterprise in the immediate post-war years was likely to suffer seriously. For subsequent falls in house prices would leave these landlords trying to let high-cost accommodation at rents determined by the relatively low-cost building of later date. Independently of these predicted price rises, the short-term prospects of construction for working-class rental were grim, simply because of the fall in real wages during the war and the atrophy of effective demand for housing that this was bound to cause.[2] These arguments held good whatever view was taken on

31

the long-term prospects of private investment in housing to let.

The ruling class could not face the prospect of a severe post-war housing shortage with equanimity. The July 1917 report of a committee of enquiry into industrial unrest had pinpointed housing conditions as a major cause and recommended 'Announcements should be made of policy as regards housing.' Indeed, the Glasgow rent strike of 1915 had already forced Lloyd George to introduce the rent control legislation embodied in the Increase of Rent and Mortgage Interest (War Restrictions) Act. The strength of the labour movement had been much increased during the war by the expansion of the shop steward movement and the growth of trade union membership from 4 million in 1913 to more than 8 million in 1919. With the return of millions of soldiers from Europe, where British and German workers had slaughtered each other for King and Kaiser, social and industrial turbulence grew apace: in 1919, 35 million work days were lost in strikes, compared with 5 million in 1918. Memories were still fresh of the success of the 1917 Bolshevik Revolution in Russia and 'from 1919 to 1921 the Cabinet was haunted by the possibility that continued strikes, especially from the Triple Alliance of miners, railwaymen and transport workers, would lead to coups in major cities.'[3]

The war-created housing backlog, the foreseen shortfall in private enterprise housebuilding for the working classes in the early post-war years, and the social turbulence in Britain before and after the Armistice were the decisive circumstances which led to a number of government housing policy decisions. One was to continue the control of house rents. Legislation in 1919 and 1920 prolonged rent control, initially until 1923, on houses below a specific rateable value built before the summer of 1919, although this was not a total rent freeze. A second decision was to introduce a subsidy on private enterprise housebuilding. The Housing (Additional Powers) Act of 1919 provided a small lump sum Exchequer payment on new private sector dwellings conforming to certain maximum size conditions. The third policy measure was to make state subsidies available to the municipalities for their housebuilding programmes and thereby to raise the annual output of the public housing sector.

On the cut and thrust of debate within the Cabinet and civil service, Paul Wilding has now provided a prolonged and extremely careful exposition.[4] It appears that the first formal proposal within the government for subsidised municipal housing was contained in a memorandum which Walter Long, President of the Local Government Board, sent to the Reconstruction Committee of the Coalition Government in June 1916.[5] From this time until July 1919, when the Housing and Town Planning Act was passed, the internal arguments concerned the duration, scale and form of the subsidy rather than the principle. There was even some support from the building industry at this time for a state programme: in May 1917, Lord Rhondda, President of the Local Government Board since December 1916, received a private enterprise deputation which said it thought the industry could meet the demand for urban housing if the state would find the capital.

With respect to the duration of the subsidy, the very first circular to the local authorities on the subject, in July 1917, made it clear that funding would be available for only a limited time period. That the need would be temporary was a conventional wisdom of virtually all the chief policy-makers, with the possible exception of Christopher Addison. A five- or seven-year period was often proposed. In November 1919, for example, Sir Alfred Mond, founder of what was to become Imperial Chemical Industries and himself the Minister of Health from 1921 to 1922, put the short-term horizon argument thus: the housing situation must be seen as the aftermath of the war and any financial losses incurred on the building programme are best regarded as a part of the cost of the war itself.[6]

With respect to the scale of public housing output and the subsidy terms, the first concrete figure mentioned was by Lord Rhondda who in early 1917 spoke of a need for 300,000 dwellings. By July, the circular we have already referred to promised the local authorities 'substantial financial assistance' with their programmes. In the same month the Joint Committee on Labour Problems After the War proposed the building of 1 million low-rent houses, with interest-free loans to the local authorities and the suspension of luxury building. At this stage in time the Local Government Board favoured a grant form for the subsidy based on the calculated difference between normal building costs and the (foreseen) abnormal post-war level. In October the Advisory Housing Panel to the Minister of Reconstruction suggested a minimum requirement of 300,000 dwellings in order to deal with the emergency at the war's end. By November 1917 Hayes Fisher, President of the LGB from 1917 to 1918, is

> more than ever convinced that anything which retards the
> measures now being taken to push on preparations, or which
> can be interpreted as an attempt on the part of the Government

to go back upon, or to 'hedge' in regard to their pledge of
'substantial financial assistance' would have the most disastrous
results and would tend largely to increase the industrial unrest
of which bad housing is admittedly one of the causes.

But a month later he is forced to admit to a delegation from the National
Housing and Town Planning Council that the Treasury is unwilling
to make promises about large-scale subsidies.

In January 1918, the Treasury and the LGB produced a joint scheme
of financial proposals, but this was roundly attacked during the following
months by figures as eminent as Addison, Lord Salisbury, Seebohm
Rowntree, Tudor-Walters, Lord Henry Cavendish Bentinck and others.
They argued that the proposal was so hedged round with safeguards that
it did not constitute a government commitment to municipal housebuilding on a scale sufficient for the need. Meanwhile at a conference in
Manchester in May–June, the county boroughs of Lancashire and the
West Riding had urged the limitation of local authority financial responsibility to the product of a penny rate, a proposal first made by the
Royal Commission on Housing in Scotland in 1917. In spite of the lack
of support from precisely that sector of government which would carry
through the programme, Hayes-Fisher in October 1918 still proclaimed
that the government wished to see 300,000 working-class dwellings built
in twelve months when the war was over—more than three times the
pre-war average annual output of the entire housebuilding industry!
Biting attacks on the Treasury–LGB scheme continued in Parliament
and in November Hayes-Fisher was elevated to the peerage, a scapegoat
for the Cabinet's lack of commitment to the public housing programme.
Auckland Geddes became the new President of the LGB.

In the same month the Armistice was signed and in December general
elections took place which returned the Coalition Government to power,
with Lloyd George as Prime Minister. There were 159 Liberals and 364
Conservatives in the new House of Commons. At the hustings Lloyd
George had declared that the government, if returned, would build half
a million working-class homes in three years through the local authorities
and the housing association movement, 'homes fit for heroes'. This was
the political commitment by the state which was a necessary condition
for council activity on a substantial scale.

In December, Geddes reported to the Cabinet on the intentions of
the municipalities and the stages their programmes had reached. Of
1806 local authorities, only 400 specified the number of dwellings their

schemes would provide and the total was only 100,000.[7] Geddes argued that the government must concede what was by now the Association of Municipal Corporations' demand for a maximum one penny rate commitment if the councils' output was to be adequate.

In January 1919, Addison took over the presidency of the LGB—the fifth incumbent in twenty-six months! His task was to transform the department into the Ministry of Health, which was achieved in June of the same year. It was Addison who revealed just how paltry were the local authorities' plans for housing at 21 January 1919, plans based on the Treasury–LGB financial scheme of a year earlier. Firm proposals to build had been made to the LGB by only fifty-two authorities, totalling little more than 10,000 houses. Final government sanction had yet to be given to a single one of these schemes.[8] The councils' unwillingness to act proved to be decisive. Circular 12 of 6 February 1919 conceded to the authorities: their demand for a maximum burden to them of a one penny rate; that schemes assisted were to be carried out under parts I, II and III of the 1890 Act; the authorities were to go to the capital market for finance; and rents were to be set as near as was possible to an 'economic' level, that is, a level which would cover capital and current outgoings.

The Exchequer subsidy for municipal housing was made law by the July 1919 Housing and Town Planning Act, the major points of which are summarised in the legislative chronology of Appendix 1. At the time the Bill was welcomed even by the 'hard faced men who had done well out of the war'—Baldwin's description of the new MPs. *The Times* said the Bill did not go far enough. Addison was to say later, under rather different circumstances, that he had to restrain the House from forcing powers on him rather than their being suspicious of those he sought to take.[9]

Half a million dwellings in three years was a huge target. If the local authorities and the housing associations were to have any chance of achieving it a complete system of building controls was necessary, something the new Ministry of Labour had argued for, in opposition to Addison's weaker demand for a simple restriction of less essential building. Yet, with the ringing of the election slogans still in people's ears and at the same time as Exchequer subsidies in their final form were decided upon, the war-time system of building controls was swept away. The possibility of target achievement had been extinguished. The abolition of licensing was decided upon by the Cabinet on 20 December 1918 and was a precondition of the construction boom of 1919–21.

The dam against five years' pent-up demand was now opened. The aggregate supply response was a surge in total output as the men, skilled and unskilled, returned from France, Germany and the Low Countries. However, by the end of the year it was clear that the unions were not willing to see an increase in the supply of skilled workers through an expansion of the system of apprenticeship, for fear that in any subsequent slump in employment their bargaining power would be weakened. This caution was later to be proved justified. The output of building materials expanded rapidly; the Committee on Trusts wrote at the time that 60 per cent of the materials needed for building a cottage were controlled, fully or partially, by trade combinations whose primary objective was to raise prices. These controls were responsible for excess profit-making but this was not inconsistent with a fast increase in the growth of the volume of output.[10]

However, the recovery of supply in aggregate was insufficient to meet the accumulation in demand and a serious price inflation began. The conditions were those of a seller's market and of course the industry supplied those sectors which offered the highest profits. The others would have to wait. Broadly speaking, the big firms found industrial building attractive and the small firms turned to repair work. The Housing (Additional Powers) Act of 1919 gave councils the powers to restrict private building in their own area but these were little used. Wilding has shown that in November 1919 senior officials at the Ministry of Labour were already aware that the government's housing programme was coming last, not first, in the queue for labour supplies.[11] And in the same month Addison conceded that 60 per cent of the trade was engaged on repair work. In spite of this, the Ministry of Health at the end of the year still expressed confidence that the half-million target could be met, through the production of 100,000 houses by September 1920 and a further 200,000 units in each of the two succeeding years.[12]

It might be thought that the local authority could bid without hindrance for the available flow of construction resources, that is, labour and materials. For under the new act the Treasury was to bear all losses in excess of a penny rate when the dwellings were rented out. In fact the authorities were severely constrained because every scheme had to be submitted to the Ministry of Health for approval where a costing department had been set up to oversee builders' tender prices to the authorities. It was claimed that the department achieved contract price reductions of as much as £80 per dwelling on average.[13] But the ministry's very success in restraining the rate of increase of prices meant that the municipalities were outbid in their demand for resources. Council housing construction was relatively unprofitable.

In contrast, it seems that land acquisition was never a serious problem. At the beginning of 1919 no land had yet been finally acquired for council building. But by August land purchases submitted for approval to the ministry were sufficient for 380,000 houses![14] Finance was a little more troublesome. Local authorities with a rateable value greater than £200,000 were required to go to the open market for capital and in the first annual report of the Ministry of Health it was admitted that the problem of raising finance was slowing down some council programmes. It was for this reason that the Housing (Additional Powers) Act permitted the authorities to fund their housing work by the issue of local bonds.

By May of 1920 there were only enough bricklayers on public housing work to build 21,000 units annually. A month later, when Addison outlined to the Cabinet what conditions were likely to be necessary to persuade the unions to raise the rate at which skilled men were being trained, it was Mond who correctly pointed out that the real problem was that only 5000 out of 50,000 bricklayers were doing local authority work.[15]

The return to *laissez-faire* in the construction industry after December 1918 had caught the municipalities in a double trap. In physical terms the output of houses was way below the half-million target required by September 1922, yet relative unit prices were far, far higher than in the pre-war situation. Table 2·1 shows that even by the end of 1922 the total number of dwellings completed under the Addison Act was fewer than 104,000 and in the three years up to and including June 1921 tender prices were about three times as great as the pre-war level.

Table 2·1 *Tender prices and completions of local authority dwellings in 1914–23*

Year	Tender prices (£)[a]	Completions[b]
1914	235	not known
1919	708	negligible
1920	881	576
1921	643	16,786
1922	378	86,579
1923	380	67,062

Sources: Prices: Appendix 3. Output: Appendix 2.

a For three-bedroom houses in England and Wales. Mid-year data.

b For Great Britain.

In spite of the underfulfilment of their government-set target, the speed of response of the local authorities was astonishing once the subsidy in its final form had been conceded. In the nine months after the passage of the Addison Act the councils had made firm proposals to build 162,000 houses, which the Ministry of Health had sanctioned. This was about seven times as great as the stock of council dwellings in 1914. Table 2·1 shows the fast rate of increase in completions: fewer than 1,000 in 1920; more than 86,000 in 1922. Moreover, the supply situation with respect to the relative profitability of council house-building had improved in 1920–1 with the slump in industrial building demand. The prices of building materials and wages in nearly all cases ceased to rise after 1920 and in 1921 they were either stationary or falling.[16] Unemployment amongst bricklayers followed the reverse direction, the figure rising from the autumn of 1920. With the reductions in their costs and with the increased competition for contracts, builders began to cut their profit margins and their tender prices. Bowley traces the start of the fall in municipal house prices to the autumn of 1920 when the peak was £930. The building slump, combined with the Addison subsidy, provided an unprecedented opportunity for a large-scale and continuing flow of working-class housing construction financed by the municipalities. It was at this point that the coalition Cabinet decided to scrap the entire programme.[17]

To understand this perverse reversal of the 1918 commitment we must look at the general economic and political situation in the country. The post-war boom was followed in 1920–1 by a tremendous slump, 'one of the most sudden and catastrophic in British history. In a single year industrial production fell by more than a quarter; unemployment rose from 2 per cent to 18 per cent of the labour force; company profits fell by more than half!'[18] The crisis strengthened the bargaining position of those within the government and civil service who wanted to see cuts in public expenditure. Between the wars orthodox economic theory suggested that under a regime of *laissez-faire*: first, there was no inherent tendency for the capitalist economy to fluctuate between peak and trough; second, Say's Law demonstrated that there could be no general condition of overproduction. Jean Baptiste Say had argued in 1803 that supply creates its own demand. Ricardo accepted this:[19]

there is no amount of capital which may not be employed in a country, because demand is only limited by production. No man produces, but with a view to consume or sell, and he never sells,

but with an intention to purchase some other commodity, which
may be immediately useful to him, or which may contribute
to future production. By producing, then, he necessarily becomes
either the consumer of his own goods, or the purchaser and consumer
of the goods of some other person.

Thereafter the assumption that the means of production would be fully
employed was never challenged—Marx excepted—until the 1930s. Public
expenditure—on housing for example—was inconsistent with *laissez-faire*
in its pure form and therefore became vulnerable to attack by the policy
theorists in production crises. It was also argued that trade union intervention in free market wage bargaining pushed rates above their equilibrium level so that, just as with every other commodity, the higher
price meant less demand with unemployment resulting. Cuts in both
public expenditure and wages were seen then as vital tactics in the
government's attempt to restore production and employment.[20]

The cost to the Exchequer of the Addison subsidy rose from £21,000
in 1919–20 to £7,952,000 in 1924–5 as the stock of 'Addison houses'
increased.[21] It might be argued that the trifling level of the sum in
1920 and 1921 could hardly have been thought a threat to the country's
economic stability. Such a view misses the point: it was not the outlay
on the subsidy which was important; it was the capital expenditure of
the local authorities on their housing programmes which was crucial.
The 1922 output alone must have required an outlay of some £75
million. This reasoning finds confirming evidence in a minute written
in 1919 by A.V. Symonds, Second Secretary at the Ministry of Health.[22]
At this time the Treasury was fighting the AMC demand for an open-
ended government subsidy. The argument it gave was that because the
rate subsidy was a known maximum, the municipalities would prove
profligate in both their designs and in the tenders they were willing to
accept, since diseconomies would be borne by the central state. Symonds
dismissed this line. The real reason, he said, that they strain at the gnat
of local diseconomies is to avoid swallowing the camel of the money
that the state must raise to fund the building programme.

The cry of profligacy was raised once again in 1921, when a justification was needed politically for terminating the subsidies. As I have
argued already, the high unit prices of council housebuilding were due
not to the diseconomies of the open-ended subsidy but to the abolition
of building controls. Bowley points out that even during the year in
which council housebuilding rose to its peak, it used only about 15 per

cent of the skilled men in the industry and 50 per cent of the bricks.[23]

> It is only possible to conclude that the course of building costs
> and employment was on the whole determined by the private
> or industrial demand, rather than by the demand of local
> authorities, for building resources in the four years following
> the Armistice.

The interest of the government in cutting back the state housing programme has now been explained. But the political power to do so was made possible by the defeats which the labour movement suffered in 1921. In that year the government ended its war-time control of the mining industry and handed the mines back to the owners, at the same time withdrawing the state subsidy. The coal-owners wished to raise the profitability of the industry by wage cuts and in April the miners struck. The leaders of the Triple Alliance of miners, railwaymen and transport workers called for a sympathy strike but, before it had begun, withdrew their support on 'Black Friday'. Three months later the miners were defeated. The collapse of the post-war boom had weakened the labour movement more generally: trade union membership, for example, was down to 5½ million in 1921 after its war-time peak of 8 million and the decline of working-class strength was reflected in 1921–4 by sharp falls in real wages.

With this background sketched in we can return to Whitehall. It was as early as October 1919 that the Chancellor of the Exchequer, Austen Chamberlain, first proposed the public housing programme be postponed because, he said, of rising costs.[24] This was barely three months after the passage of the 1919 legislation! In June of 1920 a Cabinet committee reported that postponement was impossible, because of pledges given to the local authorities. But as the depression deepened, opposition to municipal housebuilding grew more vociferous. At some stage during these months, the Ministry of Health itself reduced to 300,000 the number of dwellings they said were required and in February of 1921 Addison himself made a major concession. He 'accepted the need to limit the programme and proposed that the ministry should, for the time being, concentrate on the 172,000 houses in approved tenders and only sanction the construction of the balance of the 300,000 . . . as prices fell.'[25] Lloyd George had been trying to drop Addison from early in 1920 because of his resistance to housing cuts. In March 1921, a month before Black Friday, Addison and Austen Chamberlain agreed to limit the total commitment to 300,000 houses,

50,000 of which were to come from the subsidised private enterprise sector and the balance from the local authorities and the housing associations. But in July, the same month which witnessed the defeat of the miners, there was a dramatic shift even from the March agreement. The Cabinet accepted the proposals of its finance committee which were even more swingeing than those put forward by Mond, who had replaced Addison at the Ministry of Health on 1 April. On 14 July the commitment to houses fit for heroes was abandoned: the total number of dwellings to be completed by the local authorities was 170,000, only a little in excess of the number for which contracts had already been agreed. No new subsidy was announced. On the same day Addison resigned his position as Minister without Portfolio in protest. Later Lloyd George, in a phrase of condescending cynicism unmatched in the history of British housing policy, was to say of him:[26] 'I know that his unfortunate interest in health has excited a good deal of prejudice. He was rather too anxious to build houses.'

Marian Bowley has shown how dramatic was the slump in local authority housebuilding in England and Wales as a result of this reversal of the 1918 commitment: municipal dwelling output fell from 81,000 units in the year ending 31 March 1922 down to 14,000 units two years later.[27]

The total number of council dwellings built using the Addison subsidies was 169,300, of which all save 15,600 were completed by 31 March 1923. The total production of Addison-funded housing association dwellings was a mere 4545 and the private enterprise houses subsidised by the Additional Powers Act totalled 39,186 units. Between the Armistice and the end of March 1923 252,000 houses had been constructed, only 23 per cent of the combined total of the estimated shortage in January 1919 and the increase in the number of households during 1919-23. The promise of half a million houses had left the country with a greater shortage in 1923 than after four years of bloody war![28]

2 1921-9: the period of unstable growth

When the government cut itself loose from the Addison Act in 1921 no substitute had yet been devised. But there remained a strongly held view within the Cabinet that temporary Exchequer subsidisation of council housing was still an unfortunate necessity and this position is nicely exemplified by a quotation from Mond in August of 1921.[29]

> If I saw any real prospect of any general resumption of the
> building of true working class houses by Private Enterprise, I
> should not consider any prolongation of State assistance or any
> modification of the present policy. We have, however, to face
> the fact that Private Enterprise did not nearly solve this
> problem before the war and will not solve it in the near future . . .
> We are still some distance from the level of price at which
> working class houses can be produced freely in the ordinary
> course of trade and I do not think we shall reach that level for
> a considerable time.

Mond proposed a local authority programme of 80,000 dwellings over
the two years 1923–4, using a fixed annual Treasury grant of £3 on
each dwelling built. Some felt that this was too generous. However, the
disagreements were not quickly resolved: the flow of Addison houses
was still continuing and there was bitter strife between Conservatives
and Liberals within the government. In October 1922 the Coalition
collapsed and in the following month the Tories won an overall majority
of 77 in the general election. Andrew Bonar Law became Prime Minister
and Boscawen went to the Ministry of Health.

Preparations for a new Housing Act continued. A Cabinet committee
soon reported that there still existed a shortage of working-class houses
and that without government aid private enterprise would not build for
the class in sufficient numbers. This led to the acceptance of an extension of rent control in the private sector up to 1925, although the
interest of tenants suffered a set-back in that rents were decontrolled
whenever a dwelling was vacated. The same committee proposed a
fixed grant subsidy for both local authority and private working-class
housebuilding.

The Cabinet approved these general proposals in spite of Treasury
preference for a no-subsidy policy which, they said, would help drive
down building workers' wages and therefore reduce the money costs of
building. In March Boscawen failed to win a parliamentary seat in a by-
election and resigned as Minister. His successor, Neville Chamberlain,
made no major changes in the draft Bill and this was approved by the
Cabinet on 28 March.

A description of the main terms of the 1923 Housing Act is given in
the legislative chronology. Its main purpose was to encourage private
enterprise to build small houses either for sale or for rental. Chamberlain's
own words confirm this:[30]

> I made it clear from the beginning, both in the House and in
> Committee that I did intend this Bill to show a bias in favour of
> building houses by Private Enterprise. I did that because I was
> sincerely convinced that, in that way only, shall we ever get a
> sufficient number of houses built to make up the shortage from
> which we are suffering today.

Indeed, he must have foreseen private enterprise responding largely by
providing dwellings for owner-occupation for he was to say in May of
1923 that in his view the age of the small investor in housebuilding had
passed.[31] This doubtless accounts for the 1923 Act's encouragement of
municipal aid to owner-occupation through mortgages and mortgage
guarantees. Local authority activity was permissible only if the Minister
was first convinced that it would not trammel the work of private firms.
In the case of both sectors, the legislation was seen as a stop-gap measure
until unassisted private enterprise supply reasserted itself. For this reason
the subsidies were restricted to houses built before October 1925.

It is worth recalling that whatever the degree of his bias, Chamberlain
certainly had no objection in principle to the construction by private
enterprise of housing for municipal ownership. As a politician in
Birmingham he had been instrumental in promoting the development of
several municipal estates during the First World War. However, his
inclination towards the stimulation of house purchase is beyond question.
In a *Times* housing supplement of 1920 he had written of owner-
occupation that[32] 'every spadeful of manure dug in, every fruit tree
planted' converted a potential revolutionary into a citizen.

The most interesting aspect of the legislation was the form which the
subsidies took: £6 per year for a period of twenty years were to be paid
by the Exchequer to the municipalities on each dwelling built under the
Act. This means of subsidisation, the fixed annual grant per house,
henceforth became the dominant device for channelling funds from
central to local authority for the next forty years. It facilitated decentralised decision-making on design and the level of acceptable tenders,
for councils knew that each variation in standard or tender price of the
built form must manifest itself either in the rents tenants paid or the
rate subsidy the authority provided. The switch to this subsidy form
and the decline in municipal activity were accompanied by a reduction
in the Ministry of Health's housing and town planning staff from 1100
in 1921 to 238 in April 1923.[33]

The new subsidy could also function like a butterfly valve in controlling the volume of municipal output and thereby the scale of local government's capital expenditure on housing. This point is illustrated in Fig. 2·1.

We shall never know what would have been the effects of the Chamberlain subsidy as the single source of Exchequer payments, for political events were to lead to the introduction of a new Housing Act. In

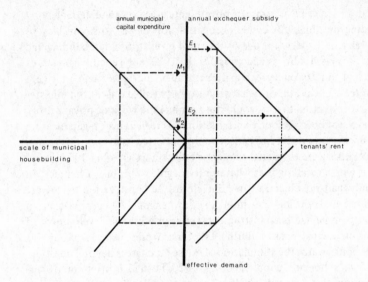

Figure 2·1 *The relation between Treasury subsidy and municipal housebuilding*

This figure demonstrates the relationship between a Chamberlain-type subsidy and the scale of municipal housebuilding. It is assumed for convenience that interest rates, construction costs and subsidies are known and fixed as is the use-value of the dwellings constructed. In the north-east quadrant, the lower the Treasury subsidy, the greater will be the tenant's rent. But the greater the rent, in the south-east quadrant, the fewer will be the number of households wishing to take up a council tenancy. In the south-west quadrant, the fewer the number of would-be tenants, the smaller is the likely scale of municipal housebuilding. Finally, in the north-west quadrant, the more diminutive the scale of building, the smaller will be the volume of municipal capital expenditure. Thus 'bouncing' off the functions, in a clockwise direction, a high annual Treasury subsidy, t_1, will be associated with a high municipal capital outlay, m_1, whilst a lower subsidy, t_2, will lead to a lower expenditure, m_2. Note that t and m would be measured on different scales.

December 1923 a fresh general election was held which gave the Conservatives 258 seats, Labour 191 and the Liberals 158. In the following months the Tories were defeated in Parliament and resigned. Ramsay MacDonald became Prime Minister as the leader of a minority Labour government. 'For the first time in history, a proletarian party became and remained the major alternative government party.'[34] However, the leadership of the party was not in the hands of revolutionaries: a majority of the most powerful figures in the party, and in the trade unions which gave the party its strength, accepted in broad terms the existing social order. They saw their task as the amelioration of the standard of life of the working class within the capitalist mode of production. That is to say, the dominant philosophy was that of social democracy. This was not inconsistent, of course, with the development of a vigorous public enterprise sector—if 'resources' permitted.

The leader of the Independent Labour Party group of MPs from Clydeside was John Wheatley, a man known for strongly held republican and socialist values and one of the chief organisers of the Glasgow rent strike. MacDonald attempted to persuade him to accept an under-secretaryship at the Ministry of Health but Wheatley successfully insisted he lead the ministry.

Wheatley's policies accepted the constraints imposed by the existing social order: the land was not nationalised; the construction industry and the financial institutions remained in the hands of the capitalist class; and the local authorities' building programme continued to be funded by loans from the capital market rather than by taxation. The difference between Labour and Conservative policy lay essentially in Labour's positive and permanent commitment to large-scale production with a quantitative plan for a ten-year period. In the very long term Wheatley wished to see the total replacement of privately rented accommodation for the working class by council housing. Rent control was seen only as a holding policy.

In order to raise public sector output Wheatley operated in two ways. First, as can be seen in the legislative chronology, the 1924 Act raised the fixed grant subsidy by 50 per cent in urban areas and doubled the period over which it was payable: the butterfly valve had been opened substantially on the demand side. Second, the conditions of supply were changed.

At the beginning of 1924 joint meetings were set up between the government, the building industry workers and their employers, at the time an unusual innovation. Wheatley's objective was to expand the size

45

of the skilled labour force on the basis of a regular and large-scale building work programme. Simultaneously the National House Building Committee was formed, composed of workers and employers. In February the Cabinet Unemployment Committee produced a report on housing which itself recommended a huge programme of construction of working-class houses and an expansion of the supply of the industry's labour. The general lines of the committee's proposals were approved, although Philip Snowden, the Chancellor of the Exchequer, was unhappy about their financial implications.[35]

In April the NHBC reported. It proposed the increase in the skilled labour force should be based on a 15-year rolling programme of house-building. Thus it was the first example in British history of long-term manpower planning. The committee also wished to have the powers to sanction materials price increases, to distribute the programme spatially and to stimulate apprenticeships. The preparation of a Housing Bill moved forward on the basis of the recommendations of these two committees. It was approved by the Cabinet in May and enacted in August. Details are given in Appendix 1. The Act included sections on the relaxation of the rules of apprenticeship, on fair wages in the building industry, and in Section IV defined its output targets. In historical perspective these were huge. In 1927, 1930, 1933 and 1936 the Ministry of Health could stop subsidy payments if during the two preceding years average annual production of dwellings by the local authorities fell short of two-thirds of the following output plans:

1925-6	1928-9	1931-2	1934-5
95,000	128,000	180,000	225,000

If the plans were fulfilled, the programme rolled forward.

After August Wheatley continued to prepare an Act on the price of building materials but in October the Liberals judged the time right to withdraw their support from the minority government and it fell. At the general election in the same month, the Conservatives won a huge overall majority partly as a result of the publication of the 'Zinoviev' letter. Baldwin became Prime Minister and Chamberlain returned to the Ministry of Health, the sixth minister in as many years. He was to remain there for five years.

Just as Wheatley had not abolished the Chamberlain Act, Chamberlain did not abolish the Wheatley Act. Conservative councils found the 1923 legislation more attractive because any municipal construction carried out was not accompanied by a mandatory rate subsidy. Labour councils preferred the 1924 Act because the Exchequer subsidy was greater. The table below shows the flow of construction under both Acts. The overall preference for the Wheatley Act is plain.

Table 2·2   *Local authority dwellings built in England and Wales in 1924–35 under the 1923 and 1924 Housing Acts (000)*

Year ending 31 March	24	25	26	27	28	29	30	31	32	33	34	35	Total
1923 Act	3·8	15·3	16·2	14·1	13·8	5·1	5·6	–	–	1·4*ᵃ*	–	–	75·3
1924 Act	–	2·5	26·9	59·1	90·1	50·6	54·6	52·5	65·2	47·1	44·8	11·1	504·5
Total	3·8	17·8	43·1	73·2	103·9	55·7	60·2	52·2	65·2	48·5	44·8	11·1	579·8

Source: M. Bowley, *Housing and the State 1919–44,* London, Allen & Unwin, 1945, p.271.
a   Transferred from the 1924 Act.

The most striking feature of the table is the violent instability in the output figures which grow steadily in the years up to 1927–8 and then plummet. To understand why this happened we need to refer to the broader political and economic context. In the year after the Conservatives returned to power the Cabinet decided to go back onto the gold standard, that is, to fix the exchange rate of the pound with respect to gold. This was seen as a means of expanding international and intraimperial trade and of restoring British finance capital to its pre-war dominance of the international economy. The rate chosen was the same as that which had existed before 1914 but this meant that British exports tended to be overpriced on the international market by about 10 per cent and domestic production found it more difficult to compete with imports from overseas. This self-imposed burden created strong pressures for wage reductions. In the same year, 1925, the mine-owners demanded wage cuts in their industry and in an important concession to organised labour, 'Red Friday', the government gave a temporary subsidy to the owners to buy off these cuts.

In April 1926 the subsidies expired and the miners refused all wage reductions. They were locked out and in May the General Strike was called. But only nine days later the TUC leadership terminated the strike without gaining a concession of any kind from Baldwin, who played the game masterfully. Thousands of working-class militants were sacked for their part in the General Strike and a few months later the miners were forced by privation to go back down the pits again. A period of unprecedented weakness in the labour movement followed and this can be illustrated by the average annual number of days lost through strikes, which fell from 40 million in 1919–26 to 3 million in 1927–38.[36]

Defeat in the industrial arena had immediate repercussions on housing policy. In 1926 Chamberlain announced that the Exchequer subsidies were going to be cut on all houses completed after September 1927: the 1923 subsidy was to be reduced from £6 to £4 per dwelling per annum, and the 1924 subsidy from £9 to £7 10s, with a proportionate cut in the mandatory rate subsidy. The butterfly valve was closed once again. In 1928 Chamberlain announced further cuts as housebuilding costs fell. On houses completed after September 1929 the Chamberlain subsidy was to be abolished and the Wheatley subsidy further diminished. As Table 2·2 shows, the response of councils to the 1926 announcement was rapid. Bowley interprets the slump in the following way:[37]

> Hesitation about starting new programmes or even completing existing ones was natural. Many authorities would decide to finish off existing programmes as far as possible in time to qualify for the full subsidy and then use the breathing space to look round before starting new schemes. Whether an authority would adopt this course or not would naturally depend on the state of the current programme, on the local enthusiasm for dealing with the housing shortage, and on the estimates of the effect of a higher rent on the demand for houses. Thus, apart from any break which would have occurred automatically with the completion of the original programmes the change in subsidy must have led to hesitation and delay until the future of costs became clear. This interpretation of the collapse in the expenditure of so many boroughs after 1927/8 is supported by the fact that it was rare for serious new investment expansion to take place until 1929/30, that is, shortly after it had become obvious that the fall in costs had more than compensated for the cut in the subsidy. The decisions, taken in 1928, to abolish the Chamberlain subsidy and to cut the Wheatley subsidy again naturally prolonged the period of uncertainty.

Before we continue the story beyond 1929 it is convenient to say a few words about rent levels and the social composition of tenants in the houses built under the legislation of 1919, 1923 and 1924. Average rents of Addison dwellings were 9–10 shillings per week and over 11 shillings per week in London. This was about 65 per cent greater than the average of controlled rents in 1921.[38] In 1926 the average rent for new houses built under the Chamberlain and Wheatley Acts was 7s 9d; in spite of the subsidy cuts, this had fallen to 7 shillings in 1928 and

6s 8d in 1929. The diminution was brought about both by a fall in building costs and by the reduction in standards which Chamberlain began to demand as soon as he took up office.[39] Using the work of Seebohm Rowntree, Marian Bowley has argued that 6–7 shillings a week was the maximum rent which the unskilled and many semi-skilled workers were capable of paying in the late 1920s.[40] Given that rents at this time did not vary with ability to pay the result was unambiguous:[41]

> There is really no doubt about how rent policy worked out in practice. The market for local authority houses was largely confined to a limited range of income groups, that is, in practice, the better-off families, the small clerks, the artisans, the better-off semi-skilled workers with small families and fairly safe jobs.

3 The return to a twofold objective

By May 1929 the Conservative administration had nearly completed its full term of office and general elections were held in which Labour won the largest number of seats but no overall majority. In June Ramsay MacDonald formed his second minority government, which was to last for two years. At the level of the international economy these were years of great crisis and turbulence, for in October 1929 the great crash began and by 1932 industrial production in the United States, Germany and Britain had fallen by 54 per cent, 42 per cent and 17 per cent respectively. At the lowest point of the trough the unemployment rate in Britain was 22 per cent. [42]

MacDonald was this time successful in excluding Wheatley from office. In any case, Wheatley's health was deteriorating and he died in the following year. Arthur Greenwood was made Minister of Health and his first action was to annul the reduction of the 1924 Act subsidy, which was to have taken effect from October 1929. The Ministry next began to prepare a new Housing Act, one which once again would make slum clearance and replacement a major activity of the local housing authorities.

In the period 1919–30 only 11,000 dwellings had been pulled down and replaced under Parts I and II of the 1890 Housing Act. 'While efforts were being made to catch up on the actual absolute shortage of houses, it seemed foolish to tear down existing houses, however bad.'[43] Under the Chamberlain Act, the Treasury contributed one-half of the loss on approved schemes. Whilst clearance had not been entirely absent from the minds of ministers during the 1920s, it was not until the autumn of 1928 that government committed itself to legislation (in the next Parliament). In 1929 slum clearance was a major campaign theme for all the parties.

Already before the election the Labour Party had decided to return to a twofold objective in municipal housing policy: to combine the replacement function of redevelopment with the growth function of general needs building. The former transformed the stock, the latter brought a net addition to it.

The preparation of the Bill and its passage through Parliament were not controversial. The details of the Act are given in Appendix 1. Its main innovation was the new form taken by the Treasury funding of clearance. In effect, a poll subsidy was introduced. In urban areas each person rehoused after a clearance scheme generated a subsidy of £2 5s per annum, which was paid by the Exchequer into the housing account of the authority in question. It was argued that this simplified the administration of the subsidy system, that it raised the Exchequer contribution above the level of the 1923 Act and that the amount of the subsidy varied directly with the size, and therefore the needs, of the family.

When the Act was in preparation it was clearly intended that the slum-dwellers themselves were to be rehoused by the municipality, unlike the replacement without rehousing experience before 1914. Their average household income was known to be lower than the average amongst existing council tenants and it was recognised that perhaps one-half of the slum population could not afford Wheatley rents. In an attempt to match the rents they would have to pay to their incomes, rent rebates based on need and income were encouraged. This must have appeared particularly logical, in that the subsidy paid by the Exchequer to councils itself varied with family size as we have seen. Later I shall return to the question of how this policy was implemented.

In terms of output the achievements of the second Labour government were distinctly modest. As Table 2·2 shows, after the peak of activity in 1927–8 when 104,000 units were built under the 1923–4 legislation, annual output for the 'growth' function never again exceeded 66,000 units. Moreover the 'replacement' function based on the Greenwood Act made very little progress in the years immediately after 1930. Up to December 1933 fewer than 12,000 dwellings had been built using the new subsidy and the total number of houses scheduled for demolition under the programmes of all the major authorities did not exceed 77,000.[44]

How can we account for these diminutive totals? My own view is that because Greenwood wished to re-introduce the replacement function, no attempt was made to raise the 'growth' output back to (or beyond) the 1927-8 maximum. But by the time the slum clearance subsidy was enacted in August 1930 and the necessary groundwork of selecting areas was under way, the international economic tempest had hit the British economy with full force and the ensuing political and economic crisis made a vigorous clearance programme impossible. Future detailed work on the official papers of the time should be able to confirm (or refute) this understanding.

In any event, during the summer of 1931 the stability of sterling *vis-à-vis* the other major world currencies was under severe pressure. Snowden, once again the Chancellor of the Exchequer, and the banking community wanted immediate expenditure cuts. The Governor of the Bank of England, at the instigation of American financiers, threatened that no overseas loans would be forthcoming to maintain the gold value of the pound if unemployment allowances were not cut.[45] The Labour Cabinet and Party split and in August a so-called National Government was formed with Ramsay MacDonald as Prime Minister and with Chamberlain back again at the Ministry of Health.

4 Filtering and clearance

Before continuing the story any further into the 1930s it is convenient to review some of the major developments in private enterprise house-building. In the fifteen years before World War I the average output of all new dwellings was about 80,000 units per year. Private enterprise building in the immediate post-war years, 1920-4, was modest, with an annual average of only 34,000 units.[46]

The figure was very substantially higher in the period 1925-33, averaging 131,000 units, and this output was fairly stable, in no year falling below 114,000 units nor exceeding 145,000 units. And then in the second half of the 1930s, the totals exceed all historical precedent: on average 256,000 houses were built annually in the six years 1934-9.

The boom of the 1930s, however, did not meet the direct housing needs of the population. Marian Bowley's data for 1934-9 show that of 1·2 million houses built in England and Wales only 26 per cent were for rental rather than sale and only 15 per cent were both for rental and with a rateable value which did not exceed £13, that is broadly speaking were built for rental to the working class.[47] Thus the inter-war years, particularly the 1930s, mark the ascendance of the owner-occupier. The reasons for this have been discussed extensively elsewhere and disagreement seems possible only in terms of the relative importance attributed to different determinants.[48]

On the demand side four factors were of most significance. First, the growth of the building societies had brought an immense expansion in the credit available for house purchase. The balance due to the societies on mortgages rose from £120 million in 1924 to £636 million in 1937 and the number of borrowers had increased from 554,000 in 1928 to 1,392,000 in 1937.[49] Second, the price of the entrance ticket to a house of one's own had been slashed. Possibly one-half of all purchases now required a down payment of only 5 per cent of the price of the house – only £25 on a £500 house.[50] Moreover, the lengthening of the repayment period from an average of fifteen years up to 20–25 years reduced the annual mortgage payment. Third, the interest rate the mortgagor had to pay fell from 6 per cent in 1931 down to 4½ per cent in 1935.[51] Fourth, those persons in regular employment found that their real incomes increased significantly because of the worldwide fall in prices, particularly primary product prices, associated with the Depression: £1 in 1933 bought 20 per cent more than it had in 1924. Moreover in Britain after 1933 employment prospects improved fairly steadily up to the Second World War.

On the supply side there are again several explanatory factors. First, as we have seen, rent control was introduced in haste in 1915 and the legislation in amended forms was reviewed throughout the 1920s and 1930s. Whilst it did not apply to new investments, the existence of price controls on the existing housing stock raised the perceived risk associated with building for rental. What had been done once could be done again. (And it was, in 1939.) Second, when choosing a safe investment with a steady flow of interest on capital, the rentier capitalist in the early nineteenth century had very few alternatives to a row of houses. By the inter-war period this situation had been transformed. With the introduction of limited liability and the growth of the Stock Exchange the capital market was now a national one. Without inconvenience, rentiers could place small sums in stocks and shares or spread their risks through investment trusts, life assurance and the building societies themselves. The relative attractiveness of investment in 'widowers' houses', so to speak, had thereby fallen. When owner-occupation funded by the building societies became a real alternative to rental for the middle class, any inclusion in the rent they were charged of allowances for management costs, maintenance and amortisation, let alone profit, made housing built to let uncompetitive but without such an inclusion, investment for rental could not compete with the capital market in attracting funds. The upper and the nether millstones! Della Nevitt has also argued that rental suffered from tax discrimination, compared to industrial investment, because investors were not permitted to amortise their outlays on housing when their tax bill was calculated.

As a result both of the fall in the annual cost of credit to the purchaser and of a decline in building costs, the weekly outlay on buying a modest house had fallen from about 12 shillings per week in 1925 to between 7s 6d and 9 shillings per week in 1934-9.[52] By 1939 about one-quarter of all householders were owner-occupiers. A sample survey in 1938-9 showed more than 60 per cent of the 'middle class' were buying their houses, and Ministry of Labour data for the previous year showed that 18 per cent of urban insured workers—manual workers generally and non-manual workers with salaries not exceeding £250 per annum—were owner-occupiers.[53]

The above analysis has been limited to explaining, for the case of the intermediate strata and the higher income sections of the working class, why housebuilding for rental was so small compared with building for owner-occupation. What still remains to be clarified is why private enterprise did so little building for rental to workers who could not afford owner-occupation. Two of the factors already mentioned—rent control and the metamorphosis of the capital market—are both relevant. In addition, building for rental to a class fraction whose employment and income was so unstable must have seemed a very high-risk proposition. Finally, we can return to an argument developed in the previous chapter that profitable investment in the construction of workers' homes would only be possible if standards were so low or densities so high that the new dwellings would have contravened from the outset the building bye-laws or the law on overcrowding as a statutory nuisance. So we can surmise that the 15 per cent of the flow of new dwellings in the 1930s which were built for private rental by the working class were let to the better-paid manual workers and the clerical workers who did not want or could not get a mortgage.

As I have said, housebuilding by private enterprise was carried out on a huge scale in 1925-33 and then almost doubled again in 1934-9.

Yet, in the 1930s at least, only some 15 per cent of the output was both available for letting and of a rateable value not in excess of £13 and only an additional 22 per cent was within this limit and available for sale. How do these output proportions compare with the effective demand for houses of different quality ranges by the population as a whole? Table 2·3 sheds some light on this question.

Table 2·3 *Increase in the number of dwellings and the number of households in England and Wales: October 1934–March 1939 (000)[a]*

Rateable value of houses	Additional houses	Estimated wastage[b]	Net addition	Additional families	Surplus
Up to £13 ('small')	517	42	475	300	175
Above £13 ('large')	748	61	687	150	537
Total	1265	103	1162	450	712

Source: adapted from M. Bowley, *Housing and the State 1919–44*, London, Allen & Unwin, 1945, p.172.
a I exclude local authority houses built for slum clearance but include 84,000 units built for general needs and decrowding.
b I have assumed the wastage was distributed between the two categories in equal proportion to additional output.

The table suggests the following process. (The subject is very much under-researched.) A huge excess of building of 'large' houses took place. These were taken up by migration of middle-class tenants from their existing houses. There was also a substantial surplus of 'small' houses built, for rental and for sale. These, too, were taken up by outmigration: probably these new dwellings were each occupied by a single household and the owners or tenants were the highest paid fraction of the manual and clerical working class. After allowance for wastage (the demolition of existing dwellings) and assuming no great increase in the number of vacant houses, the stock of dwellings existing in 1934 were redistributed within the working class so as to reduce overcrowding and multi-occupation. Bowley estimated that the ratio of private families to private dwellings fell from 1·04 in September 1934 to 0·97 in March 1939, a decrease of 6·5 per cent.[54] Redistribution must have been spatially concentrated and haphazard since it would have taken place only in those areas where substantial outmigration had occurred. The 1930s, then, were the golden age of private enterprise housebuilding, the triumph of filtering and owner-occupier suburbanisation.

Now let us return to the development of policy in the state sector. In November 1931 we had a situation in which Ramsay MacDonald was the Prime Minister of the second National Government, Sir Hilton Young had succeeded Chamberlain at the Ministry of Health, the international crisis was in full spate, orthodox economic opinion required reduction in public expenditure and the leaders of the labour movement were collaborating with the government in the pursuit of its policies. Within sixteen months—by March 1933—a stunning switch in the state's housing objectives had been broached, discussed, drafted and legislated. The growth function was jettisoned and municipal housebuilding effectively was limited to slum clearance.

The philosophy of the new policy can be found in various governmental reports and ministerial circulars.[55] It held that private enterprise output was—even in 1932—so large that councils no longer needed to build for general needs. Its role should be contained, therefore, to slum clearance and rehousing. This policy would permit cuts in public expenditure, eliminate competition with private enterprise and yet carry through the functions which the private sector was recognised as incapable of fulfilling. Unsubsidised general-needs building could continue in localities where private firms' output needed to be supplemented. The existing flow of subsidies and those subsidies on new redevelopment schemes should be channelled to the poorest fraction of the council tenant population.

Great optimism was expressed by officials and ministers on the likely scale of private building for working-class rental. We have already seen that this was unjustified. When the 1933 Housing Act abolished the Wheatley subsidy it was accompanied by a half-baked scheme to encourage building society loans to those willing to invest in working-class dwellings for rental. Wilding has shown convincingly that this was a device to disguise the negativism of the National Government's policy. Francis, a senior civil servant in the Ministry of Health, wrote at the time:[56] 'it is to our advantage to have what looks like a new scheme rather than to say that we rely entirely on private enterprise.'

Thus the 1933 legislation represented a return to the Cross Act, to the very earliest and most primitive mode of local authority housebuilding, to a sanitary policy. Bowley wrote:[57]

This optimistic policy would mean quite simply that those people
who could not buy houses but could afford to pay either an
economic, or a commercial, rent for new houses might get them,
if they happened to live in areas where local authorities were
particularly energetic, or private investors particularly enterprising.

Those who could not pay even an economic rent for new houses would go without, unless they actually fell into the slum category. The Government had gone as near to rejecting responsibility for working-class housing as it could. The principles of 1923, unwillingly abandoned after the Wheatley Act, had at last triumphed. Practical responsibility for dealing with any but the very worst housing conditions had been abandoned.

Moreover the new policy was adopted by the Cabinet when the 1931 census had just shown that in Great Britain there were 1 million more households than there were dwellings.

The effect of the changes in government and in policy was evident, in terms of the number of municipal houses which received loan sanctions, even before the new legislation received the Royal assent. The figure fell from 85,000 in 1931 to 40,000 in 1932.[58] The data on completions carried out under clearance legislation is given in Table 2·4.

Table 2·4 *Dwellings built in England and Wales 1931-9 under the slum clearance programmes ('000)*

Year ending 31 March	1931	1932	1933	1934	1935	1936	1937	1938	1939	Total
Number	–	2·4	6·0	9·0	23·4	39·1	54·7	56·8	74·1	265·5

Source: M. Bowley, *Housing and the State 1919-44,* London, Allen & Unwin, 1945, p.271.

The 1933 Act had called for local authority programmes which would abolish the slums in five years. The area surveys carried out for this purpose gave a derisory aggregate target, accepted by the Ministry of Health in January 1934, of 267,000 dwellings to be closed or demolished, 2·8 per cent of the 1931 stock of houses in England and Wales. Later revisions raised this total considerably but by March 1939 there had been a shortfall of 22,000 dwellings even with respect to the original, diminutive programme. As a result there were as many slums planned for clearance in 1939 as there had been five years earlier. The total number of replacement dwellings constructed in 1931-9 was only 23 per cent greater than the average *annual* output of privately built houses in the same period!

The switch back to a sanitary policy was accompanied by an attack on the standards of new dwellings. Chamberlain, Young and the senior civil servants all wanted house sizes reduced. At their nadir in 1932 the average area of three-bedroom houses in approved tenders was only 720 square feet, 68 per cent of their 1949 peak. The policy was defended as a means of providing houses within the means of poorer workers. Francis was more frank in private. Commenting on Circular 1238 of January 1932, which instructed the authorities to concentrate on small houses, he said:[59] 'it was directed in fact less to the benefit of the working classes than to the limitation of the number of houses to be erected and the avoidance of expenditure on houses of substantial size.' The same circular specified that proposals for new building were to be limited to housing families with children living in insanitary or overcrowded conditions and unable to rent from private enterprise. Many of the estates built in the 1930s were to become the ghettos of the 1960s, in strong contrast to the housing approved under the full Wheatley subsidy.

The familiar decanting problems appeared as slum clearance got under way: where were the workers to be housed whilst their old houses were being razed? The answer was in cottage estates built on green field sites on the periphery of the town. The solution was not always a popular one. Fares between home and work rose sharply as did journey-to-work times and if public transport was not available at the hours of day or night when it was required—in the case of shift work for example—the worker was forced to choose between his new home and his old job. If the choice favoured the latter he and his family would have to squeeze themselves into the areas untouched by the clearance programme. There were other problems—the sense of isolation, the loss of community spirit—and these were exacerbated by the meagre provision of communal facilities on the new estates.

All of these factors, in addition to the high rents charged in the council sector compared with controlled rents in the slums, could lead to strong opposition to the clearance programmes from those who were supposed to benefit, as Alison Ravetz has described in her unique, longitudinal study of the Quarry Hill Estate in Leeds.[60]

As the decade passed the proportion of flats built increased but even in the two years before war broke out the figure had risen only to about 12 per cent of new building.[61] Branson and Heinemann comment:[62]

> For the most part the blocks built at this time were severely utilitarian in character. Often five storeys high, they were usually served by concrete staircases with outside balcony access making one side both dark and noisy. The bleak paved yards were not often relieved by trees or grass. The rooms were small—a flat of three bedrooms, living-room, kitchen and bathroom had a floor

space of about 658 sq.ft. The equipment was fairly rudimentary—
hot water had to be pumped to the bath from a copper installed
in the kitchen.

I now want to look at the outcome of the Ministry of Health's advice
on subsidy concentration. In 1935 an Act was passed requiring the
municipalities to draw together into a single Housing Revenue Account
all of the rents, subsidies, debt charges and other current expenditures
associated with the dwellings they had built since the Addison Act. This
measure's chief advantage was that such 'rent pooling' enabled the local
authorities to adjust the rents they charged to the differences between
dwellings in terms of their use-values, a question to which we shall
return in Chapter 7. The new law also simplified accounting practice
since it was no longer necessary separately to balance the books of
houses built under different Acts. But in the eyes of the Ministry of
Health the main attraction of consolidating the accounts in this way
was quite distinct from these first two considerations. It was that consolidation would enable the authorities to regard all the Exchequer and
rate subsidies accruing to their housing stock as a unified funding source
for the payment of rent rebates to the poorest fractions of the body of
tenants.

In spite of Greenwood's recommendations in 1930 and the passage
of the 1935 Act, by 1938 only 112 authorities out of 1536 were
operating rebate schemes and even in these cases only a small fraction
of the authority's subsidy income was used. The Ministry's exhortations
had been ignored. The reason was that such schemes were detested by
the tenants, for their effective implementation required a means test, a
form of social control which had been bitterly fought in the sphere of
unemployment benefits. Moreover, whilst rebate schemes brought rent
reductions for those more in need, *ipso facto* they meant rent rises for
the majority of tenants. This was a second ground for opposition to
them. The two biggest rent strikes in the council sector between the
wars were in response to rebate schemes. In Leeds the tenants lost their
fight against 'Jenkinson's differentials' but the Labour Party lost the
subsequent election. In Birmingham in 1938-9 a well-organised campaign
by the tenants achieved a major victory over Liberal–Unionist plans for
a switch to slum clearance, rent rebates and rent increases, and for driving
out of higher-income households from the local waiting list and from
council tenancies where they already enjoyed them.[63]

The last major innovation in housing policy between the wars concerns overcrowding. The 1931 census had shown that in England and Wales there were 50,000 families living at densities of four or more persons per room and 180,000 families living at densities of three or more persons per room. The situation of a family living in overcrowded conditions in a house which was not technically unfit could be as unbearable as that of a family living in an unfit dwelling which was not overcrowded. In both cases the root cause was the same: the wages received by the family were low in comparison with the ruling level of rents for space, location and facilities. Thus, when the 1933 Act terminated subsidies on all dwellings except those built for slum clearance purposes, criticism was voiced immediately that this left the overcrowded in 'fit' property in a desperate plight. After all, that there still existed a general shortage of working-class housing to let was recognised in the strengthening of rent control legislation in 1933 and again in 1938.[64]

In November 1933 the AMC called for a subsidy to relieve overcrowding and in spite of opposition from the Chancellor of the Exchequer (Chamberlain!) the Cabinet in July 1934 agreed to new legislation.[65] The Act was passed in 1935 and is described in Appendix 1. On reading the small print one sees what an astonishing piece of legerdemain it was. Overcrowding was defined to exist either where persons of opposite sex above the age of nine had to sleep in the same room, husband and wife excepted, or in the case of high density per room. In the former case overcrowding could exist only in the case of one-room dwellings! In the latter case, as the legislative chronology shows, the standard set was so low that, for example, a man and his wife living in two rooms with three children of ages six months, two years and five years would not constitute overcrowding. Having defined the problem away, the politicians and civil servants proceeded to 'discover' that in England and Wales only 3·8 per cent of working-class families were overcrowded. Of these, 56 per cent were exceptionally large families and 43 per cent lived in exceptionally small houses.[66] If the definition had said living quarters should not be used for sleeping the overcrowding proportion would have risen to 9·6 per cent. Even the stringent definition gave an overcrowding rate of 22·6 per cent in Scotland![67] To cap it all, local authorities rehousing overcrowded families were subsidised only in special cases. The outcome was inevitable: by 31 March 1939 only 24,000 dwellings had been built under the decrowding legislation. The most positive feature of the 1935 Act was that it made overcrowding a punishable offence everywhere and imposed a duty on councils to abate it.

By the end of the 1930s, despite the fact that it had failed to fulfil even the original, ultra-modest target of 1934, the slum clearance programme had accomplished a great deal when compared with the earlier years of the century. Moreover, more than 30,000 dwellings were completed in 1938-9 in Great Britain as part of local authority production for decrowding and general needs, so that aggregate council output for that year was the highest on record at 121,653 units.

The last Act of the Conservative administration—by now Neville Chamberlain was Prime Minister—was in 1938 to cut the slum clearance subsidy savagely, at a time of rising building costs. As a result average subsidised rents on new building rose by 2s 9d per week.[68] At the same time access to and the scale of slum clearance and decrowding subsidies were placed on the same bases. The purpose of the 1938 Act undoubtedly was to operate the butterfly valve once again and so, in theory, to free construction industry resources for the needs of the rearmament programme as war approached. It goes without saying that no building controls were introduced on private enterprise construction of houses for owner-occupation.

5 Synthesis

We have seen that, in the years immediately preceding August 1914, approvals for local authority housing construction were running at several thousand each year and some moves were being made in Parliament for an Exchequer subsidy. The First World War was followed not only by the introduction of a very effective subsidy system but also a willingness to countenance the finance of state housing on a scale which at its first post-war peak was equal to 87,000 completions a year. This qualitative and quantitative watershed was the result of government anxiety at industrial and political unrest at the end of the war, associated as it was with the deterioration in housing conditions, and by concern that private enterprise housebuilding for the working class would fall far short of needs—at least in the first years after the Armistice. When the first inter-war depression hit the country in 1920-1, and with the labour movement weakened after Black Friday, the December 1918 promise of half-a-million homes fit for heroes was slashed by two-thirds in its implementation.

However, by now the failure of *laissez-faire* to provide model dwellings for all at unsubsidised rents was seen so clearly that no government since

1919 has ever attempted to terminate Exchequer subsidisation. Municipal powers to acquire land, raise capital finance, purchase construction output and then to manage the council stock existed before 1914. But it was the singular conditions at the end of the First World War which drove state housing in Britain through an implementation threshold with the result that in 1921–39 average completions ran at 70,000 per year, despite the fact that private enterprise housebuilding was on a greater scale than had ever been seen before.

At the political level the most novel feature of the inter-war years was the entry of the Labour Party as a protagonist onto the parliamentary stage. From 1923 onwards this party of the working class was matched only by the Conservative Party in the power it exercised in the legislature and in government. The proletariat had penetrated the fortress of the state. The political power of the working class now lay both in the strength and militance of the trade union movement and in the capacity of the parliamentary Labour Party to operate the levers of the state.

The commitment of the labour movement to improve housing conditions, and in particular to council housebuilding, was much firmer than that of the bourgeoisie and the Conservative Party, although it must be stressed again that both parties promoted production on a very substantial scale. For capital and the Conservatives state housing was seen as a means of reproducing the capacity to labour and of securing the perceived legitimacy of the social order. For the working-class movement municipal housebuilding was a means for advancing the material interests of the class. For the trade union and parliamentary leadership the reproductive and legitimatory functions also were central; moreover successful state intervention served to underpin the method and goals of the social democratic philosophy to which these leaders had devoted their political lives.

As a result of these marked differences in the degree of political commitment, local authority housing output was extremely unstable between the wars as output responded (in a lagged fashion) to shifts in the strength of the trade union movement and in the control of the state. The other source of instability was the cycle of boom and trough in the national economy, for cuts in public expenditure were seen by the wise men of the day as the rational response to a balance of payments crisis or a slump. Onto these fluctuations was imposed the switch from general needs construction to clearance and redevelopment which took place in the early 1930s as a result of the boom in speculative housebuilding. Even in the extremely favourable economic climate which existed for private enterprise building in the 1930s clearance and rehousing of those who lived in the slums was still an unprofitable way to allocate capital.

Part II

The contemporary experience

THREE

Land: site acquisition and residential densities

1 Introduction

The first part of this volume attempted to provide in a brief space a coherent and structured review of the development and implementation of state housing policy and provision in Britain during the course of the century which preceded the outbreak of the Second World War. In this second part I take the experience since 1939 and categorise it in a manner which has, I believe, a more general applicability. The subject matter is divided into four areas of enquiry:

  (i) the access to and acquisition of land;
 (ii) the production of dwellings;
(iii) the finance of development;
(iv) various questions concerning the consumption of the existing and newly completed stock, by which is meant the political economy of the allocation and use of the dwellings after they have been produced.

    Part two follows this order of treatment and so begins with the land question.

2 Powers of site acquisition

The land, with the waters upon it and the minerals below it, is unique in our capitalist society in that it is neither produced like capital nor reproduced like labour yet constitutes a commodity which is bought and sold in the market. There is nothing natural about this, of course, for buying and selling rests on ownership, a social concept. Even today most land in Britain is privately owned and the historical origins of the contemporary situation can be traced back to the feudal mode of production—to go no further— and to subsequent social cataclysms such as the dissolution of the monasteries and the enclosure movement. The result is that when a local housing authority wishes to acquire sites in order to construct new dwellings it must enter the land market.[1]

Comprehensive powers to acquire sites for local authority house-building were first introduced in the 1890 Housing of the Working Classes Act. From time to time these were amended and since 1957 councils have used the procedure contained in the Housing Act of that year which consolidated previous legislation. A full description of the legal position would require a book in itself but the basic position is fairly straightforward.[2]

When the local authority considers the houses in an area should be demolished because they are unfit for human habitation or by their arrangement dangerous or injurious to the health of the inhabitants of the area, the authority can declare it a clearance area under Part III of the 1957 Act. They then purchase the land and the buildings on it as well as any adjoining land necessary for satisfactory development of the clearance area. Purchase may be by agreement, or through a compulsory purchase order, in which case it must be confirmed by the Minister. Objections to a compulsory purchase order lead to a public local enquiry or hearing before the minister confirms—or refuses to confirm—the order.[3]

Municipalities also have the power to acquire sites other than in slum areas. This is the case with the purchase of agricultural land for estate construction on a town periphery, for example, and for the purchase of fit housing stock followed by demolition and rebuilding in order to achieve a net housing gain. These powers are exercised under Part V of the 1957 Act. Such land may be bought by agreement or compulsorily and in the latter case it requires ministerial confirmation.

Local authorities build dwellings on sites acquired not only under the housing Acts but also under the planning Acts. However, these have been of minor importance in quantitative terms and such housing developments have been set mainly within comprehensive development areas. The Community Land Act of 1975 did not change this. John Silkin, the Minister for Planning and Local Government, made the point quite bluntly:[4] 'This Act is about easing the flow of land for private development.'

3 Land prices and compensation legislation

Before we begin to look at the data available on the prices local authorities pay for their sites, it is necessary to say a little both about land prices in general and about the changing legislative provisions which govern the compensation a municipality pays to a landowner.

The theory of land rent and land prices is a difficult and controversial field of political economy. Elsewhere I have tried to develop a new theory on what determines the price paid for sites in a market situation, drawing on the best in the existing approaches whilst avoiding their extreme lack of realism.[5] One of the features of the model and of actual land markets is that the price paid for a plot varies very markedly depending on the economic sector for which the site is to be developed. The major land-using sectors can be ranked in terms of the price level which is likely to be struck between the owner of a site and a property developer who will resell the plot after completing his development. The broad ranking from highest to lowest is: financial services; retailing; manufacturing; warehousing; housing; and farming. Of course the hierarchy of bids for a specific site will depend a great deal on the existing pattern of land uses in an area and also the actual bids will be quite certainly constrained by a district's land-use zoning policy. Planning raises the degree of monopoly amongst owners in areas where high-bid uses relative to existing use have, or can expect to get, planning permission.[6] Thus Drewett has pointed out that the value of 'white land' (agricultural land not designated for any use and not in a green belt) is one-fifth to one-tenth the market value of agricultural land with outline planning permission for residential construction.[7]

To continue the analysis the following definition of a development value will be useful:

$$Vxy = Piy - Pix$$

That is to say, when we consider the conversion of a plot of land from its existing use x into another use y, then the development value of the plot (Vxy) is equal to the difference between the price in the case where the land is sold to a developer for conversion to use y (Piy) over the price paid where it remains in its existing use. With this definition in mind we can turn to consider the law governing local authority site acquisition.

If one can avoid becoming confused by the incidental minutiæ, the legal position on site acquisition prices is quite straightforward. The main provisions are contained in the legislative chronology. When the war began the 1936 Act was in effect: local authorities had to pay the market value for the land and buildings they purchased. In the case of compulsory purchase orders in clearance areas, only the market value of the site was payable, subject to certain additions for 'well maintained' houses.

During the war years some writers had advocated the nationalisation of the land and this was promised in the 1945 Labour manifesto: 'Labour believes in land nationalisation and will work towards it.'[8] This policy was not implemented, so municipalities still had to enter the private market in land, whether they purchased by agreement or compulsorily. Instead, through the 1947 Town and Country Planning Act, what the Labour government did do was to institute a planning system which gave the state veto powers over any proposed development. That is, the government introduced the negative power of development control via planning permissions. Some Fabians could then obscure this retreat by claiming that the 'community' was nationalising development rights in land.[9]

The 1947 Act also introduced development charges equal to the development value of the land, payable when permission to develop was granted. As a result, an owner would now find his selling price determined by the land's existing use. As a corollary, the Act permitted local housing authorities to pay compensation to site owners on the basis of value in existing use rather than at the market value. Simultaneously, a fund of £300 million was set up to meet claims from owners when hardship could be shown to result from the loss of existing development values. Thus the 1947 legislation established an extremely important principle in local authority site acquisition: the price councils were to pay did not include or reflect a plot's development value.

After the Conservatives returned to power, the influence of the landed interests within the party soon manifested itself and in the 1953 Town and Country Planning Act the state appropriation of development values was terminated for sales between private parties. That is, the Act abolished the 1947 development charges. However, the 1954 Town and Country Planning Act continued to permit local housing authorities to purchase sites at their existing-use value, plus any admitted claims on the 1947 'hardship' fund. This created a huge anomaly: land sold privately allowed the development value to be appropriated by the owner and the developer; but when sales were made to the municipality, *no* development value was appropriated by the existing owner.

I have never seen an explanation for the Conservatives permitting this dual market to exist and it was not until the 1959 Town and Country Planning Act that the market value principle was restored for public site acquisition. It may be that those who were instrumental in shaping the Conservative Party's housing policy successfully argued in Cabinet that an early re-introduction of market valuations into local authority purchasing was a mixed blessing. On the one hand, it would have the advantage of restoring the fortune of those forced to sell to local authorities. At the same time, it would both raise public capital expenditure on the slum clearance programme and lead to an increase in council rents merely to pay off the higher capital sums, with possible further pressures for compensating wage claims. My hypothesis, then, is that the demands of a Conservative fiscal policy and of those who paid wages took precedence over the interests of the landed classes during the 1950s when the scale of local authority housebuilding was greater than at any previous time in British history.

During the 1964–70 Labour administration there was no return to the acquisition principle of the 1947 Act! Neither the 1967 Land Commission nor the 40 per cent betterment levy changed the outlays local authorities were required to make in order to acquire sites. Thus the basic principles of compensation remained unchanged until the passage of the Development Land Tax Act in 1976. This law establishes that compensation is to be equal to market value less a site's computed tax, itself equal to two-thirds of the difference between market value and 110 per cent of current-use value. Under present legislation compensation at simple existing-use value will not take place until at least 1985.[10]

In summary, through the 1947 Town and Country Planning Act the post-war Labour administration established a situation in which housing authorities acquired their building land at existing-use value, so that tenants did not have to bear through their rents the burden of the development value of sites. This position, after modification in 1954, was reversed in 1959 and not until 1976 was there again any exemption from full market value with no prospect of restoring the 1947 position—itself a retreat from land nationalisation—until 1985 at the very earliest.[11]

The analysis of the concept of development values suggests a potentially fruitful line of research into the attitude of the building and development industry to general needs construction by the state. Let us suppose the industry regards municipal general needs programmes and private speculative building as competitive with each other. The question can then be posed as to whether the private sector has any strong predilection for one form rather than the other, since after all in either case it is private firms which carry through the construction contract. This simple view, I would argue, overlooks the fact that the profit of the developer-builder in the construction of private estates includes not only a mark-up on the costs of construction but also includes his profits qua developer, which will be some proportion of the site's development value, depending on the outcome of the bargain he has struck with the landowner from whom the land was purchased. Thus, whilst local authority general needs construction guarantees the builder construction profit, it denies him development profit. We should therefore expect the private development industry to oppose general needs programmes, but not slum clearance and redevelopment. This interest may well have been important in bringing the so-called National Government to abandon general needs building in 1933 and the Conservative government to do the same, as we shall see, in 1956. To cite the *Investor's Chronicle*:[12] 'Despite appearances, housebuilding is only partially the business of putting up houses. The houses are the socially acceptable side of making profits out of land appreciation.'

4 The evidence on land prices

This short review of the changing legislative context is now complete and it is time to look at the published information on the scale of local authority site acquisition and the price paid per acre. Unfortunately, in spite of the welcome and remarkable improvement in the quality and range of published statistics on British housing over the last twelve years, it still remains true today that we know virtually nothing about either the volume or value of acquisition!

On the scale of purchase, a research report of the Department of the Environment shows that in England and Wales in the years 1966–70 about 3000 acres of land were bought per annum, most of it under Part III of the 1957 Housing Act.[13] I know of no other published data source.

On the price paid per site, the data is a little better. The same DoE source shows that mean price per acre rose from £3200 in 1966 up to £5600 in 1970 on Part V land, and from £13,000 up to £17,300 over the same years on Part III land.[14] So sites in clearance areas were three to four times as expensive as green field locations, outside London, presumably because they were more central and the cost of purchase would have included compensation paid to owner-occupiers.

The most useful statistic covering a longer time span is presented in Table 3·1. It gives not the acreage price but the land price per dwelling, averaged over the total number of dwellings in approved tenders, including all multistorey flats.

Table 3·1   *The average cost of local authority dwellings in tenders approved in England and Wales by cost category 1963–75[a]* £

Year[b]	Estimated[c] land acquisition costs	Dwelling construction	Estimated[d] other costs	Estimated total cost	Land costs as a proportion of total (%)
1963	200	2,190	410	2,800	7·1
1964	240	2,390	510	3,140	7·6
1965	310	2,690	540	3,540	8·8
1966	370	2,830	590	3,790	9·8
1967	410	3,090	650	4,150	9·9
1968	420	3,180	740	4,340	9·7
1969	420	3,040	730	4,190	10·0
1970	420	3,230	910	4,560	9·2
1971	590	3,590	960	5,140	11·5
1972	700	4,230	1,200	6,130	11·4
1973	900	5,860	1,600	8,360	10·8
1974	1,500	7,040	1,900	10,440	14·4
1975	2,300	7,690	2,100	12,090	19·0

Source: HCS. DoE, *Housing Policy*, 1978, Technical Volume Part III, Table VIII, 13.
a   excluding New Towns. Neither interest charges on work in progress nor the professional services provided by local authority staff, e.g. architects, are included.
b   years ending 30 September.
c   subject to substantial error. The data are based on a two-year lag, e.g. 1972 figures are based on the prices of land acquired in 1970.
d   fees, site work, and ancillary buildings such as garages and shops. Subject to substantial error.

No finely judged conclusions can be drawn from these columns: the regional mix will have shifted from year to year; some years will have included more high-priced central city land than others; the number of acres per hundred dwellings in tenders approved shifted with density changes; and in any case, the data are 'subject to substantial error'. But one conclusion is plain: allowing for the two-year time-lag in the table, we can see that in the nine-year period from 1961 to 1970, the plot price of land purchased by local authorities multiplied by the huge figure of 3·5! This was in a period when there were no changes in legislation and before the land price boom of the early 1970s. As a result the proportion of total capital expenditure per dwelling that went on the land component clawed its way up from 7 per cent in 1963 to 11 per cent in 1972 in spite of substantial price inflation in the other

71

cost categories. When the private sector house price boom did take place in 1971-3, the downstream effect on municipal acquisition costs was appalling: by 1973 they had multiplied 3·3 times in only three years with the result that the land component in capital expenditure had jumped to 19 per cent by 1975.

As we saw in the preceding section, after 1959 local authorities had to pay the market price for the sites which they acquired, so it seems sensible to compare the surge in land costs in Table 3·1 with the nation-wide trend in land prices. Table 3·2 shows the movement in land prices for private residential construction in the period 1963-76.[15]

Table 3·2   *A price index of private sector housing land sales in England and Wales 1963-76 (1966=100)*

Year	1963	1964	1965	1966	1967	1968	1969
Price index	74	84	94	100	102	118	147
Year	1970	1971	1972	1973	1974	1975	1976
Price index	150	185	311	483	480	331	333

Source: prepared from HCS.

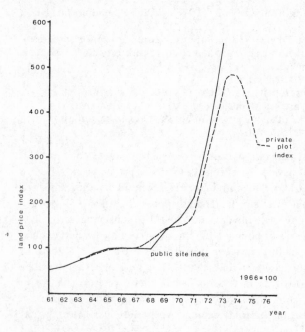

Graph 3·1   *A land price index for public and private sites 1961-76*

Graph 3·1 plots the index above alongside an index based on Table 3·1. The two series intertwine. Given the 'substantial errors' in calculating them there seems no doubt that they move together, as indeed they should for, with the important exception of local authority purchase for redevelopment, they largely comprise purchases at market price of agricultural land for development into residential sites.

The extreme and extraordinary paucity of data makes it impossible to say anything useful about either regional variations in municipal site acquisition costs or intra-urban variations. The lack of information on land sales within the private sector is understandable for secrecy is all grist to the mill of merchant professionals such as solicitors, estate agents and surveyors. The only statistics readily available derive from auction sales, the results of which are published regularly in the *Estates Gazette*. But in the public sector secrecy is not a source of profit and the information gap exists basically because so little research has been done into the data which lie in the files of every local housing authority and the Department of the Environment.

A welcome exception to the rule is the work of Richardson, Vipond and Furbey on land purchases by Edinburgh City Corporation in the period 1952–67.[16] Unfortunately, the authors failed to relate average prices either to the law on compensation costs or to the pattern of planned-use zoning in Edinburgh. From our point of view the main contribution of their work is to record the movement in acreage prices over a much longer period of time than the data in Table 3·1. In a total of forty-four purchases for which prices are available, twenty-seven fell in the period 1952–9 and seventeen fell in the period 1962–7.[17] The median value in the first group is £172 per acre and in the second group £2162 per acre, a thirteen-fold increase in the nine years between the mid-points of the two time periods! The scatter diagram is consistent, one cannot say more, with a steady linear upward trend in prices in 1952–9 and a jump to a new level in the 1960s. That is, the data is consistent with a price watershed after 1959.

5 Site prices and density of development

In Chapter 1, we came across an example of site acquisition costs which were so high to one of the philanthropic associations building model dwellings for the working class that the architect explicitly stated the need to offset these costs by building to a higher density.[18] The belief that high land prices generate high-density development is widely held amongst planners, architects, urban economists and geographers[19] and this section begins by examining that hypothesis with reference to state housing. In its most elementary form it can be formulated as follows: at any given density, the higher the cost to a municipality of acquisition of a site, the higher will be the sum of tenant's rent and state subsidy in order to meet the (notional) annual site rent. In order to offset this factor, planned densities are raised on high-cost land so that the site rent per household remains approximately constant.

But before we proceed further, some clarification is necessary on the meaning of density and on its relation to block height. As Stone has pointed out there are three commonly employed definitions of density in this country: net residential density, gross residential density, and town density.[20] In the first case we refer to the land occupied by the housing sites, the estate roads and incidental open space in the housing area. Gross residential density includes all this land as well as land used for local shopping, primary schools, other local institutes and local open space. Town density relates to all the land within the urban boundary. I shall usually refer to net residential density, which can be expressed as the number of dwellings, or habitable rooms, or bedspaces or persons per acre or per hectare.

What, then, is the relation between density and block height? Just as common sense suggests, net residential density increases with the number of storeys of the blocks constructed although, as Table 3·3 shows, density and height do not rise equi-proportionally. Each additional storey brings a diminishing number of extra bedspaces.

Table 3·3 *Number of storeys and net residential density in flatted blocks of local authority housing*

Storeys	2	3	4	5	6	7	8	9
Bedspaces per acre	64	88	109	127	141	152	161	167
Storeys	10	11	12	13	14	15	20	
Bedspaces per acre	172	176	179	182	185	187	194	

Source: P.A. Stone, *Urban Development in Britain*, Cambridge University Press, 1970, p.107.
NIESR estimates based on local authority practice.

This fall in the marginal density gain, in spite of the equi-proportionate increase in the plot ratio of a structure with storey number, is because the amount of space around the building plots must increase in order to conform with daylighting requirements and meet the greater needs for road, parking and amenity space.

However, it must be stressed again that there *is* a positive correlation between net residential density and storey height. The frequently expressed view that this is not the case is a plain error, often arising because of a confusion over density concepts. In the table, whilst net density virtually trebled as block height rose from two to fifteen storeys, the increase in gross or town density—for example in the case of a planned development in a new town—would be much smaller because land requirements off the housing sites are correlated with the residential population size.

Let us return now to the hypothesis that high land prices generate high-density development in the state housing sector. What it ignores is that local authorities do not simply buy sites and then move families onto them. The land must be cleared of any existing buildings; the site must be prepared; electricity, gas, water and telephone services must be networked; and dwellings have to be constructed. Only when we take all these costs into account can we state whether high-density development reduces the total capital cost per household of providing accommodation and thereby reduces the annual cost which has to be met from tenant rent and state subsidy.

The evidence on this comes from the seminal work of P.A. Stone and is given in Table 3·4.

Table 3·4 *Estimated construction costs in pounds per dwelling of three-bedroom housing in flatted blocks in the provinces in 1959*

Block height	Dwellings per acre	Site preparation, levelling roads and sewers	Public utility services	Dwellings including works within the curtilage	Total cost
2	20	127	153	1,617	1,897
3	26	101	145	1,940	2,186
4	31	88	140	2,199	2,427
5	35	80	136	2,394	2,160
6	38	76	133	2,539	2,748
7	40	72	132	2,652	2,856
8	41	70	132	2,749	2,951
9	42	69	131	2,830	3,030
10	43	68	131	2,894	3,093
12	44	67	130	2,992	3,189

Source: P.A. Stone, 'The economics of housing and urban development', *Journal of the Royal Statistical Society*, Series A, vol. 122, part 4, 1959, p.437.

Construction cost per dwelling rises with block height and tends to offset the fall in land acquisition costs per dwelling, particularly because of the falling marginal density gain. As a result the price of land needed to be extraordinarily high in order to justify high-rise construction on capital cost minimisation grounds. Stone suggested that land would need to be £46,000 per acre in order for a twelve-storey block to be cheaper per dwelling than a two-storey block. At the time land in provincial city centres was only about £5000 per acre. Needleman came to a similar conclusion at the same time:[21]

> Even when land is £50,000 an acre, it is still cheaper to build
> flats at three storeys rather than at twelve, and when land is as
> expensive as this the cost per dwelling is then twice that of
> houses built on peripheral or New Town sites.

Thus, save under the most exceptional circumstances, the hypothesis can be firmly rejected. In 1959, when Stone first read his important paper, he was employed at the Building Research Station of the Department of Scientific and Industrial Research. There can be no doubt, then, that the MHLG knew that high density meant high costs. If compelling reasons existed for high-density development other than the land price argument, one might have expected the state to have provided subsidies to offset, wholly or in part, the higher unit costs and so to encourage a development strategy by local authorities which cost considerations would have otherwise made forbidding. Such offsetting subsidies did exist, the most important measure being the 1956 Housing Subsidies Act. As Appendix 1 shows, the annual subsidy at that time for redevelopment work was £22 1s for flats in blocks of less than four storeys and rose (on all dwellings in the block) for each successive storey.

Rejection of the narrow cost-minimisation thesis still leaves unresolved the question as to why high-density development took place and why the state encouraged it through the structure of the subsidies available to local authorities. But before turning to this complex question it will be convenient to look at some of the data available on local authority housing densities. Graph 3·2 shows the average density of approved tenders for local authority and new town dwellings in England and Wales, excluding the GLC, over the years 1964–76. A clear downward trend is evident: the 1964-9 average is 169 designed bedspaces per hectare which drops to 155 bph in 1970-6.

Table 3·5 shows the *variation* in density over recent years.

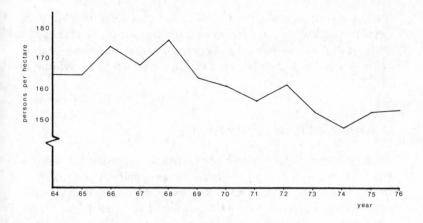

Graph 3·2 *The average density of approved tenders for local authority and new town dwellings in England and Wales 1964–76 in designed bedspaces per hectare*
Source: HSGB, HCS.

Table 3·5 *Designed bedspaces per hectare in tenders approved for local authorities and new towns in England and Wales 1970–5 (%)[a]*

	1970	1971	1972	1973	1974	1975
Under 74·9	2·9	3·5	3·2	3·6	3·6	2·3
75– 99·9	4·8	5·6	5·4	5·2	6·5	3·5
100– 24·9	8·3	9·8	8·5	9·6	10·8	9·8
125– 49·9	16·5	17·3	14·3	17·3	21·3	23·3
150– 74·9	22·7	20·4	15·5	25·7	22·3	25·4
175– 99·9	15·0	12·4	21·0	16·3	13·7	18·5
200– 49·9	9·9	14·3	12·2	10·7	10·3	7·5
250–349·9	13·1	9·6	10·3	7·0	7·5	6·9
350–499·9	5·2	4·8	7·7	3·5	3·7	2·6
500 or more	1·6	2·3	1·9	1·1	0·3	0·2
Total bedspaces	100	100	100	100	100	100

Source: HCS, supplementary tables.
a excludes the Greater London Council.

In every year more than 50 per cent of the total bedspaces fall in the range of 125–199·9 bph. The concept of a high-density development is a relative one and there seems to be no widely accepted definition for this country. The table enables each reader to calculate the proportion

77

of high-density contribution for his or her own definition. But if we were to take 200 bph as a minimum, for example, then more than one-fifth of all dwellings in local authority and new town developments in 1970–4 were 'high density', although this figure fell to 17 per cent in 1975.

6 Density, politics and planning

With this brief glance at some of the data on net residential densities complete and with the land-cost minimisation hypothesis firmly negated, let us turn to look at an alternative view of the origin of high-density development in the local authority housing sector. Here I draw heavily on the work of Peter Hall and his co-authors and on E.W. Cooney's outstanding paper on the origin, progress and downfall of high-rise flats.[22]

Post-war redevelopment largely took place in the great industrial cities of Britain where population densities were high, particularly in the slum areas scheduled for clearance, and where housing conditions were oppressive for a substantial section of the working population. So the pressure for high density redevelopment was very strong unless adequate 'overspill' schemes outside the central areas could be mounted, providing an alternative location for the families cleared from the slums, for those moving out of sub-standard accommodation not yet planned for demolition and for the annual increase in the total urban population. Substantial overspill building alone could permit low- or medium-range densities in redevelopment schemes.

Overspill could take a number of forms. First, there were the new towns planned and developed after the 1946 New Towns Act. Second, there were the expanded towns, based on the Town Development Act of 1952: voluntary agreement between an 'exporting' conurbation and an 'importing' established town led to the town's expansion so as to provide housing for those workers and their families willing to make the move. Third, cities could develop estates on green field sites within the periphery of their administrative area or they could extend their boundary if they were permitted. Fourth, authorities could build housing estates outside their own boundaries.

All four of these alternatives were pursued as any post-war history of British planning reveals. However, in the 1950s and 1960s, a coalition of interests developed which checked the implementation of an overspill strategy on a scale which would have allowed low- and medium-density redevelopment in the cities. The containment of urban Britain had the effect of reproducing in a new built form, most strikingly in high-rise development, the 'maggot numbers' of nineteenth-century accumulation and concentration.

A striking description of the compactness of the urban domain in England and Wales has been given by Hall.[23] He has defined 'Megalopolis England' as a set of sixty-three 'metropolitan economic labour areas' running on an axis from Fleetwood in Lancashire to Brighton in Sussex. This territory contains 35 per cent of the land area of England and Wales but 70 per cent or more of its population and employment and within megalopolis only 18 per cent of the area is physically developed for urban land uses.

The policy of containment was elaborated at an early stage in the first post-war Conservative administration. Cooney writes:[24]

> The advice in the White Paper of 1953 that greater emphasis should be put on slum clearance was shortly followed by increased government support for planning of green belts around the major conurbations and encouragement of housing development at higher densities than local authorities had generally been accustomed to consider . . . Overspill, as an alternative, was not of course ruled out in central government policy but definition of a proposed green belt implied that overspill would probably be at a greater distance and to that extent might be less attractive or even less feasible.

Moreover the new towns programme was virtually abandoned by the Conservatives and the expanded towns offset this reversal to only a minor degree. In any case, between 1945 and 1970 the new and expanded towns contributed only 3·7 per cent of total new housing output in England and Wales.[25] As we can see from Graph 3·1 the return of a Labour administration in 1964 did nothing to bring down the net residential densities in local authority housing schemes.

The second party within the coalition was landed capital. Roy Drewett has argued:[26] 'The landowning interests in the counties have been a major stumbling block to urban expansion in many parts of the country and this sector of society is both vocal and influential in using the political process.' Their motivation seems to have been political and ideological rather than directly economic. Landed capital, sitting on 'shire' county councils, feared the in-migration of proletarians likely to vote Labour. At the same time they could state the conservationist case against the depredations of the megalopolitan octopus. Lowe writes:[27]

> The cause of conservation offers to the dominant rural interests
> a unifying, hermetic and socially acceptable ideology through which
> social and economic change in the country may be effectively and
> legitimately resisted. The need for conservation—of villages, of
> farmland, of rural amenities and landscape—can be used as a
> disarming and formidable 'last card' in seeking to deny important
> social welfare measures.

That same 'last card' was also used by the state.[28]

The coalition's third party was the local housing authorities them-selves. Stone has suggested that many of them feared that substantial overspill outside their boundaries would bring a cut in the flow of funds they received from ratepayers and from the state as housing subsidies and rate deficiency grants, more than offsetting reductions in their own expenditures.[29] Moreover, the decentralisation of industry likely to go on alongside an overspill policy was seen as a threat to the economic prosperity of the city. This is not to say that every authority within the great conurbations checked decentralisation outside their boundaries, for we know that planning policy has been responsible in part for the overall loss of jobs and population from London and Manchester to a ring of peripheral metropolitan areas.[30] Nevertheless the fear of actually gutting the great cities, some kind of planning hara-kiri, has constituted a powerful inhibiting force, never more so today when the current crisis is perceived by many as a real urban haemorrhage. In these circumstances high-density development has been seen as preferable to the secular threat of metropolitan decline. Those anxieties have been the more acute because of the inability of central or local government to plan positively the scale and occupational composition of their employment base.

At this point it is tempting to go on to consider why high-density development manifested itself in the form of high-rise flats. But in order to begin to tackle that question we need to understand something of the nature of the housebuilding industry, which is the subject of the next chapter.

7 Synthesis

The construction of local authority housing necessitates access to the resource of land. In Britain land is owned largely by private individuals and institutions, thus the district councils must enter the land market in order to acquire their sites. The power to acquire, compulsorily or by agreement, and the terms of purchase, derive from specific Acts of Parliament. In the period 1947–59 the acquisition price was based on the market price of the land in its existing use. This excluded the development value of each plot and helped the local authorities to keep down the capital expenditure on their housing programmes. Between 1959 and 1976 the acquisition price was based on market prices which included any development value and this led to an upward shift in compensation costs. It also exposed the local authorities to land price movements brought about by the volatility of speculative building and purchase for owner-occupation. As a result the land acquisition cost per dwelling rose from 2 to 3 per cent of total capital costs in the early 1950s up to a figure of 19 per cent in 1975. In 1976 a partial return to the principles of the 1947 Town and Country Planning Act was made.

One feature of the local authority sector since the war has been the high density of much new construction. Visually this is most striking in high-rise development. The argument is frequently expressed that high net residential densities find their root cause in high land prices. In general this argument is false. No definitive study yet exists to explain the spatial pattern of densities but my belief is that redevelopment densities tend simply to reflect the historically determined concentration of people in slum dwellings, save where vigorous planning policies for overspill have been implemented. Because overspill provision was limited in the post-war decades, by the state, by the landed class and even by the urban authorities themselves, redevelopment densities have been very high, imposing on architects strictly defined design constraints in terms of bedspaces per hectare.

FOUR

Production: the housebuilding industry

1 Introduction

The political economy of the process of production of dwellings is such a vast subject that several volumes could be written on it alone. Inevitably, then, Chapters 4 and 5 can deal only very briefly with many aspects of the question, although the bibliographical references should help those who have particular interests to follow them up. This chapter begins with a description of the construction industry as a whole, the number and size of the firms of which it is composed, and the degree of specialisation in housebuilding amongst the different trades. Next follows an account of the special characteristics of the labour process and of the distinction between traditional and systems building. Section 4 deals with the peculiarities of the contractual organisation of production and relates this back to the nature of the labour process. Then there follows a brief review of some particular aspects of the production of state housing, including the form of tender, the method of payment to the builder and the scale of in-house design and construction. Section 6 looks at the time trend in the average unit prices of local authority dwellings and concludes with a brief review of changes in standards of construction since the war.

2 The construction industry as a whole

The construction industry is one of the country's largest economic sectors and in 1975 contributed more than 7 per cent of the United Kingdom's gross domestic product.[1] Table 4·1 breaks down output into its component parts and shows that housing makes up 42 per cent of the total.

Production is carried on largely by private undertakings or by the local authorities' direct labour organisations. The industry is well known for the multiplicity of its small firms and this is demonstrated in Table 4·2.

Table 4·1 *Value of output of the construction industry in Great Britain in 1976*

	£m	%
New public housing	1,798	14
New private housing	1,790	14
Housing repair and maintenance	1,786	14
Other public work	4,100	33
Other private work	3,053	25
Total	12,527	100

Source: HCS, no.21, Table 5.

Table 4·2 *Distribution of number of private undertakings, employment and net output by firm size in the UK in 1975*

Firm size by number of employees	Number of undertakings	Employment[a] ('000)	Net output[b] £m
1–19	79,527	329	1,271
20–99	8,449	315	1,404
100–2499	1,419	440	2,374
At least 2500	24	146	784
Total	89,419	1,230	5,833

Source: Business Statistics Office, 1975 census of production.
a This column underestimates total construction employment for it excludes some 300,000 lump workers, i.e. labour-only subcontractors.
b Unlike Table 4·1, this value is net of the contractors' payments for goods and services.

The data shows that whilst the firms with fewer than twenty employees make up 89 per cent of all firms they contribute only 22 per cent of total net output. At the other extreme the largest twenty-four firms are the source of 13 per cent of total output. Even this understates the degree of concentration of control in the industry for much of the work done by small firms is on subcontract in the construction projects of the larger enterprises.

It will be noticed that Table 4·2 does not distinguish the house-building sector from all other construction activities. This lack of statistical clarity no more than reflects a material fact: there is no house-building industry as such. It is not the case that within the construction

83

industry as a whole one set of firms devote themselves to housing work and another set are engaged wholly in non-housing work. A great many firms produce a range of construction 'products', housing 'products' making up only a part of the total.

There seem to be two reasons for this. First, many elements of the labour process in house production are the same as or very similar to those in non-housing work: site clearance, the erection of the steel framework of a high-rise block and plastering are three ready examples. So the technical possibilities of resource switching between product types are manifold. Second, there exist important economic reasons for multiproduct activity within firms. It is a familiar fact that the aggregate demand for construction work in Britain is subject to violent fluctuations. If one partitions aggregate demand into a three-dimensional matrix of type of work, location of work and size of contract, then it can be readily understood that the demand fluctuations for any single matrix cell are even more turbulent. One way for the firm to deal with these within-cell fluctuations is precisely by covering a number of cells, that is by taking on work over a wide geographical territory, by tendering for contracts of varying size and by engaging in the construction of a mixture of product types.

Donald Bishop has pointed to the advantages and disadvantages of this 'non-commitment':[2]

> Building organisations (professional and contracting firms) have few resources committed to the construction of any building type or any method of construction. That is, they are merely organisations capable of building, and entry to a particular market is often conditioned by an ability to finance and manage work rather than by technical considerations. There is both strength and weakness in this situation. Strength in the lack of commitment and an ability to redeploy resources without mortal damage, an attribute not to be lightly dismissed if clients wish to maintain the present characteristics of the market. Weakness stems also from this lack of commitment, in that operational units have an ephemeral nature and there is insufficient time to take advantage of training, improvement, development and management, all of which have marginal rather than decisive returns. Hence the structure of the building industry is a product of the market it serves.

Whilst it is true in general that the activity of housebuilding is not carried out by firms which build or repair only houses, it would be a mistake to give the impression that there is no specialisation whatsoever. Table 4·3 shows the trades into which the industry's firms are conventionally divided and gives the value of the housing work they do. It is clear that the general builders and the building and civil engineering contractors take the lion's share of the business with 71 per cent of the total. Amongst the specialist trades, the most important are the plumbers, the painters, the heating and ventilating engineers and the plant hirers.

Table 4·3 *Value of housing work done by private contractors in Great Britain by trade of firm in 1976 third quarter (£m)*

	New Housing Public	Private	Repairs and maintenance	Specialisation index
Main trades				
General builders	157·1	196·0	125·1	1·67
Building and civil engineering contractors	132·1	59·3	16·1	0·84
Civil engineers	11·5	9·4	1·9	0·23
Specialist trades				
Plumbers	11·5	9·7	19·0	1·83
Carpenters and joiners	4·6	3·8	8·4	1·38
Painters	5·6	3·4	23·0	1·17
Roofers	5·5	5·9	6·0	0·94
Plasterers	9·8	7·3	3·6	1·79
Glaziers	1·9	1·8	5·4	1·58
Demolition contractors	1·5	0·9	0·2	1·39
Scaffolding specialists	3·2	1·7	0·9	0·58
Reinforced concrete specialists	4·0	1·1	1·0	0·84
Heating and ventilating engineers	13·1	5·2	12·7	0·62
Electrical contractors	9·8	4·9	10·0	0·52
Asphalt and tar sprayers	2·1	1·6	1·0	0·25
Plant hirers	11·5	11·1	2·3	0·84
Flooring contractors	1·7	1·2	1·4	0·73
Constructional engineers	0·6	0·1	0·1	0·03
Insulating specialists	0·6	0·3	1·9	0·41
Suspended ceiling specialists	0·3	0·1	0·1	0·15
Floor and wall tiling specialists	0·7	0·7	0·5	0·83
Miscellaneous	3·4	2·7	4·8	0·51
Total all firms	392·0	328·1	245·4	1·0

Source: DoE, Private contractors' construction census, 1976, Table 41.

A different story is told by the specialisation index which measures the ratio of a trade's housing work to its total work divided by the same ratio for the entire industry. The figure 1 indicates no relative specialisation; values above 1 do indicate such a specialisation. Thus the plumbers, plasterers and general builders specialise most in housing work.

Whilst Table 4·3 is useful in indicating the degree of housebuilding specialisation within a trade, it tells us nothing about specialisation within individual firms and as far as I am aware there is no published comprehensive source which provides such information. On this question I am driven back to some fairly elementary and qualitative judgments. Hillebrandt suggests that the very large firms are nearly all building and civil engineering contractors with head offices in London or one of the other great conurbations and with a national coverage. Specialist contractors are smaller and have varying areas of operation around their base but the most important may work all over the country.[3] Most repairs and maintenance work for the private sector is done by small firms and the major part of repair and maintenance in the council housing sector is carried out by the direct labour departments of the local authorities. Most new housebuilding is done by medium and large firms and virtually all the rest by direct labour.

3 The process of production of houses

When we compare the process of production of houses with the production of most manufactured goods, housebuilding enjoys a number of special characteristics which largely explain the peculiarities of its organisation. In the first place the final product, the dwelling, is extremely bulky and heavy and therefore impossible to produce in a factory and transport to its site. The result is that the construction of new houses is a complex assembly industry carried out at the site where the product is to be located until its demolition decades or centuries later. The advantages of construction on site are increased, as Stone points out, because of the need to tailor the dwelling to the site and to attach it to site services.[4] The materials and components used are themselves the output of manufacturing industry and over time there has been a shift towards increased prefabrication. For example, joinery in situ has been replaced by prefabricated windows, doors, staircases and cupboards; brick and concrete construction in situ has partly been replaced by pre-cast concrete products whilst ready-mixed concrete is now used for much of the remainder.[5]

House production as complex assembly work on site gives rise to two further and associated characteristics of the industry: a relatively low degree of mechanisation and the importance of craft work. The movement of the work-force from site to site is an obvious hindrance to the use of machinery in production since it requires that the machinery itself be mobile. Furthermore, few of the housebuilding assembly tasks are capable of being carried out by machines: machines do not build brick walls nor do they lay electrical circuits. The consequence is that capital per man in the industry is lower than any other of the economy's sectors. In 1970 it was £1200 per head at 1963 prices compared with £3500 in manufacturing.[6] Plant is mainly used for earth moving and the mixing and handling of materials. The use of power hand-tools has also become widespread. Much plant is used discontinuously. The under-utilisation of machine capacity implies relatively high costs for the periods that it is in use and as a result there has been an extensive growth in plant hire companies within the industry.

The manual skills necessary for assembly and the restricted application of machines has created a continuing demand for craft workers. Table 4·4 shows the relative importance of the skilled trades in the construction industry as a whole.

In 1968 the Phelps Brown committee suggested that operatives could be categorised into the apprenticeship trades, non-craft occupations with special skills, and labourers.[7] Dividing Table 4·4 in this way gives 53 per cent in the apprenticeship trades, 19 per cent with special skills and 28 per cent as labourers. Repairs and maintenance work absorbs a higher proportion of skilled labour than does new construction. We also have some data on the proportional labour inputs to new public housing in Table 4·5.

In this discussion of the nature of the process of production of dwellings I have not yet raised the distinction between traditional and systems building. Stone has provided a definition of these two modes of the labour process:[8]

Broadly, traditional building embraces all those methods of construction in which materials and components are purchased from the market and assembled on the site into buildings and works designed to the requirements of individual clients or expected clients. System building usually implies construction by the assembly of specially manufactured or prefabricated units, or formwork or profiles to produce buildings to standard designs.

Table 4·4 *Employment of operatives by private contractors in the construction industry in Great Britain in October 1976[a]*

Trade of operative	Number employed ('000)
Carpenters and joiners	112
Bricklayers	67
Masons	5
Roof slaters and tilers	8
Floor, wall and ceiling tilers	8
Plasterers	19
Painters	64
Plumbers and gas fitters	36
Heating and ventilating engineering workers	25
Glaziers	4
Paviours	5
Bar benders and steel fixers	4
Scaffolders	12
Steel erectors and sheeters	9
Electricians	54
Mechanical equipment operators	51
Crane drivers	6
Other building and civil engineering crafts	68
All other occupations including labourers	219
Total	776

Source: DoE, private contractors' construction census, 1976, Table 17.
a Operatives are defined as men and women aged fifteen and over, including apprentices, but excluding working proprietors and administrative, professional, technical and clerical staff. The figures exclude large numbers of lump workers.

Table 4·5 *Man days per £1,000 contract value at 1963 prices of new public housing work in 1967–9*

Trade of operative	No. of man days	%
Bricklayers	12·7	17·2
Carpenters	10·6	14·4
Plasterers	4·9	6·6
Plant operators	1·1	1·5
General labourers	23·5	31·8
All other operatives	21·0	28·5
Total	73·8	100

Source: NEDO, *The Public Client and the Construction Industries*, London, HMSO, 1975, p.8.

In the early 1960s the view was very widely held that systems building would rapidly become the dominant mode within the housebuilding sector, particularly for the public sector programme. The Ministry of Public Building and Works in 1964 set up the National Building Agency specifically to promote the systems approach. The NEDC pamphlet on the construction industry published in 1964 gives the flavour of those years.

Systems building, it was said, aimed to reduce the demand for on-site craft skills by increasing the proportion of factory-produced components and by increasing the scale of site mechanisation. The saving of site labour would be partially off-set by an increase in factory labour but substantial overall economies were possible. Further advantages said to exist were saving in the time of erection, and the benefits of factory production unaffected by weather where production flows can be accurately planned, standards maintained and the working conditions of labour improved.[9]

Bearing in mind the relatively low degree of capital concentration in the industry, any move towards factory production, greater fixed capital requirements on site and the deskilling of the labour force would have both assisted the largest construction companies to out-compete the medium-sized builder and would have reduced their dependence on sub-contracting work to firms specialising in particular craft skills.

But by 1970 P.A. Stone's judgment was that:[10]

It seems clear that it is by no means easy to develop systems of factory-built construction which are more economic of resources than traditional forms of construction. For example, in spite of the hundreds of systems which have been developed in the last fifty years, especially for housing, none appears, at best, other than marginally cheaper than traditional forms.

The reasons given by Stone were the high unit costs of prefabricated units if the level of demand does not permit high capacity utilisation within the factory; the inherent cheapness in Britain of burnt clay, i.e. bricks, on which traditional building is based; and the relatively lower importance of dimensional accuracy and freedom from distortion in curing with construction in situ compared with factory-made units. Bishop has argued that even the site labour requirements of systems building are only marginally less than in traditional buildings.[11] Bricklaying, carpentry, and plastering diminish but teams of concreters and specially trained teams of fitters and assemblers become necessary. In the 1960s the systems approach was closely associated with high-rise buildings and the increase in unit costs with block height has already been demonstrated in Table 3·4.

4 The organisation of production

I now turn to look briefly at the way in which housebuilding, public and private, is organised. Section 5 will take up some of these points in greater depth for the public housing sector alone.

The demand for new housing as it is put to the industry comes over-whelmingly from two sets of clients: the local housing authorities and the developers of private housing estates. The latter group very frequently are building companies in their own right and are then referred to as speculative builders by way of contrast with the bespoke work done by those who build for the state. In either case the client writes a brief and places it before the architect he has selected. The architect then prepares a set of drawings which will meet the demands of the brief, possibly engaging the skills of independent consultants such as structural en-gineers, particularly in the case of large buildings with complicated functional requirements. The large speculative developers usually employ standardised drawings of a range of house types for their estates.

Taking just those cases where the client and the builder are in-dependent, when the architect has completed the design in detail, has made his working drawings and has drawn up his specifications of the materials to be used, a quantity surveyor then prepares the bill of quantities. This consists of a list of the quantities of all the labour and materials which the surveyor believes will be necessary in order for the architect's design to be physically realised. The working drawings and the bill of quantities are sent to those firms which have accepted the invitation to tender for the contract. The competing contractors price each item in the bill of quantities and include as well figures for pre-paratory work, overheads and profit. The client peruses the tenders he receives and selects one of them, usually the lowest. In Scotland the normal practice has been different: the job is let out in a number of contracts to separate trades.

The firm whose tender is accepted will rarely carry out the entire task using its own resources alone. It is usual to subcontract much of the work. On a typical large site the main contractor's own direct work may be only 30 per cent of the total contract.[12] Large contractors usually have only a relatively small supervisory staff in permanent employment, office personnel excepted, and engage most of their site labour on a casual basis. Needleman has pointed out that some main contractors subcontract all the trades and concentrate completely on the organisation and supervision of the subcontractors. Electrical work, glazing and gas fitting are usually subcontracted; plumbing, plastering and painting somewhat less frequently. It is usual for the main contractor to do the bricklaying, carpentry and general labour of unloading, handling, concreting, excavation and site clearance.[13]

Subcontracted work may be for labour and materials or labour only. Sugden notes that there has been a trend for a decade or more towards the re-organisation of casually employed operatives into labour-only subcontracting gangs, largely self-employed. The Lump, as it is known, provides a simply negotiated system of piece-rate working, mainly in bricklaying and carpentry.[14] Its very existence has been fought in recent years by the building unions and the political organisations of the left. Labour and materials subcontracting is carried out by the type of specialist firm listed in Table 4·3. These are invariably small- and medium-sized firms which normally retain a permanent staff who are sent from site to site.

Site organisation requires the advance planning of the entire contract, the integration of the work of all trades, the supervision of labour and the quality of work, the ordering and progressing of materials and the provision and placing of appropriate mechanical plant.[15] Supervision of the whole process is by the main contractor's site agent. Because so many of the labour tasks are mutually or sequentially dependent, the speed with which the total project is carried out can be very sensitive to delay in the component activities.[16] The building team, this ad hoc network of professional consultants, contractors and subcontractors, is usually disbanded at the end of the contract so that many problems which may have been solved on one contract may recur on the next.

Before looking in more detail at the production of state housing, this is an appropriate point to relate the nature of the process of dwelling production to its organisation. The constraints on factory production, the complexities of the assembly process, the low level of mechanisation, the existence of plant hire facilities, the absence of scale economies and the inclusion in the demand vector of a multitude of very small contracts have all combined to encourage the continued existence and viability of craft skills and small- and medium-sized firms within the industry. Small, discrete jobs appear to impose disproportionate administrative and managerial costs on large firms and this type of work is predominantly left to their smaller competitors, whether they be general builders or specialist firms although the big fish do bite at smaller bait when times are hard. The larger the contract, the more likely it is that the medium-sized and large firms will tender for it, since the demands on managerial skills and on working capital become much more substantial. But although the large firm acts as the main contractor, the efficiency of the small and medium firm leads to the subcontracting of the major part of the work to this sector and to labour-only gangs. The tendency towards subcontracting is reinforced by the turbulence of demand at the within-cell level of the matrix of space, product type and contract size. Demand instability discourages the large firm from retaining a comprehensive set of labour skills on its permanent payroll. Casual work is the result for many of the operatives although the existence within a single area of a multiplicity of demands for specialist skills permit most small to medium firms to retain a permanent work-force. Inevitably in this system the network of working relationships established during a large contract is dissolved when the contract terminates.

One feature of the organisation of production which does not appear to be determined by the nature of the labour process is the institutional division between architects, quantity surveyors, engineers and building firms. In her excellent book on the British building industry, Marian Bowley has attacked with some ferocity 'the system' as she calls it.[17] She describes three interdependent activities necessary for the completion of a building: its overall spatial design; its structural design; and the task of erection itself.

Specialisation in the various aspects is inevitable. But what is not logically inevitable is what happened nevertheless in the nineteenth century—the evolution of a system in which each specialisation was segregated into a watertight compartment in terms both of training and use of knowledge. On any particular project on which an architect was employed the relationship between the architect and the rest tended to be that of employer to employed. The architect designed his building; if he was not able to design the structure to support it he passed this problem to an engineer. The possibility that an engineer's knowledge of structures might have suggested a more economical, efficient, or even more interesting, or beautiful, building was not normally considered. Similarly, by the time the design complete with the engineer's contribution got to the builder there was no opportunity for the builder's knowledge to influence it. The process was similar as far as the builder was concerned if the project started with an engineer. It is difficult to see how any system more wasteful of technical knowledge, intellectual ability, and practical and organising experience could have been invented . . . It must also be observed that the system, with its divorce of responsibility for design from that for erection, meant that the designer had no means of dis-covering with any accuracy how much particular items of the design, or methods of arranging the layout, cost compared to some alternative solution. It might have been supposed that the quantity surveyor's function would have developed to fill the gap. This, however, did not happen. His main function remained that of developing a form of bill of quantities which would enable the contractors to estimate their total tender prices, and enable the surveyor to check these prices sufficiently to see that they were not absurd.

Similar criticisms have been expressed—less pungently—in many other reports.[18]

5 The production of state housing

Now we can turn to describe some of these issues specifically within the context of state housing provision.

Forms of tender
There are four major types of tender procedure used by local housing authorities and their relative importance is shown in Table 4·6.

Open tenders are the traditional form but have declined to less than one-fifth of the total in recent years. The contract is advertised and any firm may compete. The disadvantage is that many tenders may be pre-pared whilst only one can succeed, which is wasteful of manpower. Furthermore the lowest bid may come from an incompetent contractor who botches the job. Selective tendering was strongly recommended in the Banwell Committee report in 1964:[19]

There are most powerful arguments for limiting invitations to tenders to a realistic number of firms, all of whom are capable of executing the work in question to a recognised standard of competence; to rely on price alone without regard to competence and experience, the quality of materials and finish and the ability to comply with a programme is to ignore factors vital in securing value for money spent.

Table 4·6 *England and Wales classification of tenders in 1970–5 (%)[a]*

Year	Open	Selective	Negotiated	Package deal	Total[b]
1970	13·6	58·7	17·6	10·1	100
1971	18·0	62·7	10·6	8·6	100
1972	14·6	63·1	12·7	9·6	100
1973	17·4	52·9	19·6	10·1	100
1974	17·8	51·4	24·3	6·5	100
1975	10·7	60·8	22·0	6·5	100

Source: HCS, no.22, table XXVI.
a Tenders approved for local authorities and new towns, excluding direct labour schemes and the GLC. Percentages are in terms of the total number of dwellings.
b Ignoring rounding errors.

Thereafter government circulars recommended the replacement of open by selective tendering and as Table 4·6 shows well over half of all public housing is now built using this tendering procedure. The tender documents sent to competing contractors should be the site plan, scale drawings, complete bills of quantities, any necessary schedules or specifications and the desired completion date. Six to eight weeks is the time normally allowed for a response.

In the negotiated contract some of the drawbacks of the institutional division of design from construction are overcome. The client, usually on the advice of his architect, approaches a single contractor, often one with whom a satisfactory relationship has already developed on the basis of open or selective competitive tendering. The architect and the building firm then have detailed discussions on the type and scope of the work and its financial implications. If these prove satisfactory the architect will prepare his drawings and the contractor will then negotiate a final contract with the client. The proportion of contracts concluded under this procedure is two to three times greater in the case of systems building than it is with traditional building as the normal documentation of design and bills of quantities for competitive situations is not appropriate when a contractor may wish to use a proprietary system.

A drawback expressed about non-competitive contracts is that they weaken public accountability. There can be no doubt that a negotiated contract concluded after discussion with only a single firm virtually eliminates all price competition on that specific scheme. It is particularly interesting to see that negotiated contracts now make up more than one-fifth of total local housing authority output, in spite of the clear link which the Poulson affair revealed between the corruption of some local government officials and the letting of housing contracts. As far as I know, no one has ever investigated the form of tender procedure in the cases where corruption has been exposed and a prison sentence delivered.

The principal advantages of the negotiated contract are its appropriateness to systems building and the opportunity it gives in traditional or systems approaches for a company to modify the designs to permit more efficient construction.

Table 4·6 indicated that the package deal is the least important of the four tender categories. Strictly speaking this arrangement describes not the tender procedure but the fact that design and construction are united within a single firm. This is consistent with open and selective competition as well as with negotiation. A NEDO working party report pointed out that the deal price is often negotiated on the basis of outline drawings and specifications only; this is insufficiently stringent in their view.[20] Table 4·7 shows that the average size of package deals is usually larger than all other procedures. The proportion of package deals amongst contracts for systems building was two to six times as great as amongst traditionally built schemes in the same period.[21] Marian Bowley has written that both negotiated contracts and package deals were stimulated originally in the mid-1950s when both building

Table 4·7 *England and Wales average size of schemes by tender type in 1970–5 in numbers of dwellings*[a]

Year	Open	Selective	Negotiated	Package deal	Overall
1970	27	55	68	62	51
1971	28	53	41	78	45
1972	30	55	52	83	50
1973	30	47	61	105	47
1974	29	44	70	94	46
1975	33	52	76	65	53

Source: HCS.

a Tenders approved for local authorities and new towns, excluding direct labour schemes and the GLC.

costs and interest rates were rising and when the switch to slum clearance encouraged government to seek all means to lower costs.[22] Similarly in 1957 the state attempted to reintroduce firm price contracts and by the 1970s over 90 per cent of schemes were firm price. This fell precipitously after 1973 when the DoE bowed to the industry's demands for fluctuating prices at a time of escalating price inflation. Unfortunately this undermined the pressure on firms to comply with the agreed dates of contract completion.

Client, architect and builder

I now turn to look briefly at the linkage in municipal housing between client, architect and builder. Elizabeth Layton has proposed a model of the procedure which precedes the putting of a contract out to tender:[23]

  (i) preparation of brief by client department, for example the housing department;
 (ii) discussion of brief by officers of the client department with the architect;
(iii) preparation of layout plans and preliminary drawings;
(iv) approval of these by the relevant client committee, for example the council's housing committee;
 (v) preparation of working drawings by the architect and bills of quantities by the quantity surveyor;
(vi) despatch of tender documentation.

The NEDO working party has made some interesting comments on the role of the client.[24] They argue he should set objectives, prepare the brief and establish lines of communication for monitoring design and construction. In cases where there exists a fragmentation of responsibility for a project between individuals and departments, the basic objectives may become uncertain:[25]

> The combination of an uninvolved client and a strong contractor offering a package deal did result in one instance in the building (albeit within cost and time targets) of housing which was subsequently found difficult to let.

They therefore recommend the appointment of a co-ordinator for each project to provide the interface between client, designer and contractor.

One of the most frequent malfunctions in the linkages we are describing is the commencement of construction before full working drawings have been provided by the architect to the builder. The NEDO survey of 478 public sector housing projects built in the years 1969–71 showed that in only 39 per cent of the schemes were all drawings available at the tendering stage. Relf calculated in one case study that the total number of manhours spent on design during site operations was 846 out of a total of some 2150![26] The cause of this may be the relevant council committee imposing unrealistic design deadlines in a misguided effort to hurry a project along. The result can be inefficiency in the planning and operations of the building phase as the contractor is faced with additions to and revisions of his work programme, all of which have to be measured by the quantity surveyor and agreed with the contractor. It is also said that council committees can be too anxious to compress the period between the appointment of a contractor and the start of site work, when he should be organising his resources. A rapid move to the site may prove costly later.

Method of payment

The capital which the building firm commits to house production for the state is at much less risk than that laid out on speculative developments, for the simple reason that the former is bespoke and the latter is not. Moreover the rotation of capital is extremely rapid, far faster than in private housing construction.[27] This is because payments by a council to a contractor take place during the construction itself. In principle the client's quantity surveyor certifies each month the value of work done and the client pays the amount on the certificate, less a 5 per cent retention which is accumulated until it equals 3 per cent of the total value of the contract. When the building is complete there is a grand settlement of accounts. The cost of every item changed during the course of site work is added to or subcontracted from the tender price. All outstanding debts should be cleared—but rarely are—immediately after the end of the six-month defects liability period. The pricing and agreeing of large numbers of variations and claims is the major factor causing a delayed settlement. Variations should be priced in advance but usually are not. This is yet one more symptom of poor linkage:[28]

> there is a tendency in some sections of the industry to recoup site losses, whether due to under-pricing or to inefficiency, by raising claims against the client on the grounds, for example, of late receipt of information, altered requirements and causes of delay outside the contractor's control.

The rapid rotation of the builders' capital implies, of course, that the total working capital required for state housing contracts is relatively low.

The building cycle

With the exception of certain civil engineering projects, there is probably no other commodity in Britain today which takes longer to produce. Christine Whitehead writes that there has been a secular tendency since the war for the period from site operations start to dwelling completion to increase. She explains this by the proportionate growth of large, complex contracts and by the greater proportion of flats in total output, these taking longer to complete because they must be started (and finished) simultaneously.[29] The building period itself can over-run very seriously—that is the actual completion date can exceed the contracted date substantially. The average time from site start to completion is about seventeen months in both the private and public sectors.[30] Of course, the total building cycle is much more protracted than the site operations themselves. The NEDO working party showed that in a sample of fifteen public sector housing projects completed in 1969-71 the average length of time required for conception and design was forty months whilst the average construction period was twenty-seven months, six months longer than the average planned construction period.[31] We shall return to this question of the length of the building cycle in Chapter 5.

In-house construction

I now wish to indicate to what degree local housing authorities rely on their own productive resources in the design and building of council housing. Probably the great majority of district authorities employ their own design staff. The figures for England and Wales in 1975 show that 56 per cent of all local authority and new town housing schemes were based on the designs of their own architects both for layout and building, while 30 per cent of all schemes used the services of the authorities' own surveyor.[32] Layton has suggested that there is a strong body of opinion within the local housing authorities against using private architects except where the volume of work is too great for salaried staff to cope with.[33]

With respect to the district councils' own construction units, the direct labour organisations, the total value of their housing work in the third quarter of 1976 was £130 million, of which 80 per cent was on repairs and maintenance.[34] The value of direct labour housing work as a proportion of all housing work is only of the order of 9 per cent. In 1977-8 a fierce political battle was being fought on the direct labour question, as the private contractors saw their workloads falling with the slump.[35] One of the results of the informal Liberal–Labour coalition of 1977 was to halt legislative moves to give some freedom to direct labour departments to tender for contracts other than those awarded by their own authority and in the organs of the contractors' press direct labour is found guilty both of inefficiency and undercutting the private sector!

6 Unit prices and standards

In this, the last section of the chapter on the housebuilding industry, I want to look at the long-term trends in the unit prices of local authority dwellings and the associated question of standards. Jointly with the scale and composition of production, unit prices determine the volume of capital finance required to be raised on the market. Moreover these prices and the terms on which capital finance must be repaid are together all-important in setting the level of the tenant's rent and the state subsidy per dwelling.

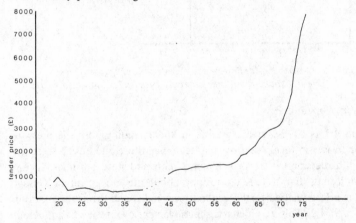

Graph 4·1 *Average tender prices of local authority five-bedspace dwellings 1914–75*
Source: Appendix 3.

Graph 4·1 presents the information on the movement in the tender prices of local authority five-bedspace dwellings between 1914 and 1975. The sharp fall in prices after the 1920 peak was followed in the depressed years of Churchill's return to the Gold Standard and of the

great slump by a price decline to about £300. Prices jumped to a new
level in the years immediately after the Second World War and climbed
fairly steadily until about 1959. In the following decade the speed of
increase was much sharper, at an annual rate of 7·6 per cent but in the
most recent period the rate of inflation has been without parallel in
peace-time, with an average annual compound rate of 16·7 per cent.

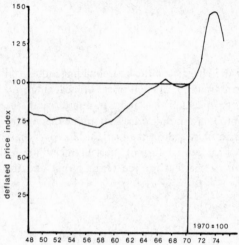

Graph 4·2 *Deflated price index of average tender prices of local
authority five-bedspace dwellings corrected for space standard shifts
1948–75*
Source: Appendix 3.

Graph 4·1 is of the greatest value in understanding both the pressure
for increases in local authority capital expenditure on housing since the
war and the upward trend in tenants' rents and state subsidies. Its disadvantage is that it tells us nothing about the movement in average
tender prices relative to the general price index and this is the function
of Graph 4·2. This graph charts the movement over time of an index of
average tender prices for local authority dwellings of a given space
standard deflated by the general index of retail prices, setting 1970
equal to 100.[36]

The most obvious feature of the graph is that prior to 1970 the
index lies below 100, 1967 excepted, whilst after 1970 it lies above
this value. Because of the way the index has been constructed[36] this
implies that the post-war trend of local authority dwelling prices has
been more rapid in its increase than the trend in retail prices generally.

There are a variety of possible explanations for this, of which the simplest is that the efficiency with which dwellings are produced, in terms of unit labour time, increases at a slower rate than is the case with retail goods and services in general. This thesis has been proposed by Michael Ball and the graph does tend to confirm his view.[37]

Our preceding discussion of the labour process in the production of dwellings is of some relevance here. It may be the case that the complexity and variety of the product and the site basis of the assembly work have together checked the pace of technical progress embodied in new machinery—the tribulations of systems building supports this—and that therefore for a given dwelling product the fall in unit labour time is less rapid than in the production of other consumer goods. If the upward movement of money wage rates in housebuilding is broadly of the same order as in the other retail goods and services sectors, the ability of productivity increases to check the transmutation of higher wage rates into higher prices will be that much weaker.

However, the trend in the deflated index is not a simple upward sweep. The gentle slope downwards in 1948-58 shows tender prices increased relatively slowly for an entire decade. This could be accounted for by a fall in dwelling standards in that period, to which I return below.[38] The surge in 1958–67 might be explained initially by the leap in the proportion of fixed price contracts in 1957–60, by the cost impact of the turn towards high-rise construction after 1956 and the reversal of the fall in standards from the early 1960s. Finally, the huge jump in the deflated index in 1972 and 1973 is almost certainly the result of a disproportionate increase in tender prices for state housing work during the private housebuilding boom of those years which itself was triggered off by the building societies' lending policies during the 'Barber boom'.

This analysis is fairly rough and ready and I hope that the fascinating shape of the index in Graph 4·2 will stimulate other economists to explore the question in much greater depth. For the present I shall limit myself to reviewing post-war changes in just one of the relevant variables—the standards of local authority housebuilding. I might add that the economics of internal planning, the standards of construction, equipment and fittings, and the built form of estates—in brief, the political economy of design—is probably the most underdeveloped dimension in the entire analysis of the housing question.

The standards of construction and equipment of local authority dwellings in the early post-war years far exceeded both pre-war standards and the building that was to follow. The paradox is that these years were a time of considerable economic hardship for the mass of the British people as they struggled to recover from a destructive war which had irreversibly transformed the world system of power relationships.

In 1944 the Dudley committee had reported on the design of dwellings and its proposals included a substantial increase in space standards in order to incorporate a utility room and a kitchen which was 'a good room' where meals could be regularly eaten.[39] The minimum recommended floor space of a three-bedroom house was 900 square feet and the calculated cost of the improvements proposed showed they brought a 39 per cent increase over the cost of a standard 1939 house.[40]

The annual report of the Ministry of Health for the year ending March 1945 stated that Dudley's advice had been embodied in the housing manual of 1944.[41] (The manual represented the government's official advice to local authorities on the siting, design, construction and equipment of their houses.) The annual report was telling a plain, old-fashioned untruth for the manual's standards were lower. However, the return of a Labour government in July 1945 brought Aneurin Bevan to the Ministry of Health and thereafter the implemented standards in fact exceeded those of Dudley. By 1948 the first Girdwood report suggested that more than one-quarter of the cost of post-war council houses was attributable to their increased size and improved amenities. Appendix 3 shows that the average area of a three-bedroom house in 1946–51 was 97 square metres (1044 square feet), 37 per cent greater than in the six years 1934–9.[42] By November 1949 the housing manual had been revised and republished to reflect the change in political attitude.

The beginning of the decline in standards can be pinpointed to Circular 38/51 of April 1951 when the Labour government was still in office but three months after Bevan had left the Ministry of Health. The circular promoted reductions in 'circulation space' whilst maintaining living space standards. Within three years the average area of five-bedspace houses in approved tenders had fallen by the astonishing figure of 11 square metres. The rapidity of the decline was the result of strong pressure from the new Conservative government which came to power in October 1951 for the production of 'the people's house', a design of 900 square feet which first appared in *Houses 1952*, the second supplement to the 1949 housing manual. Circular 37/52 also reminded local authorities of significant cost reductions which could be secured by keeping equipment installed to essentials.[43]

By 1961 a new official report on design was forced to conclude:[44]

the [Dudley] Committee in setting its minimum standards of overall dwelling sizes gave a sufficient margin to allow for the rooms to be of satisfactory shape and for the circulation space to be adequate. When, however, under the impact of economic pressures, housing standards were reviewed in 1951, this margin, which gave an important element of flexibility, was to a large extent abandoned, room sizes and aggregate living area sizes becoming in fact the operative standards. The effect of these changes was to induce a standardisation and a lack of variety in the internal design of the local authority housing of the 'fifties . . . .

Thus in the local authority field, emphasis on room sizes had focussed undue attention on working out a pattern of room areas which will comply with the standards, whereas the important thing in the design of homes is to concentrate on satisfying the requirements of the families that are likely to live in them.

At the same time the Building Research Station had found that kitchen storage provision was only 40 cubic feet whereas it had been 90 cubic feet in the early post-war years.[45] In an article published in 1965 Vere Hole demonstrated that four decades after 1920 the overall gain in designed space standards per person in the state housing sector was less than 10 square feet![46]

I have absolutely no idea of the political circumstances, but the marked decline in standards which began in 1951 eventually produced a counter-reaction. This may have originated in the civil service itself or in a quasi-official body such as the Central Housing Advisory Committee. The outcome was a decision in 1959 to set up a new design committee under the chairmanship of Sir Parker Morris. The committee's report was published in December 1961 under the title *Homes for Today and Tomorrow*.

The committee pointed to the growth of real wages since the war, the increased stock of consumer durables owned by working-class families and the burgeoning interests pursued at home by the individuals within the family. In order to match these changes they urged that there was a need for increased space and they made some stinging criticisms of the post-1950 decline. But rather than discuss the dwelling room by room—the Dudley approach—they turned their attention to activities and 'the conditions necessary for their pursuit in terms of space, atmosphere, efficiency, comfort, furniture and equipment.'[47]

On this basis it was argued that a new minimum space standard should be set in aggregate terms rather than for each separate room. The report stressed that the minimum overall floor area should not be simultaneously treated as a maximum. A corollary of the new approach was that each space should be usable for a set of activities through the year so this required much more effective heating: 'Better heating is the key to the design of homes.'[48]

The new space standard proposed was a minimum of 910 square feet plus 50 square feet of store in a five-bed-space terrace house, an increase of 60 square feet over the average size of five-bedspace houses under construction by local authorities at that time.[49] The recommended minimum heating standard was for an installation capable of maintaining temperatures of 55°F in the kitchen and circulation areas and of 65°F in the living areas (but not the bedrooms) when the outside temperature was 30°F.[50] In addition there were proposals for improved kitchen fittings, socket outlets and bedroom cupboards and for a washbasin in any lavatory not adjacent to a bathroom. These six specific improvements were costed and in aggregate they were calculated to raise the capital outlay on a five-bedspace, two-storey house by 11 per cent.[51]

However modest its proposals, I think it can be argued that the Parker Morris report was the most enlightened state paper on housing published since the war. The response of the government was perceptibly cool. The annual report of the MHLG for 1961 gave a brief summary and noted that a circular was in preparation.[52] The annual report of 1962, signed by Keith Joseph, completely ignored the document's existence! Circular 13/62 was distinctly vague: 'The Minister commends it to all housing authorities and to their professional advisers as a basis for making a fresh assessment of the sort of houses they should build in future.' In case this was thought to be too strong the circular also noted that 'Publication of the report comes therefore at a difficult time when the country is engaged in financial struggle.'[53] New standards would require 'realistic' rents and the 'less well-off' tenants should not be allowed to get their foot inside the door.

Since the Parker Morris recommendations were not made mandatory and since no additional subsidy was given for introducing them it is hardly surprising that they were not implemented. By 1964, the last of thirteen years of Conservative government, only 14 per cent of dwellings in approved tenders included all six Parker Morris standards, although 39 per cent included the floor-space standards.[54]

The return of a Labour government in 1964 brought a more positive attitude from the Ministry although it fell far short of making all six internal improvements mandatory. New public sector housing was 'normally' expected to incorporate Parker Morris space and heating standards.[55] This shift in position was reflected in the statistics: by 1966 41 per cent of all dwellings in approved tenders included all six standards and by the fourth quarter of 1967 almost 85 per cent had the new space and heating standards.[56]

In the meantime Circular 36/67 had been issued. As from January 1969 Parker Morris space and heating standards were *required* to be incorporated in public housing design although the other Parker Morris recommendations were clearly stated not to be mandatory. As Appendix 3 shows, in 1969 the average area of local authority five-bedspace dwellings peaked at 89·6 square metres, still 8 square metres less than the figure for 1949. Circular 36/67 simultaneously introduced cost norms based on current tenders, expressed in terms of building cost per bedspace, which were to be reviewed annually.[57] Housing subsidies were paid only on costs which fell within these yardsticks; moreover, no loan sanction was to be given where tenders exceeded 110 per cent of the cost yardstick. Thus the new design regime was a combination of mandatory minima in terms of space and heating and mandatory maxima in terms of permitted cost. The local authority architect was handed his circular and thrust out onto the high wire.

The new double constraint produced an inflexibility in design choice which recalls the post-1951 era of minimax dwelling spaces condemned by Parker Morris. The minima were not made compulsory where district councils bought up newly completed private estates at the request of developers in order to meet their cash-flow problems.[58] As tender prices rose at the giddy pace shown in Graph 4·1, housing cost yardstick tended to become out-of-date and this was to result in bad design as architects wrestled to stay within a cost limit which had fallen in real terms. This norm drag also became an informal way of slowing down the rate of tender approval.

Cost yardstick applied only to construction costs and excluded the continuing outlays after inhabitation of maintenance and repairs. In many cases the effect of yardstick was to secure short-term economies in capital outlay at the expense both of higher expenditure on running costs and tenant dissatisfaction over questions such as dampness, condensation, noise level and ill-fitting doors and windows.

7 Synthesis

Conventional discussions of housebuilding often begin by describing 'the scale of housing investment' and 'the proportion of gross domestic capital formation represented by additions to the housing stock'. At this juncture I ought to say why such terms have been omitted from this chapter and from the rest of the book. The synonyms 'investment' and 'capital formation' doubtlessly can have whatever meaning we wish to attribute to them. In my view these terms become most useful if they are based on two separate distinctions: between producer and consumer goods and between accumulative and non-accumulative expenditure. A producer good is, for example, a tractor or a textile machine or a tower crane, whilst a consumer good is a loaf of bread or a child's coat or a house. The distinction between accumulative and non-accumulative expenditure rests on whether (or not) an expenditure is made in order to employ the purchased good to make a profit—by starting a tool-making business for example or laying out money on a row of cottages to rent. Combining the two distinctions we get the four possible outcomes set out in Fig. 4·1.

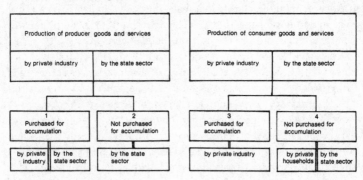

Figure 4·1 *Accumulative and non-accumulative purchase of producer and consumer goods*

In an advanced capitalist economy, production is carried out both by private industry and the state sector—and they also play the major role in accumulative expenditure. Non-accumulative expenditure is made by households and by the state. The production of consumer goods and services can be termed reproductive production since the consumption of food, clothing, accommodation, health care services and so on is the basic material requirement (in any society) for the reproduction of the labour force. Housebuilding, then, is one field of reproductive production and council housing in Britain is one form of non-accumulative expenditure on reproductive production by the British state.

Let us return to 'housing investment'. I use the term investment or capital formation in the sense of accumulative or non-accumulative expenditure on producer goods. In this sense there can be no such thing as 'housing investment'. As has been said, each one of us is able to use the term in his or her own way. But those who *do* use the term 'housing investment' should bear in mind these two points. First, housebuilding is *not* the production of a producer good. Second, in Britain since 1945 there has been very little expenditure indeed on new housing for accumulative purposes.

Having clarified my omission of any reference to domestic capital formation and having introduced the concept of non-accumulative state expenditure on reproductive production, it is time quickly to review the substantive content of this chapter.

Housing production is an activity of the construction industry, a sector noted for a multiplicity of small- and medium-sized firms, in addition to several dozen large enterprises. Construction is a complex assembly industry carried out on site, in which the volume of investment has been low so that the degree of mechanisation is relatively modest and craft work continues to be of great importance. Demand for the industry's distinct products is volatile.

The organisation of production is markedly fragmented. Design is separate from construction and site work is carried through by one major contractor and a number of subcontractors. Much employment is on a casual basis. Housebuilding for the state sector is largely done by private companies, although local government workers play a very important role in design, repair and maintenance.

The prices of council houses have increased very substantially since the war, particularly since about 1969. There appears to be a tendency for prices to rise relative to those of all other retail goods and services and this may be the result in part of a relatively slow increase in labour productivity in the industry. However, changes in internal standards and built form make measurement extremely difficult. With respect to standards, these were raised very sharply in the immediate post-war years in spite of the economic difficulties faced by the country. A brutal cut in standards took place in the early 1950s which was reversed with the gradual implementation after 1961 of the Parker Morris recommendations.

FIVE

Production: private rehabilitation and public redevelopment

1 Introduction

The process of production of accommodation in the state sector can be divided into four distinct types of activity: new building on redeveloped sites; new building on green field sites; maintenance and rehabilitation of the existing council stock; and the rehabilitation of newly municipalised dwellings. These categories are mutually exclusive but not mutually independent: for example redevelopment may generate overspill, which will require green field development, or the improvement of existing council dwellings may be perceived as competing for the same resources as does the improvement of the acquired stock. I would like to be able to present a graph of the breakdown of resource expenditure between these categories but the necessary data have never been published.

This chapter deals largely with public redevelopment, the first of my four categories, and its relationship with private sector rehabilitation. In order to prepare the ground, I wish to begin by clarifying some terms. The production process on a site which already contains dwellings can constitute either the activity of redevelopment or one (or more) of the activities of routine maintenance, repair, replacement, improvement and conversion. By replacement is meant the substitution of outworn elements or equipment, and improvement implies the installation of new elements or equipment not previously contained in a dwelling. Housing renewal itself, public or private, I shall define as either rehabilitation, that is the repair, replacement, improvement and conversion activities; or redevelopment, that is clearance and the construction on site of new dwellings; or some combination of the two. These points are summarised in Fig. 5·1.

In the absence of compulsion, owners of housing property—whether they be the state or private landlords or owner-occupiers—choose to finance housing renewal because they consider their dwellings to be either physically inadequate or economically obsolete. Physical inadequacy arises on two counts: from dwellings which were not of satisfactory construction when they were first completed, or from the process of physical deterioration. 'Adequacy' can be gauged only by means of standards and it goes without saying that these standards vary over time and space.

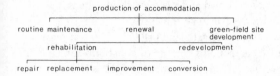

Figure 5·1 *A definition of the production of accommodation*

Given a clearly defined standard and a comprehensive survey of the existing housing stock, it would be a relatively easy matter in any area to state what proportion of dwellings fall below the minimum acceptable standard. What is far more difficult to judge is the rate of deterioration and its determinants. I do not think it an exaggeration to say that in the post-war period one of the most egregious areas of governmental ignorance in policy formulation was precisely this question, particularly the economic factors lying behind physical obsolescence. That is, how does it come about that the effective demand for routine maintenance, repair and replacement can fall short of what is necessary to 'hold' a dwelling in a stable state in terms of its physical condition? Thus housing renewal, with the exception of houses which were inadequately constructed in the first place, becomes necessary because of past failures to carry through routine maintenance and the renewal activities of repair and replacement. In that sense housing renewal has to constitute an historical schism in the life of a dwelling and, as I hope to show, the policies of the state have been aimed either at creating the social and economic conditions for that schism or at itself implementing the transformation.

An interesting study of the determinants of rehabilitation has been carried out by Kirwan and Martin in a working paper of the Centre for Environmental Studies and a restatement of part of their argument will form a useful prelude to the rest of this chapter.[1] Kirwan and Martin were seriously concerned that the rate of obsolescence could undermine progress in renewal and this led them to try to set up a simple model of private sector rehabilitation. Physical obsolescence, they point out, is due to the effects of time and use on a structure, and its rate will be conditioned by the building's nature and construction. Obsolescence can be diminished or off-set by maintenance and rehabilitation. The economic study of physical obsolescence, then, is the study of insufficiencies in the demand for maintenance—repair—replacement activities. A low expenditure is likely when:

(i) the dwelling is owner-occupied and the owner's income is low so that such expenditure is seen to be too costly;

(ii) the dwelling is owned by a private landlord who does not regard the outlay as profitable, perhaps because of constraints on an increase in rents or because redevelopment proposals impose a short life on the property;

(iii) the selling price of the dwelling, whatever its own condition, is depressed by neighbouring housing of a low quality, a form of non-planning blight;

(iv) the nature and condition of the house means that the cost of given increases in quality is high;

(v) the cost, including the cost of travel to work, of newer housing of reasonable quality is low relative to the cost of improving old housing.[2]

With these definitions and preliminary comments on the economics of housing obsolescence out of the way, I can turn to the substantive content of this chapter: to the scale and experience of rehabilitation and redevelopment and the balance between these two production activities.

2 The partitioning of housing renewal

Let us imagine that a survey has been conducted of every dwelling in the country and that we have scored the entire stock, from best to worst, in terms of each dwelling's use-value. Let us also hypothetically subdivide the stock into groups defined by each dwelling's floor area. We can then state the following proposition with real confidence in its broad truth: for any given group those dwellings falling below a specific minimum use-value can be brought up to the minimum through rehabilitation, the production cost varying inversely with the dwelling's use-value. However, if the same result were sought through clearance and redevelopment, we should find no correlation between production cost and the use-value of the dwelling which has been cleared. The point is illustrated in Fig. 5·2.

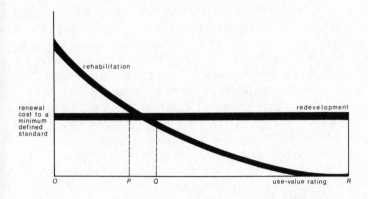

Figure 5·2 *The variation of rehabilitation and redevelopment costs with dwelling use-value*
For a given size category a very low use-value is associated with extremely high rehabilitation costs. These fall to zero for a very high rating. There is no such correlation in the case of redevelopment since clearance and reconstruction costs are independent of the original dwelling's quality. In this sense redevelopment is more cost effective in the range OP whilst rehabilitation is more cost effective in the range QR. The range PQ is indeterminate.

Obviously the actual situation is far more complex than this, nevertheless the basic relationships are true and these have constituted an implicit assumption amongst virtually all those politicians, civil servants and academics concerned with the formulation of housing renewal policy. The upshot was that it was considered appropriate to demolish housing which was totally unfit and then rebuild, whilst rehabilitation was seen as the most cost-effective measure for dwellings which were merely unsatisfactory. With respect to houses which were seriously deficient, then opinion could vary on the most appropriate course of action.

There is a second dimension to the state's renewal policies since the 1950s which I believe is central to a clear understanding of the British housing question. This requires the introduction of a concept which I call 'partitioning'. As Fig. 5·1 shows, housing renewal bifurcates on technical criteria into rehabilitation and redevelopment. I hope to show that this technical distinction was paralleled by an institutional division created and maintained by the state, a political partitioning of the set of housing renewal production activities. Rehabilitation was stimulated within the private sector through the private landlord and

111

the owner-occupier whilst the local housing authorities were discouraged from municipalisation and the consequential work of repair, replacement, improvement and conversion. Simultaneously redevelopment by the authorities was actively promoted by the state and no attempt was made to draw private enterprise as a developer into this activity. There are some important exceptions to this policy which I shall examine in Section 8 below. For the moment I want to take the partitioning thesis in its starkest form and try to explain why both Conservative and Labour governments followed the same course.

The political economy of Conservative policy requires no great elaboration. They had always viewed state housing as a measure of last resort, a stratagem to be used only where private enterprise was unwilling to act. We have already seen in Chapter 1 that since the second half of the nineteenth century it had become obvious private capital was unable to profit from pulling down the slums and rehousing their population in a decent fashion. Clearance and redevelopment had to be assigned to the council sector. However, the Tory view was that repair, replacement, improvement and conversion could and would be carried out by landlords and owner-occupiers, especially with appropriate financial incentives. Accordingly rehabilitation was reserved for private sector enterprise. Municipalisation was pure anathema.

With the exception of properties damaged and destroyed during the war, housing renewal did not begin on a large scale until the mid-1950s, when the Labour Party was out of office. Throughout the 1950s the party's policy was strongly in favour of municipalisation. Moreover men like Munby, MacColl and Eversley had argued the case for municipalisation with care and had set out the implications of its implementation in a number of Fabian papers.[3]

However, in the years immediately preceding Labour's return to office in October 1964 the policy on municipalisation was reversed. This appears first in the document *Signposts for the Sixties*[4] and the reversal was confirmed after close-fought debates at the 1961 and 1962 annual conferences. The core of the argument presented by those, such as Anthony Greenwood, who opposed municipalisation was that the 1957 Rent Act had driven up private sector rents so sharply that the compensation payments to landlords of fit property, which were related to rent levels of course, had made the policy unacceptably expensive. This volte-face was reflected in the key 1965 White Paper *The Housing Programme 1965 to 1970*, which contained no provision for socialisation of the existing rented housing stock.[5] Henceforth both Conservative and Labour parties pursued a bipartisan policy with respect to partitioned renewal, since they both simultaneously accepted the need for local authority redevelopment and rejected municipalisation followed by rehabilitation.

3 Private rehabilitation

Before reviewing the state's renewal programme it will be useful first to discuss the experience of rehabilitation in the private sector since it has had so much influence on the public sector's activities.

The housing professionals of the Ministry of Health and later the Ministry of Housing and Local Government were well aware in the years after the war's end that a large proportion of the housing stock required more or less intensive rehabilitatory work quite apart from the needs for slum clearance. In historical retrospect we can distinguish five dimensions to their strategy to stimulate private rehabilitation, all of which were designed to call forth private finance to swell those subsidies the state itself provided for this work.

First, there was the provision of improvement grants. Table 5·1 lists the main acts under which these were provided. The rationale for the grants was that by lowering the price of the housing renewal product a much greater quantity of rehabilitation work would be demanded than would otherwise occur. Table 5·2 gives the yearly data on improvement grant approvals.

The figures are fairly easy to interpret. In the first years of the improvement grant system, uptake was slow but it increased very rapidly in the late 1950s. The introduction of standard grants in 1959 is associated with a further leap in demand which holds fairly steadily until the more generous provisions of the 1969 and 1971 Housing Acts cause the number of grants to more than treble in only four years. The precipitate fall after 1973 is partially a response to the cancellation in June 1974 of 75 per cent grants in the intermediate and development areas.

The second dimension of governmental strategy for private sector rehabilitation was to raise the profitability of the private landlord's operation. This was done as a general measure through rent decontrol in 1957 and the 'fair' rents machinery of 1965. It was also related specifically to improvement in the Acts of 1949, 1954, 1959 and 1969 as Table 5·1 shows. These measures failed, for the number of dwellings

113

rented out by private landlords in the post-war period has declined without interruption and the number of grants taken up to improve accommodation which continued to be available for letting appears to have been well under one-fifth of all grants made to private owners.

Table 5·1 *Improvement grant and rent increase legislation to stimulate private rehabilitation 1949–74*

Act	Provisions
1949 Housing Act	Improvement grants made available to landlords and owner-occupiers for work costing £100–600, at 50% of approved costs. (Upper limit raised to £800 in 1952.) Dwelling had to provide accommodation for thirty years at a 16-point standard. Private landlords could raise rents by 6% of their share of costs.
1954 Housing Repair and Rents Act	A 12-point standard replaces that of 1949. The upper limit on costs is waived—but maximum grant level of £400 maintained. Minimum life reduced to fifteen years. Where private landlords received a grant they could raise their rents by 8% of their share of the expenditure. In essentially sound dwellings, landlords could raise rents by an amount equal to twice the difference between gross and net rateable value provided appropriate repairs were carried out.
1957 Rent Act	Rent control is terminated on all dwellings with rateable value exceeding £40 in London or £30 in the rest of England and Wales. All other dwellings to be decontrolled when let to a new tenant.
1959 House Purchase and Housing Act	Previously all grants had been conferred at the discretion of the local authorities. Standard grants are now claimable as of right for a 5-point standard with a minimum fifteen-year life. The maximum grant was £155 or half the cost of works, whichever was lower. Discretionary grants also given for conversion of large houses into self-contained dwellings. Local authorities permitted to make loans for owner's cost-share. Private landlords permitted to raise rents by 12½% of their share.
1964 Housing Act	Standard grants now available for a 3-point standard.
1965 Rent Act	System of 'regulated' and 'fair' rents for decontrolled unfurnished tenancies introduced.

Table 5·1 (*cont.*)

Act	Provisions
1969 Housing Act	Standard grant maximum raised by £45 to £200. Discretionary grants renamed 'Improvement grants'. Maximum raised by £600 to £1000 (£1200 in houses of three or more storeys) and approved works of repair and replacement become eligible for grant aid for the first time. Conditions of grant approval relaxed. 'Special grants' introduced for installing amenities in homes in multi-occupation. Private landlords making improvements could convert controlled tenancies into regulated ones over a five-year period.
1971 Housing Act	In the intermediate and development areas grants cover 75% of approved costs.
1974 Housing Act	Grants cover 75% of approved costs in housing action areas. Eligible expense limits for grants were raised to £3200 for improvement grants, £1500 for intermediate (i.e. standard) grants for repairs and amenities installation, and £800 for repairs grants in HAAs and GIAs.

Table 5·2 *Improvement grants approved for private owners in Great Britain 1949–76*

Year	Number[a]	Year	Number
1949–54	4,144	1969	80,263
1955–9	41,898	1970	116,379
1960–4	90,094	1971	137,364
1965	89,000	1972	224,468
1966	81,569	1973	260,364
1967	86,225	1974	173,764
1968	84,860	1975	92,512
		1976	80,164

Source: HSGB, HCS.
a   For the years 1949–64 I give the annual average.

The third dimension of strategy was to encourage improvement on an area-wide basis. The reasoning here was that owners see their dwelling as an investment and only believe that its value will augment with improvement if simultaneous improvement is taking place throughout their neighbourhood. An alternative view was that some threshold demonstration effect exists: a minimum scale of improvement in a locality is necessary before spontaneous imitative improvement is triggered off. The area approach is at least as old as Allied Ironfounders' Stockton experiment in 1953[6] and soon thereafter was taken up by Leeds City Council, an experience to which we return in Section 8 below. By 1962 the MHLG was giving advice in Circular 42/62 on the selection of streets or areas worthy of improvement and the 1964 Housing Act created the legislative concept of 'improvement areas', areas considered improvable up to a five point standard.

The zenith of this approach was contained in the 1969 Housing Act with its general improvement areas. It was intended that each area would contain about 300 houses, in reasonable enough condition so that by a voluntary process they could be improved up to the twelve point standard. For the first time Exchequer subsidies were made available to councils for environmental improvement, such as tree planting and the provision of play space and car parks. Their initial value was 50 per cent of approved expenditure up to £100 per dwelling. This cosmetic outlay was seen as seed capital which would generate voluntary improvement.

The fourth dimension was to stimulate the formation and expansion of non-profit-making housing associations. The first initiative was made by the Conservative government in 1961 when they provided a loan fund of £25 million for this purpose. However, the scale of improvement by this sector of the housing market has until recently been minimal. The data since 1967 are given in Table 5·3.

Table 5·3 *Improvement grants approved for housing associations in England and Wales 1967–77*

Year	1967	1968	1969	1970	1971	1972	1973
Number approved	1,712	2,059	3,185	4,064	6,168	6,756	5,051

Year	1974	1975	1976	1977[a]			
Number approved	5,295	5,278	13,868	19,000			

Source: HSGB, HCS.
a Estimate.

Compared with the figures for improvement by owner-occupiers and private developers given in Table 5·2, housing association improvement in aggregate has been on a fairly small scale. The 1973 White Paper, *Widening the Choice: the Next Steps in Housing*, after conceding that the privately rented sector was continuing to decline, stated that the trend to 'a municipal monopoly of rented accommodation is unhealthy in itself '.[7] A far more important role for housing associations then seemed to be in prospect and the housing action areas in localities of 'housing stress', introduced by the 1974 Housing Act, were clearly intended to be the loci of association improvement. The Housing Corporation was at the same time given powers to channel up to £750 million to the movement. The spurt in the grant figures in 1976-7 reflects the outcome of this new emphasis.

The last of the five dimensions to which I referred was the exercise of compulsory powers by the local state to secure private improvement. The powers available, for example under the 1954, 1964 and 1969 Acts, have never been used on any substantial scale for they have proven to be slow, of uncertain outcome and heavy consumers of officers' time. The Upper Holloway study documented this well.[8]

This volume on state housing is not the place for a substantial critical appraisal of the experience of private sector rehabilitation but some summary points can be usefully made. With respect to compulsion and rent increases, all the evidence points to their ineffectiveness as policy instruments. On the other hand there can be no doubt that the subsidy of private owners' repairs, replacements and improvements—on an areal basis or not—has achieved a huge number of discrete acts of rehabilitation. More than 2·2 million grants have been made in the period 1949-76. This must certainly exceed what improvement would have been carried out without subsidies, although no one has ever tried to calculate the grant-induced increment. However, we must judge rehabilitation not just in terms of before-and-after surveys of the housing stock, but in terms of its impact on people, on the working population as a whole:[9]

> For it would not be an exaggeration to say that most of the very
> evident and well-documented failures of renewal policy have come
> about as a result of national and local policy-makers thinking
> solely in terms of the stock of housing rather than in terms of the
> welfare of its residents.[10]

That is, we must reject Lord Brooke's judgment that 'the most important thing of all is to consider the interests of the houses.'[11]

From what evidence is available the grant system has largely benefited the higher income strata of the working population. To some extent this has happened through 'mediated' gentrification, a process I have analysed elsewhere.[12] But overwhelmingly it has come about by these strata improving their existing homes or buying deficient or delapidated dwellings and then rehabilitating them.

As a result, in areas of predominantly old private housing inhabited by the manual working class, both the economically active and those on pensions, rehabilitation simply has not happened on a major scale, whether the dwellings were rented or owner-occupied. The inconsistencies became particularly evident in the general improvement areas, which covered a wide range of area types. 'The implication that good and bad areas should both reach similar standards after improvement meant that the greatest expenditures and outlays were expected to be made often on the poorest and cheapest properties.'[13]

A small number of areas consumed a very great deal of the time of local authority housing and planning officials whilst vast areas of similar housing were left untouched. Where rehabilitation did take place in the areas of old housing it was because the resident population was changing, the original inhabitants being replaced by the higher income strata. Coventry Hillfields constitutes one pole of the experience and Islington's Barnsbury is a justly infamous example of the other pole.[14] Kirwan and Martin argue:[15]

Put simply, it is clear that the type of people or households involved (in residential improvement) are those that are relatively young, usually with children, usually middle-class, with above average incomes (for the area, i.e. at least equivalent to national average earnings), most probably undertaking repairs and improvement in connection with a move. The houses involved are certainly not the oldest and tend to be of the period 1900-1940. While some may have lacked some amenities before improvement, most are already reasonably well-equipped, tending to be the larger houses with gardens. The improvements are generally carried out in areas where the general standard of the residential environment is high and where the majority of houses in the area are well maintained and equipped with all amenities. But this does not appear to mean that good external environment encourages improvement in areas of otherwise poor housing conditions, since the other conditions relating to the characteristics of the households and the houses are not satisfied.

Thus the willingness of both of the dominant political parties to witness the slow asphyxiation of the big and petit housing bourgeoisie without offsetting that long march to oblivion by a vigorous municipalisation programme has slowed the improvement of manual working-class housing, has accelerated the process of decay of much of the older housing stock and has imposed severe pressures on those sections of the population who have had to continue to rely on the private landlord. In particular, the failure of social democracy when in power to progressively take into local state ownership the rented housing stock constitutes one of their greatest social failures since the war.

Evidently since an enterprising, housebuilding landlord class did not exist, the Conservative Party was compelled to invent one, but rehabilitation by the housing association movement has had little impact because of its diminutive scale. In any case the associations have done nothing that the local authorities could not have done with the same capital finance used to fund 'the third arm'. Instead, under the slogan of 'no municipal rented monopoly', one more tenure category has been established to divide the working people at the level of the consumption of the housing product, as a consequence diverting some of the most able and creative professional workers away from those authoritarian and myopic authorities where the political struggle for new production and allocation policies is most crucial.

4 Clearing the slums

We have already seen at the beginning of Chapter 3 that local housing authorities have the right to purchase slum dwellings for clearance and redevelopment, by agreement or by compulsion. In Section 4 of the 1957 Housing Act the following criteria were specified as the basis of judgment:
(a) repair;
(b) stability;
(c) freedom from damp;
(d) natural lighting;
(e) ventilation;
(f) water supply;
(g) drainage and sanitary conveniences;
(h) facilities for storage, preparation and cooking of food and for the disposal of waste water.

A house was deemed to be unfit 'if and only if it is so far defective in one or more of the said matters that it is not reasonably suitable for occupation in that condition.' Circular 55/54 stated that unfitness may be 'based either upon a major defect in one of the matters listed or upon an accumulation of smaller defects in two or more of them'. Also under the clearance area procedure the local authorities could purchase dwellings which, because of their bad arrangement or the narrowness or bad arrangement of the streets, were dangerous or threatened the health of the inhabitants of the area. Furthermore it was possible to purchase compulsorily land needed for the satisfactory development or use of the cleared area.[16] Table 5·4 gives the scale of slum clearance in Britain since the war.

Table 5·4 *Houses demolished in slum clearance in Great Britain 1954–76[a]*

Year	Houses demolished	Year	Houses demolished
1945–54[b]	77,884	1966	78,637
1955	29,488	1967	85,208
1956	39,085	1968	85,865
1957	49,752	1969	82,722
1958	59,578	1970	81,398
1959	64,423	1971	87,472
1960	62,294	1972	81,473
1961	67,256	1973	77,200
1962	69,265	1974	51,797
1963	68,724	1975	56,191
1964	71,090	1976	51,075
1965	72,118		

Source: HSGB, HCS.
a Scottish figures include houses closed.
b England and Wales only

In England and Wales the total number of slums demolished in the period 1945–76 was 1·24 million units, of which 67 per cent were unfit dwellings in or adjoining clearance areas, 7 per cent were badly arranged dwellings or those needed for satisfactory site redevelopment and 26 per cent were unfit houses outside clearance areas, knocked down using the demolition order procedure.[17]

As the table shows, slum clearance did not take place on a substantial scale before 1955. It then rapidly built up to an annual level exceeding 60,000 units and remained within the range of 60–90,000 units per year right through to 1973, since when it has fallen perceptibly. The switch into large-scale clearance in the mid-1950s was part of the Conservative government's grand strategy for housing to which we shall return and review in detail in Chapter 9. But in passing we shall mention that one of the most extraordinary features of the clearance campaign was the nature of the information base.

Samuel, Kincaid and Slater, in a *New Left Review* article, took a careful look at the 1955 White Paper *Slum Clearance (England and Wales)*, which contained the councils' own estimates of the number of slums in their areas requiring demolition.[18] These authors concluded that:[19] 'as an assessment of the amount of unfit housing in the country . . . it is worthless . . . . As the basis for a major government campaign it is derisory.' They suggested, only just tongue in cheek, that the official estimates tend to reflect the number of dwellings the state believes it can pull down in ten years. With estimate and forecast rolled into one, and given the contemporary failure to analyse the process of housing obsolescence, the 'final' abolition of the slum problem was constantly promised as attainable within a decade. In fact the first house condition survey to be sponsored by the government did not take place until 1967 and it demonstrated that twelve years after launching the great offensive (the metaphors were often military) the enemy army was still more than 1·8 million strong![20] It goes without saying that in 1967, as at any other time, the standard of fitness itself could have no absolute quality to it, but necessarily reflected both the social values of the time and the resources likely to be made available to deal with dwellings found to be unfit. For example, the Denington committee in 1966 made it clear that they did not feel justified in adding any new criterion in the specification of unfitness if it meant b.g increases in the numbers likely to be condemned.[21]

I argued at the start of this chapter that housing renewal can take two modes—rehabilitation and redevelopment. We know that in the 1950s and 1960s the attack on the slums was carried through by the second of these two modes. In the main, the slums were cleared and their sites redeveloped. In retrospect we can see that there was no continuing appraisal made of the relative economic efficiency or social appropriateness, in any sense, of pursuing the redevelopment rather than the rehabilitation mode. I believe that there were certain biases to clearance which brought this about and these can be categorised under the three heads: partitioning bias, density bias and production bias.

The partitioning bias to clear should require little comment. Local authorities had the formal power to compulsorily purchase houses for rehabilitation under Sections 96 and 97 of the 1957 Housing Act, although there was no 'rehabilitation area' procedure or 'cellular renewal area' procedure to parallel the clearance area procedure of Sections 42-52 of that Act. But until the 1970s it was the policy of government, whether Conservative or Labour, to delimit public sector activity to redevelopment. Thus, when the planning or housing departments of a council considered how to operate on an area of unfit housing, they were faced with the choice between themselves clearing or by promoting private rehabilitation. If they doubted the effectiveness of the rehabilitation mode—and we have seen that excellent grounds existed for such mistrust—then the real choice open to them was between clearance or nothing.

The density bias to clear can be simply stated. In Chapter 3 we argued that for a number of reasons municipalities sought to achieve high densities when carrying through renewal. Quite aside from the constraints on overspill, the higher the new density captured by a specific built form the faster would be the release of the citizens of a town from bad housing conditions on sites other than the one being renewed. I hypothesise that the densities promised by redevelopment substantially exceeded those offered by rehabilitation and that this produced a strong disincentive to rehabilitation. Unfortunately I know of no research which has ever explored this line of thought and so I cannot offer here any supporting evidence.

The production bias to clear took two forms. In the first place, the training of architects does not create within them the self-image of a building worker with a specific set of design skills, which is what the majority are and must be, but the self-image of the artist–genius whose sculpted forms soar above the urban landscape. Development gave the architects a free hand to attempt to stamp their greatness in the concrete form of a set of dwellings. Rehabilitation could only constitute the expression of a set of skills which *in appearance* were mundane. In the second place we know that rehabilitation work, with its heavy reliance on traditional craft labour, tends to be carried out by small contractors and by direct labour, whereas only large firms handle redevelopment contracts. So it has always been in the economic interests of the latter to push for clearance. Systematic evidence does not exist but discrete confirming examples are available. Muchnik's study of Liverpool, for instance, showed that when the Labour leader of the city council called in the National Building Agency, its programme required razing huge swathes of the existing territory.[22] The agency existed to propound the systems approach, of course, and the systems were largely the property of the big firms. Pepper has cited evidence of the large contractors' lack of interest in small improvement jobs although some interesting counter-examples are also discussed.[23] Pepper also shows that the Leeds rehabilitation programme, to which we shall return, was carried out by direct labour and four dozen small builders and that in the view of the city corporation there was little scope for large contractors to operate economically.[24] A review of the evidence produced at the trials of John Poulson and his collaborators could provide further evidence on the production bias.

These three mutually reinforcing biases to clearance had the consequence that local surveys of the housing stock became oversimplified and planners were willing to use the crudest indicators of condition since there was no need for the more thorough research which would have been the obligatory prelude to a choice between clearance and municipalisation. Land-use plans prepared by consultants reflected this: the age of buildings and their rateable values were referred to as if these alone could determine what should come down and what remain. For the same reason planners did not set up models for determining whether redevelopment or rehabilitation were most appropriate for individual houses or areas of housing. And of course the indefinite quality of the unfitness criteria meant that it was not too difficult to generate clearance areas. As a result it is likely that tens of thousands, possibly even hundreds of thousands of dwellings were demolished which in retrospect would have been better dealt with by rehabilitation, although no estimate even on a local level has ever been made of this misplaced demolition effort.

As the years passed after the return in 1955 to large-scale clearance and as experience accumulated as well as research into that experience, so there began to mount up a number of criticisms of redevelopment. One argument was that many houses were destroyed which although technically unfit were structurally sound. This was undoubtedly true. An associated thesis was that many fit houses were misclassified as unfit, a position I am not inclined to accept since where appeals were made on these grounds—by owner-occupiers for example—the great majority of determinations by the government's inspectors concluded in favour of the local authority. Yet another criticism was that too many sound houses were being pulled down in order to ensure a satisfactory size and shape of site. On this score, at least, there is good evidence available: in England and Wales the proportion of dwellings in clearance areas which were not either unfit or badly arranged rose from

4·4 per cent in 1945–54 to 7·9 per cent in 1967.[25]

A second major theme related to the dispersal of the population from a cleared neighbourhood. This formed the basis of a critique of the policy because it was said to tear to shreds a fabric of personal relationships which could take years to replace within new neighbourhoods and brought with it psychological stress and mental illness. I do not intend to review this extensive literature but it is worth noting that Parker's survey of the published research established that the social scientists came to no consistent result on the social, psychological and mental outcome of displacement. Nevertheless he concludes:[26] 'evidence from British sources seems to suggest that the break-up of existing working-class communities by slum clearance has no more than a minor and short-term effect on most people.'

An associated criticism was that during displacement a substantial minority of households did not get rehoused—the same situation which faced those engulfed by the clearance schemes of the nineteenth century. Ungerson has pointed out that:[27]

> According to Part V of the 1957 Housing Act, local authorities have to show that they can rehouse the people displaced by redevelopment schemes 'in so far as suitable accommodation . . . does not already exist.' Thus local authorities are free to impose certain rules for re-housing which exclude those people whom they consider could find alternative accommodation. This exclusion is often taken to be applicable to young, single households, furnished tenants, lodgers, sub-tenants, owner occupiers, etc. Moreover, most authorities impose some kind of residential qualification, but can vary the length of this qualification.

She cites the case of the London Borough of Southwark where a furnished tenant was required to live in his accommodation for some eleven years before displacement to qualify formally for rehousing![28] The point during the clearance process at which the residential qualification took effect varied widely between municipalities, even for nuclear families, from the initial survey by the public health inspector through, to and beyond the date of approval of the CPO. In practice both the boroughs surveyed by Ungerson were reluctantly willing to rehouse even those families which did not qualify, but the accommodation offered was the worst on the council's list of available lettings.

Two further criticisms of public sector redevelopment both turn on the extended time-span of what I shall call the gestation period: the period elapsing between the initial survey by the health inspector and re-inhabitation of the site on completion of the building contract. The complexity of the process derives from the interaction of three sets of activities:[29]

(i) the negotiations between the local state and the central state for confirmation of compulsory purchase;

(ii) the displacement process;

(iii) the design–tender–clear–construct sequence.

It will hardly seem credible to those who are not familiar with the field of housing research but we have to say that no comprehensive survey has been published on the time span of the components of this critical path network.[30] We can only report that it is widely believed that the gestation period in aggregate is extremely long, probably on average some five to ten years. Of all the factors extending the period, perhaps the most serious is the shortage of accommodation to offer to those rehoused, one of the pressures which we saw exist for high-density development.

As I said, the very protraction of the process has been associated with two criticisms: the housing loss that goes with it and the experience of redevelopment itself. The housing loss is easy to understand in principle although, once again, no published documentation exists. At some point in time, usually after the council issues its CPO, there takes place a net outmigration from the clearance area, which continues until the site is empty and then cleared. It remains uninhabited until the building contract is terminated. Thus redevelopment, the purpose of which is to raise the quality and possibly the quantity of housing, often in areas where substantial shortages of accommodation exist, as a process itself makes an area temporarily redundant in its capacity to provide living-space. The housing loss involved can be expressed in terms of the bed-space years foregone: if a site which originally contained 1,000 bed-spaces were kept completely empty for five years during the gestation period, the loss would be 5,000 bedspace years.[31]

The original population's experience of redevelopment has been extensively researched. In her study of Southwark and Brent, Clare Ungerson described the distressing tension which residents feel because they are ignorant of whether redevelopment will take place or not. Once they do know, continued stress arises from their uncertainty about whether they will be rehoused and when and where. The inhabitants are in doubt whether or not to decorate a room, repair a wall, plant the garden. Private landlords at the same time stop doing repairs and maintenance. Simultaneously people find that the area is decaying. Ungerson writes:[32]

> Other anxieties arise because of the way neighbourhoods change, due to the redevelopment process. Houses are closed up, leaving scope for vandalism, vermin and petty thieving of lead and any bits of furniture left in the houses. People living in one house amongst many empty ones worry in case they too have their windows shattered by bricks or a tramp assumes their house is also empty and tries to break in. The neighbourhood takes on a 'tatty' appearance. Gardens fill up with old mattresses, prams and other unwanted possessions amassed by any family over the years. At the same time, some houses acquired early by the council with vacant possession may be in too poor a state to re-let, in which case they are closed up and large sheets of corrugated iron or wooden slats are put over the doors and windows.

Bitterness may grow at what seems the arbitrariness of relettings policy and the lens of their perception can irrationally focus residents' anger and hostility on the newcomers who drift into the area, especially where these are a distinctive group—blacks, or Irish or squatters.

The last attack on the experience of redevelopment which I wish to examine concerns the built form of the new estates and this is the subject of Section 5.

5 The rise and fall of the tower block

One of the most visible trends in the built form of new state dwellings since the war has been the growing proportion of flats in total output. This is illustrated in Graph 5·1 for England and Wales; the Scottish data are unavailable before 1960. Three phases are readily apparent. First is the proportionate growth in flat construction in the period up to 1964. Second is the years of relative stability in 1965–72 when flats made up about half of all new municipal dwellings. Thirdly comes the phase of decline since 1972. These movements correlate fairly closely with the scale of slum clearance in England and Wales and presumably also with the proportionate scale of new building which took place on redeveloped sites. No statistics exist on this last variable.

As the proportionate significance of flat construction grew, so too

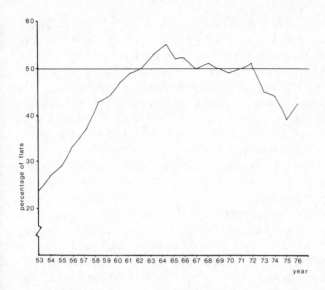

Graph 5·1 *Proportion of all public sector dwellings constructed as flats and maisonettes in approved tenders in England and Wales 1953–76*
Source: HSGB, HCS.

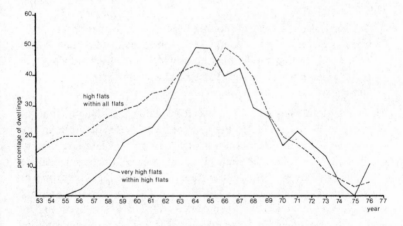

Graph 5·2 *Proportion of all public sector flats constructed in blocks of at least five storeys ('high' flats) and the proportion of high flats constructed in blocks of at least fifteen storeys in approved tenders England and Wales 1953–76*
Source: HSGB, HCS.

127

did the proportion of high flats, defined as those in blocks of five or more storeys. Graph 5·2 illustrates the relative importance of high flats and within their numbers the proportion of flats constructed in blocks of at least fifteen storeys. From a narrow statistical point of view the graph tells the high-rise story with the most brutal simplicity: an astounding growth rate up to 1964–6 and a violent decline thereafter. These Matterhorn proportions illustrate the most profound double metamorphosis in the built form of new construction in the entire history of British architecture.

The complexity of explanation in social science expands with the time available for its textual embodiment. However, I suggest that this extraordinary history can be told briefly and simply, particularly as we can draw on an article of outstanding quality written by E.W. Cooney.[33]

The rise of the tower and slab block can be understood in terms of the interrelation between four domains of activity and decision: those of the architectural profession, the local state, the central state and building capital. The original conception was that of the architects. The modern movement before and after World War II, particularly the work of Le Corbusier and Gropius, had inspired a generation of designers with the vision of towers of concrete and steel in a park-like setting with a full internal complement of social facilities available to every family.[34]

> The vertical garden city of blocks of flats in ample open space
> was to supersede the horizontal garden cities favoured by public
> policy and opinion and in doing so provide more efficient living
> accommodation and check urban sprawl with its waste of time
> and resources.

The increase in the executive power of architects within the housing field of the local state led to the concretion of these visions, originally in the world-famous Roehampton scheme of the London County Council. By the time that slum clearance became a major element in the housing strategy of the central state in 1955, the high-rise form was already being implemented on an increasingly wide scale. Graph 5·2 shows that even in 1953 15 per cent of all flats in approved tenders were in blocks of at least five storeys. The high-density demands of redevelopment, which have already been explored in Chapter 3, themselves gave a powerful impetus to the new public sector architecture. The approval of blocks of at least fifteen storeys was negligible before 1956 but by 1964 they made up one-half of all new high flats approvals.

Since high density was relatively costly the central state found itself obliged to introduce a subsidy system which would compensate for this.

As the number of high flats in approved tenders grew in the early 1950s, building capital quite naturally turned its attention to this sector of demand. Indeed McCutcheon points out that as early as 1945 a small number of firms had become involved in the innovation of non-traditional building methods for permanent houses:[35]

> Two or three well-known firms, which subsequently became substantial contractors in the multistorey field, owed their post-war debut in precast concrete techniques first to their war contracts and second to their contribution in the field of non-traditional housing in response to government invitation during the 1940s.

The persuasion and pressure of construction companies on government policy at the local and central level is the hidden thread in the skein of British housing history. Whilst no comprehensive documentation exists of the industry's influence, it does seem likely that some of the larger firms were encouraging the new trends. Not only could they draw on their immediate post-war experience in non-traditional techniques but the property boom which began in the early 1950s in the bomb-devastated centres of our great cities brought with it the high-rise office block which allowed research and development costs on the new architecture to be spread over output in two distinct sectors.

Another factor which encouraged the largest firms to promote high flats was that this form of work is not suited to the managerial, technical and financial capabilities of small and medium firms and therefore the new form itself constituted a profound advantage for the big capital sector of the industry. The increasing importance of negotiated and package deal contracts in the case of industralised building of high flats, including the use of British or licensed continental patents, was also an attraction for the very large firms as it raised their degree of monopoly. I must repeat that the precise relation between industry and government is unclear but that there was a continuing interchange no one would seek to deny or hide. McCutcheon points to the building interests of Geoffrey Rippon and Keith Joseph and the presence in the 1964–70 Labour government of advisers seconded from Costain, Concrete Ltd and Quikbuild.[36]

To sum up these brief comments on the rise of the tower block from the days of the Roehampton scheme we can say that the state's switch to a high-density redevelopment strategy took the shape of high flats because of the formal hegemony in local authorities of architects who were zealots of the modern movement, and that simultaneously this sea change in the form of public sector housing was underpinned by the material interests of big capital in raising its degree of monopoly in the competition for contracts.

How, then, can we account for the precipitate fall in the relative proportion of high flats within the flat total? Some would say that the pivot was the new legislation on housing subsidies which took effect from 1967 and terminated subsidy increments per dwelling above six storeys. But, as I have argued in Chapter 3, whilst the structure of new subsidies is critical to understanding how the central state exercises its power over local government, this structure itself requires explanation. Moreover the 1967 Act was first introduced in parliament in 1965, so the shift of ground is already taking place within the civil service in the early 1960s, precisely when industrialised building seemed to be riding high!

I believe that three different arguments were coming into play, which jointly began to tilt the balance against high rise. First, there was the mounting volume of criticism expressed by social scientists in response to the experience of the working class in high-flat accommodation. The pressure of housing need had led to a situation in which a far greater number of families with young children tenanted the new blocks than had originally been envisaged. The stress imposed on parents, and developmental problems for the child, were first expressed in an enquiry written by Joan Maizels in 1961.[37] Second, the return of a Labour government in 1964 gave the Fabians a much more influential voice in government. Within the Town and Country Planning Association, if Cooney is correct, there had for long been 'a running fire of adverse, reasoned criticism of [high flats] . . . which favoured continuing outward movement of people from the congested cities to New Towns, avoidance of high densities and provision of houses, rather than flats, for all who needed them'.[38] The philosophy of these planners and the relative weakness of the landowning class in the Labour Party (in spite of the gentleman-farmers who jostle at the table of Labour cabinets) may have been crucial in bringing about the downturn in public sector residential densities which, as we have seen in Graph 3·2, took effect from 1969. Third, those who identified with P.A. Stone's position that high-rise was costly to build and brought falling marginal density gains with block height presumably carried on the good fight within the civil service. The very marked increase in unit costs from 1959 onwards and the effect that the introduction of Parker Morris standards would have in maintaining the inflationary impetus must have amplified their voices within the internal committees of the state. I hope I am not unfair to the architects when I say that their own invective against the visual outcome of much multistorey building came after the move against high rise was well under way. What does seem to be an open question is how far the new iconoclasm was made effective by the development of non-traditional, low-rise, high-density designs and to what degree the big contractors who sold high rise now sell low rise.

In any case, that there was a shift in policy and that it was manifested in the 1967 Housing Subsidies Act is beyond doubt. In that very year the proportion of flats in approved tenders which were in five or more storey blocks fell by 3 percentage points and by a further 8 points in 1968. This evidence suggests that the Ronan Point disaster of May 1968, when several tenants died in the partial collapse of a point block after a gas explosion, largely served to administer the *coup de grâce* to a very, very sick man rather than the disaster itself initiating the malady. Seven years later only 1·2 per cent of all dwellings in public sector approvals in England and Wales were high flats, none of them in blocks of ten or more storeys. It would make for fine symmetry in my argument if I could say, as do some, that because of the property boom the big contractors lost interest in public sector housing contracts and that therein lies the explanation for the end of the high-flat age.[39] Unfortunately I do not believe that there is a shred of evidence to support this reductionist view.

6 Enter cost-benefit analysis

At the time that redevelopment was coming under attack in the 1960s an economic debate was launched on housing renewal which played an important part in what many have seen as a swing from redevelopment to rehabilitation in government policy. I wish to look at that debate in some detail.

Before doing this it is worth saying a little about the analytic technique employed, cost-benefit analysis. CBA has quite a long history although its use in this century is usually dated from its application by engineer-economists to water resource projects in the USA during the 1920s.

The basic notion is that when you have two different ways of achieving a similar outcome or when you have only sufficient funds to finance a single project from several competing alternatives, CBA offers a decision based on the future time stream of the costs and benefits associated with each choice. It is as simple as that—in principle. In the late 1950s in Britain its use was becoming quite widely discussed and by the mid 1960s economists in the civil service were using it with respect to state resource expenditures. As the CBA approach became more widely known, its use spread particularly when departments were seeking economic justification for their budgets in the face of Treasury demands for restraint or reduction. (On a personal note, in 1967–9 at the Ministry of Technology I found myself using the technique in assessing the economic viability of the British and European space programme.) Sooner or later CBA was certain to be taken up in housing analysis. In fact the story began in 1965.

In that year a book was published which later became a basic text in this field. The title was *The Economics of Housing* and the author was Lionel Needleman.[40] The last four pages of the text appeared under the subhead 'Demolition and rebuilding or renovation' and this was where the debate began. Needleman pointed out that an individual dwelling of unsatisfactory standard could be either redeveloped or rehabilitated. After citing the advantages of the latter he then put forward the following formula for choosing between the two modes 'from the purely economic view'. Prefer modernisation if:

$$b > m + b(1 + i)^{-\lambda} + \frac{r}{i} [1 - (1 + i)^{-\lambda}] \qquad (1)$$

where b = cost of demolition and rebuilding
$\quad\ m$ = cost of adequate modernisation
$\quad\ i$ = the rate of interest
$\quad\ \lambda$ = useful life of the modernised property
$\quad\ r$ = difference in the annual repair costs

The content of the inequality was also expressed in words: 'modernisation is worthwhile if the cost of rebuilding exceeds the sum of the cost of modernisation, the present value of the cost of rebuilding in λ years time and the present value of the difference in the annual repair costs.'[41] Using the simplifying assumption that r was a fixed proportion of b he then drew up a table, for different interest rates and different useful lives of the modernised property, which showed the maximum proportion that rehabilitation costs could be of redevelopment costs and still leave rehabilitation as the most favoured solution.

This was the first attempt to apply cost-benefit analysis to housing renewal questions and quickly stimulated a response from E.M. Sigsworth and R.K. Wilkinson which was published in *Urban Studies* in June 1967.[42] Their article contained some interesting material, for example on the inadequacy of making a judgment purely on economic grounds—not that Needleman had proposed this—and on the possibly protracted duration of large and comprehensive modernisation schemes. With reference to the formula itself they proposed a curious amendment. This was to include on the right-hand side of the inequality a term, c, which represented the capital value of the house before improvement on the ground that 'To extend (the life of a dwelling) means not only the investment of additional resources in renovation but the existing investment of capital which that house represents.'[43] The implications of this 'correction' are shown in Fig. 5·3.

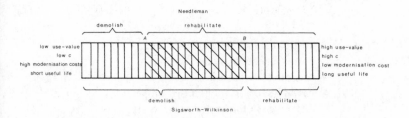

Figure 5·3 *Comparison of Needleman and Sigsworth-Wilkinson formulas for choosing between rehabilitation and redevelopment*
The dwellings to be renewed are ranked from those of the lowest use-value on the left to those of the highest use-value on the right. Suppose Needleman's inequality gives a cut-off point between the two modes at A. The cut-off point in the amended formula must be to the right of A, say at B, since it adds a positive term to the inequality's right-hand side. Thus Sigsworth and Wilkinson (so to speak) demolish $A-B$ dwellings more than Needleman purely on the grounds of their higher use-value! Indeed it is perfectly plausible that the increase in c beyond A could outstrip the fall in other right-hand-side terms in which case the 'corrected' formula would indicate 100 per cent clearance!

The error in the formulation of Sigsworth and Wilkinson was to take the value of the existing dwellings as a cost for rehabilitation but as no cost for redevelopment. Needleman made this point firmly in his acerbic reply to the two authors but to no avail for they persevered with this 'correction' in a further rejoinder.[44]

Meanwhile Needleman was working on a new paper which appeared in 1969 and was a definite advance on his first statement.[45] Two important modifications were introduced into the argument. First he took the view that the quality of dwellings in a redevelopment scheme is higher than that of modernised houses and suggested that this could be taken into account by assuming that the rent tenants are willing to pay varies accordingly. Second he recognised that the population density of the two modes can differ and in a worked example supposed the redevelopment density to be lower.[46] This could be encompassed in his inequality by introducing a term for the annual cost of housing elsewhere the shortfall of people accommodated under redevelopment.[47]

Introducing these two new factors and supposing with Needleman that the quality of redevelopment accommodation is higher and the population density lower we can write[48] modernise if:

$$b > m + b(1 + i)^{-\lambda} + \frac{r + p - a}{i}[1 - (1 + i)^{-\lambda}] \qquad (2)$$

where b = cost of demolition and rebuilding
m = cost of adequate modernisation
i = the rate of interest
λ = useful life of the modernised property
r = difference in the annual repair costs
p = excess of rent on redevelopment properties
a = annual cost of housing elsewhere the redevelopment shortfall.

The Needleman approach received an official benediction when Circular 65/69 was printed. Appendix B of that document contains a method for the choice between rehabilitation and redevelopment on economic grounds alone. The logic of the approach is precisely that constructed by Needleman:[49]

Improvement normally costs considerably less than redevelopment, but after improvement, the standard of the accommodation is likely to be lower than that provided by a newly built house or flat, and its useful life will be shorter. The maximum amount worth spending on improvement, given the cost of redevelopment, will depend inter alia on the standard of accommodation after improvement, the useful life, and the rate of interest.

The only variable in inequality (2) which is not treated is that which reflects the population density difference between the two modes, and the Sigsworth–Wilkinson paradox is neatly side-stepped: 'The cost of improvement here includes acquisition costs, as does cost of redevelopment.'[50]

With this brief exposition of the development of a cost-benefit approach to housing renewal in mind, I should now like to set down some critical reflections on the subject. But before beginning I have to say that in my view much honour is due to Needleman for being the first to introduce this technique into housing renewal decision-making.

At the time of writing it is clear that no definitive critique yet exists of cost-benefit analysis, although critical essays are available on its use in particular fields.[51] Some people (in verbal debate) argue that it should be abandoned because it necessarily relies on the concepts and philosophy of neo-classical economics. This view is mistaken. Certainly CBA grew historically within that theoretical context but it is not the case that it must perforce rely on concepts such as marginal utility, smooth aggregate production functions or the fissile productivities of the 'factors of production'.[52] Moreover we know CBA is now widely used in the collectivist countries quite free of the marginalist philosophy of Marshall, Menger, Walras and company. A second, more curious, attack is that we must reject the technique because it is a decision tool employed by the capitalist state. This argument is philosophically erroneous: to demur at the use to which a psychopath puts a hatchet is not to condemn the craftsmanship with which the axe was made. What I wish to do here is to see whether CBA, as it is formulated within the specific context of housing renewal in Britain, embodies any dangerous assumptions or fallacious arguments.

In the first place no one seems to have remarked on the extremely unorthodox structure of Needleman's use of CBA. The orthodox approach would have been to evaluate separately each of the two mutually exclusive renewal modes and then to compare the outcomes. For example the ratio in each case of the discounted benefit to discounted cost could have been calculated and the highest ratio selected as optimal. Instead Needleman poses the choice as one between redevelopment now or redevelopment later with an intervening stage of rehabilitation. If 'modernisation' inevitably gave a shorter life product, this approach might have had something to recommend it. But since there are no grounds for believing that this is always the case the approach is fundamentally mistaken. The correct approach, then, would be to calculate separate benefit-cost ratios (or net present values) and only to regard modernisation as a delaying expedient where one was sure this was appropriate.

As it is, the Needleman/MHLG approach generates the most stunning paradox. Let us take the simplest case for which, in inequality (2) r and p and a are all equal to zero. Then the inequality resolves into the decision to modernise if:

$$b > m + b(1 + i)^{-\lambda}$$
$$\text{or} \quad m < b - b(1 + i)^{-\lambda} \tag{3}$$

that is, modernise if its cost (at constant prices) falls short of the present costs of redevelopment less the discounted costs of future redevelopment, that is if the cost of modernisation falls short of the savings made by carrying through exactly the same building programme but at a later date. If b and m were equal one would choose to rebuild since obviously

$$m > b - b(1 + i)^{-\lambda} \qquad \text{where } b = m \tag{4}$$

Thus we have a clear case for rebuilding where the value of all the economic variables specified are precisely the same for each mode![53]

This crippling objection leads on to a related point. The 'saving through delay', the core of the argument, is very very sensitive to the discount rate chosen and this is shown in Fig. 5·4. This shows that even a five-year patching job gives rise to substantial savings, more than one-third of present cost at an interest rate of less than 9 per cent for example. In the case of a ten-year improvement life the same saving is effected at an interest rate of less than 5 per cent. It follows that it is crucial to establish what is the correct discount rate. The weakness of the Needleman–MHLG approach is that because there is no discussion of what the proper discount rate might be they simply assume it to be 'the rate of interest'. Whilst we can be quite sure that 'the rate of interest' is not automatically the correct discount rate it would be too ambitious here to try to state how it should be calculated. The rationale of discounting resource outlays is that later outlays, *ceteris paribus*, are lower cost than earlier outlays because postponing the use of these resources permits them to be used in the process of expansion of the resource base so that when they are drawn on at a later date they will by then have multiplied. This being so, in an economy like that of Britain, where the rate of resource expansion is very slow, the discount rate should be correspondingly low.

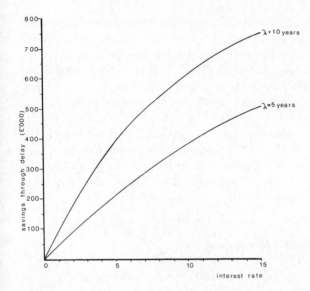

Figure 5·4 *Relation between savings through delay and the rate of interest for a five- or ten-year improvement life*
Savings through delay are defined as the value of $b - b(1+i)^{-\lambda}$ for a redevelopment scheme costing £1 million. The function is shown for interest rates in the range 0–15% and for a useful life of the modernised property of either five years or ten years.

Thus I regard the use of discount rates of 8, 10 or 15 per cent as far, far too high, particularly since they reflect high rates of inflation when the technique assumes constant prices! High discount rates, as the figure shows, favour modernisation since they raise the apparent savings through delay.

My other objection to the present use of CBA in renewal can be dealt with more briefly:

(i) CBA is of relevance only if applied to alternatives each of which can be selected and implemented. But we have seen that partitioning negated this condition in housing renewal. If redevelopment were ranked highest by its benefit-cost ratio, it could be carried through but if rehabilitation were superior it took place only if owner-occupiers and private landlords chose to do so. By ignoring this question of agency, Needleman was thereby presenting an illusory choice. This is another example of how economists can fail to locate their analysis within the statutory context of the times.

(ii) The MHLG formulation in Circular 65/69 ignored the vital question of the scale of accommodation provided by the alternative modes.

(iii) Neither Needleman nor the ministerial circular bring into their formulas and decision tables the length of the renewal mode from start to re-inhabitation. If the redevelopment process is longer and if the average population density on site during the process is lower, this should appear as a cost.

Finally we should note that there are social questions of great moment involved in the decision which CBA cannot incorporate—for example the distress associated with the renewal process and the scale of dispersal of the original community. Thus CBA can only aid decision; it cannot be a substitute for it.

7 The retreat from redevelopment

In the early 1970s government White Papers made it clear that the big-scale clearance programmes of earlier years were now anathema. Rehabilitation was to be the preferred mode of renewing the housing stock. This professed switch in policy had its origins at least a decade earlier, although for a number of years policy was formulated as a maintenance of the clearance programme alongside an expansion of improvement.

A number of the arguments which influenced this decision have already been reviewed in earlier sections of this chapter. Some thinkers proposed that the negative aspects of redevelopment called for a re-appraisal of the scale of demolition and they cited aspects such as the anxiety and area decay which accompanied clearance and the associated diminution in the supply of housing before re-inhabitation. Others argued that as the worst housing of the nineteenth century was swept away, the appropriateness of large-scale clearance diminished and by way of confirmation they could point to the perceptible increase in clearance areas of dwellings demolished only in order to provide a site of satisfactory size and shape. Moreover the debate of the economists was now opening, and this made the point that in resource terms unfit or inadequate housing was not necessarily best dealt with by destruction.

Another argument concerned what I call the 'treadmill' effect. Civil servants and the academics with strong policy interests began to conceive more clearly that the notion of a static target of slums to be cleared was scientifically mistaken. If the levels of expenditure on maintenance, repair and replacement were too low, the housing stock of low-to-middling quality could deteriorate so that finally it fell beyond the scope of effective rehabilitation. If this were taking place on a substantial scale the clearance target might have to be raised annually for an indefinitely long time period. Clearance could become a treadmill. This point of view was underpinned by the first house condition survey, conducted in 1967, which showed that after twelve years of clearance the problems of our older houses were still huge. There were still 6·3 million dwellings which were either unfit or required at least £125 worth of repairs or lacked one or more of the basic amenities.[54] It was judged that 1·1 million of the existing slums required demolition. To deal with these alone would have required a twenty-three-year programme at the 1967 rate of clearance.[55] In 1970 P. A. Stone estimated that up to 100,000 houses each year deteriorated beyond the point at which repair was worthwhile.[56]

With this background in mind we can look briefly at the 1968 White Paper *Old Houses into New Homes*.[57] Scheherazade tells us that Aladdin's lamp was stolen with the cry of 'new lamps for old!' The cunning of that ancient thief is nothing beside that of the civil servants who authored this paper. For it promised everything. The scale of improvement was to rise; the scale of clearance was to rise; yet the total of public 'investment' in housing was to remain static![58] The answer to this riddle is not contained in the paper but all three commitments are only mutually consistent if local authority housebuilding for general needs was to be slashed. If this interpretation is correct, the document, produced during a Labour administration, reflected a wholehearted switch to Tory policy of combining partitioned housing renewal with stringently constrained public sector output for all other needs.

After referring to academic CBA studies and to the Denington, Deeplish, Fulham and Halliwell reports, the main thrust of *Old Houses into New Homes* is to the general improvement area strategy with improvement based on 'the voluntary principle'.[59] A large-scale municipalisation drive was thereby ruled out. The summary of proposals refers overwhelmingly to private improvement and does not say a single word on the paper's implicit cut-back in local authority general needs building and the explicit commitment to an expanded clearance programme! Many feared at the time that the commitment to an increase in redevelopment was mendacious in spite of the Minister's promise that clearance in the 1970s would be 50 per cent greater than that of 1967.[60]

We should not therefore be surprised that Duncan, on the basis of

his survey, reported that the 1969 Housing Act, which followed the
White Paper, led councils to take a fresh look at some of their areas of
older housing and consider improvement rather than redevelopment.[61]
Because of the lags involved, Table 5·4 shows clearance only began to
fall from its post-war peak after 1971.[62]

These remarks on Command 3602 call to mind the importance to
policy of the question of public expenditure. There can be no doubt
that one of the government's grounds for favouring rehabilitation rather
than redevelopment was that it would be accompanied by a fall in
public expenditure. This is so for two reasons:

 (i) for a given total resource cost, public redevelopment embodies
     no private outlays whereas private rehabilitation does do so and
     therefore a lower public cost;

(ii) private rehabilitation of old houses by the lower-income strata of
     the working population is much more fragmentary and dilatory
     than public redevelopment, so that the total resource flow is
     lower in fact.

Thus when the government seeks to impose public expenditure constraints, as it did after the 1967 devaluation, the voices of those who
propose rehabilitation before redevelopment are sure to resound with
greater force. So, given the existence of partitioning, a switch from redevelopment to rehabilitation was always likely both to have a distri-
butional effect and a scale effect: to increase the proportion of renewal
resources flowing to the dwellings of the higher income strata, and to
reduce the total resource flow. In fact gross public 'investment' in housing
fell from £1,611 million in 1968–9 down to £907 million in 1972–3 at
constant 1973 survey prices.[63] So much for Command 3602's 'static'
public investment total!

I have argued that the retreat from redevelopment can be read into
Command 3602. The professed switch between renewal modes had become rather more explicit by 1973 in the White Paper *Better Homes: the
Next Priorities*.[64] After the ritual pronouncement that the existing slums
would be cleared within ten years, the paper states that the clearance
programme would be 'broadly' maintained at the current level.[65] (Table
5·4 shows the clearance total was to drop by one-third in the following
year.) The government then showed its true intentions more openly.
After a brief but eloquent attack on large-scale clearance, the document
continues:[66]

Some local authorities, recognising the heavy financial and social costs involved in major redevelopment schemes have begun to draw up programmes in which new building and rehabilitation are carefully integrated, house improvement being used to phase urban renewal in ways which allow continuous, flexible and gradual redevelopment on a relatively small scale. The Government wishes to encourage this concept of gradual renewal which allows groups of the worst houses to be cleared and redeveloped quickly; some to be given minor improvement and repair pending clearance in the medium term; others comprising predominantly sounder houses to be substantially rehabilitated and possibly included in general improvement areas. This approach also means that fewer homes, at any point in time during the process of renewal, are lost from the stock of available dwellings—a very important consideration in areas of housing scarcity.

It then states the need for a redirection of priorities to areas of housing stress (Housing Action Areas) to areas of decent, older housing (General Improvement Areas) and to essential repairs.

The cut-back in the allocation of state resources to unfit or inadequate housing is quite open here. The National Community Development Project, drawing on the experience of its project areas in Batley, Saltley, Coventry, Cleator Moor, Newcastle, Newham, North Tyneside and Southwark, concluded that the implementation of the White Paper's policies, through the 1974 Housing Act, was 'a systematic assault upon the housing standards of the working class as a whole'.[67]

8 Public sector rehabilitation

In the second section of this chapter the concept of the partitioning of renewal was proposed. In its simplest formulation this states that *all* redevelopment of the stock of privately rented or owner-occupied dwellings is, after compulsory purchase, carried out by the state whilst all rehabilitation of that stock is done by non-state individuals and bodies including private households, landlords, developers and housing associations. I believe that if sufficient data were available and published we should discover that an overwhelming preponderance of the resources allocated to housing renewal in Britain since the war was partitioned. In the rest of this section I want to examine some counter-examples, but before doing so it is worth spending some time discussing one form of renewal that is not covered at all by the partitioning hypothesis, the improvement of the local authorities' purpose-built stock.

As we have seen, the first council dwellings were built in 1864; more than 20,000 units had been completed before 1914; and a further 1,324,000 during the inter-war years. By the 1960s it was evident that a substantial number of these houses and flats required extensive rehabilitation, particularly improvement. Even by 1971 the House Condition Survey showed that there were 511,000 public sector dwellings lacking one or more of the standard amenities.[68]

Improvement grants have always been available to local authorities for work on their own dwellings and just as in the case of a private owner, the authority received three-eighths of the total cost of approved works from the Exchequer, within the upper bounds described in Section 3.[69] Table 5·5 shows the annual number of improvement grants received by the local authorities since 1949. Unfortunately it does not differentiate the improvement of the purpose-built stock from that of

Table 5·5 *Rehabilitation grants approved for local authorities in Great Britain 1949–76 in terms of the number of dwellings*

| Year | Discretionary | | Intermediate | Total |
	Conversion	Improvement		
1949–58	4,626	6,991	not applicable	11,617
1959	1,779	3,737	11,136	16,652
1960	1,842	8,031	33,138	43,011
1961	1,846	9,098	31,331	42,275
1962	1,754	10,052	20,498	32,304
1963	1,651	9,047	20,820	31,518
1964	1,346	11,070	20,771	33,187
1965	2,278	12,423	25,625	40,326
1966	2,312	15,648	15,760	33,720
1967	1,758	22,287	8,442	32,487
1968	1,874	28,794	10,271	40,939
1969	2,710	30,832	6,894	40,436
1970	2,890	48,031	8,547	59,468
1971	3,142	81,987	3,850	88,979
1972	3,764	128,541	4,539	136,844
1973	5,446	177,703	4,932	188,081
1974	6,803	111,908	2,712	121,423
1975	3,246	57,923	–	61,349
1976	4,752	69,996	–	74,748

Source: HSGB, HCS.

the municipalised stock.

The scale of public sector conversion and improvement was minimal before 1959 so that the House Purchase and Housing Act of that year brought a considerable surge in activity. The table shows that the annual number of grants approved between 1960 and 1969 was fairly stable in the range 31–43,000. After the 1969 Housing Act, the flow swelled once more. Many GIAs have been declared for purpose-built council estates and the municipalisation programme also boosted the figures. The cut-back in these grants has been exceptionally severe with a 60 per cent reduction in the three years after 1973.

Let us now turn back to consider the counter-examples to complete partitioning. These fall under the four heads of private redevelopment, patching, the Leeds and Newcastle experiments and municipalisation in the 1970s.

Private redevelopment need not detain us long. The only evidence that it has happened on a substantial scale is in London, where Swann has shown it to be associated chiefly with the demolition of good-quality stock followed by new building for owner-occupation at much higher site densities.[70]

The second exception to 100 per cent partitioning was patching. Some local authorities, particularly in the 1940s and 1950s, purchased large tracts of unfit housing without even the short-term prospect of clearing them. They were therefore allowed to defer demolition and in the interim to patch these dwellings to a minimum level. In fact Kirwan and Martin suggested that by 1972 only 1 per cent of local authorities had undertaken patching since grants were made available for it.[71] The biggest of the deferred demolition programmes was that carried out in Birmingham.

The area experiments in Leeds and Newcastle are the third counter-example to blanket partitioning. In 1954 in Leeds the housing committee discovered that the implementation of an extremely modest municipal-isation programme was very slow. As a result in the following year the council adopted an area-based policy of voluntary improvement up to the twelve-point standard with municipal purchase by agreement and compulsory purchase as fail-safe devices. Improvements were carried through predominantly without displacing residents and the work on the municipalised dwellings, about 45 per cent of the total, was carried out by direct labour.[72] I know of no detailed retrospective study of the 'Leeds method' which attempts to evaluate its success. It seems to be the case that the chief obstacle was the serious administrative workload necessary to secure comprehensive improvement given the nature of the statutory powers. Cullingworth has written:[73]

> In spite of the success achieved in Leeds the programme in that
> city has been held up by the lengthy negotiations which are
> necessary with reluctant owners and by the cumbersome and
> time-consuming nature of the compulsory purchase procedure.
> Elsewhere results have been generally much more disappointing.

From the point of view of the central state, then, we can see Leeds as the test-bed for the area approach to rehabilitation rather than as the operation of a genuine drive for improvement through municipalisation.

The Rye Hill scheme in Newcastle is a second case of area-based re-habilitation with a substantial role for municipalisation. This 56-acre site in the west end of Newcastle contained about 1,000 dwellings, most of them structurally sound, and in 1960 was chosen by the local planners as an experiment in 'revitalisation' rather than redevelopment.[74] In their view existing housing act powers did not permit them to carry through a comprehensive improvement programme so they sought to make Rye Hill a comprehensive development area under the 1962 Town and Country Planning Act. After some delay the Minister approved this designation in 1966 but rejected a compulsory purchase order for the area as a whole.

After the council's intentions for the area had been announced in 1960 a blighting process set in, much like those of the clearance areas we have already discussed, with the familiar characteristics of decay, Rachmanism, hostility between old and new residents and growing racialism. This was exacerbated both by administrative delay and by the planners' perverse insistence on putting the properties they municipalised into cold storage. Vandalism reduced many to shells. Davies writes of:[75]

> The over-emphasis on the environment and the rigid emphasis on
> 'phasing'—i.e. on doing the work sub-area by sub-area, using a big
> contractor, and thereby (allegedly) benefiting from various
> 'economies of scale', resulted in the refusal to modernise the
> property as it was bought lest the ad hoc work jeopardized the
> 'final plan'!

By the time of the passage of the 1969 Housing Act, the scheme had been under way for nine years and had produced seven fully modern-ised houses. In the cold light of hindsight we can categorise this planning nightmare as a clear case of a local authority seeking renewal through the rehabilitation mode but baulked from carrying it out effectively both by their own mistakes and by the partitioning strategy of the central state. All their efforts became piecemeal and all they touched turned to ashes.

In this, the final subsection of the chapter, I want to look at the expansion of municipalisation in recent years. We have already seen that by the early 1970s a policy switch had taken place which reduced the scale of clearance. Simultaneously there was a growing understanding of the failures of private rehabilitation in the older residential areas inhabited by predominantly retired and low-income workers. The combination of these factors produced the concept of housing action areas and in this context there was a quite definite weakening of the traditional opposition to municipalisation. Command 5339 declared that the government would look sympathetically at the use of powers to municipalise 'where no other action will succeed in renewing pockets of inadequate dwellings within Housing Action areas'. It is worth remembering that this was a Conservative White Paper.[76] Yet these shifts were taking place in a climate of attacks on public expenditure, which became more strident with the gathering crisis of the present political and economic order. Municipalisation was therefore exposed to quite contradictory influences.

Some indication of the scale of municipalisation, in England at least, is given in Table 5·6. The number of dwellings acquired in the years preceding 1974-5 is not known; a rough estimate is 7,000 in 1972-3 and 12,000 in 1973-4.[77]

Table 5·6 *Number of dwellings municipalised by local authorities in England 1974-7*

		1974-5	1975-6	1976-7
Acquisition under general authority	Compulsory purchase	1,790	2,470	1,756
	In acute housing stress areas	6,539	2,469	2,643
	Empty properties	14,218	5,829	2,363
	Re-acquisition	296	453	731
	Other	34	3	—
Acquisition under specific authority		2,723	8,276	8,404
Total		25,600	19,500	15,897

Source: HCS.

The most thorough research into the experience of municipalisation has been carried out by postgraduate planning students at the Bartlett School of Architecture and Planning in University College, London.[78]

One of their case studies was a broad review of the Islington programme, which appears to have been the largest in the country.[79] The clearest lesson from this study was that the council's lack of experience in re-habilitation through municipalisation was initially the cause of a number of policy errors but that as the local authority's staff went through a 'learning by doing' process their effectiveness was substantially raised, both through the clarification of objectives and the reorganisation of work methods. A simple example is that by March 1975 the authority had acquired 3000 properties but rehabilitation had actually begun on only 360. However, during the course of 1975-6 the number of ad-ditional starts rose to 1000. Other positive policy modifications were the switch away from purchase with vacant freehold possession, which had led to winkling and harassment by private owners to secure market prices sometimes five times as great as with partial vacant possession; far more systematic co-ordination of the acquisition, production and allocation processes; and the use of 'schedule contracts' in place of time-consuming individual specifications.

It seems ironical, indeed tragic, that just as councils like Islington were consolidating the 'learning by doing process', the scale of the municipalisation programme was being hacked back. Table 5·6 shows a substantial fall in the number of dwellings acquired by 1976-7 and the government's expenditure plans in 1978 indicated that local authority acquisition expenditure was planned to fall from £308 million in 1974-5 down to a forecast £92 million in 1978-9.[80] The cut-back in the programme, so soon after it had been seriously initiated, reflected the grim determination of the government to reduce public expenditure. It is to the raising of the capital finance required for local authority ex-penditure on site acquisition and housebuilding that I turn in the next chapter.

9 Synthesis

Dwelling production can be ordered into the three categories of routine maintenance, renewal and green field site development. Housing renewal itself divides into rehabilitation and redevelopment. Renewal is under-taken, by the state or by the private sector, because of past inadequacies in the level of maintenance and repair of the stock or because by con-temporary standards the use-values of new accommodation constructed in earlier decades is judged to be unsatisfactory.

The central thesis of this chapter is that the process of renewal was partitioned in the post-war years so that the overwhelming preponderance of the total flow of resources was allocated either to municipal redevelopment or private rehabilitation. Thus there has been a one-to-one correspondence between the technical bifurcation of renewal and its implementation. The origin of this lay in the unwillingness of successive governments to encourage really substantial municipalisation programmes as an alternative to redevelopment when the structural quality of unfit housing made this viable. In the case of both Conservative and Labour governments this was because the executive power wished to limit the sphere of state activity only to what it was absolutely clear the private sector could not implement.

Slum clearance first began to gather force in 1955 and reached its peak in 1971, since when there has been a substantial decline. Its scale and growth were stimulated by systematic biases to wholesale clearance, rather than councils in their own programmes *combining* redevelopment and rehabilitation. I have called these the partitioning, density and production biases. They brought the destruction of accommodation on a larger scale than a careful calculus of the relative advantages of the two renewal modes would have justified. But on precisely what scale this happened we shall never know. However, it is not the argument of this chapter that a huge slum clearance programme was never necessary. It was.

The most marked feature of the built form of the new estates was the very high proportion of flats provided, particularly high flats. This originated in the formal hegemony of the Modern Movement, the search for high-density construction and the interests of big building capital. A precipitate fall in high-flat construction took place after 1967.

A substantial retreat from the commitment to redevelopment began to take place at the end of the 1960s, signalled by the White Paper *Old Houses into New Homes*. The introduction of cost-benefit techniques into governmental analysis was one factor amongst many in changing the balance of attitudes. The use of time discounting can be seen as a technical analogue to the shortening of time horizons within the state apparatus in the context of a gathering economic crisis. Policy now stressed the objective of switching resources into rehabilitation. Because of partitioning, this promised substantial reductions in state expenditure and this was perhaps the crucial element in the timing of the shift in renewal modes. However, if grant approvals are a reliable indicator, the scale of rehabilitation itself dropped sharply after 1973

147

in both the private and state sectors. Thus the switch from redevelopment to rehabilitation was an extremely brief phase. What happened after 1973 was a cut-back in the total flow of resources allocated to renewal.

SIX

Finance: the capital market

1 Introduction

The British system of housing finance is a wonderfully grotesque monster whose anatomy perplexes even those who spend their lives in its study. This chapter and the next are primarily concerned with financial questions, so it will be useful to make a preliminary sketch of the circulation of the blood of the beast in order to clarify the context of specific arguments.

This preliminary model of the system as a whole is set out in Fig. 6·1. It addresses itself to the local authority and owner-occupier sectors only, which jointly encompass more than four-fifths of all households in Great Britain. In the process of production a stream of income is generated which is conventionally classified into profits, rent, interest, dividends, wages and salaries. The figure divides households into two groups: those which primarily derive their income from profits, rent, interest and dividends and those which rely on wages and salaries as their chief source of income. I assume the first group are overwhelmingly owner-occupiers whilst the second group are divided between the two tenure forms. Households pay a proportion of their income to the state through taxation. At the same time these taxes, with the other forms of state income, are the source of housing subsidies. The main subsidy to owner-occupiers is tax relief on mortgage interest payments, a transaction between the state and the house owner. The subsidy to council tenants is paid directly into the housing revenue accounts of the local housing authorities. Household outlays for the possession of their accommodation take the form of mortgage payments, primarily to the building societies, and council rents.

In the preceding paragraph I dealt with financial flows taking the form of housing subsidies and housing outlays on the existing stock of dwellings. The lower half of Fig. 6·1 represents the financial flows with respect to the demands for newly constructed dwellings. In the case of the local housing authorities we simply have the expenditure for site acquisition and for the completed work of the private firms undertaking the councils' contracts. All this has been discussed in Chapters 3 and 4. In the case of owner-occupiers, they must first raise mortgage finance from the building societies. With these sums, and any savings of their own, they purchase their new houses from speculative builders. Both public and private flows manifest themselves as an effective demand for the housing output of the construction industry.

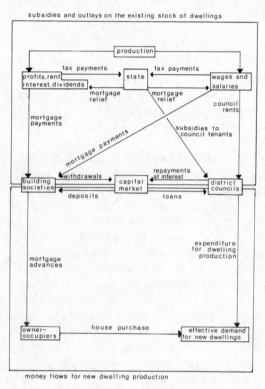

Figure 6·1 *The British system of housing finance*

Where, then, does the capital market come in? With respect to new dwelling production the answer is that under the existing social order the municipalities must raise loans from the market in order to pay their contractors' bills. Similarly the building societies rely on the inflow of deposits to provide mortgages to those who borrow from them. With respect to the transactions on the existing stock, it is the income from council rents and state subsidies which in the long run enables the local authorities to repay the loans they have taken out. Similarly mortgage payments by existing owners can be seen as the chief source of funds for the payment of interest to the building societies' depositors.

The model in Fig. 6·1 could be made much more complex in order to take into account the existence of housing associations, private tenants, rehabilitation production and the market in second-hand houses. All of the flows of this more complex circulatory system could be fairly readily estimated I believe. However, that would not serve the rather narrower interests of this chapter and will be left for some future occasion. What I do wish to do here is to set out in much more detail the present scale of public expenditure on housing, including those flows which are not incorporated in the simple model.

Table 6·1 presents the data for 1977–8. Three kinds of public expenditure are distinguished from one another. Resource expenditure includes all payments by the public sector authorities for goods and services. In 1977–8 it made up 36 per cent of the overall total, the new building programme of the local housing authorities contributing by far the largest share. Transfer expenditure covers payments for which no goods and services are received in exchange and these I have divided into two categories. Gift expenditure embraces non-recoverable transfers and in 1977–8 made up 66 per cent of all public housing expenditure, with subsidies to council tenants and owner-occupiers predominating. Loan expenditure, on the other hand, was a very small and negative part of the grand total.

With these introductory remarks complete, I now wish to turn to the main subject matter of this chapter, the scale of local authority capital expenditure on housebuilding and the way in which it is financed.

2   The scale of capital expenditure

Government accounting practices always draw a distinction between expenditures on capital account and those on revenue account. Hepworth uses the following definition:[1]

> Very broadly, expenditure of a capital nature may be described as that which is incurred on some object of lasting value even though that value may diminish in the course of time, whereas revenue expenditure is usually of a constantly recurring nature and produces no permanent asset. The cost of erecting a school by a local authority

151

Table 6·1 *State expenditure on housing in Britain in 1977-8 at 1977 survey prices*

Resource expenditure	£m	%
Local authority expenditure on:		
land	77	1
new dwellings	1,149	20
acquisitions	56	1
rehabilitation	425	8
other	74	1
New towns and SSHA expenditure	203	4
Housing administration	48	1
Total resource expenditure	**2,032**	**36**
Gift expenditure		
Exchequer subsidies to council housing	1,073	19
Exchequer funding for rent rebates to council tenants	292	5
Rate fund contributions to council housing	210	4
Rate funding for rent rebates to council tenants	95	2
Subsidies to new towns and SSHA	139	3
Housing association revenue deficit and capital grants	490	9
Rent allowances to private tenants	80	1
Option mortgage scheme and mortgage tax relief[a]	1,209	21
Rehabilitation grants from local authorities	91	2
Total gift expenditure	**3,679**	**66**
Loan expenditure[b]		
To private persons for house purchase and rehabilitation	−94	−2
To housing associations	3	negl.
Other lending	− 4	negl.
Total loan expenditure	**−95**	**−2**
Grand total	**5,616**	**100**

Source: Adapted from The Government's Expenditure Plans 1978–79 to 1981–82, vol.II, Cmnd 7049–II, HMSO, London, 1978.
a Estimate.
b Gross advances net of repayments.

is an example of capital expenditure producing an asset with a 'life', whilst the expenditure on the general maintenance of the school—teachers' salaries, cleaning, heating and lighting, etc.—is of a revenue nature.

It follows from this that local authority site acquisition and outlays on rehabilitation, redevelopment and green field development are all treated as capital expenditure whilst the maintenance of the stock of

Table 6·2 *Local authority capital expenditure on municipal housing and the loan income to finance it, in England and Wales, from 1944-5 to 1974-5 (in £m)*

Year	Expenditure	Loans	Year	Expenditure	Loans
1944–5	5	4	1959–60	229	222
1945–6	22	14	1960–1	223	216
1946–7	107	107	1961–2	250	239
1947–8	210	191	1962–3	272	268
1948–9	244	217	1963–4	354	333
1949–50	221	216	1964–5	440	426
1950–1	228	220	1965–6	495	479
1951–2	252	247	1966–7	600	582
1952–3	314	309	1967–8	656	629
1953–4	335	330	1968–9	668	635
1954–5	297	297	1969–70	661	632
1955–6	261	262	1970–1	655	615
1956–7	252	234	1971–2	656	600
1957–8	235	227	1972–3	838	736
1958–9	208	202	1973–4	1,107	981
			1974–5	1,620	1,560

Source: Local Government Financial Statistics.

municipal dwellings is conventionally treated as a revenue expenditure. Table 6·2 shows the changing scale of expenditure over time.

The seven-fold rise in expenditure since the late 1940s is a staggering increase. However, it reflects not a huge surge in the volume of construction but the powerful inflation in average unit costs, particularly in the 1960s and 1970s (as we saw from Graph 4·1).

3 The capital market

I now turn to the sources of funds for the local authorities' capital expenditure on their housing programmes. Table 6·2 shows that loan income is the predominant source and that income and expenditure move very closely together. In the period covered by the table, housing expenditure totalled £12·9 billion of which 95 per cent was financed out of loan income. As a result the authorities' gross outstanding loan debt attributable to their own housing stock rose from a total of £0·6 billion in 1944-5 to £11·3 billion in 1974-5.

Loan finance rather than taxation has been used to fund municipal housing schemes since the last century, just like the philanthropic housing which preceded it. Indeed it has been the practice for so very long that many experts can hardly conceive how it could be otherwise, a question to which I shall return in Chapter 11. For the present, it is useful to look at the different shapes assumed by these debts and here we shall be concerned with all municipal borrowing, whether for capital expenditure on housing or for any other purpose.

The forms of municipal borrowing for capital expenditure include mortgage loans, stock, local bonds, negotiable bonds, loans from the Public Works Loan Board, temporary loans, revenue balances temporarily used for capital purposes and advances from internal sources such as the authorities' superannuation funds. The means by which these borrowings are raised and their different identities in terms of security, repayment and the market in the debt have been set out by Hepworth.[2] Their relative importance is shown in Table 6·3.

Table 6·3 *Analysis of the outstanding debt of municipal authorities in Great Britain at 31 March 1977 by sources of borrowing (%)*

Source	%
Temporary loans: repayable within 3 months	9·2
repayable in more than 3 months and less than 12 months	4·0
Revenue balances temporarily used for capital purposes	9·2
Stock	5·2
Local authority negotiable bonds	3·1
Bonds/Mortgages	27·7
PWLB Loans	37·4
Internal Advances	1·7
Other Loans (including foreign currency loans)	2·5

Source: CIPFA, Return of Outstanding Debt.

Since borrowing from the PWLB represents over one-third of the debt it is worthwhile describing this source in some detail. The board is nominally an independent statutory body consisting of twelve commissioners, first established in 1817.

> The functions of the Commissioners, derived chiefly from the Public Works Loans Act 1875 (c.89) and the National Loans Act 1968 (c.13), are to consider loan applications from local authorities and other prescribed bodies and, where loans are made,

to collect the repayments. At present virtually all borrowers are local authorities requiring loans for capital purposes sanctioned by Government departments and the security consists of the rates and revenues of these authorities. Funds provided by Act of Parliament are drawn from the National Loans Fund and rates of interest are fixed by the Treasury.[3]

Appendix 4 shows the relative importance of the board as a source of borrowing since 1938-9.

Let me now turn to consider the developments in policy since the war both with respect to the sources of municipal loan finance and its cost in terms of the interest rates payable. It is important to note that the broader macro-economic context of policy is sketched in only lightly since this constitutes the basis of Chapter 10.

In the early post-war years the Labour government ensured that the PWLB supplied virtually all the external loan requirements of the municipalities so that their capital expenditure programmes would be 'financed in an orderly manner and as cheaply as possible'.[4] The rate of interest charged was very low and very stable as we can seen in Table 6·4. However, this stability did not hold for the *scale* of housing loans sanctioned, for these reflected the government's public expenditure plans and the crisis of 1947 brought a severe cut in sanctioned loans from £222 million in 1946-7 to £168 million in the following year.[5] The cut in capital *expenditure* on housing was less sharp, because of the inertia of the building programme.

The return of a Conservative government in October 1951 brought with it an immediate change in policy. In November board rates of interest were raised 'to bring them into line with market rates'.[6] The rate on loans of greater than fifteen years in length, for example, was raised from 3 per cent to 3¾ per cent. They continued their gentle upward progress, with the exception of small falls in 1953 and 1954, until the end of the decade. Furthermore, with effect from January 1953, the local authorities were no longer required by statute to raise their loan finance from the board. This substantial switch in policy was couched in the language of the freedom of choice to borrow either from the government or in the open market.[7] The first post-war stock issue for cash was made by Birmingham Corporation in the same month, at a rate which was almost 1 per cent higher than the going board rate. It was in this year, 1952-3, that the proportionate reliance on the board as a funding source began its long decline from 85 per cent in

Table 6·4 *The average rate of interest on new advances by the PWLB, and the average rate of interest on all outstanding debt of local authorities in England and Wales, from 1945–6 to 1976–7(%)[a]*

| | Rate of interest | | | Rate of interest[b] | |
Year	New advances	Outstanding debt	Year	New advances	Outstanding debt
1945–6	3·1		1961–2	6·6	4·5
1946–7	2·5		1962–3	6·3	4·6
1947–8	2·6		1963–4	5·8	4·6
1948–9	3·0		1964–5	5·8	4·9
1949–50	3·0	3·1	1965–6	5·9	5·0
1950–1	3·0	3·1	1966–7	5·9	5·6
1951–2	3·5	3·1	1967–8	7 (6·7)	5·7
1952–3	4·1	3·2	1968–9	7·8 (7·9)	6·1
1953–4	4·1	3·3	1969–70	8·9 (9·1)	6·7
1954–5	3·8	3·5	1970–1	8·1 (8·5)	6·8
1955–6	4·6	3·6	1971–2	6·9 (7·0)	6·4
1956–7	5·6	3·9	1972–3	8·5 (8·5)	6·6
1957–8	6·0	4·1	1973–4	11·6 (12·8)	8·0
1958–9	6·0	4·2	1974–5	12·5 (13·8)	9·5
1959–60	5·8	4·2	1975–6	11·6 (12·1)	9·8
1960–1	6·1	4·4	1976–7	12·3	10·4

Source: PWLB Annual Reports, CIPFA Return of Outstanding Debt.
a Outstanding debt figures are at 31 March. Financial years run April–March.
b For the years 1967–8 to 1975–6 the figures in brackets are the DoE's own estimate of the rate on new borrowing from all sources. See DoE, *Housing Policy*, Technical Volume, Part III, Table VIII.18.

1951–2 down to 8 per cent in 1959–60.[8] But we must also recognise that, with respect to the *absolute* level of borrowing from the board, 1952–3 was the peak year of the first two decades after the war, because of the Conservative administration's huge if temporary expansion of the local authority housebuilding programme. We return to this in Chapter 9.

At the end of 1954 market rates of interest began to rise. Taking advantage of their 'freedom of choice' the local authorities began to draw more heavily on the board. Consequently the proportion of new loans coming from the board jumped to 69 per cent in 1954–5. Following the first of the Conservative's 'stop-go' crises in the summer of 1955, the Chancellor of the Exchequer pronounced that the expansion of PWLB lending was a drain on the Exchequer and added to the difficulties of credit control. The Ministry's summary of his decisions stated:[9]

> To reduce the volume of Government lending and at the same time to increase the sense of financial responsibility of the local authorities, he had decided to make two changes in the conditions of lending by the Board. These were (i) that applicants for advances would be put upon inquiry as to their ability to borrow on their own credit either in the stock or in the mortgage market, before the Board decided whether or not to lend; and (ii) that the rates of interest for loans would be fixed by reference, not as hitherto to the Government's own credit, but to the credit of local authorities of good standing in the market.

The effect was dramatic. Within two years proportionate lending from the board had dropped by 47 percentage points and, as Table 6·4 shows, the rate of interest on new loans had risen from 3·8 per cent to 5·6 per cent.

Some clarification of the implication of this policy change is necessary. The fact is that for a housebuilding programme of a given size, a switch away from the board as a source of finance neither brought with it any reduction in public expenditure, nor did it lead to a fall in the borrowing requirement of the public sector, nor did it diminish, in the final analysis, the dependence of the programme on private capital. All that happened was that the cash was raised directly on the capital market by the local state rather than indirectly through the state at the centre. Now if all this is true, why on earth did anyone bother about how the transactions were routed? There seem to be three possible answers. First, Conservative policy at this time stressed their desire to rely as far as possible on the 'natural' operations of the market in the sphere of the production and distribution of dwellings. The demise of the PWLB ripped away the veil covering the authorities' real dependence on private capital and therefore had a real utility in the ideological battle. But there was also a second, material, factor at work. The rate of interest charged by the board represented the market's assessment of the central state's credit standing. When the authorities were required to raise their capital directly from the market they discovered that the rate of interest they had to pay was perceptibly higher; moreover the administrative cost and inconvenience of these decentralised placements was greater. Inevitably the higher cost of capital tended to reduce the scale of municipal housebuilding which again was an objective of government policy. More expensive credit was like the butterfly value of lower subsidies in the inter-war years. Third, a reduction in the scale of central borrowing brought with it greater flexibility in determining the value of the Treasury bill issue, a form of government borrowing which at this time was seen as a crucial determinant of the money supply because it made up a major part of the commercial banks' liquid assets.

The late 1950s saw the continuation of the new policy. In retrospect bank rate and the market rate of interest on stock issues were fairly stable, although high by post-war standards. The 1957 annual report of the Ministry noted for the first time an increased reliance on the mortgage market and the temporary money market.[10] One intervention of note was contained in the 1959 report of the Radcliffe committee on the working of the monetary system. It recommended that the board should be able to provide long-term capital at gilt-edged rates to any local authority requiring it, a reversal of the 1955 decision. The committee argued that independent action by the councils was unnecessarily expensive and that the sums required were often very large and therefore the timing of their placement in the stock market was important. Moreover, they said, the central government in any case controlled the level of local authority borrowing since about 90 per cent required prior loan sanction from government ministries.[11] The Chancellor rejected these proposals.

The combination of restricted access to board finance and the relatively high level of interest rates led many authorities to turn to the temporary money market in which repayment periods ran from as little as overnight up to 364 days. Many authority treasurers took the view that by doing this they could later substitute this short-term money for longer-term debt when interest rates fell. The argument certainly appeared rational enough at the time.

In the summer of 1961 interest rates rose to a particularly high level. Even board loans bore a rate of 7–7½ per cent. Between March and September this was associated with a jump in the proportion of short-term borrowings within the total outstanding debt from 14.4 per cent to 16·1 per cent. Substantial sums came from abroad. When they were recalled at short notice in July, treasurers were forced to seek refinancing at even higher rates of interest.[12] Consideration began to be given by the Treasury to some form of control over local authority short-term debt. The 1963 White Paper, *Local Authority Borrowing*, said that such finance was insensitive to the state's interest-rate policies and had led to the growth of large and unstable debts to foreign sources.[13]

With effect from April 1964 revised arrangements were introduced. Upper limits were placed on temporary borrowing. By way of compensation each authority was allowed access to the board for a proportion of its longer-term borrowing at a rate of interest based on government credit. In 1964–5 the quota was set at 20 per cent. For non-quota loans a higher rate of interest was charged.[14] Nevertheless, temporary borrowing continued at a high level, expressing the continued reluctance of authorities to borrow for long periods at what were considered to be high rates of interest and so the quota was raised in 1965 to 30 per cent.[15]

The quotas have since been revised several times. In 1976–7 the arrangements were that local authorities in areas designated as less prosperous had a quota of loans they could raise from the board which was equal to 40 per cent of their net capital payments in 1976–7, plus 4 per cent of their capital debt outstanding at 31 March 1976. For areas not designated less prosperous the respective percentages were 30 and $3\frac{1}{3}$. Every authority had a quota right of a minimum of £500,000. Quota loans are at rates of interest representative of those at which the Treasury can borrow. The minimum repayment period of new debt is ten years. Where authorities cannot raise money from other sources, the board continues to act as a lender of last resort. Restrictions on temporary borrowing continue to be exercised through Control of Borrowing Orders.[16]

The post-1964 regime has provided a powerful stimulant to the board's lending. As Appendix 5 shows, net borrowing by the local authorities from the board had been negative in 1963–4. In the following year their net advances jumped to 27 per cent of total borrowing and they have always remained since then between one-third and two-thirds of the councils' annual requirements.

With respect to the scale of expenditure and loan income, Table 6·2 shows that the 1953–4 peak was not exceeded again until ten years later, when a surge in local authority building took place as the 1964 general election approached. Expenditure and borrowing both increased by about 140 per cent in the five years after 1962–3 and then remained remarkably stable for the next five years, in spite of rapid increases in unit costs. A new surge began in 1972–3.

The trajectory of interest rates was rather different. Here we run into a most unfortunate data problem, for there is no time series which gives the cost of new local authority borrowing. At present the information is neither collected nor published, although for 1967–8 to

159

1975-6 we do have some DoE estimates. As a second best we can use
the data in Table 6·4, which gives the average rate of interest on new
advances from the board, covering about one-half of new net borrowing
since 1965-6. This rate moves in line with market rates since, after all,
it is based on the market rate for government credit. After peaking in
1961 the average new rate slipped back until the crisis of 1967, after
which it fluctuated around a rising trend which had no precedent in
British monetary history. As the table indicates, at it highest point in
1974-5 the PWLB rate was 12·5 per cent, or an estimated 13·8 per cent
on all new borrowing. The government's Green Paper on housing points
out that accelerating inflation and the use of restrictive monetary
measures to try to restrain it were accompanied by an exceptional increase in interest rates between 1972 and 1975.[17]

4 Internal relationships

We have seen that capital expenditure by local authorities on their
housebuilding programmes is financed from loans raised directly or
indirectly from the money market. What we need to look at now are
some of the internal administrative and accounting relationships. In the
first place it must be explained that no specific housing expenditure is
seen as tied to a specific loan. Indeed a consolidated loans fund usually
exists, which alone is seen as borrowing from the outside world. This
fund in its turn lends money to the individual spending departments,
including the housing department or its equivalent. The CLF borrows
not only to finance new projects but to refinance expiring debt, in
particular its temporary borrowing.

The rate of interest charged against a scheme is not the rate on new
advances in the year when finance for the project was raised (the
'marginal rate') but the 'pool rate'—the rate of interest on all outstanding
debt. If interest rates had remained invariant over time the two rates
would be identical. But since the marginal rate has followed a rising
trend in the past it always exceeded the pool rate which, in a sense, is
the 'memory' of all past 'marginal' rates on loans not yet repaid. The
marginal rate could be seen as hauling up the pool rate. The greater the
rate of capital expenditure in money terms in comparison with outstanding debt and the greater the volume of refinancing of old debt, the
more quickly the pool rate approached the marginal rate. As Table 6·4
shows, the pool rate moves only sluggishly in comparison with the

marginal rate. The steep downward movement in interest rates on new borrowing in 1977 for the first time since the war brought a situation in which the marginal was well below the pool rate.

The arrangements whereby the spending departments redeem their debt to the CLF are fairly straightforward. The ministerial loan sanction attached to any capital project specifies the maximum period over which a debt is to be redeemed. (Authorities can choose to redeem in a shorter period.) In the case of housing and land this is sixty years. Thus in each year a sum of money is paid by the spending department to the CLF, representing repayment of the principal of the loan plus the payment of the accrued interest. Together these are known as the debt charge and they appear in the housing revenue account of each authority as we shall see in the next chapter. The procedure in most common use is for the amount of principal repaid each year on each internal loan to rise at a steady rate, and this is known as the rate of accumulation. The maximum permitted rate is 5 per cent per annum. Since the principal outstanding is obviously greater at the beginning, it follows that the interest payments are also greater early on.

In money terms the sum of the debt charges paid over the entire redemption period far exceeds the original loan. This, of course, is because of the interest component in the charge. The ratio of the total charge to the loan I call the repayment ratio. It can be demonstrated mathematically that this ratio is a function of only three variables. When the values of these variables remain constant we can write:

$$q = 1 + i\left[n + \frac{n}{(1 + a)^n - 1} - \frac{1}{a}\right] \tag{1}$$

where q = repayment ratio i = rate of interest
       n = redemption period a = rate of accumulation

The relation is not a simple one but with a calculating machine the size of q can be very quickly established for given values of the three variables. For example, with a sixty-year redemption period, a rate of interest of 5 per cent and a rate of accumulation of 3 per cent, the value of q is 2·95. That is to say, taking typical values for the 1960s of our three variables, if housebuilding loans had been repaid on these terms throughout the repayment period, the sum repaid would have been almost three times as great as the sum originally borrowed. In these circumstances it is the redemption period which is the most

161

powerful factor determining the ratio. For example, one can recalculate q when each of the three variables in turn is reduced by one-half with the other two held constant. With the repayment period reduced to thirty years q falls from 2·95 down to 1·89; with the rate of interest reduced to 2½ per cent q falls to 1·97; with the rate of accumulation reduced to 1½ per cent, q falls only to 2·75.

Now let us look at the relationship between a loan's repayment ratio and u, the average proportionate amount made up by interest in the debt charge. This, at least, is simple: $u = \frac{q-1}{q}$. Taking the example above where q equals 2·95, the proportion which interest would make up on average of the debt charge would be 66 per cent. It should now be plain why interest can form such a huge proportion of the debt charge.

Up to this point the discussion has been conducted in terms of money values without regard for any general price inflation which may have been taking place. Since the interest rate rises in the decade after 1966-7 took place in a context of accelerating inflation, it is worthwhile trying to bring the two together. One of the basic concepts in such a discussion is the real rate of interest, which can most simply be defined as the rate of interest minus the rate of inflation.

The argument which can be made in inflationary conditions—and it is one I accept—is that whilst the total debt charge over the redemption period exceeds the original loan (when the money rate of interest is positive), this is totally misleading in that the value of each pound received is less in year two than in year one, less in year three than in year two, and so on, in terms of its purchasing power either over goods and services in general or over the commodity in particular which was purchased with the original loan. That is, the basic unit of measurement, the pound, is itself elastic: it shrinks from year to year. So—the argument concludes—we need to calculate the total debt charge in indexed terms to allow for price rises; and the simplest way to do this is to use the real rate of interest. Table 6·5 gives a simple illustration.

In order to finance a particular project a loan of £100 is raised at the beginning of year zero. The principal is repaid in equal instalments at the beginning of each of the succeeding five years. The money rate of interest is 10 per cent per annum and interest is payable at the beginning of each of the succeeding five years. The money rate of interest is 10 per cent per annum and interest is payable at the beginning of each year on the outstanding debt of the previous year. It follows that the total

Table 6·5 *A numerical example of the money and indexed debt charge on a £100 loan*

Year	0	1	2	3	4	5	Total
Loan raised	100	–	–	–	–	–	100
Debt redemption		20	20	20	20	20	100
Debt interest		10	8	6	4	2	30
Total debt charge		30	28	26	24	22	130
Indexed debt charge		27·27	23·14	19·53	16·39	13·66	99·99

debt charge is £130 and the repayment ratio 1·3. However, the rate of inflation is equal to 10 per cent per annum and therefore the total charge is also calculated in indexed terms, on the basis of year 0 prices.[18] The indexed total is £99·99 with a real repayment ratio negligibly different from one, which is the same figure as we would arrive at by entering the real rate of interest into equation (1).

To sum up the argument: the repayment ratio under conditions of inflation is misleading as it does not allow for the fall in the value of money. This can be corrected by using the real rate of interest—the money rate of interest less the rate of inflation—to calculate the real repayment ratio.

Now let us look at the level and movement of the real rate of interest since the war. To calculate this I shall use the pool rate of interest in Table 6·4. With respect to the rate of inflation the correct statistic to use—remember, there are many different rates of inflation—would be the price increases in council housebuilding. Unfortunately we do not know what these were since actual price changes reflect use-value shifts as well as simple price movements. So I shall rely on the rate of increase in retail prices. Graph 6·1 gives the results.

The overall picture is very clear. From the time of the return of the Conservative Party at the end of 1951 until the end of the 1960s the real rate of interest is low and stable. It averages 1·08 per cent per annum in 1952–69 with a standard deviation of 1·42. In the 1970s a much more rapid rate of inflation, coupled with a relatively sluggish pool rate, led to a series of negative rates. Under the conditions of the period 1952–69 the real repayment ratio would have been 1·42 and the real value of u, the real interest burden, would have been 30 per cent of the debt charge.[19]

The final topic of this section will cover the phenomenon known as

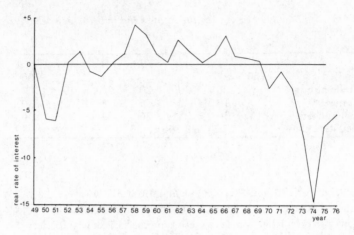

Graph 6·1 *The real rate of interest on local authority debt in England and Wales 1949–76*

frontloading, since it is a crucial element in understanding the financial crisis in state housing during the 1970s. In simple terms frontloading means that for a given gap between the rate of interest and the rate of inflation, the higher these two rates are the heavier will be the burden of debt repayment in the early years of the redemption period. Mathematically we can write that the real half-life of a series of debt charges with a given total real value varies inversely and asymptotically with the rate of interest and the rate of inflation for any given real rate of interest. By real half-life I mean the number of years elapsing until half the total debt charge is repaid in real terms. Fig. 6·2 illustrates this extremely important phenomenon of capitalism in an inflationary crisis.

5 The crisis of the 1970s

We are now in a position to consider the extraordinary impact on the debt charge of the capitalist crisis of the 1970s. Table 6·6 shows the movements in principal and interest.

The annual rate of growth in debt redemption (repayment of principal) is by no means inconsiderable, averaging 10·3 per cent. But the annual growth rate in the much larger item of debt interest is out of all proportion at 17·4 per cent. As a result the proportion of interest within

Table 6·6 *Debt redemption and debt interest on local authority dwellings in England and Wales 1969-70 to 1975-6 (£m)*

Year	1969-70	1970-1	1971-2	1972-3
Debt redemption	76	81	88	93
Debt interest	451	500	507	556
Total debt charge	527	581	595	649

Year	1973-4	1974-5	1975-6	
Debt redemption	101	116	137	
Debt interest	726	988	1180	
Total debt charge	827	1104	1317	

Source: DoE *Housing Policy*, Technical Volume, Part I, Table IV.9.

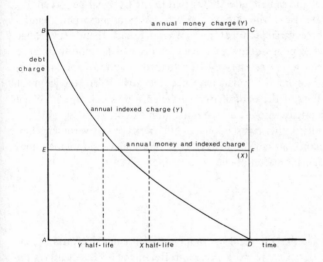

Figure 6·2 *The variation over time of the annual debt charge in money and indexed terms for two different money rates of interest*
We consider two projects *X* and *Y*, whose loan finance is redeemed in the same length of time, *A–D*; whose debt charges both take a constant annuity form; and whose real rate of interest is the same. Thus their total real debt charge is the same in both cases: the area *ABD=AEFD*. In the case of project *X* the rate of inflation is zero. In the case of project *Y* the rate of inflation is positive so the rate of interest is correspondingly higher. In these circumstances both the money value and the real value of the debt charge of *Y* will be higher in the early years of the redemption period.

165

the debt charge had risen to the unheard-of level of 90 per cent by 1975-6.

Four distinct factors had been at work. Three of these concern the capital expenditure of new estates. First, there was a marked upturn in the scale on construction after 1971-2 for three years. Second, there was a general process of price inflation which was driving up unit costs. Third, there had been a tendency until 1974-5 for unit costs in building to rise even more rapidly than prices in general. The fourth factor, of course, was the rise in market rates of interest.

Together these four variables produced the massive rise in the debt charges shown in the table. With respect to capital expenditure, a DoE study has suggested that general inflation was the most important factor, followed by the relative price effect and lastly the scale of output.[20] Yet the same study shows that in the five-year period ending in 1975-6 the rise in the rate of interest was more important than all the other three variables together.[21] What we had, then, was a huge expansion of capital outlays in money terms which went to finance schemes which were very heavily frontloaded in spite of the fact that their real rate of interest might have been negative.[22] To this we must add the swelling of the debt charge on the existing stock as refinancing drove up the rate of interest on the outstanding debt.

The impact of this crisis upon tenants' rents and government subsidies was immediate and dramatic. It is rent and subsidy which constitutes the subject matter of the next chapter.

6 Synthesis

In order to acquire sites and pay contractors for housing production, local authorities have to raise the requisite finance. These outlays on construction are conventionally referred to as 'capital expenditure' because of the longevity of the resources purchased. Capital expenditure on housing had risen seven-fold between the late 1940s and the mid-1970s, entirely as a result of the inflation in unit prices of council houses. The required finance has always been raised by loans from the money market, either directly or indirectly.

Thus whilst the local authority *develops* sites for the housing of the working population, *owns* the stock of council dwellings and *manages* this accommodation, in actually bringing the stock into existence it has always relied on private individuals, institutions and companies for the supply of the land, for dwelling production and for the raising of loan finance. Whenever we speak of 'local authority housebuilding' or 'state housing production'—convenient if misleading terms—we should always remember this symbiotic relationship between the state and the private sector, that is, the landowners and construction and finance capital. The intervention of the state has always been as developer and landlord.

In 1977 just over one-third of the total outstanding debt of all British local authorities took the form of loans from the Public Works Loan Board. Total reliance was placed on the board in the immediate post-war years but this relationship was broken by the Conservative government after 1951 and by the early 1960s, net borrowing from the board was negative. In order to reduce the local authorities' increasing use of temporary loans, access to the PWLB was renewed in 1964 and it has since supplied about half of the councils' net borrowing requirements.

With respect to rates of interest, the trend in rates on new advances from all sources has been upward since the war. After 1973–4 the rate stabilised at an extremely high level for three years and then fell sharply in 1977. The pool rate of interest has always lagged behind the marginal rate and rose almost without interruption before 1977–8.

Loan finance is raised for the totality of each authority's capital expenditure in any given year without specific loans being tied to specific projects. The Consolidated Loans Fund onlends this externally raised finance to individual spending departments at the pool rate of interest. The departments redeem their debt to the CLF over a specified maximum period—sixty years in the case of housing programmes—and this internal transfer is known as the debt charge. It is composed of the repayment of loan principal plus accrued interest. The repayment ratio and the proportion of interest within the debt charge are functions of the redeption period, the rate of accumulation and the rate of interest.

The real rate of interest on housing debt—that is to say the pool rate of interest minus the rate of inflation—was positive in the years 1952–69 but negative in the period 1969–77. In spite of this the sharp acceleration of the pool rate after 1972–3 and an expansion of local authority housebuilding at relatively high unit prices created the phenomenon of 'bunching' in an acute form with a high swelling in debt interest payments.

SEVEN

Consumption: rents and subsidies

1 Introduction

This chapter deals with the related questions of the level, trend and structure of council tenants' rents and state subsidies. It begins with a brief summary of the make-up of local authority housing revenue accounts, after which I turn to describe 'rent pooling' and the motivation underlying rent rebate schemes. With this general background complete, the main body of the text covers the trends in rents and subsidies since the war and the associated development of state policy. The final section considers whether council tenants are, in some sense, exploited.

A convenient starting point in the analysis of rents and subsidies in the state housing sector is the housing revenue account. Since 1935 each local housing authority has been required to keep in a standard format a single account for the revenue expenditure and income associated with all of the houses it rents out, including both purpose-built and acquired dwellings as well as slums 'temporarily' patched prior to demolition. Table 7·1 summarises the housing revenue accounts of all the English and Welsh districts in 1975-6.

Let us begin by looking briefly at the expenditure items. Supervision and management, which would be better termed management and services, includes both 'general' and 'special' functions.

'General' supervision and management is the management of local authority housing in the ordinary sense of the term, including rent collecting and accounting, selecting and interviewing tenants, organising transfers, and operating housing lists . . . 'Special' supervision and management, in contrast, is the cost of provision of services to tenants, such as heating in centrally heated blocks of flats, lighting and cleaning of the common parts of blocks of flats, and upkeep of estate grounds. These are in general the services for which long leaseholders of privately owned flats would pay service charges.[1]

Table 7·1 *Aggregate housing revenue account of local authorities in England and Wales in 1975-6[a]*

Expenditure	£m	%
Supervision and management	254	13
Repairs	340	17
Debt charges	1,317	66
Other expenditure	66	4
Residual: mainly change in end-year balance	10	1
Total expenditure	1,987	100
Income		
Rent: dwellings excluding amenities	839	42
Rent: amenities	17	3
Rent: other properties	36	
Exchequer subsidy[b]	799	40
Rate fund contribution	232	12
Other income	64	3
Total income	1,987	100

Source: HCS.

a   Provisional figures.

b   Includes £166m rent rebate subsidy; thus the dwelling rent figure
is net of rent rebates.

The repairs item is self-explanatory as is the residual item. Debt charges we dealt with in the previous chapter. Other expenditure includes debt management expenses, revenue contributions to capital outlay and a proportion of salaries and overheads related to housing capital works. The income items begin with rent, which is broken down into three categories. Dwelling rent requires no comment. Rent for amenities includes as its dominant element the payments for heating provided to the tenants by the council. Rent on other properties is derived from estate shops, lock-up garages and hard-standings. The Exchequer subsidy and rate fund contribution entries are, of course, the payments made to the account by the central and local state respectively. Under 'other income' the largest receipt derives from the astonishing fact that when local authority dwellings are sold, the debt charges on their original construction continue to be borne by the remaining tenants in the rest of the council's housing stock! As a corollary, where regular payments of principal and interest are made on the dwellings sold, the interest is credited to the housing revenue account.

With the exception of a brief interlude in 1972-5, local authorities have never been permitted to budget for a surplus in the housing revenue account nor is the account permitted to run at a deficit. Ignoring the

small 'other income' item, we can therefore write the implicit function:
$$E-R-S=0 \tag{1}$$
where E is equal to the expenditure total, R is equal to total rental income and S is the total of Exchequer and rate subsidies. From equation (1) we can derive:
$$R=E-S \tag{2}$$
i.e. rent is equal to revenue expenditure less subsidies. This arithmetic identity also has a limited causal significance in the sense that the total rent any single local authority raises from its tenants is determined by the sum of the expenditure items in the account less the subsidy receipts. For that reason I shall use the relation expressed in equation (2) in the remainder of this chapter.

Nevertheless, from a broader perspective, we need to realise that the causal direction is a far more complex matter, for in the development of government policy both the designed use-values of new dwellings (and therefore expenditure) as well as subsidy payments have been strongly influenced by the average rental payments which the state has perceived tenants being able and willing to bear. Thus rent, expenditure and subsidy all interact but I believe we can propose as a broad truth that expenditure is determined by the market costs of constructing and financing model dwellings at specific densities; rent is quite separately determined by what levels must be charged in order to ensure that tenants can afford to occupy the dwellings; and the subsidy payments make up the difference. The point is illustrated in Fig. 7·1. The existence of rent pooling and the variation in tenants' net incomes amends this basic relation and it is these questions I now wish to consider.

2 Rent pooling

In earlier chapters we have seen that, quite apart from changes in standards over time, local housing authorities have experienced very considerable shifts in the marginal rate of interest on borrowed finance and in capital costs per dwelling in the implementation of their housing programme. The dominant trend since World War II has been for both unit money costs and interest rates to rise. Similarly, rates of subsidy have changed markedly over the last thirty years. The result is that if the rent charged to a tenant for a house or flat were set equal to its historic level, the excess of its historic cost over the subsidy provided through the legislation in force in the year in which the dwelling was built, then the variation in rents within an authority would be huge and yet would bear no consistent relation with the relative use-values of the housing stock.

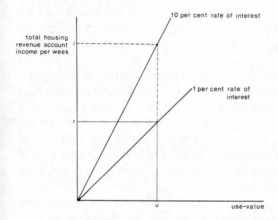

Figure 7·1 *The relation of state subsidy to the rate of interest on capital finance*

Let us suppose that the state builds dwellings with a use-value of u units and that the level of tenants' incomes permits them to pay a weekly rent of r. Given the labour productivity and profit rate of the housebuilding industry and the current costs of management and maintenance, we can derive the maximum rate of interest which could be paid on borrowed capital compatible with rent r meeting the debt charges of a dwelling with use-value u. The derived maximum is, say, 1 per cent. But let us assume that the actual rate of interest is 10 per cent. In this case r and u are compatible only if a subsidy equal to $(i-r)$ is paid by the local and central state (see a parallel analysis in Fig. 1·1).

But as we know, rents are not set on this basis. Instead the arrangement is that gross rents (rents before rebates) are set so that *in aggregate* they are equal to total expenditure in the housing revenue account less the sum of all Exchequer and rate fund contributions with the exception of rent rebate subsidies. The gross rent for each individual dwelling is then based on its relative use-value, for example the number of rooms, the total floor area, its age and aspect, whether it is a house or a flat, the range and quality of interior fixtures and fittings, the amenities available on the estate, the estate's location and 'character', and so forth. (A common procedure is for the relative gross rents to be based on the gross rateable values of the properties as estimated by the rating valuation officers of the Inland Revenue.) This procedure is known as rent pooling since it abstracts from the specific historical costs and sub-sidies of each house and thereby effectively pools the expenditure and subsidy income of the entire stock. This approach embodies an import-ant principle in social justice: within a single authority gross rents vary between habitations in a consistent way with respect to their relative size and quality.[2]

As we saw in Chapter 2, the system of rent pooling finds its legislat-ive origin in 1935 when the government required the local authorities to bring together the separate accounts of their housing estates into a single housing revenue account. We have already observed that the motive behind this innovation was not merely to introduce the principle of equity between households, it was also to enable the total flow of subsidies to be channelled towards the low-income tenants cleared from the slums after the 1930 Act.[3]

As time passed rent pooling came to fulfil another, quite distinct function. With the inflation in finance and construction costs—very considerable during the war years, fairly steady throughout the 1940s and 1950s and much more rapid since then—there was a continual upward pressure on the money subsidies required for new building. Simultaneously the continuous growth in money wages or salaries per worker meant that the historic rent of the older stock of state dwellings fell steadily as a proportion of income, although rising management, service and repair costs offset this effect. The system of rent pooling enabled the municipalities to raise the rents on the older houses above their historic levels and the surplus earned—rather like a property tax—could be transferred to the newly built stock, thereby reducing the subsidies required to bring the rent of the new dwellings down to a level their tenants could afford. The 1968 NBPI report on council rents suggested that rents from new dwellings often covered little more than half the costs incurred.[4]

The need to set the rents of newly built council housing below their full cost is demonstrated in Table 7·2, which is taken from the DoE's Green Paper, *Housing Policy*.

The table shows that the full cost of rent for a manual worker in manufacturing industry would have taken up 18 per cent of his income in 1947, 24 per cent in 1970 and the staggering figure of 36 per cent in 1976. The proportionate impact on his take-home pay would have been even higher of course. It was for this reason that a means of subsidising the full rent had to be found and the existence of rent pooling enabled this to take place with lower Exchequer and rate fund contributions that would otherwise have been necessary. Rent pooling, in effect, served as an indexing device for council rents under inflationary conditions, by reducing their money level initially and by raising them with the passage of time.

Table 7·2 *Cost rent on new houses compared with incomes in 1947, 1970 and 1976 (£)*

	1947	1970	1976
Capital cost	1,400	4,490	10,600
Loan charges[a]	51	311	1,116
Upkeep, management, etc.	10	45	140
Total annual cost	61	355	1,256
Weekly cost	£1 13s 6d	£6 16s 11d	£24.15
Average weekly earnings	£6 14s 2d	£28 18s 2d	£66.83
Cost rent as per cent of average earnings	18%	24%	36%

Source: DoE *Housing Policy*, Technical Volume I, Table I.29.
a Redemption over sixty years at rates of interest of 3 per cent for 1947, 6·8 per cent for 1970 and 10·5 per cent for 1976.

3 Rent rebates

The attempt to relate the rent paid to the municipality to the income of the household making the payment by means of a rent rebate or a differential rent has a long history.[5] Even the 1919 Addison Act indicated that rents should vary with the tenant's ability to pay and in 1930 the Minister of Health specifically recommended rent rebate schemes as the local authorities began again to take up the task of slum clearance. As we shall see in the next section, there has continued to be government pressure for the introduction of such schemes ever since the 1950s.

The system of pooled standard rents in existence before 1972[6] and pooled gross rents since 1975 has meant that external subsidies were themselves pooled amongst all the tenants, with the exception of subsidies used for rent rebate schemes. The greater the degree of pooling of the subsidy total, the greater is the effect of subsidy payments to act as an entirely generalised device to keep down rents within the council sector. On the other hand, the greater the proportion of subsidies used for rebate schemes, the more effectively is this income channelled as another welfare instrument in the state's provision for the poor.

What were the economic reasons which caused the central state so persistently to inveigle the local state to channel the subsidy flow? In Fig. 2·1 of Chapter 2 it was argued that this flow acted rather like a butterfly valve in an aircraft engine: by raising the subsidy rate, by opening the valve, a higher volume of new council dwellings were likely to be supplied by the municipalities and vice versa with subsidy cuts. But the need for a subsidy on pooled rents obviously varied considerably between tenants. Those in particularly acute need included the pensioners, the chronically sick, the widowed, the single-parent families, the unemployed and the low wage-earners with large families. Thus if a rent rebate scheme were introduced which disbursed the major part of subsidy income from new building on the basis of need, the same flows of new building could be achieved as with a higher, non-differentiated, subsidy, since the transfer to those in the most favourable economic circumstances could be set at a lower level. Similarly a new rebate scheme would permit the raising of the pooled rents of the higher paid workers in the existing stock and thereby provide greater surplus for transfer to subsidise households in the newly added stock. For the government, then, the function of rent rebate systems was to diminish the total public revenue expenditure required to stimulate the scale of municipal housebuilding which the centre wished to see achieved.

These pressures were strengthened by an increase in the *spread* of incomes in the council sector. As we saw, the first government circular on rebates came in 1930, when slum clearance was introduced as the chief element in Labour's public sector housing programme. Clearance followed by council rehousing of the dislocated population brought with it an influx of working families with incomes lower than had formerly been the case in the council sector. The need for rent rebates became obvious in these circumstances. Doubtless the slum-clearance policies of the Conservative government after 1955 continued the increased dispersion of council tenant incomes. It was Duncan Sandys who both launched the clearance programme of the mid-1950s and who attacked the 'waste' of government money on council tenants who did not 'need' subsidies. Parker has also suggested that household income differentials increased because of the post-war growth in the opportunities for wives to work, the growth in overtime in many sectors of industry and the increasing proportion of pensioners in the council sector.[7]

The drive for subsidy concentration cannot be left without referring to the hypocrisy of both political parties in arguing the case for it. The real grounds were essentially economic but the argument presented was one of 'fairness'. It was reported constantly that help ought to go only to the needy. A large number of people were undoubtedly deceived by this emotive language. But the government of the day never quite managed to explain how the principle of fairness was being applied in the rest of the housing market. This was no oversight, for if medium- and high-wage tenants did not need subsidies then certainly neither did the owner-occupiers. Yet arguments for the concentration of council subsidies were never coupled in the official literature with persuasive resolutions on the fairness of eliminating income-tax relief on home ownership. Here stands naked the true nature of arguments from principles of fairness in capitalist society: pure cant.

Why was it that the local authorities resisted with such tenacity the attempts of successive Conservative and Labour governments to persuade them to introduce allocation schemes which concentrated the subsidy on the low-income tenant? With many councils it was doubtless a question of political principle, the unwillingness to convert a subsidy to the working class as a whole into a welfare benefit. With other councils it was a matter of political pragmatism: subsidy concentration inevitably led to a rise in average standard rents and this might weaken the position of the party in power at the next local election. This argument was strongest in authorities with a large proportion of council-tenant voters.

Perhaps the most important single factor which permitted the local authorities to avoid concentrating the subsidy before rebates became mandatory in 1972 was the existence of the National Assistance Board, and after it the Supplementary Benefits Commission. An analysis in 1967 by the Ministry of Social Security showed that 21 per cent of all heads of households in council tenure in Great Britain were in receipt of supplementary benefits.[8] Each of these tenants could ask for the Ministry to include in his benefit a sum covering in full his standard rent. Most council tenants on benefit did this and as a result about 85 per cent of them were in receipt of no rent rebate from their local authority.

In this case we see that the councils did not convert their subsidy allocation scheme into a welfare benefit device because a welfare agency already existed which was willing, in the last analysis, to pay the standard rent in full. Doubtless there were conflicts between one

175

sector of the bureaucracy and another. The local office of the Ministry of Social Security wanted to see large rebates to tenants receiving supplementary benefit, whilst the local authority wanted a continuation of the practice whereby the Ministry covered the standard rent. Parker has argued that it was the Ministry, as the provider of last resort, which usually lost the tussle. The people who suffered most were those caught in the cross-fire: tenants reluctant to apply for supplementary benefits; those getting assistance at less than scale rates because of the 'wages stop'; and those in full-time work on low wages but with big families.[9]

Before leaving this discussion of the recalcitrance of the local authorities, it is necessary to mention the phenomenon of 'sorting'. The need for rebates existed because people could not afford the standard rents assessed on their dwellings. The authorities, probably in their great majority, had their own way of providing the urban poorest with relatively cheap accommodation. This was to allocate them to the poorest *quality* council dwellings. Most authorities had in their housing stock a range of quality of accommodation for any given family size. Some of the worst, for example, would be in the flats built in five-storey blocks during the period of the so-called National Government of Ramsay MacDonald, when standards were probably at their lowest since 1919. The practice was, and still is, to place new council tenants with particularly low incomes in this low-quality band of accommodation, provided vacancies existed there. It is common even today to 'send up' the most sub-standard council accommodation to the homeless families section of the housing department. Low-quality accommodation bears low standard rents, of course, and thereby the necessity of the low-income tenant receiving a rebate may be avoided.

Sorting is not merely a local practice; it has at least on one occasion been recommended to the authorities. In 1968 the NBPI report said that if council rents were based on pooled historic costs and the 1967 ministerial rebate system, existing Exchequer subsidies would be nearly sufficient to meet the total of rebates offered 'if the authorities extended the policy of letting their cheaper dwellings to the lower income tenants and allowing those with higher incomes to move into the higher rented houses'.[10]

4 The first post-war decade

With this preliminary discussion of housing revenue accounts, rent pooling and rent rebates complete, I now wish to review the main trends in rent levels, subsidy structures and government policy since 1945. A brief summary of all the legislation to which I refer can be found in Appendix 1.

The price inflation associated with the war had a relatively minor impact on council rents because of the historical basis of their determination. As a result, whilst money earnings doubled between 1936 and 1946, rents rose only from about 7s per week to 9s per week.[11] This second figure may well have influenced the new Labour government's subsidy policy, for the legislation of 1946 was designed so that Exchequer and rate fund contributions would together lead to an average rent on new houses of some 10s per week. The central and mandatory local subsidies were set at £16 10s and £5 10s per dwelling per year over sixty years. Thus the subsidy form introduced in 1923 was still in favour. A clutch of special subsidies, such as those for flats on expensive sites, were also provided.

In these early post-war years the causal link between subsidy and the building and finance costs of new dwellings was a recurring theme. Thus in June 1947 it was decided that the current subsidy would remain unchanged because, although building costs had risen, there had been a cut in the PWLB rate on new loans to the local authorities.[12] However, subsidies remained constant even when construction and interest costs were rising together (in 1948) and when it was admitted (in 1949) that outlays on repairs, maintenance and management were higher than in the original estimates.[13]

With the exception of the innovation of improvement subsidies to local authorities in 1949, the first major change in government contributions did not come until the Housing Act of 1952. The Conservative government elected in the previous year had decided on a substantial increase in municipal housebuilding. As building costs had continued to move up and since the new government itself had raised the rate of interest on PWLB finance, an increase in the rate of subsidy was a necessary condition of greater willingness on the part of the councils to expand their programmes. The butterfly valve was opened: the standard annual subsidy per dwelling was set at £26 14s to be supplemented by a rate subsidy of £8 18s. Consequential alterations were made in the special subsidies. As Appendix 5 shows, there was a sharp increase in total government payments to authorities in England and Wales under post-war legislation from £13·2 million in 1951–2 to £23·8 million in 1953–4.[14] 1953 was an interesting year for it witnessed the first expression since 1945 of the pre-war concern with relating rents to the tenants' ability to pay. The 'advantages' of such schemes were described in a report of the Central Housing Advisory Committee chaired by the Minister of Health, Henry Brooke.[15]

Governmental pressure for an enlarged scale of state housebuilding had all along been planned merely as a temporary device until speculative housebuilding should begin to reassert its old power of the 1930s. So when the rate on PWLB finance fell in 1954, the administration took the opportunity to announce subsidy cuts which would take effect with dwellings completed after All Fools Day, 1955. The new general standard subsidy was £22 1s from the centre and £7 7s from the rates. Hardly had they begun to operate when board interest rates were raised sharply with the summer crisis of 1955.

5 Subsidies for high-density redevelopment

A very substantial policy change came in 1956 which we shall examine in more detail in Chapter 9. The Conservative Cabinet decided to continue the reduction in the scale of municipal housebuilding and at the same time to switch its dominant function from general needs construction to redevelopment. The Housing Subsidies Act cut the subsidy on houses completed for general needs purposes to £10 per annum. (In December 1956 an order abolished even this contribution other than on one-bedroom houses.) For houses and flats built for slum replacement there was no change in the existing government subsidy of £22 1s. It was this Act, too, which for the first time linked the subsidy per dwelling on flatted blocks to the number of storeys, thus giving a tremendous stimulant to high-rise schemes. Slum-clearance subsidy would still be paid on a dwelling, even if cleared families were moved into old local authority stock, thereby underpinning the 'sorting' practices of housing management.

A second feature of the new municipal policy was the renewed attempt to stimulate wider adoption of differential or rebated rents as well as rent pooling.[16] For the first time the local authorities were given a direct financial incentive to channel their subsidy as the Minister, Duncan Sandys, made plain:[17]

Unless local authorities will exercise more discrimination in giving rent relief to their tenants, there is bound to be a continued misuse of public money. At present, councils are discouraged from introducing differential rent schemes by reason of the fact that, no matter how much they increase their revenue from rents, they still have a statutory obligation to pay into the Housing Revenue Account a fixed contribution from the rates. We therefore propose to abolish this obligation. This will allow local authorities, if they so desire, to use any savings they may make to reduce the rate burden, and will give them for the first time an incentive to adopt realistic rent policies. . .

The proposed changes in the subsidy rates will have the effect of slowing down the annual growth of Exchequer expenditure on housing.

In Circular 29/56 information and advice was given on differential rent schemes with details of those already in operation.

From the end of 1956, then, the rate fund contribution became either a voluntary subsidy towards the overall reduction of rent levels or a voluntary subsidy on specific items—the warden's wages in sheltered housing, for example. The result of this decision was to introduce marked disparities between authorities in the proportionate size of the contribution. Labour councils, of course, tended to set a higher subsidy level than Conservative councils. In 1965–6 about 70 per cent of the housing authorities in England and Wales made either no rate contribution, or one which was less than 5 per cent of their total housing expenditure; about 20 per cent made a contribution in the range of 5-10 per cent of expenditure. On the other hand, amongst the Scottish authorities the 1965–6 average rate contribution was 35 per cent of expenditure.[18]

The subsidy reduction of 1954, the abolition of the general needs subsidy in 1956, the now voluntary nature of the rate fund subsidy on new houses and the constant money value of subsidies per dwelling at a time of cost and interest rate inflation had a startling effect on the ratio of the income from Exchequer and rate fund contributions to total housing revenue expenditure; in other words the proportion of the total expenditure bill that was met by the central and local state. Graph 7·1 shows that the ratio remained very stable in the years 1949–50 until 1955–6 inclusive at a level at which something over one-third of expenditure was met by the state authorities. Thereafter the ratio plunges until the year 1962–3, after which it remained stable for the next nine years at the 25–27 per cent level. In spite of this decline the absolute value of all Exchequer subsidies climbed steadily from £48·2 million in 1955–6 up to £84 million in 1966–7, an annual compound rate of growth of 5·2 per cent.

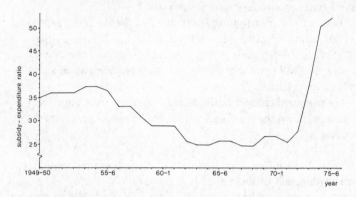

Graph 7·1 *The subsidy–expenditure ratio for local authority housing in England and Wales 1949–50 to 1975–6*
Sources: IMTA, HSGB, HCS.

Over the same period the annual rate of growth of weekly rents was 7·7 per cent. This must have been markedly higher than the growth rate of the take-home pay of manual workers. During the 1960s most municipalities had general rent reviews every two, three or four years, although these were more frequent at the end of the decade as inflation became more rapid. The data on rents are given in Table 7·3. It should be noted that the rent concept used in this table is not the same as rent as it is understood by most council tenants: the table excludes amenity payments, e.g. heating costs, and rates. So the 'rent' a tenant pays will often be considerably higher than the published figures. This, of course, does not diminish the accuracy of the table, which in effect denotes the rebated payments for the use of the dwelling *per se*, before heating charges and before payment of the local authority's property tax.

In spite of Sandys's incentive to municipal introduction of differential or rebated rents, they made slow progress in the face of tenant resistance. The most notable post-war struggle against such schemes took place in St Pancras, London, in 1960.[19] In the local elections of May 1959 a Conservative council was returned to power in the borough. In July it approved a new rent scheme which set minimum and maximum rent

levels based on each dwelling's rateable value and simultaneously introduced rebates designed to bring down the rent paid to one-fifth of
gross income after certain allowances were deducted. The overall intention of the scheme was: (i) to raise average rents sufficiently to eliminate
the rate fund contribution (70 per cent of which was paid by industrial
and commercial enterprises); and (ii) to raise very considerably—in many
cases by a factor of two or three—the rents of those households, 52 per
cent of the total, paying the maximum rent.

Table 7·3 *Average weekly rebated rents of local authority tenants
in England and Wales 1949–76 (£)*

Year	Weekly rent	Year	Weekly rent
1949	0·48	1963	1·27
1950	0·50	1964	1·35
1951	0·54	1965	1·45
1952	0·59	1966	1·59
1953	0·64	1967	1·78
1954	0·67	1968	1·93
1955	0·70	1969	2·08
1956	0·80	1970	2·33
1957	0·87	1971	2·52
1958	0·95	1972	3·05
1959	0·99	1973	3·31
1960	1·05	1974	3·39
1961	1·11	1975	3·85
1962	1·21	1976	4·43

Source: IMTA Housing Statistics, HSGB, HCS.
Note: Since there were no mandatory rent rebate schemes before
1972, the term 'weekly rebated rent' only takes on real meaning
from that year. Nevertheless both before and after 1972 the data are
the averages of *all* rents, net of any rebates which the tenants received.
For the period 1949–56 the data are my own estimates based on IMTA
statistics and are for April–March financial years. (Thus the 1949
figure is actually the April 1949–March 1950 datum.) The 1957 figure
is for September of that year and all data thereafter are for the month
of October.

In August of 1959 a United Tenants Association was formed to fight
the scheme and it proceeded to launch a number of marches, picketings,
demonstrations and a 16,000-signature petition. The rent scheme began
in January 1960 and the UTA response was to advise tenants to with-
hold the increase. Many hundreds did so. In the same month the council
decided to serve notices to quit on tenants in arrears. The first batch
were soon served and court cases began in May. The UTA decided only

a limited number should face the eviction threat and eventually this task was shouldered by two households, Don Cook and Arthur Rowe and their families. At 5 am on 22 September the bailiffs, supported by 800 police, attacked and after a one to two hour battle the evictions were complete. That evening 14,000 people marched on St Pancras Town Hall and there followed bitter fighting between demonstrators and police until midnight. The following day the Home Secretary banned all public processions. In November the council made concessions involving a loss of £15,500 in rental income. This, plus the evictions, brought a situation where many more tenants began to pay off their arrears. In view of these circumstances the UTA leadership felt obliged to switch their policy to avoid eviction and to strive to return a Labour council in the next elections. These took place in May 1962. The victorious Labour group five months later accepted the Conservative scheme, although increasing the value of rebates. The St Pancras rent strike was over.

By 1961 the new strategy had been in operation for five years. In the eyes of the civil service and the Conservative leadership certain defects had become apparent. First, rebate schemes were still relatively unimportant in their overall impact on the structure of tenants' rents. (The continuing commitment to subsidy channelling is made clear in a Conservative Political Centre pamphlet published in 1960 which advised that[20] 'a desirable development is for all tenants to pay the economic rent, with the Exchequer and rate fund subsidy, if any, available as a rebate in deserving cases.') Second, the provision of subsidies only for slum clearance and the housing of the elderly was proving to be too inflexible, particularly since it was realised that housing shortages were by no means at an end and that general needs requirements were not fully met by speculative building. Third, the distribution of subsidies between local authority areas was quite irrational.

The last point is worth expanding. I have already pointed out that pooling introduced an important principle of equity in rent determination by attempting to relate standard or gross rent to the use-value of a property. But pooling took place only within the boundaries of each separate municipality. No mechanism existed for the joint pooling of all the nation's council rents. Thus an authority with a stock predominantly composed of pre-war and early post-war dwellings would be charging average (historical) rents much lower than an authority which had been engaged in large-scale construction from the mid-1950s when costs were higher and the subsidy expenditure ratio was falling. Similarly rents would be much higher in areas like London, where construction costs were more expensive. The distribution of Exchequer subsidies bore no systematic relation to these spatial variations in average rents.

A new Housing Act received the royal assent in 1961 and was intended to remedy these defects. In recasting the subsidy system it attempted to create a more public expenditure-effective tool for implementing the government's political-economic objectives. Subsidies were to be paid on all local authority dwellings approved for that purpose by the Minister. This was the means by which greater flexibility would be achieved. In addition there were to be two rates of standard annual subsidy, £24 and £8 per dwelling paid over sixty years, although all subsidies committed under the Act could be reviewed in not less than ten years. The higher rate was paid only to authorities passing a financial test of need, that is where the notional rent income from its housing stock—set equal to twice the aggregate gross rateable value—fell short of the housing revenue account expenditure total. This needs test obviously was devised so that local authorities with relatively low historic expenditure would receive a smaller subsidy flow on new building, thereby forcing them to raise average rents more rapidly than would otherwise have been the case. Substantial average rent increases were probably seen, too, as likely to lead to the introduction of rebate schemes so as not to price out the tenants on low incomes. The Act also revised the system of special subsidies.

The most informed criticism of the Act has come from the civil service itself. The DoE's *Housing Policy* Green Paper points out in retrospect that averaged over all completions the new subsidies were worth only £10–12 per dwelling.[21] They applied to less than half of the total building programme and were heavily concentrated in urban areas with high land costs and a large proportion of high-rise developments. The anomalies were that rateable values were only a rough guide to notional rent resources; that these values were not adjusted on an annual basis; that authorities with high values yet in great housing need would receive a low basic subsidy and that the subsidies were fixed in money terms.

6 Rent and income

Government exhortations to the local authorities to introduce rebated rents had by no means come to an end. The May 1963 White Paper promised that if proper rents were charged subject to rebates for those who needed them, the state would be prepared to see that local authorities received whatever subsidies they needed to carry through their housing responsibilities.[22] A working party was set up by the Ministry to study costs and the rent-paying capacity of tenants. In the same vein Labour's 1965 White Paper *The Housing Programme 1965 to 1970* said that:[23] 'Help for those who most need it can be given only if the subsidies are in large part used to provide rebates for tenants whose means are small.' This advice was given flesh in Circular 46/67 of June 1967, entitled *Rent Rebate Schemes*. (The logic of this Labour scheme was the model for the rebate provisions of the 1972 Housing Finance Act.) A year later the Prices and Incomes Board added its voice to the crescendo: it put forward the idea of a uniform rebate scheme with its own separate account into which all Exchequer subsidies were to be channelled.[24]

All of these proposals to relate rent net of rebate to need were couched in terms of household income usually adjusted for family size. Naturally this stimulated much curiosity about what proportion of income was, in fact, spent on council rent. The DoE has published data for 1936–76 on what proportion average council rents make up of the average pre-tax earnings of men in manual work, excluding rates.[25] Since the war the figure has stayed fairly close to 7–8 per cent of income. The Family Expenditure Survey publishes similar data. Unfortunately this information is virtually useless if only because gross income is simply not available for the payment of rent, it is only post-tax income which is so available.

With respect to rent as a proportion of post-tax earnings the only nationwide information that I know of appeared in the NBPI report already referred to. In 1968 the board conducted a survey amongst the tenants of twenty local authorities in Great Britain. Some of the results are given in Table 7·4.

The average weekly rent paid in these authorities was £1.94. The average weekly net income of the 156,280 tenancies in Table 7·4 is £17.14. This gives a rent–income ratio of 11·3 per cent in 1968.

Returning to the question of the introduction of rebate schemes, it is worthwhile enquiring what effect this continual stream of advice since 1930 had had on municipal practices. The answer at the end of the 1960s was: precious little. Admittedly the proportion of authorities employing some kind of differential rent or rent rebate scheme had risen from only about 5 per cent in 1949 up to 45 per cent in Scotland and 53 per cent in England and Wales by 1968.[26] However, the NBPI report showed that the rebates paid out in 1966-7 still only made up 8 per cent of the total subsidy paid into the housing accounts of the authorities.[27] In the same year about 9 per cent of council households were receiving rebates.

Table 7·4 *Average net weekly incomes in 1968 of a sample of local authority tenants in Great Britain[a]*

Components of income	Pensioners[b]		Non-pensioners[b]	
	Persons reporting item	*Average amount they received (£)*	*Persons reporting item*	*Average amount they received (£)*
Husband's take-home pay	3,120	9·26	117,620	16·53
Husband's self-employment income[c]	180	1·28	2,860	16·30
Husband's bonuses, etc.[c]	–	–	5,720	1·16
Wife's take-home pay	3,290	6·33	48,610	6·30
Family allowances	–	–	44,110	0·90
Widow's pension	3,430	4·72	7,950	5·86
Disability pension	1,720	4·03	4,260	3·13
Service or firm's pension	10,950	4·22	2,390	2·79
National Insurance retirement pension	18,670	6·25	1,240	5·37
Maintenance allowance	–	–	1,860	3·58
Any other income[c]	3,490	1·65	3,910	3·40
Total no. of tenancies	23,120		133,160	

Source: NBPI (1968), Statistical Supplement p.62.
a Excludes tenancies where 'head of household' was receiving unemployment, sickness or supplementary benefits.
b The division between pensioners and non-pensioners is based on the status of the 'head of household'.
c Gross, not net, income. The gross items amount to 3 per cent of the total income of £2·68 million.

7 Subsidies and inflation

In the chapters on site acquisition and dwelling production we have seen that land price and construction cost inflation perceptibly quickened after about 1959. Interest rates were also following an upward trend. In these conditions the Chamberlain system of a constant money subsidy defined by Parliamentary legislation was no longer appropriate. It became apparent that in some way subsidy and cost had to be tied together. Systematic spatial variations in building costs underpinned this view. It was this link that the Housing Subsidies Bill was intended to forge. The Bill received its first reading in 1965 when the new Labour government was committed to a huge expansion in local authority housebuilding as well as to partial implementation of the Parker Morris recommendations on improved standards. Thus when the Act finally received the Royal Assent in 1967—a general election intervening in 1966—the unit subsidies were very much higher than even the £24 level of the 1961 Act. The basic feature of the Act was that the subsidy met the cost difference between borrowing on the approved cost of a housing scheme at a 4 per cent rate of interest and borrowing at the representative rate of interest which was calculated from municipal new borrowing rates generally. Approved costs were those which fell within newly computed housing cost yardsticks which varied between regions. The subsidy stimulant to high-rise construction was very markedly weakened in comparison with the 1956 Act.[28]

Average subsidy per dwelling completed jumped immediately to about £67 and this had increased threefold to £187 per dwelling in 1971 as building costs and (up to 1970) interest rates rose.[29] Because of this and because of the increase in the rate of local authority completions, the aggregate Exchequer subsidy paid out rose from £84 million in 1966-7 to £192 million in 1971-2, a compound rate of growth of 18 per cent per year. In spite of this the total subsidy-expenditure ratio of Graph 7·1 remained stable at about one-quarter. Government economists suggest that rent increases in 1967-8 to 1971-2 on the starting stock were nearly sufficient to cover expenditure increases in spite of debt refinancing at high interest rates. Gross subsidies to the newly built stock through rent pooling had evidently come to an end, at least for some years. Rents on additions and acquisitions were sufficient to cover only 45 per cent of revenue expenditure.[30] In spite of this the compound annual rate of increase of average weekly rent was 9·6 per cent as it rose from £1.59 in 1966-7 to £2.52 in 1971-2.

Already in the mid-1960s the development of policies to combat inflation was becoming a major concern of government and sharp increases in council rents were feared as a stimulant of 'excessive wage demands' as the phrase goes. The July 1966 White Paper, *Prices and Incomes Standstill* (Cmnd 3073), asked local authorities to give a lead in preventing or postponing rent increases. As a result only twenty-one out of over 1200 English housing authorities did increase rents during the standstill period.[31] In November the councils were asked to avoid or limit increases during the period of severe restraint. By the following year the government took the view that some increases were unavoidable but after several authorities had announced very substantial rises the Prime Minister, Harold Wilson, decided to refer these to the National Board for Prices and Incomes. After the board had reported, recommending staged increases, the Prices and Incomes Act was passed in 1968 making increases which were not approved by the Minister unlawful. Circular 37/68 advised that an average increase of more than 7s 6d per week or an increase of 10s per week on an individual dwelling would normally be unacceptable. Alternative measures such as a reduction of working balances or an increase in the rate of accumulation were proposed. Now the pressure to introduce rebate schemes took a new form when it was made clear that introduction or extension of a scheme would be accepted as a justification for a rent increase under the prices and incomes policy.[32] Once more subsidy channelling and average rent increases went hand in hand. In 1969 came the passage of the Rent (Control of Increases) Act which took effect from 1 January 1970. Rent increases exceeding an average of 37½p per week or a maximum of 50p per week in any fifty-two week period required the Minister's agreement. But with the return of the Conservative Party to power in 1970 a revolutionary new innovation in the system of rent determination and subsidy payment was put in train, which finally manifested itself as the Housing Finance Act of 1972.

With respect to council housing the main provisions of this exceedingly complex Act are contained in Appendix 1. The existing arrangements for settling rents and subsidies were abolished. Rent increases were immediately set in train which were to continue until levels reached the 'fair rents' determined by newly established rent scrutiny boards. A mandatory rent rebate system was introduced. Rebates became available subject to income, family circumstances and 'fair rent' to all tenants, including those receiving supplementary benefit. With respect to subsidies, the essential feature was that any difference between 'reckonable' housing revenue account expenditure and rent income should be met by the Exchequer and the local rate fund in prescribed proportions. All subsidies payable under earlier Acts were terminated and replaced by the new provisions. As rent rose relative to reckonable expenditure, subsidies would be withdrawn. Housing revenue account surpluses were encouraged and above a balance of £30 per dwelling they were to be paid to the Secretary of State. A new 'rising cost subsidy' applied to all new reckonable expenditure and quickly became the dominant element

The objectives of the Act were unmistakably within that consistent policy pursued by the Conservative Party since 1956. First, the Act sought to achieve a cut in the Exchequer subsidies made available to the state housing sector below what they would otherwise have been. The government of the day did not inform the public about how much these planned reductions were likely to be but that relative cuts were budgeted for is clear from the fact that the Act introduced a very steep average rent rise of £1 per dwelling per week as from October 1972 with a further 50p rise one year later. The Conservatives were confident that the 'fair rents' set by the rent scrutiny boards would be well above existing levels because the boards were to use the much higher 'fair rents' in the private sector as a comparison. Moreover, for the first time in the history of the state sector, local authorities were to regard their housing stock as an 'investment' on which a rate of return could be earned.

The second objective of the Act was to channel state subsidies to the low-income tenants by means of the new rebate scheme. The principle of the scheme was that a minimum rent was set and where this was exceeded by the 'fair rent', the difference was covered in full by a rebate. (Rents excluded the amenities charge and rates.) The minimum rent was based on the 'fair rent', the family's actual income and a bureaucratically defined notional minimum family income. If all had gone according to plan, in the fourth year of the Act's operation as much as 62 per cent of the subsidies paid would have been for rent rebates, a massive internal redistribution of subsidy in comparison with the situation in the late 1960s.[33] The government's July 1971 White Paper *Fair Deal for Housing* (Cmnd 4728) made it plain that the Conservatives hoped the net rent of a council house would increase so sharply for high-wage tenants that a mortgage would begin to appear more attractive. This general encouragement to owner-occupation was buttressed by encouraging building society practices which improved the mortgage prospect of those with high earnings but low capital, i.e. skilled workers. At the same time restrictions on the sale of council houses to tenants were removed. These measures and the Act itself were intended to initiate the slow dissolution of the public rental sector with respect to the relatively high-wage working class. The intention to raise a surplus over costs on the council dwellings occupied by high-wage tenants, compared with the substantial subsidy they would receive as new owner-occupiers, was presented as 'a fairer choice between owning a house and renting one'—a grotesque distortion of the truth.[34]

The third objective of the Act was to channel the total subsidy paid to those housing areas where the need for new public construction was most pressing. This was to be done by running down the existing historically determined subsidies through the device of the 'residual subsidy' and by making the 'rising costs' subsidy the major government contribution after the rent rebate subsidy. The rising costs subsidy was associated with some very important and positive features of the Act. The subsidy was paid as a contribution to 'reckonable expenditure' and this included for the first time costs incurred before dwelling completion, higher interest charges on old debt and current expenditure on maintenance and management. In addition to the existing government contributions to local authority improvement, one-half of loan charges on improvement work was to be included in reckonable expenditure. As we have seen in Chapter 5 the partitioning of redevelopment and rehabilitation was being modified in the early 1970s and this made it essential for the financial system not to give a bias to redevelopment as a relatively high subsidy earner. Civil service economists are now clear that subsidy bias towards the form of investment or vis-á-vis the balance of current and capital costs must be avoided.[35]

Any assessment of the implementation of the Housing Finance Act is made difficult because it was in unconstrained operation for such a short time. The new system had met very widespread criticism and opposition from tenants' associations and from Labour councils. Their hostility had been aroused above all by the rent increases, the pressure on councils to earn surpluses and the ideologically conceived stripping of subsidies from high-wage tenants. The exemplary struggle of the councillors and townsfolk of Clay Cross was the high point of the movement in spite of the national Labour leadership's disapproval of outright refusal to implement the Act.[36] It was undoubtedly as a result of these movements that after the Labour Party returned to power in 1974 a rent freeze was imposed in March, halting the advance to 'fair rents'—in the event only a very small number of 'fair rents' had been determined by the rent scrutiny boards—and in 1975 the same government replaced the Act with new legislation. Since the Act received the

Royal Assent only in July 1972, the financial year 1973-4 alone was witness to its untrammelled progress. What is certainly beyond doubt is that its period of operation is associated with an extremely rapid rate of increase of average rents: in the two-year period between October 1971 and October 1973 they rose from £2.52 to £3.31, or by 31 per cent.

One of the features of the 1972 Act which was not later repealed was the mandatory rebate system. This brought with it a change in the role of the Supplementary Benefits Commission. In the two financial years 1972-4 supplementary benefits were made on the assumption that the tenant paid a rebated rent and so he or she had to claim the rebate from the council. From the year 1974-5 onwards, benefit was assessed on unrebated rents whilst the tenant paid the full gross rent to the local authority. As a corollary the local authorities made block payments to the SBC to broadly equate with the total rebates tenants eligible for supplementary benefit would have received if they had claimed them separately.[37] By 1976 945,000 tenants in England and Wales were receiving rent rebates and 1,132,000 were receiving supplementary benefit. Together these two groups made up 44 per cent of all local authority households. The total rebate granted including re-imbursements to the SBC was equal to £223 million in 1975-6. It is estimated that about one-quarter of tenants who qualify for rebates do not take them up.[38]

Now let us look at the 1975 Housing Rents and Subsidies Act. It cancelled the 'fair rents' principle of 1972 and municipalities reverted to charging 'reasonable rents' based on historic costs with rate fund contributions at the local authority's discretion. The new subsidy system consolidated existing subsidies at their 1974-5 level; gave a new capital costs element paid at 66 per cent of the debt charge on reckonable capital expenditure; and met 33 per cent of increases in the debt charge of pre-1975-6 debt due to refinancing. The Act also included a special element subsidy for the financial years 1975-7, in order to make less acute the need for sharp rent (or rate) increases at the end of the rent freeze in 1975. We should also note that the scale of subsidy per £1000 of loan charges was the same for new building as it was for acquisition or improvement, thus avoiding subsidy bias. However, unlike the 1972 Act, it contains no standard subsidy for management and maintenance costs.

As both the 1972 and 1975 Acts related new subsidy payments to the costs of debt refinance and to the reckonable costs of new building, acquisition and improvement, it is convenient to look at rent and subsidy trends since the early 1970s as a continuum. The most astonishing feature of the period is shown in Graph 7·1: the subsidy–expenditure ratio rose from 28 per cent in 1972–3 to 52 per cent in 1975–6. This was associated with a gargantuan increase in Exchequer subsidies: from £277 million in 1972–3 to £973 million in 1975–6. And yet all of this took place at a time when average rebated rents were increasing, in money terms, at a faster rate than ever before, in spite of the 1974 rent freeze. Between October 1971 and October 1976 they rose at an annual compound rate of 12 per cent.

What was happening? Well, of course, we have already seen that forces beyond the sphere of housing were impacting at the same time all along the line of site acquisition, construction and finance. The period of rapid inflation in the economy since about 1969 had brought with it unprecedented unit price increases in land and construction output, as we have seen in Graphs 3·1 and 4·1. Simultaneously, after 1971–2, the PWLB rate of interest on new advances rose by almost 5 percentage points in as little as three years, as Table 6·4 shows. With the exception of debt refinance, all this would not have mattered a fig if there had been only a small building programme, for this would have meant that these unique absolute increases were not being embedded in the debt charge item of local authority housing revenue accounts. But, as fate would have it, the municipal housebuilding programme had been cut to the bone by the year 1973, and in the next three years there was a rapid expansion in the number of starts, the bunching of individually front-loaded capital expenditures we have discussed in Chapter 6. At the same time there were substantial increases in the wage and salary costs of supervision, management, maintenance and repair. Finally we have to reiterate that these cost rises were immediately transformed, partially at least, into subsidy transfers from the Exchequer to municipal housing accounts only because of the abandonment from 1967 onwards of Chamberlain-type subsidies. Indeed if the council housing sector had gone through the inflation of the 1970s with fixed annual money subsidies per dwelling based on, say, 1967 unit prices and interest rates, there would have been virtually no local authority housebuilding at all by 1975 or even earlier, with incalculable consequences in terms of political and social unrest and in the deflationary effect on aggregate demand in the economy as a whole.

8 Are council tenants exploited?

Among the political organisations of the Left in this country there is a very widespread view that tenants are systematically exploited in the state housing sector. This section explores that assertion which typically is accompanied by reference to the fact that the largest entry in the expenditure column of housing revenue accounts is the debt charge and within that the payment of interest predominates.

If we cannot develop a clear statement of what we understand by the concept of exploitation then it is quite certain that we shall not be able to advance the argument one way or the other. So the starting point that I shall choose is the work of Karl Marx, primarily because he has an extremely lucid position on the nature of the exploitative process.[39] What follows is a very brief summary of the Marxist argument. It is essential to keep in mind that when Marx uses the term *value* he understands by it the labour socially necessary to produce goods and services: one can visualise value as labour so to speak crystallised in commodities as they are produced.

In the capitalist mode of production, the total value of the output of goods and services in an economy in a given time period derives from the value of existing materials and equipment which is transferred into that output and the value *created* by the application of labour during production. However, the produced value necessary merely to replace the reduction in material stocks and to make up for the depreciation of equipment (c), plus that required to ensure the reproduction of the labour force (v), is less than total value produced (t) and the difference is called surplus-value (s).

$$t - [c + v] = s$$
or
$$t = c + v + s$$

Surplus-value originates in the labour of the work-force during the process of production but is appropriated, in the form of profit, by the capitalist class because, whilst created value is equal to $[v + s]$, the wages workers receive are equal only to v. Not all of surplus-value or profit is retained by the industrialists: some portion is paid out in interest and dividends and some in rent to the owners of land. The worker is exploited because he produces surplus-value without appropriating it.

On this basis let us return to the original question: are council tenants exploited? Evidently, since council tenants are members of the working class, it follows that they *are* exploited—as workers. But by the same argument they are certainly not exploited as tenants. For in the Marxist sense it is only workers, through the payments for their labour power at the point of production, who can be exploited. In that sense it is logically impossible for them to be exploited as consumers, as purchasers of wage goods, including the commodity 'accommodation'. Since the Left assertion is that municipal tenants are exploited through their rental payments we can confidently insist that this view is entirely mistaken in the strict Marxist sense.

What I wish to do here is to propose an alternative approach to the concept of exploitation in capitalist society. The principal continuity with the Marxist system is that it still treats the appropriation by the owners of property of all (or part) of the surplus product as exploitative. The break with Marx is that it does not identify the form of such appropriation as limited only to the wage contract, although this may still be the dominant form. Any means by which such surplus-appropriation is achieved is regarded as exploitative. This permits the inclusion not only of landlords' profits, which are difficult for the strict Marxist approach to incorporate, but also state taxation receipts used to pay incomes to the owners of property—for example the capital subsidies in assisted areas. Exploitation, then, I understand as any social process which permits the owners of private property, whether it be real or financial, to appropriate part of the flow of national income so as to increase the value in constant prices of their capital. The qualification 'in constant prices' is added since, for example, the money deposits of a financier lending at interest could obviously augment, whilst these deposits were rendered virtually worthless in a situation of inflation. Thus the calculation of whether or not the value of capital has increased as a result of surplus-appropriation needs to be done in terms of the original purchasing power of such capital.

Let us see how this approach can be applied to the council housing sector. The only expenditure item in the housing revenue account which could constitute a source of surplus-appropriation is that of the debt charge—the payments to the providers of loan capital. In Section 4 of Chapter 6 I argued that only in 1952–69 was the real rate of interest on such debt positive and in that period the real interest burden would have been about 30 per cent of the debt charge. The debt charge itself averaged about 68 per cent of total revenue expenditure in England and Wales in those years so the real interest burden, the exploitative element, was about 20 per cent (·30 times ·68) of that total. But, of course, rents do not equal the expenditure total since it is partially funded by the flow of Exchequer and rate fund subsidies. Graph 7·1 shows that in the period under consideration the subsidy-expenditure ratio averaged 30 per cent. Since the flow of subsidies exceeded the exploitative element it follows that council tenants were not exploited during this period. After 1969 the real rate of interest became negative and the average subsidy–income ratio rose so that exploitation still no longer took place, although cost increases and frontloading pushed rents up fast. If this analysis is accepted certain conclusions can be drawn:

(i) council tenants are exploited as wage-workers but are not exploited as tenants;

(ii) the continuous attempts to strip relatively high-income workers of subsidy receipts would have had the effect, if successful, of exploiting this group of tenants and therefore driving them towards owner-occupation;

(iii) the Housing Finance Act, if it had been implemented under relatively stable financial conditions, would have had the effect, through the surpluses it sought to generate, of introducing the exploitation of council tenants for the first time, at least since 1945.

(iv) under the relatively stable conditions of the period 1952–69 about two-thirds of state subsidies were necessary because of the exploitative elements in the municipalities' housing revenue expenditure. That is, the great part of the subsidies 'wasted' on council tenants, as the slogan went, merely acted as transfers to meet the exploitative item of real interest.

(v) the surplus-appropriation which has taken place through the system of state housing capital finance has not constituted a burden on council tenants as payers of rent but on the working class as a whole as payers of taxes.

9 Synthesis

In the case of any single authority it is convenient to regard rent as set by the expenditure less subsidies of the housing revenue account. But from a broader and long-term perspective we can argue that expenditure is determined by the costs of constructing and raising finance for model dwellings; rent is set at a level which permits tenants to afford to occupy their accommodation, whilst subsidies make up the disparity between the two. From this perspective state subsidies are the dependent variable. One of the functions of rent pooling and rent rebates is to reduce the size of the subsidy flow necessary to bring down rents on new dwellings to a level their tenants can afford. A specific function of channelling subsidy payments to the poor is to raise the relative rents net of subsidy of the better paid workers. This serves to make owner-occupation more attractive to them, thereby narrowing the spectrum of the working class for whom state housing is provided.

The upward trend in costs since the war has brought with it a continued growth in subsidy payments as well as in rent levels. Rent per dwelling increased at an average annual compound rate of 8·6 per cent since 1949, outstripping the growth in post-tax household earnings. The trend in unit prices and interest rates eventually led to the abandonment of Chamberlain-type subsidies and since 1967 the level of subsidy has been based on reckonable expenditure per dwelling. As a result of this more flexible approach, not only rents but subsidies too have become more sensitive than in the past to market interest rates. The return in 1973–6 to a high-interest regime drove up both rents and subsidies at an extremely rapid rate.

The final section of the chapter asks whether council tenants are, in some sense, exploited. It is proposed that exploitation can be understood to include any process which permits the owners of property to appropriate the surplus produced in the economy. Such surplus-appropriation did take place in the period 1952–69, when the real rate of interest was positive. However, the exploitative burden of the debt charge was met not from tenants' rents but from taxation.

Council houses are built because of the state's commitment to maintaining the reproductive production of accommodation for the working class. Because, under the present social order, this is carried out within a market context, the state has to raise from its taxation receipts the funds necessary to bridge the gap between historic costs and rents, a gap which in part has existed because of surplus-appropriation by finance capital.

EIGHT

Consumption: council house management

by Fred Gray

1 Introduction

This chapter examines aspects of the management of the public housing stock. In the field of management, local authorities, as the responsible bodies, are the dominant force and have considerable autonomy from central government and discretionary power over households.

This situation has a number of consequences for the study of management policies and practices. Of necessity research has to be carried out at the local level. Since local conditions, responses, structures and processes may vary, in reviewing the national situation generalisations have to be made whose appropriateness varies from area to area. On the other hand, since the mid-1960s a considerable amount of research has been undertaken in a range of local authorities. Piecing together the jig-saw of evidence should therefore allow the construction of a fairly clear picture of the general character, basis and consequences of management policies and to take some account of variations.

However, a further confusing factor is that the housing researcher often tends to subject to closest scrutiny the unusual and abnormal, perhaps illustrating his point with the best (or worst) examples he can find. As far as housing management is concerned, research has often concentrated on the most restrictive and paternalistic authorities, the poorest estates, the worst excesses of management policies and practices, and the tenants and prospective tenants most restricted by management. Such an emphasis may ignore the immense benefits state housing has provided for large sections of the population, and that from the point of view of many tenants council house management rarely impinges on their lives in anything but a satisfactory manner.

Throughout it should be borne in mind that some local authorities depart from the situation described below. Basildon, for example, is somewhat unique in basing the management of the dwellings under its ownership on the philosophy that 'working people should control their own lives'.[1] A further point arises from the exceptional case. Management assumptions, policies and practices are not immutable and impregnable but are susceptible to positive change under certain conditions. Even so, it should be stressed that one of the remarkable conclusions to emerge from a study of the available evidence is that, despite seemingly great variation in detail, essentially similar features and consequences, and underlying assumptions, structures and processes appear to operate in the majority of places.[2]

2 The dwelling stock and the social structure of the council sector

This section draws out some pertinent features concerning the dwelling stock and the social characteristics of the occupants of public housing in Britain.[3] While most of the information concerns Britain, or England and Wales, throughout it should be borne in mind that at other scales of analysis there are often immense variations from national or aggregate figures. These variations exist at a number of levels: between north and south, between regions, between urban and rural and inner city and suburb, and finally both between and within estates. Unfortunately detailed discussion of such variations has to be necessarily foregone because of both lack of suitable quantitative data and insufficient space. However, variations in social and dwelling characteristics from one area to another do draw forth (and also reflect) different management activities. This is a theme which will become clearer in later sections.

In 1976 32 per cent (or 6,557,000 dwellings) of the housing stock in Britain was rented from local authorities or new towns. This varied from 54 per cent in Scotland to 22 per cent for the south-west region of England. The distinction between local authorities were often even greater, with older urban areas typically having high, and suburban and rural areas low, proportions of council dwellings.

Turning to the age distribution of council dwellings, in 1975 4 per cent were built before 1919 (including municipalised dwellings acquired in the post-war period), 25 per cent between 1919 and 1943, 48 per cent between 1944 and 1965, and 23 per cent after 1965. Again differences between local authorities are great. For example, in 1976 6 per cent of the council dwellings in Basingstoke were built before 1944 and 68 per cent after 1965. In Chelmsford 21 per cent of dwellings were pre-1944, 59 per cent 1944–65 and 20 per cent post-1965. In Barking, 46 per cent were built before 1944 and 31 per cent between 1944 and 1965.

Nationally, the percentage of council dwellings of different types in 1975 was as follows: 1 per cent detached, 36 per cent semi-detached, 30 per cent terraced houses, 30 per cent purpose-built flats or maisonettes, and 3 per cent other flats and maisonettes.[4] Yet again, dwelling types varied greatly from local authority to local authority. For example, in 1976 the proportion of council dwellings consisting of flats in Stoke, Hull, Leicester and Ipswich were 14, 19, 20 and 22 per cent respectively. In contrast, the figures for Kensington and Chelsea, Camden, Hackney and Southwark were 96, 95, 93 and 88 per cent.

Another important characteristic of dwellings is size, which is perhaps best assessed in terms of number of bedrooms. In 1976 for England and Wales, 17 per cent of council dwellings were of one bedroom, 29 per cent of two, 51 per cent of three, and 3 per cent of four or more. Differences between local authorities are again notable. For example, the figures for the London boroughs were 23 per cent of dwellings one bedroom, 36 per cent two bedrooms, 38 per cent three bedrooms and 3 per cent four or more bedrooms, with the relevant percentages for non-metropolitan districts being 15, 26, 57 and 2.[5]

A number of points of interpretation should be made. Differences between local authorities in tenure, age, type and size of dwellings reflect a myriad of national and local factors operating at different times over the past sixty years. For example, councils building largely at a time when the national framework emphasised construction of high-rise flats are today left with a legacy of particular dwelling types, which in turn create particular management needs and demands in terms of, for example, allocation and tenant response. To an extent, however, the nature of the dwelling stock in any local authority can only be understood in terms of unique local factors, including patterns of land ownership and availability, the political control of the council, ideologies concerning the value and purpose of public housing, actual and perceived housing need at particular times, slum-clearance activities, and so on.[6]

A further point concerns contrasts with other tenures. The age distribution of the council stock does mean that local authorities and council tenants are rarely faced with the difficulties often associated with managing and living in pre-1919 dwellings (in 1975 27 per cent of all dwellings in Britain were built before 1919). Turning to dwelling type, although purpose-built flats give rise to their management problems and requirements for both owners and occupants, at least the public sector does not generally suffer the difficulties of converted flats which tend to be more dominant in the privately rented (and particularly furnished) tenures. Moving to dwelling size, the relatively large percentage of one-bedroom accommodation (in 1971 only 2 per cent of owner-occupied dwellings were of this size) reflects dwellings purpose-built for old people. At the other end of the range, the council sector contains the smallest proportion of dwellings with three or more bedrooms of all the tenures. Because the public sector contains a disproportionate number of large households there is, in absolute terms, more overcrowding in the council sector than in other tenures.

One criticism of the public dwelling stock is that, with the notable exception of short periods following the two world wars, the quality of council dwellings has often been poor.[7] This has occurred for the often complex reasons indicated in other chapters. In consequence many council dwellings and estates are characterised by a number of undesirable features. These include high densities, poor design, 'minimum standards' which become maximum standards, cheap materials, and so on, which sooner or later result in a set of management problems, and sometimes poor living conditions, which would have been less likely if the quality of new construction had been higher. One tangible indication of this situation and the inadequacy of programmes of repair and maintenance in the sector is that in 1976 44 per cent of inter-war council houses (546,000 dwellings) and 11 per cent (371,000 dwellings) of post-war public sector houses were in need of repairs costing £250 or more. (Compared with 38 per cent and 3 per cent respectively in the owner-occupied sector.)

Nevertheless, it remains the case that other indices reveal that the public sector does not suffer the same magnitude of physical dwelling problems typical in other tenures. For example, in 1976 only 1 per cent of council dwellings could be statutorily defined as unfit, 1 per cent had no fixed bath in the bathroom, 3 per cent had no inside lavatory, and 6 per cent lacked one or more basic amenities. These figures compare favourably with the aggregate figures for all tenure (5, 5, 9 and 9 per cent respectively) and a smaller proportion of dwellings in the local authority sector suffered from such problems than in all the other tenures (with the one exception of a slightly lower level of lack of amenities in the owner-occupied sector).

The foregoing discussion indicates that council tenants generally occupy relatively recent purpose-built and self-contained dwellings, and typically do not suffer from a lack of basic amenities. Against this it may be argued that the physical dwelling stock is often less adequate and desirable in terms of dwelling type, construction standards, estate layouts, densities, building materials, repairs and maintenance, and so on. It is at the level of individual estates or parts of estates that such problems are most manifest.

Who then is housed in the public sector? The authors of the 1977 *Housing Policy Technical Volumes*, on the basis of detailed analysis, conclude that the characteristics of council tenants[8]

are very diverse, whether measured in terms of type of household, age, income, or socio-economic group. Tenants of local authorities do however include a distinctly higher proportion of the larger families (i.e. those with three or more children) than other tenures, and a higher proportion of older one-person or two-person households than other tenures, except for those who rent unfurnished from private landlords.

As later sections indicate, large families and old people tend to be favoured in the selection process whereby households are admitted into the council sector. In contrast, entrance policies and practices tend to work against large proportions of single working people and childless couples becoming local authority tenants.

Although the social characteristics of tenants cover a wide range, in fact the council sector tends to provide accommodation for, and be dominated by, poorer households in Britain. Average incomes for household heads and wives in public housing are about 25 per cent below those for owner-occupiers. (In contrast, total household incomes for both tenures are closer, reflecting council households with three or more earners, such as where adult children stay in the parental home, sometimes because of the lack of alternative housing.) Similarly in 1975, 35 per cent of council households had economically inactive heads. This figure, which rose from 25 per cent in 1968, results, amongst other factors, from the increased proportion of council tenants over retiring age and the greater numbers of single-parent households receiving supplementary benefit in the local authority sector.

Turning to socio-economic groups, in 1971 81 per cent of council households could be classified as manual (as opposed to non-manual) households. In the owner-occupied sector the corresponding figure was 46 per cent, and for all tenures, 58 per cent. Indeed, over the last ten years the proportion of manual workers finding accommodation in the tenure group has steadily increased. This is most clear in the case of households with heads in unskilled manual occupations, where the proportion living in council dwellings increased from 52 per cent in 1971 to 59 per cent in 1975. Evidence concerning incomes for 1975 also indicates that 'the *majority* of low income families are in council housing'.[9] Thus 40 per cent of household heads with gross weekly incomes of less than £15, 45 per cent with incomes between £15 and £30, and 39 per cent with incomes over £30 and up to £50 were council tenants. In contrast, despite the size of the tenure, only 9 per cent of household heads earning over £70 were local authority tenants.

Although the data should be treated with some caution, the *Family Expenditure Survey* does indicate that over the last two decades the role of the council sector in providing housing for low-income households has rapidly accelerated. In 1953–4, of all households in England and Wales in the bottom quarter of the income distribution, only 16 per cent were council tenants. By 1965 this had risen to 29 per cent, and in 1976 to 43 per cent. Looked at another way, the percentage of council households with incomes within the lowest quarter of the income range for all households rose from 20 per cent in 1953–4, through 26 per cent in 1965, 33 per cent in 1976. In other words, even taking into account the growth of the sector during this period, the income characteristics of local authority tenants have undergone drastic changes, from being biased away from the lowest income groups in the mid 1950s to strongly emphasise this very group twenty years later. The reasons for this important development are complex, but include the evolution of public housing as the chief 'welfare' tenure, and concomitant changes in policies, attitudes and in management itself.

These data indicate that commonly held views of council tenants as relatively well-off households require substantial modifications, and instead support Murie's statement[10] that 'council housing in Britain does provide the major source of housing for the worst off'.

Despite the validity of this general conclusion, two points of qualification should be made. For various reasons, many of which are to do with local authority housing management, some groups of poor households, and particularly those without children and below retiring age, tend to be excluded from the council sector, and are in consequence pushed into often very poor housing conditions in the private tenures. Second, as we have seen, housing conditions within the council sector itself are not uniform. As later sections exemplify, it is often the least well off and most needy households who, once admitted to the council sector, are allocated the most inferior and inadequate dwellings.

It is appropriate to conclude this section by discussing a number of other issues concerning the relationship of housing management to public housing and council tenants. The first concerns the extent to which local authority renting is a hindrance to household mobility. The available evidence indicates that while about the same proportion of both council tenants and owner-occupiers are mobile each year, council tenants tend to move far shorter distances and less often for employment-related reasons than owner-occupiers. On the basis of such evidence it is sometimes argued that housing management policies and practices restrict inter-urban moves by council tenants.

As we shall see, local authority housing management does exert a crucial influence on who moves, when and where. However, this is not to argue that without present-day management activities the patterns of residential mobility amongst council tenants would be radically different, and that moves for employment reasons would be made more often. Indeed, the opportunities for employment-related long-distance moves by council tenants may be minimal for a number of other reasons. These include, for example, the high proportion of economically inactive local authority households, and the relatively low level of this sort of residential mobility for all manual households (whether council tenants or not) who, as we have seen, comprise a majority of local authority households. In addition, it may equally be argued that the various costs and constraints involved in owner-occupation may in fact operate to reduce labour mobility in that tenure. In summary, the factors determining employment-related mobility (or lack of it) are complex, and the precise paths of cause and effect are not, as yet, satisfactorily established.

A second concluding point concerns the cost of housing management. 'General' management costs are those incurred in managing and supervising the sector, and include selecting tenants and allocating dwellings, running waiting lists and transfer and exchange systems, rent collecting and accounting, offering housing advice to tenants and prospective tenants, carrying out housing research, and so on. Unlike the owner-occupied tenure, where the cost of management is borne by the household concerned, management charges in the council sector are shared by all local authority tenants. This fundamental difference means that from the individual household's point of view no management charge is incurred on moving into or within the council sector compared to the often immense cost experienced by people moving to an owner-occupied house. In addition, of course, many private sector management institutions—such as estate agents—exist in order to extract profit—a motive absent in the public sector.

Over the last decade, general management and supervision costs have risen dramatically (and more than general inflation) from £6·5 per dwelling in 1967–8 to £28·6 per dwelling in 1975–76. This increase is partly due to the labour-intensive nature of management (earnings rising more steeply than retail prices) and because an increasing number of staff have been employed in 'welfare' activities such as running housing aid centres and in undertaking research. Interestingly, 'general' management expenses are greater in London than elsewhere, perhaps reflecting the proliferation of housing advice and research in London housing departments compared with other places. A further explanatory factor of rising management costs may be that in recent years, as the council sector has aged and increasingly evolved as a welfare tenure for those unable to become owner-occupiers, so the task of running the sector has become more difficult and expensive. Nevertheless, despite the increase in costs, the 1975–6 average weekly management and supervision expenses of less than 60p per dwelling appears extremely low both in absolute terms and if set against management costs in the owner-occupied sector.[11] Indeed, for reasons suggested elsewhere in this chapter, there are strong grounds for arguing that in many local authorities there should be greater investment in information gathering and giving, the reform of management policies and practice, and the training of housing staff.

Finally in this section is is appropriate to say a little more about repairs and maintenance, an issue closely related to council house management. Local authorities have a statutory duty to decorate, repair and maintain the exteriors of council dwellings. There is greater variation between local authorities concerning interior decoration, repairs and maintenance, with some obliging or allowing tenants to undertake all but major work while others retain complete control over such activities.

As with management costs, from the late 1960s there have been rapid increases in the costs of repairs and maintenance borne by local authorities. In 1967–8 the average expenditure per dwelling was £22·1 and in 1975–6 £67·2. Even allowing for inflation, local authority charges to housing revenue accounts for this item rose by 48 per cent between 1967–8 and 1975–6. Much of the increase from the 1960s may be explained by the rising costs of materials and labour.

Local authorities, even with similar dwelling stocks, vary greatly in their expenditure on repairs and maintenance. However, high flats,

flats containing common facilities such as lifts and walk-ways, very new dwellings and non-traditional designs, all tend to increase the need for and costs of repair and maintenance. Such developments may become a considerable burden both for occupants and councils. If repairs and maintenance are postponed or inadequately undertaken (a situation occurring in many authorities in response to public expenditure cuts and attempts to economise[12]) the results may be detrimental to tenant satisfaction, and contribute to the downward spiral of deteriorating buildings, unpopular dwellings and estates, vandalism, and, a lowering of expectations and a worsening of attitudes of both tenants and managers. In the longer term, attempts to rehabilitate and improve such areas may prove more expensive than if repairs and maintenance were carried out promptly and when required.

Apart from delaying repairs and maintenance, a related response to increasing costs and public expenditure cuts have been restrictions on the activities of Direct Works Departments and attempts by local authorities to place the burden of maintenance and repair on tenants themselves. This may be done either by charging for work on top of rents or by encouraging tenants to carry out repairs and maintenance themselves.

Against this situation, some positive features of the repairs and maintenance issue should be noted. Work by the National Consumer Council[13] indicates that in 1977 half the repairs for council tenants were completed within two weeks, and that a significantly smaller proportion of council households, compared with households in all tenures, waited longer than six months for the completion of repairs. In addition, over half of council tenants carried out some work themselves. Indeed on average in 1976-7 council tenants themselves spent more on repairs than did local authorities. However, one of the additional problems, apart from those suggested above, to be faced if there were wholesale movement from local authority to tenant responsibility for repairs is that low-income households, the elderly, and so on, might all experience considerable difficulties in maintaining the dwellings they occupy.

3 Council house management : an overview

The management of council housing in Britain rests in the hands of local authority housing departments,[14] their associated officials and elected representatives. Perhaps of all the aspects of state housing, it is management which, in an immediate sense, allows local authorities the greatest degree of discretion and autonomy from external forces, and particularly central government. In this field local authorities operate with a minimum of legal control, the legislative framework being phrased in such way as to allow considerable freedom in deciding who should be housed, when and where.

It is this situation, which in part derives from the view that local authorities best know the local context and how to meet needs and fulfil management responsibilities, which helps explain the often great variation in the details of management policies and practice from area to area: 'Local authorities have almost a free hand in devising policies to suit their own areas, particular housing problems, resources, political beliefs, aspirations and prejudices.'[15]

For many years central government has set out guidelines to management through a series of circulars and reports.[16] This activity has, however, been advisory rather than supervisory. Local authorities may ignore legislation or recommendations, or implement them in a fashion contradictory to the intentions of central government.

An additional reason for the autonomy and discretion allowed local authorities is that in theory at least the managers are accountable, through the ballot box, to tenants and the general public. Indeed, at times the managers argue that they operate in the interests of rate-payers, or the community at large,[17] which may necessarily involve sacrificing the interest of individual tenants or would-be tenants. However, the chain of accountability is long—from voters through councillors, housing committee, housing department, individual officials to tenant—and ineffectual, if it is exercised at all. In addition, there is considerable evidence that the managers of the council sector, as in other fields, may operate in their own self-interests[18]—which may, in turn, involve political popularity, minimisation of the demands made on the council sector, and easing of management responsibilities and activities, and so on—rather than for existing or potential tenants.

An associated question is who, or what, holds the determining power shaping and controlling management policies and practices. The relationships between the various actors and bodies involved in management is little researched, but appears to vary both spatially and historically. At one extreme, local councillors and elected members of the housing committee may select tenants and allocate dwellings themselves, with little or no regard for the recommendations of the housing department.

205

Today such cases appear relatively rare.[19] More typical is the situation in which elected representatives instruct a department to carry out a particular policy, the details being left to officials. At the other extreme individual officials, such as housing investigators, may be able to decide the fate of applicants without recourse to other officials or an explicit policy.

Whatever the precise relationships between the various actors in the management sphere, there is considerable scope for informal processes and discretion, of one sort or another, which, as already noted, may reflect either individual or group beliefs, assumptions and prejudices about correct management policies. The discretion may be masked by a superficially objective policy but revealed when a particular policy or procedure is not adhered to:[20]

> Discretionary power is mainly used in the interests of the
> administration itself, serving both ideological and managerial
> ends. The effect is to obscure the basis on which decisions are
> made and to weaken the ability of prospective tenants to
> challenge them.

For various reasons suggested below, individual tenants have relatively little power or control over management. This is seen in many ways, including typically restrictive tenancy agreements,[21] lack of security of tenure,[22] and inability to positively control either selection or allocation processes. What power or bargaining position individual tenants do have is essentially negative (for example, deciding not to accept the tenancy of a house) and often a by-product of management decisions and activities themselves (for example, an applicant may refuse to move from a clearance scheme until he has been offered the dwelling he wants). Even then, managers often appear to go to considerable lengths to circumscribe or deny the power of individuals.

Management involves a number of varied responsibilities and obligations which tend, at times, to be contradictory. The immediate purpose of the council sector is, of course, to provide housing for people. A situation of qualitative if not quantitative scarcity, and the absence of the relatively hidden mechanisms at work in the private sector matching (or mis-matching) people and dwellings, necessarily involves decisions, by managers, as to who should be admitted to the council sector, and who should get which sort of housing. Mediating between the demands of households and the supply of dwellings is, therefore, a major management task, and a principal concern of this chapter.[23]

Here it should be stressed that the mediation of demand and supply invariably necessitates concentration on demand. In the short term at least, supply is outside the direct control of the managers (although at times household movement within the sector may be manipulated to create particular sorts of vacancies) and it is demand which is necessarily organised and controlled. The production of council houses is the concern of other chapters of this book, but in the context of management it is worth stressing that decisions about the quantity and quality of building are influenced by central government, and other external pressures such as the wider economic situation. Councils may wish to build large numbers of high-quality dwellings, but be thwarted in their attempts by external pressures.[24] Against this, other evidence indicates that local authorities are themselves partly to blame for differential dwelling quality. Through persistent under-investment in repairs and maintenance and because of particular allocation policies, local authorities may ensure the production and continuation of low-status dwellings.[25] The causes of 'ghetto' or 'slum' estates are discussed in more detail later in this chapter.

Management also involves a number of other major responsibilities and property management tasks. These include maintenance and repair of dwellings, efforts to ensure that property is kept in good order by tenants, that rent arrears and non-payments are minimised, the 'best use' is made of available dwellings, and so on.[26] Responses to these various tasks may be cross-cutting, and influence selection and allocation decisions and attitudes towards tenants.[27]

> Councils, for the most part, are preoccupied with behaving as
> efficient landlords—balancing the account, furbishing the
> properties, governing arrears. They prize above all a good (i.e.
> solvent, tractable, clean and quiet) tenant and tend to favour him,
> as any private landlord would. Because he is deemed likely to
> treat it carefully, he is generally given one of the authority's
> newest and best houses.

This preoccupation may influence the local authority's views on who should be offered a council house, and what sort of dwelling it should be. Rather than being solely based on the 'need' of households (however this is defined) selection and allocation may reflect, in part at least, the desire of the local authority to minimise management tasks.

Managers operate within a number of other constraints. It would, of course, be naive to suggest that housing officials are an independent professional group acting in a neutral or detached manner. The majority of the staff in housing departments receive little or no training, and few are professionally qualified.[28] Instead, new staff are typically 'shown the ropes' by longer serving officers as and when time allows. Attitudes and behaviour are thus handed down from one generation of managers to another, with little thought about the wider implications of particular activities and action. In addition, managers are typically middle class or 'respectable' working class, their values and assumptions tending to reflect this situation, and often conflicting with those of tenants and prospective tenants. On a related point, as Damer[29] notes, housing officials hold an ideology with complex historical origins, which legitimates their beliefs and actions and mystifies both managers and managed. This ideology, as we shall see, has been relatively slow to change over time, despite evolution in society and within the council sector itself.

Public opinion, or the managers' perception of public opinion, also has an influence on managerial activity in a number of ways. For example, those seeking to enter the sector and gain access to a scarce resource are in a situation of potential if not actual conflict with each other, either individually or as groups. In managing demand there is a tendency to acquiesce to the strongest groups. Consequently, newcomers may be excluded in favour of locals, the inarticulate in favour of the vocal, and so on. Similarly, managers have regard to schisms between existing council tenants, and again minority groups (such as 'problem families', the 'disrespectable', the 'troublesome', the 'undeserving') lose out in favour of majority groups. Nevertheless, as noted below, the actions of the managers may operate to create and accentuate divisions amongst tenants and prospective tenants, rather than simply being a response to what already exists.

A further aspect of management which should be discussed in this section is the perhaps rather obvious but nonetheless important point that tenants as well as property are to be managed. The continuation of this assumption in the post-war period is well illustrated by an examination of restrictive and paternalistic tenancy agreements and the handbooks often issued by local authorities to tenants. For example, a 1950s handbook asserted:[30] 'Keep your home clean and tidy. Endeavour to have some method of cleaning as you go along; . . . Regular bed times for children and adults, except on special occasions. Sit down properly at the table.' In some local authorities the situation changed little two decades later. For example: 'The collector calls on you on a specified day—regard him as a friend, for your welfare is his concern.'[31]

Such paternalism appears usual rather than rare,[32] although it takes a number of forms, at times leading to aggressive and abusive treatment of tenants by managers. Typically, however, it stresses 'fairness' but strictness, the interests of the community over those of the individual, social and community training, education in home management, attempts to produce 'good' and 'respectable' tenants, and so on. Although appearing oddly out of place in the last quarter of the twentieth century, nonetheless, it remains a very real influence on council house management policies and practice. To understand something of its development, and the origins of some of the other management features discussed above, it is necessary to examine the historical roots of council house management.

4 The origins of management

The origins of many present-day management policies and practices may readily be traced back to the nineteenth century, when the management, control and education of the working class was explicitly accepted as a necessity, although there was some debate as to the correct methods of doing this.[33] In the field of housing management during the fifty years surrounding the end of the century one name, that of Octavia Hill, looms large. Evangelistic and paternalistic, and with a considerable band of dedicated followers, Octavia Hill's policies were originally applied in the management of renovated privately rented property. Under this system 'philanthropy and business are very judiciously combined and the results are very satisfactory'.[34] With the wholesale introduction of public housing after World War I, there were simply no tested sets of ideas about management which might be used in the council sector other than those of Octavia Hill.

The Octavia Hill system emphasised the need for direct management of tenants, education away from ingrained slum habits to citizenship, rigorous pressures to avoid rent arrears, weeding out of unsatisfactory tenants, and so on. The starting point was that:

> the tenants must be considered as well as the houses . . . (for)
> provision is seldom made against the social evils which the
> tenants themselves may bring in their train. The only way to avoid
> these evils is to secure good management . . . (involving) care for
> the tenants as well as for the dwelling.[35]

Contemporary authors illustrate the assumptions and resultant policies well:

> Tenants brought up in slums have engendered slum habits—uncleanliness, thriftlessness, brawling, destructiveness, etc—and such habits are not easily given up . . . slackness in the payment of rent is more frequently due to carelessness and thriftlessness than to hardship.[36]

> they rejected even poor persons who were known to be dishonest or disorderly or in other ways undesirable. They restricted their field of choice to the more decent people among the needy labouring classes, to people whose faults were attributable to ignorance rather than to inherent vice.[37]

> By weeding out of vicious tenants and the gradual and unconscious training of those who remain . . . tenants have learned new and better habits and have become decent citizens.[38]

Immediately after World War I, under the guidance of the Housing Department of the Ministry of Health, the Octavia Hill system was taken as the model for the then infant housing authorities facing the task of management for the first time. Contemporary Ministry of Health advice in 1920 illustrates the sudden realisation that management was a necessary feature of the provision of public housing:[39]

> The question of making adequate provision of working-class houses is one which intimately concerns a very large proportion of local authorities at the present time. Many of these bodies have in the past had little or no experience of owning and controlling property of this kind, and they doubtless realise that their work will not cease with the erection of houses but that, on the contrary, a number of problems will inevitably arise when the question of managing property comes under consideration.
> With regard to management by local authorities, it will be impossible to lay down any detailed scheme of management which would be generally applicable to the housing undertakings of all local authorities. So many factors have to be taken into account . . . that it will probably be best for each local authority to work in detail its own plans.
> It cannot, however, be too strongly impressed upon local authorities that direct management is essential to success . . . The

association of these two functions (rent collecting and letting
and supervision of property) in the one department undoubtedly
results in better tenants and fewer losses than where they are
exercised in two separate departments. Whatever system is adopted
arrangements will have to be made for carrying out the following
objects:

(1) The careful selection of tenants;
(2) The elimination of unsatisfactory tenants;
(3) Constant supervision of the property and its occupants by
    officials directly employed and paid by the owners;
(4) Systematic and punctual collection of rents.

Here we see the origins of many basic management features which exist
today, including local autonomy, the establishment of all management
functions on one department, housing managers as a professional group,
the need for the management and training of tenants, careful selection
and allocation, and so on. The noteworthy point is that, despite a rapidly
changing society and considerable changes in the council sector itself,
with a few changes in terminology the above illustrations of the assumptions and practices of 1920 might well be used to describe many
management policies and practices today. The grading of tenants, the
exclusion of certain sorts of household, the development of waiting
lists, the use of housing investigators, authoritarian and paternalistic
attitudes, and so on, may all be seen as developments deriving from
these first roots. As a 1967 official report noted,[40] the Octavia Hill
system 'was highly successful and has had a profound influence upon
modern thought on housing management'.

The relationship between central and local government is particularly relevant to an understanding of the evolution of management
policies and practices from 1920. Once granted, local autonomy allowed
housing authorities to easily ignore or side-step the recommendations
and advice of central government which has been noticeably more
liberal, and increasingly so over time. Residential qualifications are a
case in point. As early as 1949 the Ministry of Health urged[41] local
authorities that:

whatever system of selection is adopted, care should be taken
that factors not relevant to housing need, such as length of residence
in the area or the date of application, are allowed to weigh only
in deciding between applicants whose claims on grounds of need
are equal.

211

The autonomy and conservatism of most local authorities in this direction is well demonstrated by the fact that in 1977 central government again found it necessary to recommend almost identical policies to local authorities.[42]

A similar situation exists regarding grading of tenants and management of unsatisfactory tenants. Until the Cullingworth Report of 1969,[43] central government provided at least tacit support for grading. For example, the 1939 report[44] argued: 'In our opinion the grading and placing of tenants of different standards are of the highest importance.' Similarly, a 1967 report[45] on Scottish council housing argued: 'If the problem family are living in a new scheme where their behaviour is particularly noticeable and offensive, it may be advisable to move them into older accommodation.'

However, central government has invariably been against more extreme forms of managing unsatisfactory tenants. The 1939 report,[46] for example, while accepting the need for grading suggested the value of:

> separating unsatisfactory families from one another, so far as this
> is possible, and interspersing them amongst families of a good
> type . . . (as such) the introduction of the Dutch method of
> dealing with difficult tenants, based on complete segregation,
> is neither desirable nor necessary in this country.

At the local level, however, the 'Dutch method' survives in many authorities, and indeed in some has been introduced in the 1970s. In 1977 Birmingham's housing committee decided to concentrate such tenants in selected areas, the chairman asserting:[47]

> At the moment these irresponsible families are spread out like a
> lot of little sores. If we have to put up with them we might as
> well put them together and create a few big sores where they
> can shout obscenities and fight with their own kind.

Present-day management policies and practices are then, in part, simply a continuation of what has for many years been accepted and practised at the local level, and assumed to be correct by housing managers as a group.[48] Council house managers have relative freedom in this respect, and until recently there has, perhaps, been little need for them to change their activities.

Nevertheless, the context within which management takes place has evolved in a number of respects. For example, the very range of quality and type of council houses in many local authorities (which simply did not exist in the 1920s) has made it increasingly possible for the managers to match status of tenant with quality of property. As the Cullingworth Report[49] notes, 'A local authority with a small range (e.g. all post-war houses) sees no need for careful grading.' To an extent grading has been facilitated by the increasing complexity of the dwelling stock. Similarly, local authorities, over time, have been forced to house families which in the past would have been excluded, and this has resulted in an increase in low status households and drawn forth a particular management response.

A further example of the changing context of management is that increasingly some local authorities experience considerable difficulties in filling their lowest quality and least desirable stock, although whether falling-off of demand would have occurred if dwelling quality had been better remains a debatable point. This topic is examined in more detail later. However, it is worth noting that the problems experienced by some authorities have not been eased by the rigidity of council house management. Despite falling demand many authorities have been slow to change their selection and allocation policies and practices, but have instead retained procedures formulated in a time of grossly greater demand than supply.

The following two sections examine the management of household movement within and into the council sector. Conceptually it is useful to view decision-making concerning who gets what housing in two stages. The first step, discussed in Section 5, concerns the *selection* of households deemed suitable or eligible to enter the local authority sector, or, in the case of existing council tenants, move from one dwelling to another. Once households are selected for movement, the next management task involves the *allocation* of specific dwellings to particular households. Such activities are examined in Section 6.

5 The selection of households

As already suggested, historically the sorts of households selected to enter the council sector have tended to evolve somewhat over time. In the early 1920s local authorities chose who they thought would be the most satisfactory tenants. These were typically 'better-paid artisans'.[50] Other households, perhaps in greater need, were excluded, it being hoped, at least by central government, that those groups' living conditions would improve as they occupied the dwellings vacated by new council tenants. In other words, council building was a means of facilitating filtering in the private rented sector.

In fact, however, the local authorities' hands were tied in terms of who they could house. As the 1939 CHAC report[51] points out, between 1919 and 1924: 'the cost of production had not reached the level at which even with the aid of subsidy houses could be let at rents within the means of the lowest paid workers.' The general point arising out of this specific instance, that the characteristics of the dwelling influences who can be selected for the council sector, is something which occurs later in the history of selection. For example, the 1924 Housing Act dwellings were built at lower unit costs, and were therefore let at lower rents and 'the local authorities were thus able to draw upon poorer sections of the population for their tenants.'[52] In turn, the 1930 Act introduced another principle: 'The slum house was to be demolished and the tenants moved to a new house; the very poorest were to be rehoused.'[53]

The post-war period has also witnessed several swings in the central government framework, so influencing the sorts of dwellings built, and the households selected by local authorities at any particular time. Such developments have been accompanied by changes in the ideas about whom should be offered a council dwelling, and indeed, in the purpose and function of the public sector. Increasingly today the council sector is viewed both locally and nationally as a welfare net for those unwilling or unable to provide themselves with adequate private sector housing. The severest critics of these developments argue: 'from creditable and idealistic origins it has descended to a miserly output of often poorly designed and constructed homes for "underpriviledged" groups.'[54] Indeed many of the present-day features of the sector, including the sale of council houses, discussed later in the chapter, and the definitions of need employed to select households, fit well into this interpretation. Concerning central government activity, a paradox emerges. As noted in the previous section, central government has consistently been liberal in its management recommendations and advice, yet only rarely has it given local authorities the resources to provide large numbers of good quality dwellings, a prerequisite for easing, for example, selection and allocation policies.

Given the general demand and supply situation in the council sector, the selection of households necessarily involves decisions about which households should, or should not, be offered a council dwelling. A range of policies and practices are used to control demand, remove some households from consideration, and so ration housing to particular groups. Households typically favoured in the selection process are those conforming to a particular conception of housing need. This conception stresses factors such as overcrowding, ill-health, sub-standard housing and sharing. Consequently: 'the "need" of the applicant household is assessed in relation to the physical suitability of its present housing circumstances.'[55]

A number of consequences follow from this conception. Selection does not take account of factors such as 'social' need and differential vulnerability in particular housing conditions. For example, old people unable to cope with a large but physically adequate dwelling may be excluded from selection. Other households falling outside such definitions are usually excluded. In effect many wish to become council tenants but have no chance of selection, the long-term effect being the formation of specific social patterns in the council sector[56] contrasting strongly with the private tenures.

The details of selection processes are best understood if the four major sorts of demand managed by officials are discussed in turn. These four groups are: people living in dwellings to be demolished by the local authority; the homeless; other households wishing to move into the council sector; and, families already living in a council house but who wish to move to another dwelling in the control of the same local authority. In England during 1975, of the 260,000 households entering the council sector, 18 per cent came via slum clearance activities, 9 per cent were rehoused as a consequence of homelessness, and 64 per cent from the ordinary waiting list. The remaining 9 per cent constituted 'key workers' and other priority groups.[57] Throughout, it should be remembered that the degree of formality or informality, whether decisions are made by elected representatives or professional managers, and the precise details of administration, procedure and rules vary considerably from area to area. In addition, although the mediation of supply and demand is an underlying explanatory feature, other factors, such as management needs, the beliefs, assumptions and prejudices of the managers, and so on, may cut across this responsibility to infringe upon who is offered a council dwelling. Finally, it should again be stressed that the legislative framework to selection allows considerable local autonomy and discretion.

People in clearance dwellings

The background and nature of slum clearance is not the direct concern of this chapter.[58] It is, however, important, in so far as people displaced by the clearance activities of local authorities often constitute one of the largest sources of demand experienced by councils, particularly in large and old urban areas. Local authorities have a duty to rehouse people made homeless as a result of local authority demolition activity. However, this duty is less than precise. Although given legislative force by the Land Compensation Act 1973, it exists only where suitable alternative accommodation is not available. In effect, local authorities are allowed some choice in whom they rehouse, and typically various groups are excluded for the immediate reason that the housing authority believes alternative accommodation to be available. Excluded groups often include single people, newcomers to the local authority, latecomers to the clearance area, couples without children, lodgers, sub-tenants, former council tenants with a history of rent arrears, and households otherwise thought 'unsuitable' for the council sector (sometimes including single parent families).[59]

Apart from being a means of reducing demand for the council sector the underlying reasons for these particular groups being excluded are rather complex. In some situations the absence of a large stock of small dwellings precludes the possibility of housing single people. 'Unsuitable' households may be turned away because they represent a potentially considerable drain on management resources, a means of minimising likely rent arrears and disturbances, and so on. Newcomers and latecomers may be rejected for reasons of 'fairness', while for other minority groups it may be because they are viewed as 'undeserving'. In effect, various factors discussed in previous sections, such as other management responsibilities, managerial ideology and personal beliefs and prejudices may influence the selection process.

In most local authorities the decision as to who should be excluded is made by housing investigators or visitors[60] who interview the household concerned whilst still living in the dwelling to be cleared. The visit is a means of assessing the family, dwelling, conditions of the furniture, household cleanliness, rent arrears, and so on, remarks typically being made on an official form under headings such as 'type of applicant' and 'cleanliness'. Housing investigators may inform applicants that they are ineligible. A number of studies reveal that individual or group prejudices and beliefs figure in deciding who to exclude:

the underlying philosophy seemed to be that council tenancies
were to be given only to those who 'deserved them', and that only
the 'most deserving' should get the best houses . . . Moral
rectitude, social conformity, clean living, and a 'clean' rent-book
on occasion seemed to be essential qualifications for eligibility—at
least for a new house.[61]

This situation may be viewed as a continuation of an historically
accepted role, although it is worth noting that most housing investigators receive little training (the post sometimes being promotion for a
successful rent collector). The long-term consequences of these policies
and procedures in many towns is the increasing concentration and
segregation of various relict social groups in the shrinking and low
quality private rented sector.

The homeless
It is only since the passing of the Housing (Homeless Persons) Act 1977
that housing authorities have statutory duty to provide accommodation
for certain groups of the homeless. In previous years homelessness
tended to be viewed as a responsibility for social services departments,
the infamous policy of placing families in 'bed and breakfast' accommodation often being a typical response to the problem. Housing authorities
sometimes tended to ignore homelessness for a number of reasons,
including the shortage of housing, fears that accepting responsibility
would attract more homeless people to the area, and the notion that
homelessness was intentional . One of the standard texts on housing
management suggests, for example, that homelessness 'does not diminish
the importance of seeing that the system is not abused by families
endeavouring to obtain a house out of their turn'.[62]

The effect of the 1977 Act is difficult to judge. Some liberal authorities were already doing more than the Act statutorily required them
to do. Indeed, as with other legislation in the management field the Act
contains loop-holes allowing authorities considerable freedom in the
handling of homelessness. For example, the Act stresses the distinction,
in terms of who should be housed, between 'priority need' and non-
priority need, and between the intentionally homeless and the uninten-
tionally. Although a Code of Guidance[63] goes some way to defining
these groups, final decisions are left in the hands of local authorities,
and there is no default sanction built into the Act. The available evidence[64] indicates that some local authorities still reject certain groups

in priority need and employ stringent notions of 'unintentional' homelessness. In effect, many of the groups excluded from rehousing because of clearance are again excluded if homeless, for underlying reasons which are essentially similar in both cases.

Other households wishing to move into council housing

The third sort of demand managed by local authorities concerns other households at present outside the council sector seeking to become council tenants. Yet again the statutory framework is vague, the only requirement for local authorities being to secure that 'reasonable preference is given to persons who occupy insanitary or overcrowded houses, have large families, or are living in unsatisfactory conditions'.[65] Apart from 'overcrowding', which is statutorily defined, the phrasing of the legislation, with terms such as 'reasonable preference' and 'unsatisfactory housing conditions' allows for considerable managerial choice. In addition, at times even overcrowding may be ignored or by-passed for one reason or another.

The typical response of local authorities is to manage this demand by means of a waiting list, essentially a device which ensures queueing for dwellings. Waiting lists may be in various forms. At times they are unstructured and informal, the decision as to who should be offered a dwelling being determined on 'merit' by an official or councillor.

Merit schemes are defended on the grounds that 'councillors and officials have personal knowledge of the individual circumstances of each applicant and that the greater flexibility it gives is a useful instrument in ensuring that the right size and type of house is allocated to each family.'[66] At their worst, however, merit schemes are open to abuse and favouritism, and may mean that people are selected for subjective and personal reasons. P.C. Brown[67] indicates the difficulties of the merit system in the following fictional scene: 'Well then, one windy day after we'd been waiting fifteen years I chased a councillor's hat, and so we got a council house.'

Such merit systems appear relatively rare, particularly in large authorities. More typical are formal waiting lists, according to which applicants are ordered according to specific criteria such as date of applying (date-ordered schemes) or nature of present accommodation and household, where points are given for factors such as overcrowding and unsatisfactory housing. Superficially these more formal waiting lists, and in particular points schemes, appear neutral and fair. In practice, however, they have been subject to considerable criticism,[68] which is not so much directed at the concept of waiting lists, but more to their actual nature and consequences in most local authorities.

Waiting lists, in practice, are an inadequate means of assessing housing need, yet they perform this function for local authorities. People in housing need may fail to register on the local waiting list because of the complexities of form filling and applications, or through lack of knowledge or misknowledge (such as 'the landlord would not allow it'[69]). In addition, although appearing neutral and objective, waiting lists are open to a variety of informal practices and policies. Lewis,[70] for example, argues of points schemes: 'They are sometimes imperfectly applied; they become rapidly outmoded; they are often incomplete and commonly include a discretionary area within the rules themselves.' Managers, for their own purposes, may distinguish between sub-lists such as 'live' and 'dormant', 'open' and 'closed', 'householders' and 'non-householders', 'priority cases' and 'non-priority cases', and so on. While fostering the image of openness, fairness, routineness and selection according to need, those selected for a house may in reality not conform to these critera 'since comparatively few people get housed from the top of lists anyway, the values built into them have little relation to housing prospects'.[71] Instead various groups are able to side step the waiting list, and in effect jump over the queue of households. These include special groups, such as 'key' workers needed by local government and perhaps local industry, former servicemen and policemen, 'medical cases', and so on. In the context of local discretion, it is relevant to note that the definition of medical cases again appears subjective and sometimes irrational, being more a reflection of persistence on the part of the applicant and administrative convenience than on objective assessment of the impact of present housing conditions on health: 'Persistence, not merit, is rewarded and by proving not only housing need but also a capacity to cause trouble, rehousing often follows.'[72] In these circumstances, the surface image of the waiting list is contradicted by the very informal processes and discretion condemned in merit schemes. In those authorities where demand greatly outweighs supply the waiting list appears a most ineffectual and subjective instrument of selecting households, at least from the viewpoint of would-be tenants on the list. In these circumstances, the discretionary power of local authorities to rehouse special cases may result in a slight or non-existent turnover in the list.

When people from the waiting list proper are rehoused, the particular rules employed clearly influence who is to be selected. For example, a waiting list stressing length of residence may result in older people tending to come to the top of the list, whilst in lists stressing existing housing conditions, large families may come more to the fore. The point which emerges is the freedom allowed authorities in deciding exactly who to select from the list. Interestingly, there is some evidence to suggest that as the population on the waiting list changes, so local authorities may amend the rules of selection to maintain particular groups in a specific position. One illustration of this concerns a local authority which increased the residential qualifications necessary so as to avoid rehousing large numbers of Asians;[73] another concerns an authority in London which changed its rules in respect of homelessness as more families faced housing need in this way.[74]

Those excluded from the council sector through waiting list rules and policies tend to include similar groups to those excluded in the management of homelessness and rehousing from clearance dwellings, although owner-occupiers also appear to be rejected in many authorities. In general, the greater the excess of demand over supply the more restrictive are waiting lists.[75] In contrast those lists which are more open and informative are often run by authorities with less pressing demand. The actions of Manchester Corporation, which in 1977 introduced a new 'rehousing list' system, giving all those on the list considerable information about the position in the queue, the details of their points and the sort of housing for which they are eligible, may be viewed partly as a response to lessening demand.[76]

The movement of existing tenants

The final sort of demand managed by local authorities comes from existing tenants wishing to move within the council sector. Such households can either transfer from their present home to a vacant dwelling, or agree to exchange their dwelling with one or more other households who also wish to move. Typically the demand for transfers and exchanges far exceeds the number of council tenants who succeed in moving.[77] Again the managers are in a powerful position to decide who should move, and if an application is refused the only appeal is to officials who made the original decision of rejection.

One constraint on selecting tenants is simply lack of administrative resources: there may be insufficient staff to fully consider and plan all the required moves. Another constraint is lack of suitable property. For example, there may simply be few if any vacancies in dwellings of a particular size. Similarly, applications for transfers show clear patterns favouring the most popular areas, estates and dwelling types. Not only may there be few of these dwellings available, but also if all applications were granted the result, in many authorities, would be vacant dwellings of a low status in undesirable areas which would be difficult and perhaps impossible for the local authority to let. Lewis[78] quotes the example of one local authority where, for this very reason, transfers were not considered from multistorey flats until the occupant had lived there eight years.

Despite this situation, many authorities refuse transfers or exchange applications on the grounds that the applicant is not suitable for the dwelling or area considered. Not only does household size figure in such refusals (for example, a small household requesting a large dwelling) but so does the nebulous factor of the 'status' or 'quality' of the household. The grading of the status of a household is essentially similar to that carried out when households displaced by clearance schemes are to be rehoused. Grading reflects the beliefs and assumptions of managers discussed above, and is an interpretation both of the 'desserts' and suitability of the household and the extent to which it will constitute a drain on administrative and financial resources. Grading typically runs through a 'school-report' system ranging from 'excellent' through four or five other classifications to 'poor' or 'unsuitable'. Those with a low status are rarely offered a transfer or exchange, yet for reasons discussed elsewhere in the chapter, such tenants are often in poorer quality and lower status property. In effect grading reduces the demand from existing council tenants considered as legitimate by managers, and ensures occupants for the worst of the council dwelling stock.

Having considered the four principal groups of demand managed by officials or councillors, it remains to note that the treatment of each group necessarily impinges on other groups. For example, if clearance households are offered accommodation this results in a slower turnover of the waiting list (the reduction in slum clearance in the 1970s has probably done more to reduce waiting lists than any other factor). Typically, each of the four groups is given a different priority. Because of statutory obligations and the ability of households to hold up clearance schemes, families in clearance areas are often given priority over other groups. At the other extreme, the homeless, and to a lesser extent those on the waiting list, if they are offered a dwelling, have little control or power to influence the type and locations of the property they are allocated. They may be offered the accommodation refused by other groups.

This complex system of priorities, which is often informal in the extreme, varies from authority to authority and over time, depending, for example, on the amount of clearance, the number of homeless families coming forward, the vacant dwellings available, the perceived priorities of the managers, and so on. Layering across these priorities in selection is a similarly complex and informal system of queues for different sorts of dwellings. Such queues may be categorised in terms of the size of the property, and its location, type, age and reputation. The length of particular queues depends on the availability of dwellings with the relevant characteristics and the demand for households. In turn demand is typically determined by the quality and status of particular dwellings and areas, this heterogeneity being recognised by both managers and households.

6   The allocation of dwellings

Those households which successfully pass through the web of selection mechanisms, queues, eligibility filters, and other policies and procedures will eventually be offered a dwelling by the local authority.[79] Managers try to ensure that the housing allocated meets a household's needs in terms of size, type, location and amenity. For example, with the important proviso that suitable vacancies are available, old people will be offered purpose-built accommodation and large families with children will be allocated houses (rather than flats) with sufficient bedrooms.

A major constraint, experienced to a greater or lesser extent by all authorities, is simply that the requirements and desires of all applicants are unlikely to be fulfilled by the vacancies available at any point in time. Necessarily managers are forced to make decisions about which households should have their needs met, and which should be offered unsatisfactory accommodation. The framework to decision-making in this respect is often complex. Local authorities will have at their disposal a range of dwelling types, including new dwellings, 're-lets' made vacant through the movement or death of existing tenants, municipalised former private sector dwellings, and houses in clearance areas which have only a short life. The mix between the types of dwellings, and in terms of other factors such as location, popularity, size and so on, varies both spatially and over time. Thus in the 1960s the domination of flats in building programmes resulted in much housing of children in what are now recognised as unsuitable dwelling types.[80] Similarly, as building programmes have been cut, so local authorities have been forced to rely to a greater extent on housing people in re-lets. For example, in England and Wales between 1971 and 1975 533,000 dwellings were added to the council stock (mainly through new building) and 655,000 were re-lets vacated by tenants who did not occupy another council house.[81] These additions and vacancies govern the number of households able to enter the council sector. Existing council tenants may, of course, occupy these 'initial' vacancies, but in most circumstances the chains of moves in the sector resulting from such transfers are eventually terminated by a new tenant occupying a vacant dwelling. Because of the nature of previous building, selection and allocation policies, it is sometimes the case that re-lets tend to be clustered in particular areas, with, for example, a considerable exodus of people from unpopular flats, or the population of an inter-war estate tending to age and leave the council sector over a relatively short period of time.

This situation results in a further complexity in allocation. In order to minimise non-payment of rent, it is necessary for managers to find tenants for property, even if it is unpopular. Yet tenants, or potential tenants, are naturally enough for the most part unwilling to accept what is considered as inferior accommodation. Many applicants may refuse to occupy low status dwellings, the task for local authorities then becoming one of locating households prepared to accept such housing. A number of strategies are employed in attempting to overcome this problem. One is to limit the number of refusals of offers each household may have, thus pressurising applicants to accept what is offered. With a similar aim, housing visitors may attempt to guide the preference and choices of particular households towards low-status dwellings. For example, Corina[82] provides detailed evidence of how visitors:

> point out to an applicant that the chance of making a successful
> application, or the chance of avoiding a long wait, might be
> increased by 'being realistic' and not entering the 'competition'
> for desirable estates with a very low tenancy turnover.

It should also be stressed that applicants have different degrees of power or ability to control the dwellings they are allocated. For reasons already suggested households from clearance areas may be able to pressurise managers into giving them the dwellings or areas they want. In contrast, homeless families tend to be in desperate need, and sometimes quickly accept dwellings which households in a more sure position would have rejected. Transfer applicants tend to be allocated relatively high quality dwellings, partly because such households are viewed as a more secure management proposition, and partly because they are unlikely to wish to move to dwellings which represent a worsening, or at least no improvement, of their housing conditions.

Another, related, aspect of the bargaining position of households is a consequence of local authority grading of tenants, a phenomenon which appears widespread, if often denied by managers themselves. Grading of both new and existing tenants is not only a means of selection, but also a device to guide the allocation of dwellings and match households and property together according to the management views of the suitability of particular sorts of applicants for particular types of property. The following remarks made by housing investigators in Hull during the early 1970s[83] reveal the factors considered in assessing households, and may be taken as an illustration of the practices in many local authorities:

'Excellent tenant, suitable for new property.'
'Fairly good type—suitable for new or post-war re-let.'
'Poor type, will need supervision—suitable for old property
... seems to have taken over the tenancy of this house and sat
back until rehoused.'
'Fair only—suitable for pre-war property.'
'A good type of applicant—this is not a long haired person. Suitable
for a post-war re-let.'

Research from a number of authors demonstrates the effectiveness of grading in guiding allocation policy and in determining who gets what dwelling.

An underlying reason for grading does seem to be an attempt to ensure applicants for the least popular and lowest quality dwellings, and hence legitimate allocation activities that are necessarily difficult and inequable given differential dwelling quality. As already noted, local authorities with only a small range of dwellings available rarely find it necessary to employ grading to guide allocations.

However, grading may also be viewed as a consequence both of the historically accepted managerial role of managing tenants as well as dwellings, and as an attempt to fulfil other management functions. To quote from a management textbook[84]: 'It will be appreciated that the personal suitability of the applicant and his wife are a guide to the type of dwelling to be offered.' Thus grading may be explained or rationalised in other ways, including: making supervision of unsatisfactory tenants easier; being an incentive to improve (with the promise of a reward in the form of a better dwelling in due course); as a deterrent to other potentially unsatisfactory tenants; as a means of minimising disturbance and protecting other tenants; a way of reducing the level of rent arrears from 'bad-payers' and the subsidy payments to low-income households; and a method of maintaining the quality of high-status dwellings ('if we let it to a problem family they would wreck it'). At times these views may be held so strongly that the local authority secures low-quality accommodation for the purpose of housing unsatisfactory tenants. Short-life properties in clearance areas may be used in this way.

7 Related issues

Despite inadequacies in selection and allocation and other aspects of council house management, as we have seen most council tenants have gained considerably from the existence of state housing. Particularly for lower income households, council tenants experience considerably better housing conditions than they might expect if in the private sector. Similarly, because allocation is, however indirectly and imperfectly, on the basis of need rather than income and market position, housing inequalities in the council sector are not so harsh and blatant.

Nevertheless, as already suggested, rather than being homogeneous in its social geography, the council sector reveals a clear internal spatial patterning of people. The most noted aspect of this tendency is for various minority groups, such as 'unsatisfactory tenants', 'problem families', black people, single-parent families, the low status, and so on, to inhabit the poorest and lowest status areas and dwellings. In most local authorities areas exist which have been variously termed as 'ghetto', 'sink', 'stigmatised', or 'residual' estates.[85]

To an extent the existence of such areas may be viewed as both a perhaps unintended product of other managerial activities, particularly of grading tenants, and the struggle to obtain better quality dwellings amongst tenants themselves, with the least powerful losing out in favour of the more powerful. Over time these processes have a snow-balling effect, being taken from the direct control of managers. With the increasing reluctance of households to move into such areas the managerial task becomes one of filling its least desirable housing, typically ensuring a captive demand. Ghetto estates may, then, become a self-fulfilling prophecy.

However, the causes of ghetto estates are invariably more complex than this. The notion of 'problem families' is a product of society-wide assumptions and attitudes rather than being internal to council house managers. In effect both managers and tenants may be responding to a situation with society-wide roots. Thus distinctions between the 'deserving' and 'undeserving', the 'respectable' and 'unrespectable' poor have long existed and serve to divide council tenants into a number of competing factions.[86] Nevertheless, ghetto estates may be viewed as a form of punishment, a device for disciplining and the social control of other tenants, a means of legitimating managerial assumptions and activities, and providing scapegoats for a variety of issues. Byrne,[87] for example, shows how the occupants of a ghetto estate were blamed both for the deteriorating conditions of their own dwellings and rent increases in the council sector as a whole, when, in fact, the local authority concerned had failed to provide sufficient resources for the maintenance and repair of the worst dwellings, and when rent increases were a product of separate processes.

Unless a local authority deliberately sets out to produce or acquire low-qualtiy dwellings, invariably present-day ghetto estates were constructed at a time when the central government financial framework imposed on local authorities resulted in low-quality dwellings. Problem areas and problem tenants may be partly a consequence of this original state of affairs. For example, post-war, high-density flats with large concentrations of families with children have specific demands and needs which, for various reasons, are not met by local authorities. As a result the tenants and area become recognised as a 'problem' and attitudes and responses evolve accordingly.[88]

Despite the absence of market forces allocating people to dwellings, it remains the case that in the council sector the least powerful are often excluded altogether from the council sector, or occupy the lowest quality and poorest status housing. As already suggested, households excluded in the selection process are forced into private tenures, which may, in the case of those on low incomes or experiencing other difficulties associated with the wider housing, social and economic systems, involve becoming trapped in appalling housing conditions. Those who are ineligible for council housing are not necessarily those least in need, and indeed often include minority groups experiencing immense housing and social disadvantages. In the struggle to gain access to good-quality council housing those who fail are often groups for whom the welfare state, the education system, and so on, are also of little if any positive benefit. Indeed, to fully understand the position of such groups in relation to council house management requires an explanation of capitalist society itself, rather than a mere explanation of managerial activity.

Two examples of such groups are black people and single-parent families. In the latter case managerial assumptions and individual and group prejudice regarding the 'undeserving' poor have some impact on the sort of dwelling allocated for reasons suggested above. In addition, however, the operation of selection and allocation policies and practices tends to operate against the interests of single-parent families for other reasons. Thus residential qualifications and points systems which stress factors such as overcrowding and bedroom deficiency tend to favour other groups since such households are often more mobile and of a below-average household size.[89]

Black people have been observed to be under-represented in the council sector, and if in the tenure group then in generally poorer dwellings than white people.[90] Discrimination on the basis of colour appears to be but one factor contributing to this situation, and then usually a product of attitudes and assumptions held in wider society rather than being consciously formulated and implemented by housing managers. Typically black people are also members of other groups discriminated against in managerial activity. In the past as immigrants they experienced the same reactions faced by white newcomers to a local authority. More recently black people have tended to enter the council sector as a result of homelessness. Relatively little clearance has occurred of private sector housing occupied by a large proportion of racial minorities. Similarly they tend to be well down waiting lists. As noted above, the homeless, and consequently black people, are often allocated low-quality dwellings.

Black people not only have an inferior bargaining position than many whites, but in addition their experience and knowledge of the council sector may be slight, and their housing conditions prior to entrance to public housing often worse. Both factors, and others, tend to lead to managers offering inferior housing, and to black people accepting what is offered. In contrast, white people are typically in a position to acquire more desirable dwellings. In consequence, despite aspiring to similar housing as white and rarely choosing low-quality and low-status housing for reasons of preference, black people are often allocated relatively inferior and sometimes stigmatised dwellings.

The solution (in so far as the solution is to be found in the reform of council house management alone) for both single-parent families and black people, and for similar groups, may be to make explicit biases operate against them, even if these are a by-product of other processes, and then to ensure that their knowledge and opportunities are made the same as for other households entering the tenure.

One contextual feature of management noted above is that tenants and would-be tenants are relatively powerless in terms of controlling or directly influencing managerial activity: whatever power households do have is often a consequence of the decisions and activities of managers themselves. The extreme reluctance of either elected members or officers in many local authorities to impart any degree of effective control to tenants themselves is partly a consequence of the origins of council management in the 1920s. Tenant participation schemes initiated by the local authority may be little more than a means of placing the burden of repairs and maintenance on tenants without a concomitant increase in tenant rights.

With some notable exceptions[91] tenants themselves have usually been ineffective in challenging management activities and assumptions. Instead, change when it has occurred has more often been the result of external pressure, as with the liberalising of selection rules to find occupants for the least-liked dwellings. The existence of various divisions between tenants and households seeking to enter the sector (for example, between the deserving and undeserving) has tended to mitigate against united attempts to challenge managerial activity. However, the policies and practices described above have accentuated whatever divisions already exist: 'Once the norms are established people tend to concur, adjusting their own definitions and behaviour to conform.'[92]

In effect, the managers provide the rules and context within which tenants are able to challenge managerial activity. Invariably, whatever protest occurs is individualised into concerns about position in the queue, the dwelling allocated, other tenants who obtain better accommodation, and so on. In addition, those with most to gain from changing management policies and practices are often minority groups with a weak bargaining position. Furthermore, the complexity of policies and practices, which often take place behind closed doors according to unwritten principles which are little understood by anyone apart from the managers themselves, adds a further dimension to the difficulties experienced by tenants' organisations.

Perhaps of all the aspects of management the domination of the tenant by the manager is seen most directly in tenancy agreements. As the National Consumer Council[93] has shown, with notable exceptions, these tend to be one-sided (stating the tenant's obligations to the authority rather than vice versa), containing wrongful exclusion of council liability (for example, concerning who is responsible for repairs), paternalistic, punitive and incomprehensible. It is also relevant to note in this context that local authorities have almost complete powers to evict council tenants for whatever reason the authority itself decides on. Yet again the central notion emerges that the tenant as well as the property is to be managed according to the decisions of managers.

Closely associated with this notion are the definitions of need employed to guide the selection of households and allocation of dwellings. Taken together, and along with a number of other features discussed above, the general point arises that despite all its actual and potential benefits the council sector may be positively harmed by managerial ideology and activity, which in this sense may be viewed as one aspect of the ideology and functioning of the wider housing system. An illustration of this is the notion that the council sector is a second-best tenure, fit only for those incapable of becoming owner-occupiers. This ethos has gained considerable power amongst managers, tenants and non-tenants, and at national and local levels. The result has been to view the council sector as a welfare service, and the concomitant, in many quarters, is the sale of council houses and the reduction of the tenure group to a minimum.

The sales debate is centrally related to the management of state housing in a number of ways. One argument for sales is that it is a means of removing paternalistic and restrictive management and increasing individual housing freedom. However, this is to accept both that owner-occupation always offers choice and personal control[94] and that the inadequacies in council house management cannot be resolved through reform of the council sector itself. The selling of council housing also has a direct impact on the remaining council stock and the social geography of the public sector. As Murie[95] well demonstrates, those tenants who are able and willing to buy are better-off and already privileged tenants in the best council housing (typically good-quality houses with gardens). Many low-income households cannot afford to buy, and other tenants live in dwellings (such as flats and 1930s clearance estates) they would not wish to purchase even if given the opportunity and resources.

The long-term effect of sales is likely to be a reduction in the range of households in the council sector and a lowering of the average quality of dwellings remaining in local authority ownership, thus resulting in a further stigmatisation and ghettoisation of the council sector, with decreasing choice for those who remain or wish to become tenants. Council house sales operate to cream off the best dwellings and higher income and status groups from the local authority tenure. In addition, the ability of the council sector to meet changing needs, desires and expectations is lessened; the number of households who can move within or into the tenure group is reduced (sales reduce re-lets); and concentration on public housing as a welfare sector alone would make any reform of management less likely. On this last point, as Karn[96] notes, the evidence indicates that: 'good management of heavily stigmatised "welfare" housing is extremely difficult and . . . the social environments created are very destructive of the lives of residents.'

Council house sales are, then, linked to the increasingly experienced problem of difficult-to-let housing which, paradoxically, often exists hand in hand with long waiting lists and homelessness. As indicated earlier, reactions to this problem are varied. At one extreme the maintenance of a captive demand, ensuring that those tenants with the least power occupy low-status dwellings. Once there, grading and various rules attempt to keep tenants immobile.

At the other extreme, some authorities respond to essentially the same problem by liberalising selection rules. Manchester has already been mentioned, and a further example is Southwark, which in 1977 proposed the introduction of a 'filtering-up' system, whereby many applicants, particularly young people, are offered a difficult to let dwelling 'with the promise of a better one, if they pay the rent, in due course'.[97] Discussing the housing needs of groups such as couples without children, single working people and students, and mobile households, previously excluded from council housing, the 1977 housing Green Paper suggests a similar solution:[98]

> The needs of some, though not all, of these people can often be
> met by using property which is difficult to let to families. As
> local pressures on housing relax, some authorities are finding that
> certain types of housing . . . can be suitable for others in need of
> accommodation.

In essence, the lessening demand eventually forces changes in management. The crucial question arises of whether change is progressive or detrimental to the long-term development of the state sector. One conclusion to emerge from a study of council house management is that poor-quality welfare housing may lead to negative and inadequate management (and vice versa), further stigmatisation, a narrowing in the range of households wishing to enter the tenure, and so on, in a downward spiral that makes positive change in management, and the tenure itself, even less likely. Positive evolution in council house management is possible, but to be achieved requires a particular political stance, an understanding of the issues involved, training of staff, involvement of tenants, and not least the development of public housing of high standard for all who wish it.

8 Synthesis

This chapter has examined the nature and consequences of state control over the consumption of public housing—a topic perhaps best described as the management of consumption.

At an early stage in the provision of public housing central government relinquished to the local state much of its potential control of management, and its influence over issues such as who should be housed, when and where.

Precisely why consumption has primarily been managed by local authorities is a question which has received scant attention. In part the answer lies in the view held by both central and local state that local authorities were and are the organisations best able to assess local needs and implement decisions. Moreover, in the first decade of this century, the ability of central government to directly provide the organisation, manpower and knowledge necessary to undertake the management (or, indeed, the building) of state dwellings at the local level was almost certainly very restricted.

During the intervening decades to the present day, local autonomy in the management field has continued, and perhaps has been strengthened. Yet this very autonomy has contained its own inconsistencies. For instance, the interests of central and local state in council house management do not always coincide. Local authorities have, on occasion, been able to ignore at will the wishes of national government. The beliefs and assumptions of council house managers have been slow to change over time, and even today retain elements found in the Octavia Hill system of the late nineteenth and early twentieth centuries. In general local control, whatever the political complexion of the local authority, has resulted in conservative, restrictive and paternalistic management assumptions, policies and practice, and the withholding from tenants of any substantial control over their own housing situation. In part this rigidity of management over time exists because local authorities, and even more so local managers, as a professional or semi-professional group, have to a degree been insulated from pressures for change (whether political, economic or ideological), for example because of the excess demand for the product whose consumption they manage.

Local autonomy and the strength of management ideology have, then, an important influence on management policy. In turn managerial practice itself exerts a crucial impact on the nature of the public sector and its occupants. For instance, during the post-war period, movement out of the tenure group to the seemingly preferable pastures of the owner-occupied sector; the growing dominance within council housing of poorer sections of the population and groups such as the elderly, unskilled, and single-parent families; and the increasing problem of difficult-to-let, poor quality and low status dwellings are all, in some degree, a product of council house management.

In consequence, although the attitudes and assumptions of managers and the surface image of policies have tended to remain relatively stable over time, in reality management has increasingly evolved away from the original function of 'eliminating' unsatisfactory tenants and providing housing for 'respectable' working-class families, to trapping the least powerful in the most unsatisfactory dwellings and confirming the sector as a residual 'welfare' tenure, with its occupants being labelled in a similar fashion. To use the terms employed in Chapter 10, the council sector has tended to evolve away from a reproductive function, to an increasingly legitimatory one. Council house management has itself shadowed this profound change in a complex network of cause and effect.

Part III

Policy

NINE

Housing policy since the war

1 Introduction

Earlier chapters in this work have covered the experience of state housing since the Second World War by looking separately at processes such as site acquisition, production, capital finance and various aspects of the consumption and management of council dwellings. This chapter will draw together these elements by reviewing in a chronological sequence the development of housing policy since the war. The period 1945-78 is divided into four sub-periods: 1945-51, 1951-64, 1964-70 and 1970-8.

2 1945-51: housing and the Anglo-American alliance

On 7 May 1945 the war with Germany came to an end and three months later the war with Japan also. In between times a general election in Britain on 5 July had brought a Labour government to power with a majority over all other parties of 146 seats. Attlee became Prime Minister and he chose Hugh Dalton as his Chancellor of the Exchequer, Ernest Bevin as his Foreign Minister and Aneurin Bevan as his Minister of Health.

Ralph Miliband has described a new radicalism which appeared during the war so that in 1945 there was 'a deep popular expectation of new beginnings'.[1] However, within the Labour Party the socialist fervour of the grass roots was not shared by the leadership and this was demonstrated at the Party's annual conference in December 1944. The Executive's main economic resolution contained no reference whatsoever to public ownership, although it did specify the need to transfer to the state the power 'to direct the policy of our main industries, services and financial institutions'. In spite of Executive opposition a composite resolution was carried calling for 'the transfer to public ownership of the land, large-scale building, heavy industry, and all forms of banking, transport and fuel and power'.[2]

Once in power the Labour Cabinet did pursue a policy of extensive nationalisation, including the Bank of England, coal, gas, electricity, the railways, part of inland transport, cable and wireless and, half-heartedly, steel. Miliband argues that these measures were carried through by the government largely in order to create a better-regulated peace-time economy and that they left intact the main citadels of power and privilege. Rogow, too, proposes that throughout its period of office the Labour government was moving towards a goal of essentially liberal planning.[3] In the same vein Dow describes the economic philosophy of the government in its last years of office in the following way:[4]

> Unemployment could be cured by the management of total demand, inequality by redistributive taxation, and monopolistic restrictions by selective nationalisation; while a control over investment would ensure effective influence over the pace and direction of economic growth. If all this was done, there would be no need to go in for complete government planning, nor to supersede the price system: consumers' choice was indeed a positive good to be preserved. Interventions could be made piecemeal, wherever particular interventions seemed required.

Thus there seems to be widespread agreement that, in power, the Labour leadership sought the goal of an effectively and rationally managed capitalism. The dirigiste character of policy, moreover, had been much strengthened by the experience of the war, the successful conclusion of which was in part founded on a huge increase in the planning powers of the state at the economic, military and social levels. As we shall see the employment of some of these powers was continued in the post-war housing programme.

At the time the new government took office the housing situation was extremely grim. The 'Blitz' of 1940 and the flying-bomb attacks which began in June 1944 had entirely destroyed 200,000 dwellings and had damaged 3½ million more, 250,000 of which were uninhabitable. Meanwhile, since September 1939 the population of Britain had increased by a little over a million. In addition to these new needs there was the backlog of local authority housebuilding which was required to meet the demands of the pre-war slum clearance and overcrowding abatement programmes and this amounted to a need for 500,000 dwellings. Moreover there must also have existed an extensive backlog of maintenance and rehabilitatory work.

Against this it is necessary to recall that building work had not entirely ceased during the war years. Approximately 153,000 new houses had been completed since 1939. Most of these were under construction on the day the war with Germany broke out, although some 3000 new agricultural cottages were also built during 1943–5 by the local authorities. There had also been a determined attempt to repair war damage even whilst the bombs were still falling. For example, even before the flying-bomb attack against South-East England had begun, 103,000 badly damaged houses had been restored to use throughout the country, 1¾ million dwellings had received 'first aid' repairs and 1¼ million dwellings had received extensive repairs.[5]

To sum up, the war had brought with it vast destruction, a severe fall in building output and an increase in the population, all of which was compounded by the existence of a pre-war backlog. If we take the March 1945 figures of the Ministry of Reconstruction as a minimum requirement, then 750,000 new dwellings were needed at that point in time to provide a separate dwelling 'for every family desiring one' and 500,000 new dwellings were required to complete the slum clearance and overcrowding abatement programme.[6] Even on the giddy assumption that within three years of the war's end the annual rate of completions could have been running at, say, 330,000 houses a year, it would not have been until the year 1950 that these needs could have been met, not counting the new needs generated after 1945.

Before we turn to consider the achievements in the building of new, permanent houses, some reference needs to be made to the other measures adopted to increase the occupiable stock of accommodation, many of which were set within a short-term perspective. There were seven categories:

(i) In 1944 a decision was taken to proceed with the immediate production of temporary housing, making extensive use of prefabrication. These dwellings were provided and owned by central government but their management was left in the hands of the local authorities. By the end of 1948, when the programme in England and Wales came to an end, 124,455 houses had been erected.[7] A small number were still occupied thirty years later.

(ii) The war-time task of the repair of severely damaged unoccupied dwellings was continued and by March 1950, 142,712 such dwellings had been repaired, 76 per cent of them by the local authorities.[8]

(iii) A similar effort was the rebuilding by the local authorities and private builders of houses which bombing had destroyed. By

March 1950, 39,208 units had been provided in this way.[9]

(iv) The repair of occupied dwellings continued after the war.
Between April 1945 and March 1949, when the work came
to an end, 775,000 such units had been dealt with by the local
authorities.[10] The number repaired by private builders is
unknown. At its peak in 1945–6, at least 133,000 operatives
were employed by the local authorities alone on war-damage
work.

(v) There were substantial achievements in the conversion and
adaptation of existing premises, including houses and war-time
hostels built for factory workers. By the end of March 1950,
123,419 units had been made available, 63 per cent by private
builders.[11]

(vi) The requisitioning of empty properties took place on a modest
scale: by March 1948, after which time the measure was put
into reverse, 27,694 houses had been taken over for residential
purposes.[12] The 1945 Silkin Report on the conversion of
existing houses, which could have provided the starting point
for the development of a municipalisation programme, seems
to have been given short shrift by the Ministry.[13]

(vii) In the 'national emergency' situation in the first years after the
war, a few thousand temporary huts were put up. More important,
many of the service camps built during the war were used for a
time: by March 1950 this had provided 22,195 units of accommodation. Their use had largely been in response to squatting,
which began in them in May 1946, although Circular 174/46
urged that local authorities should take firm action to prevent
the spread of the movement. When the squatters took over a
number of empty blocks of flats in London, five of the organisers
were arrested.[14]

I now return to the permanent housebuilding programme, the output
data of which are given in Table 9·1.

At the very beginning of the period in question the simple and
sensible decision was taken that local authority housebuilding in the
early post-war years was to exclude slum clearance and redevelopment.
This was just as it had been after the First World War. It did not exclude
the possibility of purchase followed by patching, with a weather eye
on clearance in the medium term, as in the case of Birmingham.

As far as the division of responsibility between the local authority
sector and the speculative builders was concerned, it was the state

Table 9·1 *Permanent dwelling output in Great Britain 1945–51*

	1945[a]	1946	1947	1948
Local authority starts[b]	n.a.	163,518	155,779	139,457
Local authority completions[b]	1936	25,013	97,340	190,368
Private completions		31,297	40,980	32,751
		1949	1950	1951
Local authority starts[b]		162,248	169,217	170,857
Local authority completions[b]		165,946	163,670	162,584
Private completions		25,790	27,358	22,551

Source: Local authorities:private communication from the DoE.
Private sector: ABCS.
a   Local authority data for England and Wales only.
b   Includes the Scottish Special Housing Association after 1945.
Starts data are estimates.

sector which was chosen as the main instrument of policy. It was argued that housing output should be directed to those in greatest need and that only the local authorities allocated new dwellings on this basis.[15] The councils, too, were seen as inherently plannable. Bevan put it in this way:[16]

> if we are to have any correspondence between the size of the building force on the sites and the actual provision of the material coming forward to the sites from the industries, there must be some planning. If we are to plan we have to plan with plannable instruments, and the speculative builder, by his very nature, is not a plannable instrument.

Michael Foot, Bevan's biographer, comments: 'In fact, unknown to Churchill and the Tories, most of the housing experts at the Ministry of Health had been moving along undoctrinaire paths towards this same conclusion before Bevan arrived on the scene.'[17] In general, speculative building was intended to make up at most one-fifth of the total housing output in each local housing authority;[18] in 1945–6 some authorities were discovered to be ignoring this and the Ministry of Health imposed restraints on them.[19] In fact Table 9·1 shows that in terms of completions it was not until after 1947 that the one-fifth benchmark took effect.

In spite of the talk of planning, there is no evidence that the Labour government set any *targets* for housing starts or completions, the sine qua non of a serious attempt to plan. It is true that in the summer of 1944 the Coalition Cabinet instructed the local authorities to build 100,000 units in the first year of the European peace and 200,000 in the following year,[20] a figure reduced in 1945 to 220,000 units to be completed by all sectors within two years of the end of the war.[21] But thereafter, with Labour in power, there was no attempt to set up a balance sheet of needs and annual completions targets broken down by sector and region. It is all very well to insist, as Foot does, on Bevan's hate and distrust of statistics and his 'elementary cunning' in keeping secret his targets;[22] but a more plausible explanation is that the Parliamentary leadership simply had no confidence in its own will and ability to keep to any quantitative plan.

In order to comprehend the government's year-to-year management of total housing output and the division of that total between the state and private sectors, we need to know a little about the controls they operated. As Dow says: 'Controls were retained at the end of the war for one overriding reason—that without controls, it was believed, there would be a repetition of the open inflation that had followed the first world war.'[23] With respect to materials—timber and steel for example— each firm would receive an allocation of the total supply available, based generally on their pre-war consumption. The share-out was administered by the existing trade associations.[24] With respect to the scale of output, a licensing system existed for work done for private owners, a device inherited from the war-time Defence Regulation 56A. Any item of work exceeding a fixed upper cash limit could be carried out legally only if it were licensed by the local authorities or the Ministry of Works. As the list below shows, these limits were subject to change:

Period	Limit (£)
August 1945 – July 1948	20
July 1948 – July 1952	100
July 1952 – January 1953	200
January 1953 – January 1954	5000
January 1954 – November 1954	1000

Licensing was scrapped in November 1954. As the upper limits indicate, in the years 1945–51 licensing covered all new private dwellings. Public sector work required no licence but in any case all such construction had to receive loan sanction and tender approval. After April 1947 the regional offices of the Ministry of Works could set earliest starting dates for all private and public sector projects.

The fear of post-war inflation was particularly sharp because of the labour and materials shortages from which the economy suffered at the war's end. During the period 1939–45 not only the construction industry but also the building materials and household equipment industries had been stripped of their labour assets in preference to those sectors with a higher war priority. By August 1945 they were operating well below their capacity levels. In the case of construction, the 1939 labour force had exceeded 1 million operatives but six years later had fallen to only 337,000 men. Rapid demobilisation and the creation of new training schemes helped but at the same time the emergency pro- grammes described above, particularly the repair of war damage, generated heavy demands on the available manpower. By March 1947, although the workforce on new housing work had risen above 200,000 men, this was still about 100,000 short of what was required.[25] With respect to materials there were, from time to time, shortages in the supply of plasterboard, asbestos, cement, brick, iron castings, lead sheet and pipe, paint, steel and, most acute of all, softwood. In fact the timber shortage even led to such design changes as the elimination of the use of timber on ground floors.[26]

Well before the termination of hostilities, there had been some am- bitious thinking about the contribution of non-traditional construction to output, particularly as it was argued that reliance on extensive pre- fabrication economised on skilled labour and short-supply materials.[27] Indeed, the wildest optimism was possible: a Communist Party pamphlet pronounced that 'The greater part of the houses can be constructed at a great speed in factories without interference by bad weather.'[28] Presumably this was the basis of their view that 1½ million new perma- nent houses could be *completed* within three years of the end of the war![29] As it transpired the new technology was itself an intensive con- sumer of some materials in short supply and it was relatively costly.

I shall now look briefly at the legal and financial context within which local authority programmes operated. With respect to site pur- chase, the 1946 Acquisition of Land (Authorisation Procedure) Act was a useful measure for it brought a streamlining of acquisition procedure, reducing the time required to bring land into council ownership. With respect to compensation for compulsory purchase, as we saw in Chapter 3, the 1947 Town and Country Planning Act was a most significant advance, for its final effect was that council tenants (or the taxpayers) would not bear the development values of land in their rent payments (or their taxes).

As far as capital finance goes, the immediate post-war situation was very satisfactory, viewed in historical retrospect. Given the scale of local authority housebuilding sanctioned by the government, virtually every penny that the municipalities required could be, indeed had to be, raised from the PWLB. Interest rates were extremely low. At the end of the war there was a bipartisan view that money rates should be kept down and this policy was at first successful. Even after the Bank of England ended its active phase of monetary intervention in August 1947, market rates remained low.[30] The PWLB rate on loans for periods in excess of fifteen years were:

August 1945 – June 1946:	$3\frac{1}{8}$ %
June 1946 – January 1948:	$2\frac{1}{2}$ %
January 1948 – November 1951:	3 %

The cost of council housebuilding had jumped markedly since 1939, as we have already seen in Graph 4·1. About one-fourth of the increase was the result of high standards; the rest was due to the general inflation of prices during the war. The average tender price for a three-bedroom house in 1945 was £1045, £1.07 per square foot, compared with the 1939 figures of £376 and £0.47. (Between 1945 and 1951 the average cost per square foot shifted slowly upwards at an annual simple rate of 4·2 per cent.) This meant that the post-war subsidy levels would have to be much higher if rents were not to rise disproportionately and the 1946 Housing (Financial and Miscellaneous Provisions) Act introduced a standard annual subsidy of £16 10s per dwelling, to be supplemented by a compulsory rate contribution of £5 10s. The ratio of central to local subsidy was thereby raised to 3:1. The subsidies were set so as to give an annual net rent of about 10s per week.

We are now in a position to review the scale of year-by-year output and its relationship with broader political-economic developments. Preparations for the post-war period had begun as early as March 1943 when all the local housing authorities in England and Wales had been asked to prepare a programme for the first year following the peace.[31] By the time the Ministry of Reconstruction had presented its White Paper on housing in March 1945 the municipalities throughout Britain had already acquired, or were in the process of acquiring, land sufficient for the erection of 662,000 dwellings.[32] A year later only 194 out of 1469 authorities in England and Wales had no scheme under way.[33]

Table 9·1 shows that in 1946, the first year for which the data exist, the total number of starts exceeded 163,000, an unprecedented historical achievement. Completions, of course, moved ahead in a lagged fashion but the table shows a powerful and uninterrupted surge in 1945–8 from 200 units to 25,000 to 97,000 to 190,000. In spite of the labour and materials shortages, municipal housebuilding had responded to the critical need of the British working-class with an urgency and vigour which few save the most optimistic could have hoped for. It was in the midst of this great leap forward that, like a re-run of the Coalition movie of 1920–1, the Cabinet decided to chop back and contain the municipal housing effort.

Britain's trade and payments situation at the end of the war was a most desperate one. During the conflict the sterling balances—our debts to the Commonwealth countries—had risen to £3500 million. Simultaneously the volume of our exports had fallen to less than half their pre-war level and our invisible earnings had also been greatly reduced. We were therefore running a substantial deficit on our balance of trade. In part this was covered by the lend-lease agreements with the United States, but these were terminated in the most abrupt fashion six days after the peace with Japan!

The Labour administration turned to the US government for succour. The nature of the Anglo-American alliance in the new age that followed the defeat on a world scale of fascism is, of course, complex. To treat it here in a single paragraph inevitably means the presentation must be crude. But not to treat it at all would guarantee that we failed to understand the conflicts between state policies which required for their successful implementation substantial claims on the country's economic resources. And *that* is the crux of British housing history between 1945 and 1951.

Successive British administrations strove to maintain the nation's role as one of the great world powers. This power manifested itself in many forms: in the use of our currency as a means of payment in world trade; in our political domination of huge areas in the Americas, in Africa and in Asia; and in the stationing of our air, sea and land forces in the four corners of the earth. These imperial ambitions were threatened by the growth in the strength of the Soviet Union, by the development of communist, socialist and nationalist movements in every continent, and by the increasing industrial power of the other great capitalist nations—the defeat of Italy, Germany and Japan could already be seen as merely a temporary set-back in the expansion of their industrial might. Success in the attainment of this strategic goal, in an age of our own relative decline, was seen to depend critically on our alliance with the United States, at that time—and still—the most powerful nation in human history. The alliance, then, was the single, fixed point about which all other governmental philosophy and policy pivoted.

As a consequence, when the most violent tensions were generated between our ambition and our means to fulfil it and when these tensions took form in some financial, military or political crisis it was to the US and to institutions like the IMF, which it controlled, that the government turned for aid, and if conditions were imposed in the granting of such aid, finally we did not nor could not flinch from accepting them.

As I say, in the payments crisis of 1945 the government turned to the United States for assistance, and sought a dollar loan. A sum of $3750 million was agreed upon but the conditions, even after some tough bargaining, included the immediate acceptance of the Bretton Woods conference recommendations and the restoration of the convertibility of sterling within one year.[34] From the US point of view this would imply a weakening of British trading hegemony within the Commonwealth. The alliance had its own internal divisions of interest! Convertibility was re-introduced in July 1947. Before the end of August, $3·6 billion of the $5 billion credit guaranteed by the US and Canada had been exhausted, both through the continuing current account deficit of 1946-7 and the flight of capital from the pound into the dollar when convertibility made this possible. Convertibility was suspended again on 20 August 1947.

In the midst of the crisis the demand for public expenditure cuts became strident. The president of the Federation of British Industries insisted: 'We must accept the need for curtailing capital expenditure on long-term capital projects—housing, schools, hospitals', and the *Manchester Guardian* pronounced that 'The main issue now is not whether we are building as many houses as we could, but whether we can afford to go on trying to build as many as we are doing.'[35] A number of deflationary measures were taken and amongst them was a cut-back in the housebuilding programme. In August the Prime Minister announced some 'postponement' of the general building programme. In fact the local authorities had already begun reducing their new commitments. As a consequence the number of municipal dwellings approved but not started fell from 101,000 on 1 April 1947 to 42,000 precisely one year later.[36] Table 9·1 shows that municipal starts fell by 15 per cent between 1946 and 1948. Attempts were made to obfuscate the economy-housing link by talk of 'a better balance' between starts and completions and by plaints of the timber shortage.[37] Foot calls this a 'concealment of the reality'.[38]

As the American loan was in process of exhaustion, assistance in a new guise was being devised. In June 1947 General Marshall had made his speech at Harvard where he raised the call for very substantial medium-term aid to Europe. There is no doubt, historically, that this new initiative was directed towards correcting the post-war economic and political crisis in Western Europe, thereby reducing the likelihood of Communist-led governments coming to power, particularly in France and Italy. 'The long-term solution proposed was a "strong production effort" by each country, directed particularly at the modernisation of its equipment and at the expansion of exports, especially of exports to the American continent.'[39] In consequence the Organisation for European Economic Co-operation was established in April 1948, Britain being one of the member states. In November 1947 Cripps had become the Chancellor of the Exchequer and one year later he was to make plain his and the Cabinet's commitment to the Marshallian strategy:[40]

> You will see, then, that as long as we are in this impoverished state, the result of our tremendous efforts in two world wars, our own consumption requirements have to be the last in the list of priorities. First are exports . . .; second is capital investment in industry; and last are the needs, comforts and amenities of the family.

He was more discreet about military expenditure.

In May 1948 the local authorities were told to go ahead on the basis of the current number of houses under construction.[41] We now know that the annual maximum number of completions which the Chancellor was willing to countenance was 200,000 units.[42] As can be seen from Table 9·1, completions in 1949, 1950 and 1951, respectively, were 191,736, 191,028 and 185,135.

In 1949 there was yet another payments' crisis, this time the result of the American recession and speculation on the devaluation of the pound, much prompted by the IMF. In September the pound was, indeed, devalued and in October a decision was taken to cut the 1950 housing programme by 12½ per cent, almost entirely within the speculative housing sector. The cut was reversed, however, before it was ever implemented.

The same year also witnessed a new departure: the Housing Act for the first time approved the provision of grants for improvement or conversion, whether by a local authority or by a private person. The immediate response was minimal. It seems curious that there was no initiative at this point to explore the possible link between successful improvement policy and municipalisation. The first Fabian pamphlet on the subject did not appear until 1952.[43]

In February 1950 a general election resulted in a fall in Labour's overall majority in Parliament to six seats. The dominant event of the year was the outbreak of the Korean War, which was followed by a huge increase in Britain's war expenditure: the 1950–1 estimates had been £700 million and these were raised by £1100 million over a three-year period at the urgent request of the US government.[44] As a proportion of national product, war expenditure rose from 7 per cent in 1948 to 10½ per cent in 1952.

In January of 1951 Bevan left the Ministry of Health to become the new Minister of Labour and in October of the same year a new general election was held and the Conservatives returned to power. Sir Winston Churchill became Prime Minister and chose R.A. Butler as his Chancellor of the Exchequer and Harold Macmillan to take charge of housing.

3 1951–64 : regression to the philosophy of Chamberlain

At their annual conference in 1950 the Conservatives had for the first time agreed on a proposal to construct 300,000 dwellings per annum in Britain. From the autumn of 1951 Macmillan eagerly set about achieving this objective and so the first phase of what became thirteen years of Tory power we can call the phase of expansion, running from 1951 to 1953. In the private sector this was implemented by the progressive relaxation of licensing—Defence Regulation 56A was finally revoked in November 1954—and by the abolition of development charges in 1953 so that speculative builders could appropriate the development value realised when land was switched from farming to housing. Table 9·2 shows the surge in private completions.

But more effective in raising output was the response of the 'plannable instrument' of local authority activity. The Ministry set building targets for the councils and stimulated fulfilment by increasing in 1952 the level of subsidies. Unfortunately output growth was also engineered by a brutal reduction in standards in the shape of 'the people's house' which brought with it a fall in the indexed average unit prices of new dwellings until 1958 (see Graph 4·2). Total local authority and private completions in Britain expanded from 185,000 units in 1951 to 264,000 units in 1953. This was achieved with relatively little strain on the construction industry itself.

Table 9·2 *Permanent dwelling output in Great Britain 1952-64*

Year	Local authority starts[a]	Local authority completions	Private completions
1952	219,183	186,920	34,320
1953	231,001	229,305	62,921
1954	196,388	223,731	90,636
1955	164,578	181,331	113,457
1956	139,859	154,971	124,161
1957	140,810	154,137	126,455
1958	109,804	131,614	128,148
1959	133,369	114,324	150,708
1960	112,879	116,358	168,629
1961	109,547	105,529	177,513
1962	124,099	116,424	174,800
1963	151,645	112,780	174,864
1964	159,127	141,132	218,094

Source: Private sector: HSGB. Local authority sector 1952-60 inclusive, private communication from the DoE. Thereafter HSGB.
a Local authority starts 1952-7 inclusive are estimates.

What I find most remarkable about the phase of expansion is that the Conservative Cabinet did not permit the grave balance of payments deficit of 1951-2 to check their positive housebuilding policies. They took office in November 1951 at the height of the Korean crisis and with a package of measures including a small increase in Bank Rate, hire purchase restrictions, some curtailment of fixed investment and drastic import cuts they engineered a recession which, with a fall in import prices in 1952, brought the foreign payments balance back into surplus. At that point the spurt in public and private housebuilding which was already under way helped pull the economy out of the minor slump.

The second period of Conservative governance in the housing field was the phase of policy reformulation from 1953 to 1956. In retrospect we can see that a clear and comprehensive strategy was under construction in those years which broadly represents a return to the philosophy of Chamberlain and the 'golden years' of the 1930s. The strategy had several dimensions and much of it was revealed for the first time in the 1953 White Paper *Houses: the next step.*[45]

First, output in Great Britain was to be stabilised at about 300,000 dwellings per year.

Second, new housebuilding for general needs was, in large measure, to be the preserve of the private sector.[46]

> One object of future housing policy will be to continue to
> promote, by all possible means, the building of new houses for
> owner-occupation. Of all forms of saving, this is one of the best.
> Of all forms of ownership this is one of the most satisfying to the
> individual and the most beneficial to the nation.

Moreover, it was argued, private enterprise activity would 'lighten the ever-growing burden of housing subsidies'.[47] Then, as now, the civil service refused to recognise tax relief on mortgage interest as a public expenditure.[48]

Third, total local authority output was to be controlled so that it made up the shortfall of private enterprise activity below the 300,000 target. The form that this forward control took was a system of allocations by the Ministry of permitted starts. In October 1955 the Minister decided to end these. In my view this was because the existing sanctions on council building and the new subsidy structure which was being introduced made them redundant.

Fourth, large-scale housing renewal was to be stimulated, but in a partitioned framework. Repair, improvement and conversion of the existing privately owned housing stock was to be encouraged by grants and by permitting rent increases tied to improvement. This policy was implemented through the 1954 Housing Repairs and Rents Act.

Housing renewal by means of clearance was to be the preserve of the local authorities: they 'should be encouraged in future to concentrate their main housing efforts on slum clearance and overspill building, which only they can tackle effectively'.[49] The 1954 Housing Repairs and Rents Act facilitated the administrative procedures and also called for councils to submit their own estimates of the size of the slum problem and their proposals for dealing with it. These estimates, for what they were worth, appeared in 1955 in Command 9593. In legislation in the following year the terms of compensation for the owner-occupiers of unfit property were improved. With respect to redevelopment densities, it was policy that these should be high although overspill arrangements would continue to be necessary. As a result the proportion of flats within total municipal output rapidly advanced from the early 1950s, whilst the proportion of flats in the built form of very high towers and slabs advanced with astonishing speed from the late 1950s.

Fifth, the only sector of general needs which the housing authorities were positively encouraged to build for was that of the elderly, so that the proportion of one-bedroom dwellings within the total mix of accommodation provided spurts up rapidly from the mid-1950s.

Sixth, the subsidy arrangements were changed several times in 1955-6 so that by the end of 1956 no subsidies at all were available for general needs construction, with the exception of one-bedroom dwellings, and redevelopment subsidies were designed to encourage multistorey building.

Seventh, continual pressure was exercised on the authorities to make them pool their rents and concentrate the flow of subsidies towards the poor. At the same time the real value of the subsidies on newly constructed houses was falling whilst the rate subsidy was no longer mandatory so that the subsidy-expenditure ratio fell from 36 per cent in 1955-6 to 26 per cent in 1962-3. Since costs were rising sharply from 1959 the average annual rate of increase of rents net of subsidy was as high as 7·7 per cent in the decade after 1955-6.

Eighth, the local authorities were firmly thrust back into the capital market. In the period 1953-5 councils were permitted to use their own judgment in deciding whether to raise finance on the market or from the PWLB. Then in October 1955 the government decided that board lending should only be a resource of last resort and the proportion of finance raised on the stock and mortgage markets increased rapidly. Dow has pointed out that 'In the thirteen years since policy deliberately aimed at low rates of interest, the authorities moved a long way towards the conscious adoption of the opposite policy of dear money.'[50] Thus reliance on the money market became increasingly expensive.

My ninth and final point is that in the period 1953-9 the government created and then maintained a dual market in land: land purchases by speculative builders were at market prices whilst compulsory purchase by the local housing authorities received compensation only at value in existing use.

The period from 1956 to 1961 witnessed the implementation of this grand strategy and I think of it as the phase of policy stability. The only important shift during these years was the return in 1959 to market values in compensation for compulsory site purchase.

With respect to the scale of production, Table 9·2 shows the long retreat in municipal output after 1953 right through to 1961. Graph 9·1 plots public sector and total completions data for 1951-64 and shows with what astonishing precision the Conservatives maintained their 300,000 target in the years 1953–61, save that in 1954 they overshot and, for reasons examined below, they fell short in 1958–9.[51]

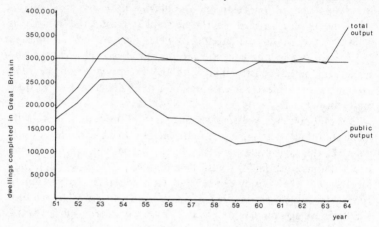

Graph 9·1 *Public sector and total completions of permanent dwellings in Great Britain 1951–64*

I would very much like to be able to show the breakdown of municipal production between the four basic categories of redevelopment, new building on green field sites, maintenance and rehabilitation of the existing council stock and rehabilitation of newly municipalised dwellings. However, the requisite data are not published by the DoE. Nor can one distinguish between new dwellings constructed in pursuit of slum clearance and those produced as net additions to the housing stock, the replacement and growth functions described in Chapters 1 and 2. Nevertheless we can be quite sure that the downward trend in total local authority output was accompanied by an upward trend in units completed on redevelopment sites and in overspill schemes, for the scale of slum clearance in Britain rose from 29,000 dwellings cleared in 1955 up to 71,000 units in 1964.

I have already pointed to the sharp downturn in total completions in 1958–9 and to this I now turn, for it is the manifestation of the only occasion in the entire 1951–64 period when cuts were made in local authority housing production because of macro-economic policy considerations.

The 1955 boom peaked nicely for the May general election and after the Conservatives were returned to power they began to introduce deflationary policies, first in July, then in the October budget, and again in February and April of 1956.[52] The economic effects of the Anglo-French military invasion of Egypt in that year were slight but a new crisis shook the markets in August–September 1957, a crisis which Dow describes as 'entirely one of confidence'.[53] There had been a bout of speculation against the pound in anticipation of it 'floating' below the existing rate of $2.80, in part stimulated by a substantial German payments surplus and by official British declarations on the dangers of 'wage inflation'. An immediate response was to raise Bank Rate to 7 per cent. Hard on this came from Peter Thorneycroft a decision to impose a 'ceiling' on public investment, to hold it constant in money terms at its 1957–8 level for two years. But as part of the package the local authority housing programme was to be slashed. Accordingly, a circular was issued by the MHLG in November 1957 which said that municipal expenditure on new housebuilding was to fall to 80 per cent of the existing level by 1959–60.[54] Table 9·2 shows that 1958 starts dropped by 30,000 below their 1956 and 1957 level.

However, because of a fall in world commodity prices there was a huge improvement in the balance of payments in 1957–8 and by mid-1958 cautious expansionary policies began to be pursued. Thorneycroft's 'ceiling' was dismantled. In part this was a response to high, regionally specific, unemployment. By November 1958, therefore, a new circular is recommending an expansion in municipal starts.[55] Table 9·2 shows that these leapt by 23,000 units in 1959 though the consequent effect on completions was diffuse. The April 1959 budget was strongly expansionary in a year which witnessed the third successive victory for the Conservative Party at the polls. In 1960 and 1961 starts were pushed back down again to their 1958 low point.

From the housing policy perspective the year 1957 was remarkable not only for the decision to cut state housebuilding but also for the Rent Act. This legislation permitted rent decontrol on properties with a relatively high rateable value and decontrol upon vacation for the rest. The objective was to make investment in existing rented property more attractive by raising rental income. This explosive device had a long fuse for the Tories but the immediate implications were ominous for those who found it difficult to compete in an open market 'for the permission to inhabit the earth'. This was the case with the pensioners. The general needs subsidy for one-bedroom flats to which we have already referred was intended to facilitate the displacement of the old from their homes as decontrol bit deep. There can be no doubt on this point for it was explicit ministerial policy![56]

I now wish to turn to the last three years of Conservative power, the period 1961–4, which can perhaps most aptly be described as the phase of policy reconsideration. The most striking innovation, although several years were to pass before it brought forth fruit, was the attempt through the 1961 and 1964 Housing Acts to stimulate the formation of the old-style housing associations and the new-style housing societies. The 1964 Act was also the first act to introduce improvement areas. Housing societies were intended to provide new unsubsidised accommodation for those who could not or did not wish to become owner-occupiers. The corollary was that local authority rental should be directed entirely at those fractions of the working-class forced by their financial circumstances to rely on subsidised accommodation. The 1961 White Paper, *Housing in England and Wales*, was perfectly explicit:[57]

> The Government's aim is to secure that there will be houses for
> sale and houses for rent in sufficient numbers to keep pace with
> the rising demand of a prospering society. As real incomes go up,
> more and more of this need, both for sale and to rent, should be
> met by private enterprise. For those who can neither afford to
> buy their own homes nor to pay economic rents there will be
> the 3½ million publicly-owned houses—increasing in number
> as local authorities continue to build for the needs which only
> they can meet.

From all this we can deduce that council tenants who were not judged to require a housing subsidy had no place being in the municipal sphere. The question was: how to expel them? The ready answer came: realistic rents! Realistic rents meant not only that subsidies should go only to the poor but that the ubiquitous council tenant with a Jaguar, that monster created by the Welfare State, should not be permitted to derive any advantage from the pooling of historic rents. As we saw in Chapter 7 it was for this reason that the 1961 Housing Act introduced a double-rate subsidy for new local authority housebuilding. Councils with relatively low HRA expenditures relative to gross values, the result of vigorous earlier building programmes, were to receive an annual subsidy per dwelling only one-third of that in other districts. The 1957 Rent Act aimed, in part, to drive the needy out of the private market and into the arms of the state; the 1961 Housing Act attempted to drive the affluent worker out of their council houses *into* the market.

The second innovation in the 1961 Act—the parallel with the legislation of 1935 is very clear—was to introduce greater flexibility in allocating subsidies for new council dwellings. Subsidies became payable on all houses approved for that purpose by the Minister. Local authorities would have to demonstrate a genuine need to build but henceforth subsidies could be paid not only for redevelopment schemes, old folks' flats and overspill but also for accommodation provided in the relief of overcrowding or unsatisfactory conditions in multi-occupied dwellings.

Another substantial shift in position, an early sign of the gathering storm, was that in 1964 the government permitted the authorities to have greater resort to the PWLB. Large-scale sales of short-dated stock by local authority treasurers who were convinced interest rates would fall was making the money supply more difficult to control. In order to check this, access to the Board was facilitated, reversing the post-1951 trend.

Finally, I should comment on the very strong upward trend in municipal starts after 1961. The economy's expansionary burst which began in 1959 came to an end by mid-1960. In spite of a slight recovery in the first half of 1961, deflationary policies introduced in that year brought with them a mild recession[58] and 1962 was a year of stagnation so that in October the Chancellor of the Exchequer, Reginald Maudling, announced a series of stimulatory measures including an increase in public expenditure for the following year.[59] The new course was already reflected in 1962's starts. Maudling's dash for growth continued into 1963, in which year real output exceeded that of 1962 by 5-6 per cent.[60]

In 1963 came the publication of a new White Paper: *Housing*.[61] The only real innovation it contained was to state the need for setting up a housing corporation to encourage the formation of housing societies. Of more immediate consequence was the decision to increase total British housing output to 350,000 completions each year. A few months later, with a certain insouciance, the Minister raised the objective to 400,000.[62]

Not only was this planned increase on the performance of earlier years compatible with a state-engineered boom but the Conservative Party was well aware that the housing question might prove to be their Achilles' Heel in the forthcoming election. The 1957 Rent Act had by 1964 reduced the number of controlled tenancies by half and had been accompanied by extremely serious abuses, especially in the 'Rachmanism' of London, yet it had brought no renewal in rental construction. The Labour Party seized on the huge decline in new building for rent to belabour their adversaries. In any case the consequence of the decisions taken in the White Paper was that by 1964, when the Tories were edged out of office, starts by the municipalities, these 'plannable instruments', were running at a higher level than in any year since 1955.

4 1964–70 : the birth, brief life and death of the national housing plan

The Labour government which took office in 1964 remained in power until 1970. It would be a mistake to characterise the development of their policy positions during thirteen years of opposition as a replication of Conservative housing strategy. The housing question had not yet been elevated to a level where it was 'above politics'. Nevertheless the social democrats had clearly converged towards the Tory perspective.

This convergence was as true for its omissions as its positive acts. There was no return to the principle embodied in the 1947 Town and Country Planning Act that local housing authorities could compulsorily purchase land at existing-use values, in spite of the powerful surge in land prices during 1964–70. Another example was the government's unwillingness to establish a municipalisation programme, a policy which had been one of the most important features of Labour's proposed social reforms in the 1950s, before its abandonment in 1961. Consequently the practice of partitioning housing renewal continued and the improvement of the existing stock still relied largely on the incentives of rent increases, grants and area-based rehabilitation. The system of 'regulated' and 'fair' rents on unfurnished lettings introduced by the 1965 Rent Act and the grant increases and general improvement areas of the 1969 Housing Act both make this clear.

The most dramatic shift in the Labourist posture was in their understanding of the complementary roles of council housing and owner-occupation. The steady increase in the scale of owner-occupation which had occurred since the 1920s would have necessitated any elected government, whatever its political complexion, accepting this sector's existence and continued growth. But the Labour government went much further than this: building for owner-occupation was not merely *one* of the forms of housing provision, it had become the *only* normal, natural, progressive form of tenure. Council housebuilding was to be provided only for those sections of the population for whom speculative development and mortgage finance were inefficacious. This was made crystal clear in the 1965 White Paper:[63]

But once the country has overcome its huge social problem of slumdom and obsolescence, and met the need of the great cities for more houses let at moderate rents, the programme of subsidised council housing should decrease. The expansion of the public programme now proposed is to meet exceptional needs; it is born partly of a short-term necessity, partly of the conditions inherent in modern urban life. The expansion of building for owner-occupation on the other hand is normal; it reflects a long-term social advance which should gradually pervade every region.

As an adjunct to the new line the government also pressed ahead with option mortgages and leasehold reform.

As we have seen, this attitude has always been closely associated with a view which insisted local authority subsidies should be channelled towards the needy, and this also was expressed in the 1965 White Paper. Two years later the first government-recommended rebate scheme was published.

Before I turn to consider the promise and the achievement of policy in these years let us look briefly at the macro-economic context in which it was set. The dominant characteristics of the period 1964-9 appear to be:

(i) an extremely slow average annual rate of growth in national output;

(ii) a recurring tendency for the balance of payments to run into deficit on the combined current and long-term capital accounts;

(iii) repeated crises of confidence in the par value of sterling with accompanying waves of selling which were checked, temporarily, either by recourse to substantial short-term borrowing from the central banks of the other advanced capitalist countries and the IMF or, in November 1967, by devaluation itself;

(iv) constant pressure from the Treasury and the City for public expenditure cuts. The rationale included three lines of argument which were not necessarily mutually exclusive: that such cuts would reduce the public sector borrowing requirement, thereby mitigating domestic credit expansion with a consequent favourable effect on the rate of price inflation; that cuts were necessary to free the physical and human resources required for investment, exports and import substitution; that cuts were deflationary through the employment and income multipliers and would thereby bring down imports;

(v) a series of neutral or deflationary budgets and mini-budgets;
(vi) policy under various guises for wage and salary restraint and price controls;
(vii) an ominous upward trend in unemployment and a very sharp rise in market rates of interest after 1966-7.

What, then, were the plans for state housing under the new Labour government and how successful were they in achieving them? Table 9·3 provides some of the output data we require to answer this question. Immediately we can see that local authority starts ran the most turbulent course, rising by 28,000 units in two years then falling back again by 60,000 units in the following three years. Let us look back at the plan which set this fading rocket on its trajectory.

Table 9·3 *Permanent dwelling output in Great Britain 1965-70*

Year	Local authority starts	Local authority completions	Private completions
1965	163,946	151,305	213,799
1966	166,644	161,435	205,372
1967	191,985	181,467	200,438
1968	170,948	170,214	221,993
1969	149,394	162,910	181,703
1970	131,506	157,067	170,304

Source: HSGB, HCS.

Soon after Labour's entry into office the civil service began work on a housing plan which many saw as complementary to the National Plan which the Department of Economic Affairs was preparing in order to chart the direction of Britain's growth in aggregate output. In spite of strong pressure in Cabinet from the Chancellor of the Exchequer, James Callaghan, for reductions in the public sector programme, starts were permitted to rise modestly in 1965 and by November the new national housing plan was ready: *The Housing Programme 1965 to 1970*.

The fundamental objective was to raise the rate of housebuilding so that by 1970 annual completions for the United Kingdom would be equal to 500,000 units, divided equally between the private and public sectors. In the paragraphs on 'the essential requirements for carrying through the programme' the document was replete with determined phrases on ensuring the availability of land, the modernisation of the construction industry and the re-organisation of the subsidy system but on two points it was silent and these were to prove to be its fatal weaknesses:

(i) speculative builders were only likely to construct at a rate of one-quarter million units per year if the flow of funds from the building societies to house-buyers was sufficient—in a context of rising dwelling prices—to finance the realisation of their output. The plan presented no means of control over the societies' flow of loans;

(ii) the public sector could build only as many dwellings as the Ministry of Housing and Local Government permitted. The capital finance required in real terms, let alone in money terms, would be greater than in any previous period of the country's history. Public expenditure on this scale could only be seriously contemplated if aggregate real growth was on target and if such outlays were not inconsistent with the Keynesian techniques which were employed to guide an economy as open, in terms of trade and payments, as that of the United Kingdom. These necessary conditions were not fulfilled.

The most important innovation which accompanied the plan was a new method of subsidy provision in the state sector. After 1959 unit costs of construction were increasing at more than 7 per cent per annum, in part as a result of the partial implementation of the Parker Morris recommendations for improved internal standards for council houses. Moreover there were widespread arguments that uncertainty about the level of rates of interest on capital loans was discouraging a vigorous building programme. In 1967, for the first time since the Addison Act, the value of state subsidies per dwelling was tied to the construction and finance cost of municipal housebuilding—just as it always had been for subsidies to owner-occupation—and the subsidy per dwelling was far, far greater than that laid down in the 1961 Act. The turn of the tide against system-built high-rise flats was concretised in the 1967 Act's termination of additional subsidies per flat for blocks exceeding six storeys in height. The fall in approved tenders for high flats after 1966 was precipitous.

Let us now turn, then, to the plan's outcome. This is summarised in the brutal lines of Graph 9·2. The starts data show that the turn towards misfortune took place in 1967–8. I have already described the general features of the travails of British capitalism at this time. In spite of these difficulties Table 9·3 shows clearly that local authority starts advanced very rapidly in the first two years of the plan period. Public sector housing was sheltered from the bleak wind of the earliest cuts because of the Prime Minister's personal commitment to 'a magnificent housing drive'[64] and because of the fall in private starts in 1965–6 with

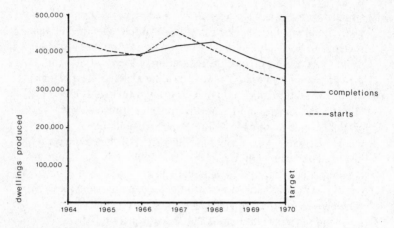

Graph 9·2 *Permanent dwelling starts and completions in the UK 1964–70*

the introduction of Selective Employment Tax and the shortage of mortgage finance from the building societies.[65] The scale of slum clearance rose from 71,000 units in 1964 to 86,000 units in 1968. Concurrently the MHLG had introduced an interesting scheme for allocating new starts on a needs basis and 130 local housing authorities, most of them in the great conurbations, whose needs were considered most critical, were given 'a complete green light' on new tender approvals.[66]

But in 1968 the national housing plan had its back broken. The pound sterling was an internationally accepted means of exchange and store of value. Any belief on the part of the market that it would be devalued vis-à-vis gold, or the dollar for example, immediately led to waves of selling. The continuing deficit in our balance of trade and on long-term capital account fed these fears and exposed the currency to destabilising speculation. In 1967 exports were stagnant, partly because of the recessionary phase in West Germany and the slow growth in US output. Imports, however, were much more buoyant than had been hoped for, especially since manufacturing output was actually falling. The Middle East war and the dock strikes exacerbated the underlying situation so that from the end of May 'sterling came under almost unremitting speculative pressure.'[67]

Sterling was devalued on 18 November and in the attempt to give the devaluation a pay-off the government's objectives were oriented towards shifting productive resources so as to raise private investment, to increase the volume of exports and to cut the volume of imports. The logic of this Keynesian world view was that public expenditure should be cut, including public outlays on wage goods if this were politically feasible. The axe fell in January 1968, when the government announced that it would cut the public sector housebuilding programmes of 1968 and 1969 by 16,500 units in each year.[68] Table 9·3 shows this was a vast understatement. The decision was undoubtedly facilitated by the fact that building society lending was at record levels in 1967 and 1968.[69]

The cut-backs were made the more effective by Conservative gains in the local elections of April 1967 and May 1968: they were only too ready to co-operate with Labour's new housing strategy. The Ronan Point disaster of May 1968 also slowed down the preparation of briefs and designs as authorities reappraised their attitude towards high-rise systems building.

The scrapping of the national housing plan in January 1968 was followed with extraordinary alacrity by the publication of that most notorious of White Papers, *Old Houses into New Homes*.[70] In summary, the document's substantive content was to describe the new phase of state-induced private, voluntary rehabilitation. In addition to this there was a promise that the scale of slum clearance would be increased and there was also an implication that general needs construction by the local housing authorities would be reduced. In retrospect we know that with the passing of the 1969 Housing Act, which followed the White Paper, many authorities began scaling down their clearance plans. *Old Houses into New Homes* marked a turning point away from public sector redevelopment to private rehabilitation with all the public expenditure savings that this implied and in that sense we must see it primarily as a response to the perceived change in priorities in macro-economic policy. By 1970 local authority starts were lower than in any year since 1962 and the national housing plan had been underfulfilled by 28 per cent.

5 Housing policy in the 1970s

There has probably been no other period in modern British history when the impact of broad macro-economic trends on the sphere of housing has been starker or more powerful than has been the case since the late

259

1960s. The difficulty which the political economist faces in treating this relationship is in giving a coherent account of what *did* happen at the level of the national and international economy. In comparison with this, the analysis of the housing question is child's play.

The macro-economic symptoms, at least, are incontrovertible: tremendous volatility in interest rates on new borrowing around a high average; rapid increases in money wages and domestic prices; a slow rate of growth in employment and a strong upward movement in the trend of unemployment; marked volatility in the balance of payments both on capital and current accounts; slow growth in real gross domestic product at factor cost: an unprecedented rise in the foreign currency price of imported oil; a substantial shift downwards in the value of sterling vis-à-vis the currencies of the other mature capitalist countries; a substantial increase in money terms in public expenditure, the public sector borrowing requirement and the money supply.

The central impact of the crisis on the local authority housing sector was in raising the unit prices of land and construction output; in lifting the rate of interest on new and outstanding debt; and in persuading the government and senior civil servants at particular turning points in economic policy that state housing production had to be cut back (or held down) in order to reduce both effective demand and the public sector borrowing requirement. An indirect articulation between the national economy and municipal housing was the effect of the crisis on private housebuilding which then, in its turn, imposed shocks on the council sector. Let me now turn to consider developments in housing policy in the 1970s, cross-referring to the evolving crisis wherever it seems most appropriate.

Table 9·4 provides the British data on dwelling starts and completions in 1971–6. It shows that the Conservative administration which came to power in June 1970 under the leadership of Edward Heath was quite content to allow the decline in municipal starts which began in 1968 to continue through to 1973, their lowest point since the war. This attitude must have been underpinned by the sharp rise in unit construction costs which seems to have taken place from about 1969, particularly when we remember that costs and subsidies were tightly linked by the 1967 subsidy legislation.

Tory philosophy towards the respective roles of state housing and private housing appears to me to have been broadly the same as that adopted after the mid-1950s and which I have described in Section 3. But under Peter Walker, the Secretary of State at the newly created

Table 9·4 *Permanent dwelling output in Great Britain 1971–6*

Year	Local authority		Private sector	
	Starts	Completions	Starts	Completions
1971	114,650	134,000	207,438	191,612
1972	99,583	104,553	227,964	196,457
1973	87,290	88,148	215,748	186,628
1974	120,894	103,279	105,931	140,865
1975	133,661	129,883	149,128	150,752
1976	124,447	129,202	154,652	152,181

Source: HCS.

Department of the Environment, the Conservatives set out to be much more systematic in implementing their policy objectives, particularly towards rent and subsidies. This was the origin of the July 1971 White Paper, *Fair Deal for Housing* and the 1972 Housing Finance Act which followed it. The new legislation sought to place council rents on a free market basis, to tie subsidies to reckonable expenditure, and to introduce subsidies for rent rebates to tenants with low incomes. The new method of rent determination and the channelling of a proportion of the subsidy total to the poor was intended to rationalise Exchequer revenue outlays, to reduce them below what they would otherwise have been and to raise sharply the rents of the higher wage strata of the working class so that they were more likely to become owner-occupiers. Access to owner-occupation was encouraged in a number of other ways, such as facilitating the sale of council houses.

The Labour retreat from redevelopment which began in 1968 and the apparent 'switch' to rehabilitation continued to be vigorously pursued by the DoE. *Better homes: the next priorities*, the White Paper of June 1973, presented the arguments for this persuasively. Slum clearance peaked in 1971 with 87,000 units demolished and by 1976 the number had been cut to 51,000 (see Table 5·4). As we have seen, the new philosophy was accompanied by a huge fall in the number of local authority starts: they declined at an average annual compound rate of 12 per cent in the six years after 1967.

It must be recognised that the 'switch' was accompanied by a considerable expansion in rehabilitation grants to local authorities. These rose from 59,000 in 1970 up to 188,000 in 1973. But three years later they had slumped again to 75,000. The experience with municipalisation was similar. The data for England suggest that the Conservatives, in a sharp reversal of their former policies, permitted about 7000 acquisitions in 1972–3 and two years later this number had increased to 26,000 annually. But thenceforth the programme was reduced.

Thus we can see that what most commentators presented as a welcome switch from redevelopment to rehabilitation, from axe to scalpel, was in fact a retreat from slum clearance accompanied by a huge cut-back in new local authority building, with only a temporary surge in the scale of rehabilitation in the private and municipal sectors. The 'switch' in fact constituted a remarkable withdrawal of construction resources from housing renewal. This withdrawal was not counterbalanced by the expansion of the housing association movement, which was signalled in the April 1973 White Paper *Widening the Choice*, although from now on new building by the voluntary movement, save for the renewal context, really began to take on substantial proportions.

Let us now move back again to the wider economic context. In both 1970 and 1971 the balance of payments was unusually favourable. Moreover in 1970 there had been a remarkable increase in real disposable income as the total wage bill in money terms rose by about 12 per cent. In spite of this, output growth was sluggish for the year-on-year increase in real output at factor cost in 1970 was only about 1½ per cent.[71] The budget of 1971 included a wide range of tax reductions and on 14 April the Bank of England published *Competition and Credit Control* which indicated that as from September a new regime of more flexible controls would be introduced. All existing ceiling limits on lending would be removed although the banks and finance houses would be required to observe a fixed minimum reserve ratio. At the same time interest rates had been falling for eighteen months from their very high level of 1969 so that by the autumn of 1971 Bank Rate stood at 'only' 5 per cent. This was the period when the real rate of interest became negative for the first time since 1951. The budget, the new expansionary phase in monetary policy, the fall in interest rates—all went to stimulate the most spectacular boom in property development and property investment since the war.

In particular the building societies benefited very substantially from the fall in interest rates. By reducing relatively slowly the mortgage rate they charged to home-owners, they were able to build up a very valuable interest rate differential with respect to the other institutional borrowers with whom they competed in the money market. As a result there was a very strong inflow of funds and the societies' willingness to on-lend quickly brought both a great leap forward in speculative building as well as soaring increases in land and house prices. The value of their loans for house purchase increased from £2 billion in 1970 to £3·6 billion in 1972. In the same two-year period private housing starts rose by 38 per cent from 165,000 to 228,000 units and the index of the average price of new dwellings purchased with building society funds rose from 100 in 1970 to 144 in 1972 to 198 in 1973.

We have already seen in Chapter 3 that this period brought with it a rise in land costs at such an inflationary rate that the proportion of state housing capital expenditure which went towards the site element rose from 11 per cent in 1970 to 19 per cent in 1973. This was undoubtedly a side effect of the property boom I have been describing. We have also seen that unit local authority construction costs rose with great rapidity in this period, particularly in 1972 and 1973 in indexed terms. Once again the state of demand for the multiple products of the construction industry was in part responsible as contractors pushed up the minimum profit margin they were willing to accept in tenders for local authority work. An additional and powerful determinant of the explosion of costs was the rapid increase in hourly wage rates and materials prices in an economy where inflation was increasingly the centre of government anxiety.

At the beginning of 1972 unemployment was at its highest level since the winter of 1947 and so the budget was strongly reflationary. The Conservative commitment to curbing public expenditure led them to seek growth through the expansion of consumer expenditure. This was in part the cause of a rapid deterioration in the balance of payments so that, once again, the structure of market interest rates was subjugated to the ebb and flow of speculation in sterling, which had been floating since August 1971. In June 1972 a run on the pound had been followed by an effective devaluation of 7 per cent and Bank Rate raised from 5 up to 6 per cent. In October Bank Rate was replaced by minimum lending rate, based on the rate of interest earned on the government's sales of Treasury bills. MLR was set at 7½ per cent and raised to 9 per cent two months later. The great surge in interest rates was well under way. In November tripartite talks on prices and incomes had broken down and a freeze was imposed on pay, prices, rents and dividends.[72] Council rents were excluded precisely because the Housing Finance Act of July 1972 was passed in order to raise these sharply, thereby reducing the relative level of government subsidies.

In the two years 1972 and 1973 gross domestic product had grown by almost 8 per cent, much of this growth concentrated in the latter

263

part of 1972 and the early months of 1973. But by mid-1973 inflation had risen to an annual rate of about 9 per cent and the balance of payments was in deficit. In May the government announced a number of expenditure cuts. Not fortuitously, *Better Homes : the Next Priorities* was published a month later. By now local authority starts were at their lowest for some thirty-five years. In July, with the pound sinking in face of speculative pressure, MLR was raised by the astonishing amount of four percentage points up to 11½ per cent. Market interest rates were by now higher than at any time since at least World War I. The downward shift of the pound fuelled the inflationary process yet it had not ended the foreign payments crisis; indeed it may have exacerbated the short-run trading position. In 1973 as a whole there was a most serious current account deficit, in part the result of a 65 per cent rise in non-oil commodity prices, the highest ever recorded.

The sharp upward shift in rates of interest from October 1972 had first eroded, then reversed the favourable interest rate differential of the building societies, particularly with the government urging them to hold down the rate they charged to mortgagors. In the second quarter of 1973 there was a slump in the number of new mortgages granted. As the year passed the demand for new housing by owner-occupiers increasingly gave cause for alarm. The huge price rises had soaked up the increased value of mortgage funding and higher interest rates on these high-priced units made mortgage repayments doubly burdensome, particularly for first-time buyers. At the same time the increases in unit construction costs and interest charges on working capital was eating into contractors' profits. The sword fell in the following year, 1974, when private starts sank to their lowest level since the mid 1950s in what was probably the sharpest reduction in private building in the peace-time history of British housing.

At the end of a year to remember, the OPEC leaders decided to quadruple oil prices. This was followed at home by the miners' strike of February 1974 and Heath's consequential decision to go to the country. No party secured an overall majority in the general election but as the largest Parliamentary group the Labour Party formed a new government in March 1974.

With memories still fresh of the failures of 1964 –70, the Wilson Cabinet firmly turned its collective face away from a national housing plan or programme. What followed was a series of ad hoc housing measures set within a philosophy which converged ever more closely with that of the Conservatives.

The first act of the government was to freeze all residential rents for the rest of the year as part of its counter-inflationary policy. The March budget was mildly deflationary but an exception was made of local authority housing construction, primarily because of the collapse of the private sector's activity. The authorities were encouraged to raise their rate of building and to buy completed but unsold houses from the speculative developers. As Table 9·4 shows, municipal starts rose from 87,000 in 1973 to 134,000 in 1975. While this was happening work was under way on new legislation to replace the Housing Finance Act and this received the Royal Assent in 1975 as the Housing Rents and Subsidies Act. Council rents were once again to be based on historic cost levels and the authorities were permitted to determine their own rate fund contribution. Subsidies continued to be based on reckonable expenditure and the system of rebated rents with its own specific subsidy was also retained. The Act was seen as an interim measure, whilst new policies were under consideration within the context of a housing finance review launched in 1975 by the new Secretary of State at the DoE, Anthony Crosland.

In 1974–5 the national economy was in the most critical condition. The rate of inflation was well into double figures. The balance of payments was deeply in deficit, much of it because of our inelastic demand for imported energy sources. Unemployment followed a strong upward trend to levels not seen since the 1930s and by the beginning of 1976 had reached 1·2 million persons or 5·2 per cent of the labour force. In these conditions the government's MLR was essentially a device for regulating the flow of short-term foreign capital. The growth of gross domestic product was actually negative in 1974 and in both years the public sector deficit was huge and unplanned. Without it the slump would really have assumed awesome proportions.

The effect of the shift in market interest rates since late 1972 has already been set out in Table 6·4. The average rate on new borrowing from the PWLB rose from 6·9 per cent in 1971–2 to 11·6 per cent in 1975–6 and in the same period the rate on outstanding debt rose from 6·4 per cent to more than 10 per cent. At the same time as this was taking place, we have seen that the number of starts in the council sector increased in two years by 47,000 units above the nadir of 1973. The unit prices of the new dwellings had been driven up so fiercely by the general and relative price inflation of the 1970s that even these modest absolute output levels of less than 130,000 units per annum had major capital expenditure implications. These capital outlays at high interest rates reflected itself in a violent increase in debt interest, which in England and Wales rose from £556 million in 1972-3 up to £1180 million in 1975-6. Because the debt charges were directly linked to Exchequer subsidies the latter rose in the same period from less than £300 million to almost £1 billion whilst the subsidy-expenditure ratio soared from 28 per cent up to 52 per cent, even though rents were increasing in the five year period after October 1971 by 12 per cent per annum.

Price inflation in the capitalist countries since the late 1960s had brought about a renewed interest in the relation between the money supply and changes in the price level. There can be no doubt that sophisticated versions of the quantity theory of money were now gaining much wider currency in banking circles, in the IMF and in the Treasury. (In its most extreme form it is argued that if the government permits only a modest expansion in the supply of money all the other policy objectives will follow—in time.) This line of reasoning began to express itself as a belief that targets for domestic credit expansion (DCE) should be at the centre of government's macro-economic policy.

In terms of financial accounting DCE is identically equal to the public sector borrowing requirement (PSBR) less public sector borrowing from the private sector plus bank lending in sterling to private and overseas sectors. PSBR, in brief, is equal to the excess of public current and capital expenditure over taxation receipts. From all this it follows that the strengthening of monetarist theories in policy formulation at a time of high inflation in itself is very likely to be accompanied by a strong prejudice in favour of tight controls over public expenditure.

The year 1976 began with the Labour government, in its Letter of Intent to the IMF, for the first time setting a DCE target. At the same time it was seeking an agreement with the trade union movement on a second stage in prices and incomes policy. This was cemented in May after the government in the previous month had announced tax cuts said to total £1·3 billion. But by this point the pound was once again in serious difficulties. We were still running a huge current account deficit (of £1·5 billion for the year as a whole) and sterling had been declining with respect to the dollar ever since the Smithsonian agreement in December 1971 had set the parity at £1 : $2·6. By December 1976 the rate had fallen to £1 : $1·68. In March to April there was a particularly striking collapse of the floating rate which was eventually staved off with an agreement in June 1976 by the international bankers to make available standby credits of $5 billion. The full price of this agreement became apparent only in the following month when the Chancellor of the Exchequer, Denis Healey, announced cuts of £1 billion in previous public spending estimates for 1977-8. Of this total £150 million was to be hacked out of housing expenditure by the local authorities, including resource cut-backs in municipal housing construction. Healey's rationale was that PSBR had to be cut and—like Cripps— that sufficient resources had to be available for manufacturing industry to achieve export-led growth, a fascinating insight into an economy with 1·2 million unemployed and extensive excess capacity. (In passing it is worth remarking at this point on an extraordinary periodicity—I hesitate to call it a cycle—in cuts in local authority housing construction since the war for the purposes of macro-economic policy. There is a clear eight–ten year pulse: August 1947, November 1957, January 1968 and July 1976.)

The aftermath of the July measures can be seen in Table 9·5. Resource expenditure, largely the districts' capital expenditure on municipalisation and new building, fell by 23 per cent in the two years after 1975-6, at a time when private starts were still only making a faltering recovery from the amazing slump of 1974.

Table 9·5 *Resource and gift expenditure on local authority housing in Britain 1972-3 to 1977-8 in £m at 1977 survey prices*

Year	1972-3	1973-4	1974-5	1975-6	1976-7	1977-8
Resource expenditure[a]	1844	2029	2324	2317	2115	1781
Gift expenditure[b]	754	1070	1535	1564	1687	1670
Ratio of resource to gift expenditure	2·45	1·90	1·51	1·48	1·25	1·07

Source: The Government's Expenditure Plans 1978-9 to 1981-2, Volume II, London, 1978.
a The total of what the Treasury calls local authority housing investment.
b The total of central government subsidies and rate fund contributions to local authority housing and rent rebates.

The table also introduces the concept of the ratio between resource and gift expenditure on municipal housing. From 1972 to 1973 the ratio follows a steep downward path from 2·45 to 1·07 so that by

1977–8 we had arrived at the absurd position in local authority housing finance where about as much was spent in state subsidies as was spent on dwelling production. The crisis of the 1970s can thus be seen from the following perspective: the international context of the British crisis of managed capitalism led to the introduction of monetary measures which automatically generated a vast swelling in state gift expenditure whilst the continued pursuit of an increasingly monetarist policy led to a massive cut-back in state resource expenditures.

The peak of the money crisis was reached in October 1976, when a second collapse in the floating rate led to an increase in MLR to 15 per cent. In December, as the IMF discussed a further $3·9 billion loan, a further round of public expenditure cuts totalling £1 billion were announced. This time housing was exempted. After the end of 1976 interest rates once again demonstrated their volatility and they fell continuously through to the autumn of 1977. In large measure this was explained by the current account surplus of the second half of 1977 in a year which witnessed a growing inflow of North Sea oil, stagnant real total output and falling real personal disposable income as Stage II of the social contract took effect.

6 The Green Paper of 1977

The housing finance review which we have seen was initiated by Crosland in 1975 was not published until after his death. It appeared in June 1977 as *Housing Policy: a Consultative Document*. It was followed by three technical volumes which, in my view, constitute the clearest and most sophisticated contribution to the narrowly economic analysis of the housing question heretofore published by the civil service. In what follows I wish both to comment on the basic philosophy of the Green Paper and also to summarise the main conclusions it arrives at specifically on local authority housing.

What first should strike the reader are the omissions—what was left unsaid. The document gives us no analysis of the land market nor the production of dwellings nor the location of new developments nor the sources of local authority capital finance. The major interests of the text are in what I have called questions of consumption. In that sense it is not a housing policy at all, but merely some elements of such a policy. The fact that so much was excluded implies that there is no commitment to change in these spheres and a conservative position on land, the organisation of production and municipal capital finance implies an essentially conservative strategy towards distribution and exchange. We should also note that scant attention is paid to the privately rented sector as this is dealt with in a separate review. Similarly the Scottish situation is covered in another document.

An associated weakness is the hesitant way in which the question of housing need is dealt with. An attack is made on the straw man of the central state laying down in detail what the local authority should be doing[73] and the point is made repeatedly that the housing problem manifests itself in quite different ways up and down the country. When this is allied with the facile treatment of housing need and stock obsolescence it soon emerges that 'a national approach' may be positively harmful.[74] This line produces a housing policy document which offers absolutely no indication of the scale of resource allocation, private and public, over time that is necessary to deal with our housing problems nor of how the existing system of finance, production and consumption will match the changing pattern of human need. The government abrogates its responsibilities. The hidden thread in the skein of *this* argument is the public expenditure crisis, although the paper never whispers a word on the massive cuts under way as it was being written.

The anodyne text of the paper assures us that the great majority of households dwell in perfectly decent homes and its bland conservatism indicates that policy should essentially be a tidying-up operation. So it comes as no surprise to the reader that the main thrust of the argument is that no radical change is required in the main policy area with which it deals at length, the question of the structure of subsidies.[75]

On the rare occasions when the prose of the Green Paper becomes lyrical it is always with reference to home-ownership. We are coolly informed that for most people owner-occupation is 'a basic and natural desire'.[76] Now this is plain verbiage. To take the specific pattern of wants of a part of the population, even if it be the majority, at a certain time in a certain society and to elevate it to the level of a fundamental trait of the human personality is psychological nonsense. The reason why so many families prefer owner-occupation is not the manifestation of some drive folded deep in the cortex but because home ownership has offered complete control of one's living space (as long as the mortgage is repaid!), very considerable mobility in the case of the wish to change house or job, built forms of relatively low density, in most cases with gardens, and the promise of a financially appreciating asset. Finally, owner-occupation is the chief means in our society whereby social prejudice in all its forms, the bane of the British working class, can realise itself in a social and spatial distancing from that half of the population systematically excluded by the building society movement from the provision of credit for house purchase.

The glorification of home ownership in Command 6851 leads to certain policy conclusions: the continuation of the existing subsidy system including tax relief at higher than basic rates; the need for measures to provide easier access to owner-occupation for people who 'find that they fall just short of current requirements for a mortgage';[77] the necessity to stabilise the flow of mortgage finance, about which the paper is prematurely self-congratulatory, and to widen the sources of finance to include life and pension funds; and the stimulation of building for sale by local authorities.

What, then, is seen to be the function of the local housing authorities? Here the philosophy developed since the time of Chamberlain at last takes a central position in Labour's strategy. Aspiration to home ownership is an inherent desire but since this is blocked for so many by the system of mortgage finance and as the decline of the private rental sector continues, the council sector is still required to fulfil the residual function of providing for those who cannot help themselves. 'The public sector will continue to play the major part in dealing with the most pressing housing problems. Public resources must be used economically and efficiently, and applied where most needed . . . In the course of the next decade a growing number of local authorities should have very largely dealt with their backlog of bad housing conditions. As this occurs, the overall level of public sector housing investment should decline in response to changing circumstances.'[78]

However, the decline of private rental and the growth of municipal difficult-to-let dwellings and whole estates does have one positive policy result. The authorities are strongly encouraged to build for categories of household of a far broader range than has traditionally been the case. In particular, improved access is recommended for the elderly, the disabled, the handicapped, young and middle-aged single persons, one-parent families, mobile workers, apprentices and students.

Perhaps the most genuinely innovative proposal in the Green Paper is that for locally determined housing strategy and investment programmes, although this is unfortunately coupled with the absence of a national strategy for matching housing resource allocations to housing need: 'each local authority should draw up a strategic statement backed by statistics on the local housing stock and households and expected changes over the next few years, and a programme for its own proposed housing investment.'[79] The housing investment programmes (HIPS)

> will set out the authority's proposals for investment in the whole range of its housing activities for the following four years, within the context of the expected activity of other public housing bodies in the area and private housebuilders. The HIPS will be revised each year. This system will make it possible to identify the most urgent problems, and to allocate resources to each authority on the basis of informed judgements of priorities.[80]

Investment is defined as clearance and demolition, new building, acquisition, renovation, conversion, home loans and the making of improvement grants to private householders.

But what the rest of the document makes plain is that the HIPS will be placed under the most careful scrutiny for their public expenditure implications. Gradual renewal is promoted as a strategic demand, as it properly should be in the great majority of districts. But allied with this is the absence of any serious consideration of the role of municipalisation in local strategies, the abandonment of opposition to council house sales save under quite specific circumstances, the intimation that council rehabilitation budgets be spent only on basic improvements and there is the ominous phrase that 'The Department of the Environment and the Welsh Office will consult local authority representatives about the scope for introducing greater flexibility into public sector ("Parker Morris") housing standards.'[81]

In the sections on rent subsidies the document introduces a useful distinction between general assistance which 'meets some part of housing costs without regard to an individual householder's ability to pay'[82] and, by implication, needs assistance which would include SBC funding for the mortgage repayments of distressed home-owners, rent allowances in the private sector and rebates. With respect to rebates, the government proposes that the Exchequer should in future meet 90 per cent of the total rather than the present 75 : 25 division between the centre and the districts.

With respect to Exchequer subsidies to municipal housing revenue accounts as a whole, two matters of concern are clearly dominant in the consciousness of the Department. The first is the continuing variation between authorities in revenue expenditure per dwelling which, legitimately, is taken to be associated with substantial variations in their

271

subsidy needs.[83] (We have already seen that the 1961 Act with its low-level subsidy was the first, if hamfisted, attempt to deal with this aspect of local authority housing finance.) These were the same grounds for the Housing Centre Trust's interesting proposal for a national rent pool, which is the subject of a quite unconvincing critique in the Green Paper.[84]

The Department's second concern is that of the relation between subsidies, rents and incomes should the trend of interest rates stabilise or fall. Our analysis of front-loading showed clearly that even with stable interest rates, the real burden of the debt charge falls rapidly over time.

The Department clearly believe that the interim arrangements of the 1975 subsidy legislation in a post-bunching era will generate a flow of subsidies higher than they will deem necessary, particularly if the scale of local authority housing development is kept low, although this aspect is not voiced. With a stable interest rate trend, 'Additional costs arising from new investment would be very largely offset by the fall in the real value of payments on existing housing debt. With falling interest rates, the amount of general assistance required would decline in real terms.'[85]

The government's proposals for the provision of Exchequer subsidies to the municipalities reflect these concerns. They are sketched out only briefly but basically turn on a suggested annual review of each authority's housing revenue account. The idea is that the extra 'admissible' revenue expenditure in the following year would be settled in consultation with the authority and that an appropriate increase in the local income from rents plus rate fund contribution would also be agreed. Where the extra costs fall short of the increased local income, the existing subsidy would be cut by that difference, and vice versa, where extra income falls short of extra costs. The internal balance of the local contribution would be determined locally. As a guide to what would constitute a reasonable annual increase in that contribution 'the Government consider that over a run of years rents should keep broadly in line with changes in money incomes.'[86] Clearly this system combines great flexibility in its treatment of costs alongside a very much closer control of the periphery by the centre.

If interest rates remain relatively low, authorities with small building programmes will find their Exchequer subsidies very substantially reduced. Here the document, for the first time in any state paper, begins to discuss the equity of the general assistance provided to local authority tenants and to owner-occupiers. The suggestion is made that perhaps there should be some minimum level of general assistance to the housing revenue account related to the rate of mortgage tax relief.[87] In this volume I do not at any point try to make comparisons of the subsidy flow to each tenure sector but I must point out that all existing studies—including the work in the Green Paper's technical volumes—contain a fundamental flaw in their method. For all of them base their comparisons, in a more or much less sophisticated manner, on the flow of assistance to households. This does not provide a proper basis for judgment on equity which needs to be founded not on money receipts but on what the resident pays, after subsidy, for what he gets. Payments are equal to gross rents and mortgage repayments less subsidy. What the resident gets reflects both use-values of dwellings he occupies in his adult life as well as the asset acquisition which takes place only in the case of the owner-occupier. Research along these lines is an essential starting point for discussions of equity in the field of general housing assistance.

Perhaps the most positive aspect of Command 6851 concerns questions of management, maintenance and tenant control.[88] The paper argues strongly for advances in the ability of the council tenant to exercise greater control over his internal and external environment. Such changes might include: greater security of tenure; improved tenancy agreements; the termination of unnecessarily restrictive management practices; the publication of allocation schemes; the tenant's right to carry out internal improvements; the right to sub-let without lodgers' charges; tenant participation in the framing of estate rules and regulations; and some control by tenants over the allocation of voids. Perhaps, for the tenants, the least attractive proposition in this sphere is that they should take over estate-wide management functions. Nor should we be blind to the fact that the basis for some of these measures in part lies with the escalating trend in unit management and maintenance costs in housing revenue accounts.

All policy documents reflect the place and time of their publication. *Housing Policy* is no exception. Both in what it does not contain and what it does contain it is deeply conservative. For it is the philosophical product of a political party whose national leadership has shifted to an understanding of the priorities and structures of housing policy which plainly stands at the terminus of the long tradition of Mond, Chamberlain, Macmillan, Sandys and Walker. Peter Shore, the Labour Cabinet and the highest echelons of the civil service have at last succeeded in taking the politics out of the housing question. Moreover it is a document which appears at a time when the hegemony exercised by the

Treasury in economic policy analysis requires the most stringent control over public expenditure, particularly over the allocation of state resources to the production of a subsidised wage-good.

TEN

State housing and state policy in historical retrospect

1 Introduction

This analysis of the historical and contemporary experience of state housing in Britain is now largely complete. In carrying it through, the greater part of the work has consisted of empirical propositions specific to a certain time and place, such as the views of a particular minister, the effects of a given Act of Parliament, and the data series for a defined variable. The objective of this chapter is to move back from the specificities of the experience so as to present the entire history in a far more abstract way. This more distanced perspective draws on the 'synthesis' section of Parts One and Two of the volume which already contain in them most of the concepts I wish to employ here.

But before beginning, some introductory remarks are necessary on the conceptual framework within which I locate the origins and nature of policy. The policy which we are considering is that of the British state, more specifically those policies which, in the final analysis, are formulated and implemented by the legislative and executive institutions of government. It is not possible, then, to theorise about housing policy without at the same time incorporating the contours of a theory of the state. Such theory is usually implicit in the books on housing policy under which the shelves of our great libraries groan. My intention is to make an explicit statement.[1]

The starting point is Marx's concept of the capitalist mode of production which, in brief, refers to a set of property relationships within the sphere of the production of goods and services. In this mode, in its pure form, the *means of production* in the economic activities of primary production, manufacturing and distribution and the finance necessary to employ them, are owned and controlled privately by capital, that is, by the class of capitalists. Capital also purchases the *labour power* of the working class, whose only means of existence is the income from this labour. Capital then sells the produced goods and services at a price which exceeds the sum of its outlays on labour and the means of production and thereby appropriates a surplus, net profit. Of course, it is extremely unlikely that when we examine any specific society the 'pure' mode would hold universal sway. Existing property relationships may include sectors which are relics of previously dominant modes of production such as feudalism, or productive activities which are outside the cash nexus, such as domestic labour.

The classes in a society are defined by reference to these property relationships and, in the case of Britain, capital has been the dominant class for several hundred years. The principal interest of this class and the fractions of which it is composed is the accumulation of capital both at home and abroad.

The most important feature of *laissez-faire* capitalism is that in the very process of its development it creates certain self-destructive trajectories, both at the political and economic levels. The dominant class comes to perceive this and therefore embarks on the reconstruction of the existing institutions and powers of the state in order to seek to resolve these contradictions.

Included amongst the functions of the state in maintaining the economic and political stability of the social formation and at a more mundane level in promoting the accumulation of capital in a direct manner are:

(i) social investment: expenditures made to provide the large-scale infrastructure necessary for production, thereby raising the productivity of a given quantity of labour;

(ii) reproduction of labour: expenditures made in order to ensure the supply of a trained, healthy work-force where and when it is required by capital;

(iii) ideological legitimation: the operations of the state through the research and education system, and the state-controlled media, to inculcate in the population an acceptance of the legitimacy of the social order;

(iv) material legitimation: state activities in the production and distribution of wage-goods which raise the living standards of the working class for the same purpose as (iii) above. Ideological and material legitimation together constitute the organisation of consent by the state;

(v) internal repression: the physical suppression of internal opposition using the police, the judiciary and, if necessary, the armed forces.

It is worth remarking that any single specific activity of the state may serve more than one of these functions.

The relation of the state to the dominant class requires further elaboration. The simple instrumentalist or diabolist perspective is that the state exists merely as a tool of capital, as an apparatus formed to carry out the instructions of the capitalist class. To repeat the formulation of the *Communist Manifesto*: 'The executive of the modern state is but a committee for managing the common affairs of the whole bourgeoisie.'[2] This view must be rejected with respect to modern Britain. An alternative position is to emphasise the relative autonomy of the state from capital. This involves an exposition of the objective role the state plays in the maintenance of the social order and in underpinning the accumulation of capital whilst recognising that it constantly seeks to appear to be above class interest and that it does not act at the beck and call of capital. Relative autonomy is likely to be greater when the capitalist class contains fractions between which there is an equilibrium of power. Poulantzas writes:[3]

> the capitalist state assumes a relative autonomy with regard to the bourgeoisie . . . For this relative autonomy allows the state to intervene not only in order to arrange compromises vis-à-vis the dominated classes, which, in the long run, are useful for the actual economic interests of the dominant classes or fractions; but also (depending on the concrete conjuncture) to intervene against the long-term economic interests of *one or other* fraction of the dominant class: for such compromises and sacrifices are sometimes necessary for the realization of their political class interests.

What bearing on this does the growth of working-class power have? The last hundred years in Britain have witnessed the rise of the organised trade union movement and, since the turn of the century, the development of a party which purported to be 'the party of the working man'. As a result, working-class representatives have entered the institutions of the state on a substantial scale, both through membership of the legislature (the Houses of Parliament), through membership of the government itself, and finally through a place in the central locus of governmental power, the Cabinet. Undoubtedly the outcome of these advances has been to strengthen the state's autonomy relative to the dominant class. However, the entry of the proletariat into the inner circle of state power has certainly not yet constituted a challenge to capital as a whole, although individual fractions may have suffered. This is because the ideology of the Parliamentary Labour Party and even more so of Labour Cabinets has been predominantly a social-democratic one,

one based on conceptions of the fruitful co-operation of capital and labour to their mutual benefit.

It goes without saying that few of these representatives subjectively held a diabolist view of their role: they did not see themselves as the tool of the capitalist class. For the majority Parliament and government were a path whereby both to pursue their own ambitions and to secure substantial material advances for their class. Yet, objectively, the gains they have achieved, because they were locked into a social-democratic world view, have been entirely consistent with the functions of the state under capitalism laid out above, particularly those of reproduction and material legitimation.

Considering the intermittent presence of working-class representation in government and the influence on all governments of the trade union movement, I suggest that the term 'ruling class' is no longer scientifically accurate in characterising capital. Nevertheless, taking into account the power exercised by the capitalist class in the sphere of the private production of goods and services and in their control of the ideological products of privately-owned newspapers and television, given the class affiliation of the state elite, and considering the strength of social democratic philosophy within all sections of the labour movement, it does seem to me to be correct to describe capital as the hegemonic class.

In the discussion so far I have implicitly been appraising the state at the central level. The state at the local level fulfils the same functions. The main difference is that the elected representatives at the periphery more frequently include people either of a clearly socialist orientation or, in contrast, men and women with strong landed or petty bourgeois interests. As a result some councils, the 'red enclaves', may attempt to pursue against the central state—particularly when a Conservative government is in power—socialist policies, notwithstanding that they would recognise that socialism in one district is a chimera; or, in the second case, a local council may move slowly on central measures aimed at securing material advances for the working class.

With these introductory comments completed, let us now turn to consider the evolution of state housing in Britain since the second half of the nineteenth century.

2 Housing policy in historical retrospect

By now I have written at such great length that it becomes possible to write with brevity. The following theses encapsulate my views on state policy with respect to state housing.

1   Production provides the material basis of human life. The fundamental requisites of the process of production are nature, human labour and the produced means of production, that is, materials and the instruments of work. The capacity to labour must itself be brought into existence, developed and maintained both within the family and outside it. This activity, the repro-duction of labour power, therefore embraces both domestic labour and certain categories of production itself. By the term reproductive production I understand human activities which fall in the sphere of production and which, at the same time, are reproductive. Amongst these are included the production of shelter, food, clothing, and education and health care services necessary for the reproduction of the capacity to labour.

Thus the construction of dwellings is one of the major activities of reproductive production and it follows that in capitalist society the analysis of the housing question must comprehend both the building of housing as a specific area of commodity production for profit *and* the consumption of housing as a prerequisite for commodity production in general.

2   The ability of the working class to purchase wage-goods rests on the productivity of its labour and the scale of the appropriation of its product by the propertied classes.

3   Because of the disparity between the price of a dwelling and the wages or salaries of labour (which itself reflects the material fact that dwellings cannot be consumed piecemeal), it has never been possible for workers to purchase a house or flat outright from their income. Even when workers save, in most cases they will wish to set up a separate household before these savings have accumulated sufficiently to make outright purchase possible. As a result, in modern Britain at least, the working class has relied on rented accommodation or on borrowing money at interest to finance house purchase.

4   In comparison with other wage-goods, the use-value which can be purchased through housing rent is reduced by the relative importance of ground rent, by repayment ratios typically exceeding unity because of the slow turnover of rentier capital and by the relatively slow rate of growth of labour productivity in the production of dwellings.

5   The level of wages before the First World War and the price of rental accommodation led to a situation in which the use-values of workers' dwellings were so low, particularly in the case of the poorer strata, that their residential environment and mode of life created a series of contradictions within the British social formation through the ravages of disease against all classes, through the reduced productivity of the work-force and through criminal violence and social discontent.

6   As a response to these contradictions the state intervened in a number of ways in shaping the construction of the urban environment. The failure of private enterprise housebuilding made it imperative for the state to stimulate compensating activities which in the British case took the form of municipal development of model dwellings for the working class.

7   The state acted as developer, owner and manager of these dwellings. For the purchase of land, for construction and for the supply of capital finance it relied, and still does rely, on the private sector.

8   State housing provision contributed to the functions of labour reproduction and material legitimation, although the relative importance of the sector was very small indeed before 1919. In addition slum clearance without rehousing, certainly in the nineteenth century, can be seen as a repressive policy instrument.

9   At the end of the First World War the state executive faced a severe legitimation crisis as well as the prospect of continuing reproductive contradictions. This led to an enormous expansion in the scale of municipal housebuilding at subsidised rents using the existing legislative powers. The surge in production acted to breach an implementation threshold so that even at its lowest point local authority annual completions never fell below 16,000 units after 1920 in spite of the long boom in speculative building.

10 The origin of state housing lay in the resolution of contradictions. However, while this was taking place a political movement was being created, the trade unions and the Labour Party, whose membership saw state housing provision as a direct means of advancing the material interests of the working class within the existing social order. These advances simultaneously served the state's legitimatory and reproductive objectives as well as under-pinning the political philosophy of social democracy.

11 Thus since at least the First World War the political leadership

of both the capitalist and the working classes has accepted a partial role for state housing development. However, the commitment of the working-class movement has traditionally been far stronger and thus the scale of construction reflects the changing balance of class forces both in terms of the mass movement and in terms of parliamentary and local council power, most clearly in the inter-war period. The other source of instability was the cycle of boom and slump in the national economy.

12   The switch to clearance and redevelopment in the early 1930s reflected conservative thinking that private building, filtering and public redevelopment together could solve the housing problem.

13   In spite of the considerable increases in real wages and salaries since 1945, it remains the case that speculative redevelopment followed by rehousing and speculative building for rental to the working class is relatively unprofitable. Moreover, the pre-existing privately rented sector has declined continuously.

14   However, this rise in real incomes and the development of institutions providing mortgage finance has brought with it, since the mid-1920s, a spectacular rise in owner-occupation.

15   During the period 1945–51 the state directed the flow of house-building resources largely into local authority construction. But the Labour government's imperial ambitions in military power, trade, direct investment and finance brought a situation in which the commitment to dealing with the massive post-war housing shortage was severely constrained.

16   Since 1953 the role of state housing has been perceived by the leadership of both major political parties, when in power, as the residual activity of carrying through what speculative building for owner-occupation and private rehabilitation were unable to achieve. After 1954 there was a substantial switch into the replacement function—redevelopment and overspill construction—and provision for the elderly.

17   This continued after 1964 under the Labour government, although on a markedly higher scale. But the clearance of much of the worst unfit stock and the continuing economic crisis since 1967 led to a major withdrawal of resources from local authority housebuilding.

18   State housing requires state expenditure, both for capital outlays and revenue subsidies. The scale of these outlays reflects not only changes in political power but also the national economic

conjuncture and the theoretically perceived relationship between it and state expenditure.

19 Before the acceptance of John Maynard Keynes's theories, the orthodox response to crisis was to cut state expenditure. In the golden age of Keynesianism, during the two decades following the Second World War, changes in the flow of state expenditure were seen both as one means of regulating aggregate demand, positively or negatively, and as a way of shifting productive resources from one economic activity to another. In the last decade state expenditure and monetary developments have been perceived as closely intertwined and the monetarist response to inflation has been to attempt to restrain expenditure in order to control domestic credit expansion at the same time as interest rate policy has raised revenue subsidies. The effect was to reduce dramatically the balance between resource expenditure and gift expenditure on state housing in the five years after 1972–3.

20 The extension of owner-occupation into the better-paid and securely employed strata of the working class and the residualist strategy of the central state is leading to a relative growth in importance of the legitimatory rather than the reproductive function of state housing provision. This is partially offset by the contraction of the privately rented stock.

21 The housing conditions of the working class have been transformed since the first decades of the nineteenth century. But more than a hundred years after the passage of the Lodging Houses Act and more than half a century since the first social democratic government took office, there still remains a tremendous housing problem in Britain. The next chapter shows how a socialist government should solve it.

ELEVEN

A strategy for the future

1 Introduction

In this last chapter I wish to turn away from the delightful, sunlit path of analytic critique and retrospective wisdom and strike off into a lonely and unmapped territory. Rather than proposing incremental advances on our present system I wish to enquire: in the event of a socialist government taking power in this country, in the short- or medium-term future, what strategy should they pursue with respect to state housing?

Let me clarify this. I wish to suppose that because of a continuing crisis in the conditions of material and cultural welfare of the British people and because of a transformation of their perception of the relation between these conditions and the organisation of our society, huge political advances have been made by the Left. Struggle within the trade union movement and within the constituencies has brought a series of major victories for the socialist membership of the Labour Party at all levels, including the parliamentary Labour Party. Simultaneously there have been big gains for the Communist Party and other socialist parties. These advances in the work-places and localities have led to the election of a Labour government committed to a major democratic transformation of British society by means of a transitional programme with a coherent socialist goal.

The economic elements of this phase include: selective nationalisation of the most important oligopolies, the big banks and the insurance companies; the termination of the role of sterling as a reserve currency; the ending of overseas military expenditure; the use of import controls to help secure balance in our foreign trade and payments; the introduction of price controls; agreement with the unions on collective bargaining to ensure increases in real wages without price inflation; and a return to the full employment of labour and productive capacity.

What, then, should be the housing strategy of such a government during these years of transition? By strategy I do not mean to try to specify here, for example, what the scale of housebuilding should be nor how it should be distributed between redevelopment, and general needs construction, nor what should be the financial value of general assistance subsidies and so forth and so on. Instead I want to try to set out the main principles which should guide policy and the central changes in ownership and control which would be required in order to implement those principles. Strategy, then, provides the framework on which specific programmes for site acquisition, building, capital finance, subsidy payments, and management can be constructed.

It is worth saying at the outset that I do not believe that the imitation of foreign models—East German, Hungarian, Swedish, Yugoslav or what you will—can provide a ready-made blue print for British policy. We must invent our own road to socialism and we must, indeed, define our own final objectives. This is not to deny the potential usefulness of inter-national comparative research East *and* West. Finally, before turning to the substantive content of this chapter. I should note that I have found no contemporary and comprehensive document on future housing policy in this country produced by any of the socialist parties or groups. I must also make reference to an important omission. In these proposals I do not examine what changes will be required in the personnel and organisation of the state apparatus, for example in the Department of the Environment. This should not be interpreted as a belief that the departments can be given a vastly different political programme and simply be left to get on with it. However, with a limited understanding of the decision and administrative processes in the civil service it would, for the present, be presumptuous of me to make specific recommen-dations for the reconstruction which would undoubtedly be necessary.

2 Production for human need

The first principle of the state's total housing strategy should be one of political philosophy rather than one of political economy: the scale and character of productive activity should be directed so that it fulfils human need. The more pressing are those needs, the higher should be the priority attached to meeting them.

The determination of supply on the basis of income and wealth—the economic mechanism of the effective demand for housing in the form of dwelling purchase and rental—should be allowed to continue to operate only where it does not conflict with a pattern of supply based on need alone.

How might such a principle be implemented? What I envisage is that the government will prepare a seven-year basic planning document which will enable it to identify the changing scale of housing needs and the resources necessary to tackle them. The document will contain three sections: the first will deal with the existing stock of dwellings, the second with households in relation to their housing and the third with the future size and character of private and public housing resource expenditure. As time passed the document would be updated on a rolling basis. The existing local authority HIP returns could be developed to provide much of the district-level information which would be required for the national planning document.

The first section, on the stock, would essentially attempt to define existing and anticipated physical problems. These include:

(i) the number of unfit dwellings;

(ii) the number of dwellings lacking one or more amenities, amongst which central heating would be included;

(iii) the extent of serious disrepair and the rate at which this is increasing as a result of shortfalls in the necessary level of maintenance and rehabilitatory work;

(iv) the number of dwellings which, whilst not unfit or lacking in amenities, constitute an oppressive physical environment for owners or tenants;

(v) the number of existing dwellings likely to be demolished each year as a result of town development, road widening schemes and so on;

(vi) the number of vacant dwellings.

All the information would be classified by tenure and district. The current series of National Housing Surveys can be extended to provide the basic data for this section. The information search would also provide an excellent opportunity for locality-based political and community groups to assist in identifying district and sub-district problems.

The second section of the basic planning document will deal with households. Its chief purpose will be to identify the ways in which the existing stock fails to meet household needs beyond the narrowly physical conditions to which we have referred above. This takes place in a number of ways and a thorough understanding of mismatching between people and dwellings will require substantial innovations in funded research as well as popular involvement in policy discussion. The areas of enquiry are:

(a) The degree of overcrowding. (The present statutory definition of overcrowding, which we inherit from the 1935 Act, is entirely inappropriate and an alternative definition will have to be established and used for the policy document.)

(b) The extent to which private tenants are paying exploitative rents. This will provide essential background information for the municipalisation programme.

(c) Shortages of accommodation for the frail elderly, the handicapped and the disabled. This is an area in which the local authorities have already made substantial advances.

(d) The amount of unwanted sharing such as a single-parent family living with another family; or several households having to use a common bathroom, water closet, or kitchen; or a married couple living with their in-laws.

(e) The scale of homelessness.

(f) The degree to which existing accommodation, particularly the new structures built since 1945, has become inappropriate to the changing patterns of residential life. What I have in mind is that both the local authorities and the speculative builders in the past have catered largely for the nuclear family. The deviants, so to speak, have had to rely on the private rental sector. This sector is disappearing whilst the variance of household types is increasing. The time has come when the district councils, those plannable instruments, should actively explore what range of built forms— new and converted—are most appropriate to these developments, actual and potential, in the spectrum of households. These include not only the nuclear family but also cohabiting couples, both heterosexual and gay; single-parent families; one-person households in the case of single men and women as well as for those who are separated, divorced or widowed. I also include those people who wish to share accommodation with friends in some kind of commune or community setting, situations, for example, where two or more people wish to live together combining private territories, typically the bedrooms, together with a shared kitchen, or garden, or living area, or children's room or all of these things. Managerial and moral conservatism in the local authority sector and financial and moral conservatism in the owner-occupied sector have clearly restricted popular choice in these areas. We have already entered the age of contraception and the sexual taboos of the Victorian era are in dissolution. The time has come for this evolution to be recognised in design. The nuclear family is and, I suspect, will remain the dominant form of home life but the range and absolute size of household minorities increases by the year and this has to be reflected in the pattern of the residential stock.

With respect to the analysis of households I have so far limited the discussion to the situation at the time the basic planning document is prepared. The document must also prepare demographic forecasts for the seven-year planning period. These will include the natural increase in the British population, its household composition and the scale of immigration and emigration. Attempts must be made to specify the net increase in population and its composition by county and district (in Scotland by region and district) and this spatial location forecast would draw not only on the existing situation in the base period but also on forecasts for the spatial location of employment growth which would be under simultaneous preparation in the Department of Industry. In my conception of the powers of the socialist state in the transitional period this ministry would have the capacity to regulate every substantial expansion of employment in all economic sectors on the basis of a national space-plan for employment and industrial growth, paving the way for the final solution of the regional problem.

One of the major difficulties the demographic forecast will run into arises from the fact that supply creates its own demand, both in a spatial sense and in terms of shifts in household composition.[1] For example, if the municipal authorities constructed well-designed grouped flatlets at reasonable rents for single adults of all ages, it is quite certain that people would come forward wishing to occupy them. If building for household minorities took place on a substantial scale it would certainly affect the trend and breakdown in the population's headship rates.

In the third section of the basic planning document the demographic information would be compared with the stock survey to arrive at an estimate of the production requirements necessary to deal with the existing situation in each district, whilst the household increase and growth of disrepair forecasts would be used to plot the future expansion of needs. Using these comparisons a *minimum* annual production programme could be derived which would do nothing more than prevent the existing situation from growing any worse. A number of hypothetical programmes more ambitious than the minimum could then be formulated and spatially defined and it would eventually be the task of the legislature and the government to choose between them. It would be at this point that the interdependence of supply and demand would be recognised by, for example, incorporating in each hypothetical programme an alternative household minorities production programme. The alternative plans would define the construction balance between green-field site building, redevelopment and rehabilitation. As we have already seen, this will require clearly defined decision rules on the proper choice between the two renewal modes! I shall return later in this chapter to the questions of how the chosen production programme would be distributed between the various tenure groups and how the policy would be implemented.

3 The land question

In Chapter 3 we reviewed some of the problems which site acquisition has posed for local authorities in their building programmes. One of these was the political process of containment, historically associated with high-density building. If the spatially defined housebuilding plan described in Section 2 is implemented, the phenomenon of containment will have been avoided. It goes without saying that the preparation of programmes for employment and housing expansion must draw on what is best in the British tradition of regional and urban planning, such as compactness of the urban environment, short journey-to-work times and ready access to the countryside. With respect to residential densities, we need to know a great deal more about the relation between density, construction costs, built form and the quality of life associated with these variables. I have no specific proposals to make on these matters save that I find it disturbing that almost 20 per cent of all public sector dwellings are still built at densities of 200 designed bedspaces per hectare or more. It is also worth noting that the socialist government will most certainly seek to expand the provision of free pre-school nurseries for the children of all those parents who wish to use them. Estates must be designed to incorporate these facilities as well as such facilities as shops, a community centre, a pub, a launderette, where appropriate.

The second major criticism I have made of the present situation concerned the huge absolute and relative increase in capital expenditure on site acquisition. The long-term solution to this, I suggest, can be provided by the appropriation of the land for the people as a whole by means of nationalisation.[2] Land in the possession of owner-occupiers must be excluded: if it were not, the right-wing forces within the country would quite surely seize on this measure as a magnificent propaganda weapon against the government. Farmland should also be excluded with the exception of the big estates already rented out to tenant farmers. All other land, by a single, swift Act of Parliament, would be denominated as 'community freehold'. The structures on the land would not be included.

Compensation would be paid to owners, whether individuals or institutions, as government bonds bearing a fixed, untaxed, annual income over twenty years based on the potential ground rent of each plot in its existing and unchanged use. (So derelict land would receive no compensation.) These securities could be traded on the stock market and therefore could be sold for cash if the owners so desired. Where appropriate the government could choose to redeem its bonds for cash at any point in their twenty-year life at a discount based on market trading. Government agencies, statutory undertakers and nationalised industries would receive no compensation.

The state would issue leaseholds to the individuals or institutions owning and using the buildings on each plot of land, for which it would charge ground rent. Where ownership and use are separate, it would be the owner's responsibility to pay the ground rent. The income from this ground rent would supply the cash flow necessary to honour the government's bonds. In this way land nationalisation would impose no financing requirements on the state budget. Former landowners who continued to lease the land from the state would find, for twenty years, that their rental payments and bond income precisely offset each other, provided there was no change in use. As time passed there would be a surplus of rent income above compensation which could be credited to the district council.

The titles to use all land held in community freehold would be maintained by a Central Land Board and it would be to this body that the local authorities turned as they required sites for their housing programmes. The CLB would be well prepared for this since it would have been involved in the preparation of the basic planning document because of the land requirements it generates. The CLB would require the municipalities to meet the appropriate annual ground rent and this would appear in the expenditure column of the housing revenue account to be met out of rents or subsidies. These payments would cease twenty years after the passing of the Act. In the meantime they would be relatively low as they would be based on fixed money values in existing and unchanged use. As is the case now, special subsidies would be necessary for particularly expensive sites, although they would no longer be required for derelict sites.

The use of nationalised land has now been dealt with. This still leaves the question of the acquisition of owner-occupied properties in the case of slum clearance and municipalisation. I propose here no change to the existing legislation with the exception of a series of paragraphs written into a new consolidating Act which sets up a procedure for the compulsory acquisition of slums for their subsequent rehabilitation parallel to the existing procedure for redevelopment. One more nail will have been driven into the coffin of partitioning. Limited compensation for the municipalisation of non-slum privately rented property would be paid to individuals as twenty-year annuities. With respect to privately owned farmland—the other major exception to community freehold—when acquisition became necessary for green-field site development either for municipal housebuilding or speculative development, the CLB would then acquire it and rent it out to the users in the manner already described.

4 Dwelling production

In Part Two of this volume the critical survey of the context and development of policy and its implementation pointed to a number of problems associated with the production of state housing. These included: violent shifts in the demand for renewal output and general needs construction; the ephemeral nature of operational units; the semi-casual character of the industry; the institutional division of architects, quantity surveyors, engineers and building firms; corruption amongst councillors and officers in the letting of contracts; the fragmentation of client responsibility; over-runs in the construction period; the slow rate of growth of productivity and the associated relative increase in production costs; the disproportionate increase in tender prices in booms; the partitioning of renewal; the failures of rehabilitation in the privately rented sector; the bias to clearance; the excessive length of the gestation period in redevelopment; and the oppressive form of much design.

It must be confessed immediately that no miraculous socialist panacea exists to remedy all these ills and I shall not play the quack by producing one myself. The political economy of housebuilding, and more broadly of the construction industry within which it is embedded, is far too complex and my understanding of it far too slender for me to urge any list of simple solutions. However, it is now possible to draw on a carefully argued analysis written by the Construction Study Group of the National Executive Committee of the Labour Party: *Building Britain's Future*.[3] What I shall do here is to set out first what seem to be the most important reforms proposed by the booklet and then to suggest some additions or reformulations.

After reviewing the importance of the industry, the crisis which it faced in 1977 and the underlying problems, *Building Britain's Future* turned to argue the case for specific propositions for change. Amongst them we can find:

1 The Construction Industry Manpower Board should establish registers of employers and employees in the industry and it would match registered employees with job oportunities offered by registered employers. Such employees would be entitled to fall-back pay, redundancy payments, pensions and so on based on length of service on the register, and they would be encouraged to join appropriate trade unions. Public sector contracts should be granted only to registered employers.

2 A proportion of future public expenditure on construction should be guaranteed against spending cuts with a 'reserve shelf' of programmes which can be implemented as economic policy requires.

3 A Public Procurement Agency should be established to co-ordinate the letting of public sector construction contracts and to act as agent in executing capital works programmes.

4 The public sector should make much more use of continuity and serial contracts and thereby move away from competitive tendering.

5 Direct labour organisations should be managed professionally as municipal enterprises, with reformed accounting procedures. They should be allowed to compete for any public work in their locality. Industrial democracy should be extended within them.

6 A publicly owned National Construction Corporation should be established, based initially on the acquisition of one or more major contractors, to compete in national and regional construction markets. The Corporation should operate as a state holding company with its activities organised into several separate enterprises. Its aim would be to establish a public enterprise base in each of the major

291

     specialised sub-sectors of large-scale construction work and in each regional construction market.

7 The development of workers' co-operatives should be encouraged through an extension of the Industrial Common Ownership Act and the establishment of the Co-operative Development Agency.

8 Mineral rights and a major part of their associated production facilities should be nationalised. A new state holding company, the Building Materials Corporation, should be established. It would acquire Pilkingtons, BPB Industries, one or more major cement manufacturers, London Brick, and one or more manufacturers of non-fletton bricks, ceramic tiles, concrete roofing tiles, clay pipes, concrete slabs and sanitary equipment.

9 The design and production of buildings should be more closely integrated. The education of construction professionals such as architects, civil engineers and quantity surveyors, should be taken out of the hands of professional institutions and controlled by a body representing the whole industry, perhaps the Construction Industry Training Board.

Building Britain's Future provides a valuable contribution to the development of socialist policies in the construction field. Indeed it is the *only* comprehensive published document of any intellectual weight at all. There is much in it that I accept without any serious comment. The proposal for a register of employers and employees is a familiar one although some consideration needs to be given to whether employers might recruit unregistered labourers and craftsmen and what could be done to check this if it happened on a substantial scale. With respect to point 4 above, there do seem to exist advantages in continuity and serial contracts even if the scope for their use is narrower than the document appears to suggest.

Point 7, the proposal for the development of workers' co-operatives, deserves high priority and will require little in the way of central resources. Point 8, the nationalisation of the commanding heights of the building materials industry, with its extraordinary degree of concentration, is likely to be included in the programme of any socialist government. Finally, I agree that the integration of design within the production institutions is most desirable. However, the document has certainly not made out a serious case for transferring the responsibility for professional education to the CITB.

The two most important areas where I differ from the policy document concern the extension of public ownership and the question of work-load stabilisation. With respect to ownership, the proposals on DLOs are very weak and require strengthening by permitting the organisations to compete for private as well as public contracts both within and outside their own district, including rehabilitation work on either a large or small scale. In the latter case much would have been done to curb the activities of unscrupulous small builders which overprice shoddy rehabilitation work done for owner-occupiers, work which in the worst cases is abandoned before completion. Also worthy of exploration is the formulation of multi-district DLOs.

If the DLOs are unshackled and their average efficiency brought up to current best practice standards, it would facilitate the decision to nationalise *none* of the great construction companies, building materials excepted of course. The arguments against nationalisation that have been put to me are strong and I find them convincing. They are:

 (i) the centralisation and concentration of construction capital has
     still not proceeded so far that nationalising one firm, or even
     two or three, would cover more than a relatively small proportion
     of total value-added output;

 (ii) the real construction assets of the large building and civil engin-
     eering firms are land, work-in-progress and plant. The first of
     these the state will have secured through its land programme, the
     second the government would not want; and the third could be
     acquired in a selective fashion by setting up a publicly owned
     plant hire company;

(iii) the big companies have their own long-established internal hier-
     archies of power and function including the claims maximisers
     and tax minimisers. Nationalisation might tend merely to repro-
     duce these structures and functions. By building up the DLOs the
     local state could create its own systems of incentive, enterprise,
     accountability and management;

(iv) since the state is such a substantial customer for the private sector,
     since it would own the land and most building materials production,
     considerable leverage exists for influencing the activities of big
     building capital without having to nationalise.

Taking these various considerations into account, I recommend the side-stepping of the Benn–Holland strategy in the construction industry and, as an alternative, the development of a network of efficient DLOs.

In my view the least convincing feature of the Labour Party document concerns the stability of demand as it is put to the industry. The paper makes not one single reference to the need to control private demand for construction output and this leaves the public sector ful-filling, in part, a residualist role. In terms of their recommendations, the authors simply do not seem to recognise that private and public demand are competing for the same resources. Moreover there is absolutely no indication that public sector demand will stabilise: *Building Britain's Future* would permit a 40 per cent cut in forecast public expenditure on construction after a lapse of two years, an in-stability more violent than even the Labour government has permitted![4]

I suggest that the means by which to control the scale of construction supply for private and public agencies is through a system of building licensing. In order to do this effectively and with the minimum bureau-cracy possible, a critical review of the British experience before 1955 would be extremely useful.[5] The basic notion is that work done above some minimum contract sum, for example £10,000, would require a licence before it began. Licences would be issued freely except where the demand on the industry's resources, by area and contract type, appeared to threaten a rise in relative prices because of the inelasticity of supply response to a surge in demand.

Whilst licensing can act to check a too rapid growth in demand, it cannot guarantee that the demand is there in the first place. With respect to the stabilisation of demand for housebuilding, we must turn back again to the basic planning document. One of its objectives is, precisely, to set out a programme of construction activity for general needs and housing renewal which is well defined by year and by area. We should now add the requirement that it generate a relatively stable work-load for the industry, at the very least at the regional scale.

However, stability in the set of figures in a planning document is by no means identical with a stable flow of expenditure for industry output in the real world. This raises the question of plan implementation, the discussion of which was postponed in Section 2 above. My conception of the task of the basic planning document is that it provide a strategy for the matching of housebuilding activity to clearly defined social needs. That strategy must define the scale of housing resource expendi-ture by the state over the plan period. Definition of the total planned building programme as well as the specific role of public housing together imply the minimum input of the private sector if the plan is to be fulfilled. Implementation, then, requires certain levels and types of defined activity in both the public and the private spheres.

In the public sphere, the plan might fail for two reasons: first, an economic crisis leading to the abandonment of the alternative strategy and the housing programme along with it; second, a refusal to implement on the part of the local state. The first difficulty is, of course, not a weakness of the housing plan *per se* but concerns the whole conception of the alternative economic strategy which was sketched out in Section 1. This book on housing is clearly not the place for an exposition and critical analysis of the viability of the alternative strategy. All that can be done is to state unequivocally that such an alternative policy appears to me to be the only feasible means for our country to escape from the combination of stagnation, inflation and de-industrialisation which are the outcome of existing policies. But I must frankly reiterate that without a successful alternative economic strategy, the housing plan which must lock into it will almost certainly prove to be abortive.

The second threat to implementation in the public sphere operates much more at the political level. In the case of districts controlled by Conservative, Liberal or Scottish National Party councils, there might well be a refusal in some cases to carry through the national plan's requirements in their own area, in spite of the fact that the plan would have been partially formulated by drawing on local initiative. This difficulty will arise not only in relation to housing, of course. It is bound to arise wherever the implementation of socialist policies relies on positive activity by local state apparatuses. One form of response would be to create an alternative agency capable of acting in default of the council. In the housing field this would require the formation of a National Housing Corporation with a full range of powers to plan, purchase land, erect dwellings and manage them. A disadvantage here would not only be the slow pace of any such response but also the image of central Goliath and local David that would be conjured up by the bourgeois media with damaging political effect. A second form of response would be to use the blocking action of the local state as the basis for political struggles to reverse such policy, conducted by locally based social and labour movements and the left political organisations. The disadvantage here is that implementation could still be baulked by a recalcitrant council, at least until the next round of local elections. On balance it is the second of these alternatives which I prefer.

The successful implementation of the national housing strategy will also require substantial new building for owner-occupation. This will be particularly the case in the first planning period when much state resource expenditure will need to be channelled into municipalisation of the privately rented sector in order to eliminate rental exploitation and to deal rapidly with the abominable physical standards which still mark

295

out that sector. If the government's economic policy succeeds in keeping the general level of interest rates down to a sensible level— something existing governments have not yet done—I foresee no short- fall in the supply of mortgage finance for the private sector to play its role. Indeed the government will probably wish to introduce a system of arealy defined mortgage rationing to ensure that speculative building and DLO building for sale do not arrogate resources to themselves on such a large scale that the public sector programme would be inhibited. To rely on building licencing alone to achieve this purpose would be unwise since it would result in needlessly high selling prices.

5 Development finance

Whatever the eventual size of the building programme, it is clear that the district authorities will continue to require a substantial flow of finance in order to fund their expenditure on new building, municipali- sation and improvements of the purpose-built stock, although site acquisition costs will be replaced by rental payments out of the housing revenue account to the Central Land Board. How will this finance be raised? I propose here a return to the principle adopted by the 1945-51 government: all such funds should be borrowed directly from the Public Works Loan Board, thereby completely severing the *direct* relationship between local authority housing finance and the national and inter- national money market. The release of monies by the board would be based on the known building targets for the districts.

But we must not make the mistake of believing that the development finance problem has been magically spirited away by a wave of the scholar's pen. Local authorities may no longer need to enter the money market but instead the board itself will have to raise the funds required for the district's housebuilding programmes. This brings us to the fasci- nating and much broader question of how a socialist government will raise the money required for all the forms of public expenditure which become necessary as a result of the entire set of its strategic choices.

For my own part I am convinced that once the government has implemented the measures necessary to ensure the full employment of the labour force and the full use of the economy's industrial capacity, thereafter public expenditure must be financed largely out of taxation, including taxes on the surpluses earned by publicly owned enterprises. If this were not the case, the government would be driven into borrowing not merely from private savings out of income but would also have to borrow from the banking sector. The effects of this if it is undertaken on a very substantial scale are likely to be highly inflationary, since excess demand on the country's productive resources would be combined with a rapid increase in the money supply.

Let me assume, then, that the major part of public expenditure is financed out of taxes and a minor part from borrowing. Now I know of no reason in economic logic why any sum of money spent by the state on productive activity—the building of a battleship, the construction of a house, the labour of a teacher in a primary school, the work of a physiotherapist in a health clinic—has to be seen as 'properly' financed out of taxation rather than out of public borrowing, or vice versa. Of course, their outcomes are dissimilar. A military exercise cannot be confused with a surgical operation. Some activities are not priced— secondary schooling for example—whilst others such as much present-day nursery care are. Some expenditures are visibly materialised in a long-lasting object—a school textbook for example—whilst others are not, such as the labour of the teacher who instructs his pupils from the textbook. But none of these very real and important differences demonstrate that public expenditure on a specific good or service is only 'properly' financed in one fashion rather than another.

This is not inconsistent with an explanation of why it was found convenient historically to fund the major part of local authority capital expenditure on housing by means of money market loans. This form of finance gave the local state some autonomy from the centre; the accommodation was priced (the rent) so that it was possible to repay the loans raised, whilst the capital outlay could not be met from the rents *without* loan finance because of the disparity between the workers' income stream and the sale price of his dwelling; finally at times of rising state expenditure it was possible to implement programmes with a slower rate of growth of tax receipts than would otherwise have been possible.

An extremely important conclusion can be derived from the non-existence of a necessary one-to-one relationship between specific resource expenditures by the state and specific ways of raising the finance required for those outlays. This conclusion is: when an expenditure is made on a good which is priced it is not 'improper' that the price be set independently of the mode in which the finance was raised. In the specific case of PWLB loans for the districts for their housebuilding programmes, the terms of repayment of the loan can be decided independently of the way in which the board raises its finance, whether this be by cash quotas from the Treasury or from borrowing on the money market, or both. In the limiting case where all public expenditure on capital or revenue account is funded from taxation, the break between the mode of raising loan finance and the terms of its repayment is unmistakable.

This brings me to the question of what repayment terms the board should be required to impose on its loans to the districts. Here the discussion in Chapter 6 will be of assistance. It was argued that a loan which did not exploit the tenants would be one in which the rate of interest on the loan is variable and equal to the rate of inflation, and that is my proposal. The inflation rate could be calculated on, let us say, a three-year moving average so that there would not be sharp year-by-year changes in the interest rate on the outstanding debt with a consequential impact on gross rents. With respect to the repayment period and the rate of accumulation, which with the rate of interest jointly determine the time-stream of loan repayments, I see no good reason for abandoning the present conventions.

This proposal, for funding all district expenditure on new building, municipalisation and major improvement though PWLB loans at a zero real rate of interest, seems to be financially feasible if only one condition is met. This is that the alternative economic strategy succeed in keeping the rate of price inflation down to a low and stable rate, let us say in the range of 3 to 5 per cent per annum. If the rate of inflation were as high as we have seen in Britain over the past ten years, the money rate of interest on board loans would be so great that interest payments would continue to dominate housing revenue account expenditure and surges in inflation would trigger off powerful front-loading effects with steep increases in gross rents and the necessity for countervailing increases in the state subsidy. Here is one more example of the impossibility of introducing socialism in one sector. The new government will stand—or fall—by the entire set of its strategic choices and their implementation and each of these is interdependent with every other.[6]

6 Rents and subsidies

The categories employed in the local authority's housing revenue account will need to be little different from those that exist now. With respect to expenditure, items will still be included to cover management, services and repairs. The existing outstanding debt charge will also continue for as long as these loans still remain to be paid off. But with respect to new capital outlays and the refinance of expiring debt we shall no longer see the term 'debt charge' but two items: loan repayments including principal and interest to the PWLB and ground rent payable to the Central Land Board.

I believe that the new system of development finance, the improved efficiency of the building industry, the changed terms of municipalisation compensation and the nationalisation of land will jointly have the result of generating costs per additional dwelling much lower than would be the case under our existing arrangements.

With respect to housing revenue account income, this will continue to be derived from rents plus subsidies and in aggregate will be required to equal total expenditure, as is the case today. Gross rents on individual dwellings will be based on the relative use-values of the stock.

The aggregate gross rental income in each district will be identically equal to the expenditure total less the revenue from central and local state subsidies. The total state subsidy will be divided into two elements: general assistance and rent rebates. General assistance, when paid, should be based on a comprehensive definition of newly incurred reckonable expenditure. However, I believe it should be a medium-term policy objective of the socialist government to eliminate altogether general assistance subsidies, including the tax relief on mortgage interest.[7] It is essential we make a complete break with the present system, whereby the working class is taxed in order to enable the state to pay out very substantial transfer incomes in the form of housing subsidies only for this to be re-transferred to loan repayments. Taxation should be used to direct funds above all into resource expenditure to reverse the process of de-industrialisation and, in the sphere of state reproductive production, to construct and run hospitals and clinics, the schools and the nurseries for which such great need exists and to build on a planned basis the new and improved dwellings which are necessary to eliminate housing need as we presently understand it.

As for rent rebates, I anticipate that procedures will continue broadly in their present form. However, it is quite sure that as the economy returns to a full employment situation the number of tenants needing rebates will diminish. One of the singular advantages of the alternative economic strategy is that the growth of the economy raises the income from taxation at the same time as it reduces the level of transfer benefits it is necessary to pay.

299

One subsidy-innovation which I would very much like to see implemented is that with households whose members are senior citizens, council accommodation would be rent-free. A condition would be that the members of that household had satisfied some minimum period of residence as council tenants, say ten years, before retirement age. One of the great psychological as well as economic advantages of owner-occupation is the prospect of free accommodation after the mortgage is repaid and I think council tenants should benefit from a similar prospect.

I have not yet referred to the existing levels of general assistance subsidy paid into the housing revenue accounts. If these are left unchanged it should be possible to move rapidly to the elimination of general assistance on new capital expenditure. Consideration could also be given to transferring the Exchequer subsidy between districts to achieve what the Housing Centre Trust have sought to do by means of a national rent pool, that is to deal with a situation where HRA expenditure per dwelling varies widely between districts and is insufficiently compensated by relative subsidy receipts.

7 Access, allocation, tenants' rights and tenants' control

In Chapter 8 an analysis was carried through of the negative features of council house management with respect to access, allocation and tenants' rights. It was noted that whilst these defects are fairly general there is substantial variation in their severity. They include: the employment of residential qualifications in determining access to a district's stock; the accompanying lack of inter-urban mobility; the exclusion of household minorities from access; the obscure nature of allocation systems; the social and racial prejudice reflected in discretionary decision-making and some points systems; the development of ghetto estates for which the 'Dutch method' is in part responsible; the lack of mobility within districts; the effect of council house sales in underpinning the ideology of council housing as a welfare net and reinforcing ghettoisation in the internal geography of the municipal stock; the long chain of accountability from councillors to tenants; the individuation of tenants who feel they are unjustly treated; the weak and essentially negative powers exercised by tenants; the lack of formal security of tenure; and the obscure, paternalist and punitive character of tenancy agreements.

The material basis for many of these negative aspects of management has always been the inadequate size of the council stock. Queues always exist when there is a shortage of supply, and where demand and supply are not equated by a pricing mechanism. It still remains the case today that the stock lacks the full range of dwelling types in the required numbers and that much of it is of low quality. In that sense the production measures discussed in Section 2 of this chapter—the planning of stable output levels to meet housing need in a comprehensive sense, including a much more creative and positive attitude to construction for household minorities—should in themselves change the stock and new output context within which management operates. But to operate *only* at the material level will not be sufficient.

In proposing policies for change in the sphere of access, allocation, tenants' rights and tenants' control it is now possible to draw on some very positive initiatives which have originated in the DoE's Housing Services Advisory Group and the National Consumer Council.[8] In what follows I have been much influenced by their work and by the basic principle set down by Basildon District Council: 'working people should control their own lives.'

With respect to access (registration with a district or borough as a would-be tenant) I believe this should be open. Anyone who is willing to provide the required information for a district's allocation scheme should have the right to register. No restrictions should be placed because of existing tenure, household type, race, place of residence, or for any other reason. An annual fee would be payable to cover the costs of operating and updating the register and to keep down the scale of multiple registrations. The DoE should ensure that a minimum quantity of information in a standardised form suitable for computer analysis is recorded on each registration card to facilitate research and the planning process.

Allocation would be based on a points system. This system would be prepared and published, after full public discussion, by a commission composed of councillors, local government housing staff and representatives of local tenants and residents associations. Each registered household, including existing tenants seeking transfers, would know their point score. The system would be revised from time to time in the light of experience and changing popular attitudes. No system, of course, could contravene national legislation against racial, religious or sexual discrimination. It is extremely likely that such an approach would give a strong weighting to local residence, thereby blocking inter-district mobility. In this case a 'council quota' of the flow of vacancies should be established, perhaps one-fifth of the total, which the local authority would have full right to allocate, guided by but not determined by a published points system of their own.

Registration would be sorted into queues for the different types of accommodation available. The queue categories and eligibility rules would be decided on by the same tripartite commission referred to above, once again after exhaustive public discussion. A periodically up-dated computer printout would be available in every public library of the district listing households in each queue by code number, ranked by their point score. As new dwellings and re-lets became available they would be offered to whichever household was at the head of the appropriate queue. A variation on this scheme would be to give the tenants' association on each estate the right to select tenants for a quota of the vacancies on each estate as they became available. The DoE would establish a National Exchange Bureau whilst the districts would run a local exchange bureau. The government would ban the sale of council houses.

With respect to the rights and powers of sitting tenants, each local tripartite commission would draw up a tenants' charter where one did not already exist. The charter would have to be compatible with national legislation covering the same ground. Its basic elements would ensure that tenants had the right:

(i) to security of tenure in law with a clear specification of the grounds for possession orders;

(ii) to a written tenancy agreement as a balanced contract between landlord and tenant;

(iii) to undertake their own maintenance, repairs and, with the council's written permission, structural alterations and additions. In no case should the tenant's rent be raised as a consequence;

(iv) to take in lodgers with no increase in the gross rent;

(v) to form estate management co-operatives where tenants so desired.

Finally, on these questions of council house management, it would clearly be necessary to expand at the central and local level the resources devoted to management tasks above their existing levels and there needs to take place a small revolution in training for state housing management.

8 Final comment

The development of a socialist policy on the housing question in Britain must be comprehensive in its ambit. In one sense such a requirement has been met in this chapter since I have tackled successively the areas of the overarching planning philosophy and practice, the housebuilding industry, development finance, rents and subsidies, and management and tenants' rights. In another sense, however, the ideas presented here are restrictive in coverage for I have dealt largely with the council sector and have written little about the dominant component of the British housing stock, owner-occupied dwellings. This restricted focus is entirely because my research over the last four years has primarily dealt with state housing. In a future study of the debtor's triangle—speculative building, mortgage finance and owner-occupation—I hope to be able to extend and deepen the prescriptive work so that it embraces both of the main housing tenures in this country.

Appendices

Council housebuilding: a summary legislative chronology from 1851 to 1978

The chronology is not a comprehensive précis of the entirety of every Act but seeks to summarise the main provisions with respect to council housebuilding in England and Wales. Scottish legislation in most cases is broadly similar.

Lodging Houses Act, 1851. Familiarly known as Shaftesbury's Act. The first to be passed dealing with the housing of working people as its main object. It permitted local authorities to purchase land and to erect or purchase and repair buildings suitable for lodging houses wherein the sexes were to be segregated. Finance could be raised from the rates, by borrowing from the Public Works Loan Commissioners or through mortgages taken out against the security of rate income. Rents were not to be beyond the means of workers nor yet constitute an indirect means of giving relief to the poor.

Labouring Classes Dwelling Houses Act, 1866. It allowed local authorities to borrow from the PWLC for the purchase of sites and the erection or improvement of dwellings for the labouring classes. The loan's repayment period was not to exceed forty years nor the rate of interest to fall short of 4 per cent.

Artisans' and Labourers' Dwellings Improvement Act, 1875. Familiarly known as the Cross Act. Its chief purpose was to permit local authorities to purchase and clear areas of unfit dwellings. The authority was to draw up improvement schemes, to carry out the street planning, paving and sewering of the land and to sell or lease it to builders. Those who had been displaced during clearance were to be rehoused on site. The possibility of rehousing by the local authority was reluctantly conceded. If the authority did build it was to resell the houses within ten years. Capital could be raised through the rates or by borrowing but it was assumed that no subsidisation of council properties would be necessary. Executant authorities: in London, the Metropolitan Board of Works and the City Commissioners of Sewers; in the provinces, the Town Corporations.

Public Health Act, 1875. It laid down the principles for the purchase of land by local authorities and it was under the provisions of this Act that local authorities made their housing bye-laws, most of which took the form of adopting the model bye-laws issued by the Local Government Board in 1877.

Artisans' and Labourers' Dwellings Act (1868) Amendment Act, 1879. The 1868 Torrens Act contained no provision for the payment of compensation to owners whose condemned houses were to be demolished. The amending Act changed this. The original Bill had also contained a clause, passed in the Commons but expunged by the Lords, which permitted local authorities to rebuild on the sites where individual insanitary houses had been demolished. This right was restored.

Artisans' and Labourers' Dwellings Amendment Act, 1879. Amended the Cross Act. Arbitrators were to assess compensation for property which had previously been a nuisance on its value after the cost of the removal of the nuisance had been deducted. Authorities were also relieved of the necessity of replacing dwellings on the cleared site but could do so elsewhere and so let or sell the cleared land more profitably for commercial purposes.

Artisans' Dwellings Act, 1882. Amends the Cross Act so that an obligation exists to 'rehouse' only half the total population displaced.

Housing of the Working Classes Act, 1885. Following the report of the Royal Commission on Housing it consolidated the existing law, lowered the rate of interest on PWLC loans for improvement and extended their repayment period. In amending the Lodging Houses Acts it provided the definition previously lacking. Lodging houses 'shall be deemed to include separate houses or cottages for the labouring classes whether containing one or several tenements'.

Housing of the Working Classes Act, 1890. The most important single item of legislation before World War I in its scope and in its use by local authorities for housebuilding purposes. A consolidating and amending Act. Part I dealt with unhealthy areas—the subject of the Cross legislation.

The rehousing provision in London remained at not less than 50 per cent. Outside London there was now no rehousing obligation. Local authorities were not to undertake rebuilding themselves without the express approval of the authority confirming the improvement scheme— the Local Government Board or the Home Secretary. Any such dwellings built were to be resold within ten years. As far as possible 'all expenditure shall ultimately be defrayed out of the property dealt with'. Part II covered unhealthy or obstructive houses and consolidated and amended the Torrens legislation. Part III had to be adopted by an authority to take effect. It provided for local authorities to erect, convert, alter, enlarge, repair, fit up, furnish and supply lodging houses for the working classes, the term defined to include separate houses or cottages. The local authority was to manage these dwellings and charge reasonable rents for them. In London the executive authorities under Parts I and III of the Act were the London County Council and the Commissioners of Sewers of the City of London.

Housing of the Working Classes Act, 1900. Amended Part III of the 1890 Act. Urban councils were not permitted to erect or purchase lodging houses outside their own district, and the metropolitan boroughs were now permitted to use Part III of that Act.

Housing of the Working Classes Act, 1903. Extended the repayment period of loans taken out by local authorities for housebuilding from a maximum of sixty years to eighty years.

Housing and Town Planning Act, 1909. It terminated the requirement of Part I of the 1890 Act for authorities to resell within ten years any dwellings they had constructed in redevelopment areas. In addition it was no longer necessary for Part III of the 1890 Act to be adopted by any authority before it took application.

Housing and Town Planning etc. Act, 1919. Widely referred to as the Addison Act. The duty was imposed on local authorities of surveying the needs of their area and making and carrying out plans for the provision of houses needed after the assent of the Ministry of Health. Councils were responsible for the fixing of rents but the Ministry had to approve them. Up to March 1927 they were to be based on the controlled rents of pre-war housing, allowances being made both for the superior use-value of council dwellings and for variations among tenants in their ability to pay. All losses up to the product of a one penny rate were to be borne by the municipality and any further losses by the Exchequer.

Acquisition of Land (Assessment of Compensation) Act, 1919. An amending Act. Land acquired compulsorily for public purposes was to be priced at its market value with no allowance for the fact that acquisition was compulsory.

Housing (Additional Powers) Act, 1919. One purpose of the Act was to provide a subsidy to private housebuilders. In addition it gave local authorities the power to stop private building in their area when this interfered with the supply of labour and materials available for public housing schemes. Councils were also empowered to raise finances for their housing programme through the issue of local bonds.

Housing Act, 1923. Widely referred to as the Chamberlain Act. It introduced Exchequer subsidies to housebuilding in a new form. The subsidy was available both to private enterprises and to the local authorities on dwellings built within specified lower and upper limits of size, equipment, etc. Its value was £6 per year per dwelling payable for twenty years. No accompanying rate subsidy was required. The capital value of the subsidy at a 5 per cent interest rate was £75 and in the case of building for private rental or sale this could be given to the builder as a lump sum. There were no limitations on the rents at which houses were let nor on the prices at which they might be sold. But the subsidy was available only on houses built before 1 October 1925. Moreover, local authorities were permitted to build only if they convinced the Minister that this was preferable to untrammelled private enterprise. With respect to slum clearance, the Treasury contributed one-half the annual loss on approved schemes. The Act also permitted councils to extend mortgages to individuals who could not raise building society finance and to guarantee payments by individuals to the building societies.

Housing (Financial Provisions) Act, 1924. Widely referred to as the Wheatley Act. The Chamberlain subsidies continued to be available for houses completed before October 1939. Houses built by the local authorities and housing associations under the 1924 Act were to receive £9 per dwelling per year in urban parishes and £12 10s per dwelling in rural parishes, in both cases for a forty-year period. The Exchequer grant was conditional on the municipalities contributing a subsidy from the rates of 50 per cent of the centre's. There was no longer any requirement to prove that building did not compete with the efforts of private enterprise. The subsidy level was to be reviewed every two years. Average rents were to be fixed in relation to controlled rents in pre-war houses, unless this led to a rate subsidy of more than £4 10s per dwelling per year. The Act envisaged a huge growth in local authority building. Section IV empowered the Ministry to stop its subsidies if house completions were fewer than 190,000 in the two-year period 1925–6, 255,000 in 1928–9, 360,000 in 1931–2 and 450,000 in 1934–5.

Housing Act, 1925. A codifying measure. The Conservatives did not restore the 1923 Act's pre-condition of non-competition with private sector housebuilding.

Housing (Revision of Contributions) Act, 1929. In 1928 the Conservatives had decided that the Wheatley subsidy would be reduced after September 1929 from its 1927 level of £7 10s per year to £6 per year. This Act annulled that decision.

Housing Act, 1930. Sometimes referred to as the Greenwood Act. The criteria for denominating clearance areas were redefined. An obligation was imposed on councils to rehouse all those displaced by slum clearance schemes. Annual subsidies were to be paid as follows: in urban parishes £2 5s per person rehoused, for forty years; in agricultural parishes £2 10s per person rehoused, for forty years. When the cost of acquiring and clearing sites exceeded £3000 per acre an additional subsidy of £1 5s per person per year was payable for those rehoused in flats. The annual rate contribution was fixed at £3 15s for forty years per house or per flat, irrespective of the size of the Treasury contribution. In the case of houses provided by rural district councils for the agricultural population, the county council was obliged to pay £1 per year per house for forty years. Rents had to be reasonable and the municipalities were empowered to grant rent rebates although their housing accounts had to balance. Every authority with a population of more than 20,000 was to produce a general statement of its plans for dealing with slum clearance and for the provision of more houses in the following five years. The exercise was to be repeated every five years. The Act also laid down criteria for 'Improvement Areas' where wholesale demolition was inappropriate.

Housing (Rural Authorities) Act, 1931. An emergency measure enacted in July 1931 to give a supplementary subsidy to rural areas financially unable to meet their own housing needs. Fewer than 2000 houses were completed under the terms of the Act.

Housing (Financial Provisions) Act, 1933. The Wheatley subsidy was repealed on all dwellings for which plans had not been approved by 7 December 1932. Each local authority was required to produce an area survey to assist in the abolition of the slums over a five-year period. These surveys replaced the 1930 Act five-year programmes. In addition a building society scheme was introduced providing cheap finance for investment for rental by private enterprise.

Housing Act, 1935. It became the duty of local authorities to survey the extent of overcrowding in their areas and to prepare plans for providing sufficient accommodation. When the five-year programme to abolish the slums had been completed a five-year programme to abolish overcrowding was to follow. Subsidies to the municipalities to diminish overcrowding were available only in three special cases: if it was necessary to build flats, a subsidy graduated to site cost was offered; a subsidy not exceeding £5 per year per dwelling could be given to individual municipalities if their programmes and financial resources meant the burden imposed on the rates would be untenable; where new houses were provided to reduce overcrowding amongst agricultural workers a subsidy of £2–£8 per dwelling per year for forty years could be given, with a mandatory proportionate rate contribution. Overcrowding was defined to exist where either: (a) it was impossible for persons of opposite sex of at least ten years of age (excluding husband and wife) to sleep in separate rooms. Kitchens were counted as rooms if they could be used as living rooms; or (b) the number of persons per room, counting children less than one as nought and children of one to ten as one-half, exceeded two in a one-room dwelling, three in two rooms, five in three rooms, seven and a half in four rooms, ten in five rooms. The act also made some changes in the terms of compensation in compulsory purchase and required the introduction of a single HRA for each authority.

Housing Act, 1936. An amending and consolidating Act.

Housing Act, 1938. A uniform subsidy was established both for slum clearance and decrowding. Dwellings built towards either purpose were to be subsidised by £5 10s per year per dwelling for forty years. The rate contribution was to be one-half of the Exchequer's. The three special case subsidies of 1935 were maintained but with changes in their levels.

Housing (Temporary Accommodation) Act, 1944. Provision made for the expenditure of £150 million on the manufacture and erection of temporary houses.

Housing (Temporary Provisions) Act, 1944. The scope of housing subsidies payable under the Housing (Financial Provisions) Act, 1938, on houses provided in connection with slum clearance and overcrowding, to be extended to houses built before October 1947 for general needs provision.

Town and Country Planning Act, 1944. Temporary provisions made for local authorities to acquire land at less than market values.

Building Materials and Housing Act, 1945. Financial provision was made for the Ministry of Works to bulk purchase building materials and equipment, including complete prefabricated houses. The 'prefabs' could be supplied to local housing authorities at reduced prices. The Ministry of Works could carry out any housing work undertaken by these authorities.

Housing (Financial and Miscellaneous Provisions) Act, 1946. A standard annual subsidy of £16 10s per house provided, to be supplemented by a mandatory contribution of £5 10s from the rates, payable over sixty years. Special subsidies were payable for houses for the agricultural population, housing in impoverished areas, flats on expensive sites, blocks with lifts and houses built on sites where subsidence was a risk. An extra capital grant payable on certain relatively high-cost permanent prefabricated houses.

Acquisition of Land (Authorisation Procedure) Act, 1946. This expedited acquisition procedure by reducing the period of time involved, the number of notices that had to be served and the number of interests that had to be treated.

Town and Country Planning Act, 1947. The basis of compensation under compulsory purchase was laid down as the value of the land in its existing or restricted use.

Housing Act, 1949. Empowered the authorities to provide housing accommodation for any member of the community, not exclusively for 'the working classes'. The Act also provided financial assistance for the improvement or conversion of houses whether by a local authority or a private person. Approved proposals carried out by the local authority received Exchequer contributions of three-quarters of the annual loss estimated to be incurred, payable annually for twenty years. Subsidies were made available for hostel accommodation provided by an authority and for houses constructed in stone or other materials to preserve the character of the surroundings.

Housing Act, 1952. The standard annual subsidy was increased to £26 14s to be supplemented by a rate subsidy of £8 18s. Consequential alterations were made in the other rates of subsidy. The minimum annual sum housing authorities were required to carry to the Housing Repairs Account was raised to £8 per dwelling.

Town Development Act, 1952. This enabled authorities of small towns at a distance from large and congested urban centres to carry out planned expansions in order to house people from those congested areas and to facilitate the building of factories to provide them with work near their new homes.

Housing Repairs and Rents Act, 1954. The law relating to clearance orders and the compulsory purchase of unfit houses was amended and a new standard of fitness was laid down. Housing authorities were required to estimate the size of their slum problem and to submit to the Minister their proposals for dealing with it. On improvement grants, the minimum standard to be met was reduced to a twelve-point specification and the life qualification of the property was reduced to fifteen years. A patching subsidy for houses with a five- to fifteen-year life was also introduced.

Town and Country Planning Act, 1954. The basis of compensation when local authorities compulsorily purchased land was the value in existing use plus any admitted development value in 1947. Ex gratia supplements were permitted for small owners suffering loss through having made no claim in 1947 for loss of development value.

Housing Subsidies Act, 1956. Exchequer subsidies on new local authority building were extensively revised. The subsidy for general needs construction was cut to £10 per annum for dwellings other than flats in blocks of four or more storeys. Dwellings provided to replace slums were to receive an annual sum of £22 1s, and those provided under town development schemes were to receive £24. In both cases the sums paid were raised to £32 for flats in four-storey blocks, £38 for flats in five-storey blocks and £50 for flats in six-storey blocks rising by £1 15s per flat for each storey in excess of six.

Slum Clearance (Compensation) Act, 1956. Owner-occupiers of unfit houses were compensated as if the property were fit, provided it had been purchased between September 1939 and December 1955. Where a small shop or business formed part of a dwelling, owner-occupiers and tenants with a lease exceeding one year were to receive full compulsory-purchase value.

Housing Act, 1957. An Act to consolidate the various enactments relating to housing other than on financial matters.

Housing (Financial Provisions) Act, 1958. Consolidated previous financial legislation.

House Purchase and Housing Act, 1959. The system of discretionary grants was continued on houses with a life of at least thirty years, whether for improvement or conversion. Standard grants were also introduced based on bringing houses with at least a fifteen-year life up to a five-point standard. Exchequer contributions were no longer to be based on estimated loss but on cost: they were equal to the loan charges which would be payable on three-eighths of the capital outlay up to a maximum of £310. For the first time the subsidy was available even on dwellings built with a government subsidy.

Town and Country Planning Act, 1959. The basis of compensation for compulsory purchase was to be assessed, once again, on the rules laid down in the 1919 Acquisition of Land Act—that an owner should receive for his land the value he could expect to get for it in the open market.

Housing Act, 1961. The system of Exchequer subsidies was recast. Subsidies were to be payable on all local authority dwellings approved for that purpose by the Minister. There were to be two standard rates. One rate of £24 per dwelling per year was payable on new dwellings built in local authorities when a sum equal to twice the aggregate gross value for rating purposes of all Housing Revenue Account dwellings fell short of the expenditure total in the HRA. The second rate, of £8, was payable when that test was not met. For local authorities with this notional deficit the sum of £24 was increased if the rate levy per £ of rateable value was higher than the England and Wales average. All the other special subsidies were adjusted at the same time. All subsidies committed under this Act could be reviewed in not less than ten years' time.

Land Compensation Act, 1961. A consolidation measure which repealed and re-enacted the provisions of the Acquisition of Land (Assessment of Compensation) Act, 1919 and certain subsequent enactments.

Housing Act, 1964. Patching grants were raised and standard grants became available for work up to a three-point standard.

Housing (Slum Clearance Compensation) Act, 1965. Continued the provision for owner-occupiers of unfit property purchased by them between 1939 and 1955 to be compensated at market values.

Housing Subsidies Act, 1967. Introduced an entirely new pattern of subsidies. They became payable on all approved dwellings for which local authorities had resolved to accept tenders on or after 25 November 1965. The subsidy met the *difference* between borrowing on the approved cost of a housing scheme at a 4 per cent rate of interest and at the representative rate of interest which was calculated from municipal borrowing rates generally. The pattern of supplementary subsidies was simultaneously adjusted, including the abolition of any subsidy to offset the extra costs to the local authority of building above six storeys.

Prices and Incomes Act, 1968. Made it unlawful for a council to increase rents unless the increases were in accordance with proposals approved by the Minister. Ceased to have effect after 1969. Section XII, which allowed local authorities to increase rents without serving a notice to quit, remained in force.

Rent (Control of Increases) Act, 1969. Came into force on 1 January

1970. Rent increases exceeding an average of 37½ new pence per week or a maximum of 50 pence per week in any fifty-two week period required the Minister's agreement.

Housing Act, 1969. The level of grants for rehabilitation was raised. The Exchequer continued to pay the housing authorities three-eighths of the loan charge incurred by the expenditure but the latter's permitted maximum was raised to £400 for standard grants and £2000 for discretionary grants which were renamed improvement grants. For flats in three-or-more-storey blocks and for properties acquired by an authority for improvement or conversion the maxima were higher.

In addition the definition of unfitness was amended to include bad internal arrangement; and under Part V of the Act virtually all owner-occupiers of unfit property compulsorily purchased received market value in compensation.

Housing Act, 1971. Provided enhanced rates of grant for improvement work completed before 1974 in assisted areas.

Housing Finance Act, 1972. It introduced a wholly new rent and subsidy system. Rents were to be determined using the concept of 'fair rent' innovated in the private sector by the 1965 Rent Act and modified to the minimum extent necessary. Fair rents were to be initially estimated by the local housing authorities but their final determination was to be the responsibility of Rent Scrutiny Boards. Provisions were made for a progression to fair rents, broadly requiring that gross annual rent income per dwelling should rise by £26 in each year after 1971-2 until the fair rent level was reached. A mandatory rent rebate system was introduced.

The concept of reckonable expenditure was introduced which included, with specified exceptions, all loan charges for land, new building and acquisition of houses; one-half of loan charges on improvement work (in addition to improvement contributions); higher interest charges on old debt; and current expenditure or management and maintenance. Exceptions were new building costs in excess of yardstick; improvement and acquisition costs in excess of approved limits; and repair and maintenance costs in excess of limits set by the central government in 1974-5. For the first time costs incurred before dwelling completion were also eligible for subsidy.

With respect to subsidies, the essential feature was that any difference between reckonable housing revenue account expenditure and rent income should be met by the Exchequer and the local rate fund in pre-scribed proportions. Non-reckonable expenditure fell on the rate fund. All subsidies payable under earlier Acts were terminated and replaced by the new provisions of which the residual subsidy was in effect a tapering out of existing subsidies. As rent rose relative to reckonable expenditure, subsidies would be withdrawn. When a surplus was pro-duced over and above a working balance of £30 per dwelling, it would be paid to the Secretary of State and when these payments exceeded rent allowances paid to the authority, the Secretary was to repay one-half of the excess to the local authority's rate fund. A new 'rising costs' subsidy applied to all new reckonable expenditure. It quickly became the dominant element and in 1972–3 90 per cent was funded by the Exchequer, scheduled to fall to 75 per cent in 1975–6.

Housing Act, 1974. It introduced Housing Action Areas. Within these improvement contributions were raised and councils had the power to compulsorily purchase housing in order to deal with landlords un-willing to improve.

Community Land Act, 1975. It extended the powers of the 'land authorities' to acquire, by agreement or compulsorily, land which is suitable for development either by themselves or others.

Housing Rents and Subsidies Act, 1975. The 'fair rent' concept was abandoned and local authorities were once again to charge 'reasonable rents' based on historic costs and to make rate fund contributions at their own discretion. The main new subsidies were: (i) basic element, consolidating all subsidies paid to housing revenue accounts in 1974–5 to continue at the same money amount; (ii) new capital costs element, paid at 66 per cent of the debt charge at the pool rate of interest on reckonable capital expenditure on land, new building, improvement and acquisition; (iii) supplementary financing element, paid at 33 per cent of the increase in the debt charge on pre-1975–6 housing debt resulting from an increase in the pool rate; (iv) special element paid only for 1975–7 to authorities otherwise obliged to make sharp rent increases at the end of the rent freeze; and (v) high-cost element paid to auth-orities with exceptionally high costs.

Development Land Tax Act, 1976. Local authorities have the right to compulsorily acquire land at its market value less development land tax. The tax is paid on the realised development value, with a number of exceptions, and initially is chargeable at $66\frac{2}{3}$ per cent on the first £150,000 and at 80 per cent on the remainder.

Housing (Homeless Persons) Act, 1977. Local housing authorities henceforth have a statutory duty to provide accommodation for certain groups of the homeless.

APPENDIX 2

The annual output of permanent local authority dwellings in Great Britain 1864-1976

Year	Starts	Completions
1864–90		89 p.a.
1891–1914		900 p.a.
1915–19		not known
1920		576
1921		16,786
1922		86,579
1923		67,062
1924		19,586
1925		23,862
1926		49,508
1927		83,948
1928		120,492
1929		69,677
1930		73,268
1931		63,996
1932		79,013
1933		68,156
1934		72,343
1935		57,326
1936		70,486
1937		87,423
1938		92,047
1939		121,653
1940		60,926
1941		20,122
1942		5,985
1943		4,095
1944		4,922
1945		3,364
1946	163,518	25,013
1947	155,779	97,340
1948	139,457	190,368
1949	162,248	165,946
1950	169,217	163,670
1951	170,857	162,584
1952	219,183	186,920
1953	231,001	229,305

Year	Starts	Completions
1954	196,388	223,731
1955	164,578	181,331
1956	139,859	154,971
1957	140,810	154,137
1958	109,804	131,614
1959	133,369	114,324
1960	112,879	116,358
1961	109,547	105,529
1962	124,099	116,424
1963	151,645	112,780
1964	159,127	141,132
1965	163,946	151,305
1966	166,644	161,435
1967	191,985	181,467
1968	170,948	170,214
1969	149,394	162,910
1970	131,506	157,067
1971	114,650	134,000
1972	99,583	104,553
1973	87,290	88,148
1974	120,894	103,279
1975	133,661	129,883
1976	124,462	129,202

The data for 1864–1914 are my own estimates of the annual averages.

The data for 1920–39 are for the year ending 31 March, i.e. 1920 means 1 April 1919 to 31 March 1920.

The data for 1920–30 exclude a small no. of houses built in England and Wales which received no state subsidy.

The data for 1940–4 are an amalgam of England and Wales data for the year ending 31 March and Scotland for the year ending 31 December.

Average tender price, floor area and price per square metre of five-bedspace dwellings in approved tenders in England and Wales 1914-75[a]

Year	Price (£)	Area (sq metres)	Price per sq metre	Year	Price (£)	Area (sq metres)	Price per sq metre
1914	235	n.a.	n.a.	1939	376	74·3	5·06
1915–18	n.a.	n.a.	n.a.	1940–4	n.a.	n.a.	n.a.
1919[b]	708	80·3	8·82	1945	1045	91·0	11·48
1920	881	80·3	10·97	1946[c]	1163	95·4	12·19
1921	643	76·6	8·39	1947	1230	97·2	12·65
1922	378	75·1	5·03	1948	1281	97·8	13·10
1923	380	73·6	5·16	1949	1294	98·0	13·2
1924	408	75·8	5·38	1950	1302	97·7	13·33
1925	444	75·1	5·91	1951	1366	95·9	14·24
1926	432	74·3	5·81	1952	1386	88·0	15·75
1927	408	72·8	5·60	1953	1384	85·2	16·24
1928	361	71·3	5·06	1954	1383	84·9	16·29
1929	346	69·9	4·95	1955	1418	84·8	16·72
1930	331	68·4	4·84	1956[d]	1472	84·7	17·38
1931	334	70·6	4·73	1957	1486	84·4	17·61
1932	295	66·9	4·41	1958	1485	83·9	17·70
1933	305	69·1	4·41	1959	1515	83·3	18·19
1934	305	69·1	4·41	1960	1611	83·3	19·34
1935	308	69·9	4·41	1961	1786	83·4	21·41
1936	312	69·1	4·52	1962	1967	84·3	23·33
1937	357	72·1	4·95	1963	2129	85·2	24·99
1938	360	74·3	4·85	1964	2303	85·5	26·94
				1965	2579	86·4	29·85
				1966	2782	87·8	31·69
				1967[e]	2951	88·0	33·53
				1968	3023	89·2	33·89
				1969	3159	89·6	35·26
				1970	3402	89·2	38·14
				1971	3864	89·3	43·27
				1972	4575	89·1	51·35
				1973	6173	89·0	69·36
				1974	7261	88·9	81·68
				1975	7984	88·6	90·11

Source: Girdwood Reports (1948, 1950, 1952), MHLG annual reports, Handbook of Statistics, HSGB, HCS.

a From 1914 to 1967 the data are for three-bedroom dwellings and thereafter for five-bedspace dwellings. Note that 1 sq metre equals 10·764 sq feet.

b 1919–39, mid-year data for non-parlour houses. Data estimated from graphs in the Girdwood Reports.

c 1946–56, annual data calculated as simple average of quarterly data.

d From 1956 third quarter houses constructed by new tradition methods are included.

e Hereupon data said to exclude GLC contracts.

APPENDIX 4

The Public Works Loan Board as a source of local authority borrowing 1938-9 to 1976-7

Two tables are presented. The first covers local authorities in England and Wales in the years 1938-9 and 1946-7 to 1959-60. It presents gross borrowing figures—borrowing *not* net of repayments. The second table covers local authorities in the United Kingdom in the years 1962-3 to 1976-7. It presents net borrowing figures so entries can be negative. The data required to produce a single table do not appear to have been published.

Local authority gross borrowing in England and Wales 1938-9 and 1946-7 to 1959-60 (£m)

1 Year	2 Total new loans	3 Advances from PWLB for new capital purposes	4 3/2 as %
1938–9	129·8	19·9	15
1946–7	149·9	95·4	64
1947–8	266·9	214·2	80
1948–9	287·3	215·1	75
1949–50	307·5	247·3	80
1950–1	340·4	280·7	82
1951–2	397·9	337·7	85
1952–3	473·9	366·4	77
1953–4	494·8	272·9	55
1954–5	491·4	340·3	69
1955–6	511·9	311·9	61
1956–7	501·0	109·1	22
1957–8	470·7	105·2	22
1958–9	463·7	36·3	8
1959–60[a]	486	40	8

Source: MHLG Annual Reports.
a Estimate.

Local authority net borrowing in the United Kingdom 1962–3 to 1976–7 (£m)

1 Year	2 Total net borrowing	3 Net advances from PWLB	4 3/2 as %
1962–3	541	−35	—
1963–4	658	− 7	—
1964–5	845	232	27
1965–6	967	535	55
1966–7	1052	543	52
1967–8	1090	371	34
1968–9	1174	476	41
1969–70	1087	537	49
1970–1	1296	688	53
1971–2	1414	829	59
1972–3	1562	924	59
1973–4	2560	978	38
1974–5	3309	1121	34
1975–6	2439	1149	47
1976–7	1993	613	31

Source: Financial Statistics.

APPENDIX 5

Government contributions in respect of permanent local authority housing in England and Wales 1945-6 to 1976-7 (£m)

Year	Pre-war legislation	Post-war legislation	1972 and 1975 Acts	Rent rebate subsidies	Capital grants for post-war houses	Contribution to council improvement conversion	Total
1945–6	14·1	–	–	–	–	–	14·1
1946–7	13·5	0·2	–	–	neg.	–	13·7
1947–8	13·0	1·7	–	–	4·4	–	19·1
1948–9	12·9	5·4	–	–	15·1	–	33·4
1949–50	12·2	7·9	–	–	4·5	–	24·6
1950–1	12·0	10·5	–	–	0·9	–	23·1
1951–2	11·8	13·2	–	–	0·3	neg.	25·3
1952–3	11·7	18·0	–	–	0·3	neg.	30·0
1953–4	11·7	23·8	–	–	0·1	neg.	35·6
1954–5	11·6	30·4	–	–	neg.	neg.	42·0
1955–6	11·6	36·6	–	–	neg.	neg.	48·2
1956–7	11·1	39·2	–	–	neg.	0·1	50·4
1957–8	11·0	42·0	–	–	neg.	0·1	53·1
1958–9	11·0	46·7	–	–	neg.	0·1	57·8
1959–60	10·9	49·2	–	–	neg.	0·2	60·3
1960–1	10·8	50·2	–	–	–	0·3	61·3
1961–2	10·8	52·8	–	–	–	0·5	64·1
1962–3	10·8	55·2	–	–	–	0·7	66·7
1963–4	9·4	58·6	–	–	–	1·1	69·1
1964–5	9·3	63·6	–	–	–	1·3	74·2
1965–6	9·0	68·7	–	–	–	1·4	79·1
1966–7	8·4	73·9	–	–	–	1·7	84·0
1967–8	7·6	86·5	–	–	–	2·0	96·1
1968–9	7·1	100·0	–	–	–	2·6	109·7
1969–70	6·6	118·9	–	–	–	3·1	128·6
1970–1	6·7	149·9	–	–	–	4·2	160·8
1971–2	5·8	179·8	–	–	–	6·8	192·4
1972–3	–	–	207·4	61	–	8·8	277·2
1973–4	–	–	209·1	130	–	22·5	361·6
1974–5	–	–	477·8	151	–	32·0	660·8
1975–6	–	–	763·0	179	–	31·0	973·0
1976–7	–	–	875·5	208	–	30·2	1113·7

Source: MHLG Annual Reports, HCS.

Notes

1 Before 1914: accumulation, contradiction and reform

1 E.J. Hobsbawm, *Industry and Empire*, Harmondsworth, Penguin, 1971, pp.27, 42.
2 Ibid., pp.86, 158.
3 Alexis de Tocqueville, *Journeys to England and Ireland*, J.P. Mayer (ed.), London, Faber, 1958, p.108.
4 Wohl suggests that it was not until the 1880s in Britain that poverty was seen as the root cause of poor housing conditions. As an example of this position he cites the medical officer for Hampstead who argued that the origin of the housing problem in London was the overwhelming fact that the city was inhabited by a majority of people divided by just one or two weeks' wages from starvation. See A.S. Wohl, 'The housing of the working classes in London 1815–1914', in S.D. Chapman (ed.), *The History of Working-class Housing: a Symposium,* Newton Abbot, David Ampersand Charles, 1971, p.38. In the same volume Chapman's essay, 'Working-class housing in Nottingham during the Industrial Revolution', demonstrates for a single town the difference in the housing conditions of the high-wage lace makers and the poverty-stricken hosiery workers.
5 Karl Marx, *Capital*, volume 3, New York, International Publishers, 1967, p.774.
6 David Harvey, in an early sketch of the exercise of monopoly power in housing sub-markets, has assumed that high incomes systematically outbid low incomes in the demand for dwellings. His failure to incorporate the economic power inherent in over-crowding invalidates his sequential space packing model. See *Social Justice and the City*, London, Edward Arnold, 1973, pp.168–71.
7 J. Hollingshead, *Ragged London in 1861*, London, 1861, p.118.
8 Cited by the Earl of Shaftesbury, *Hansard,* CXV (new series April 1851), c.1260–1.
9 Enid Gauldie, *Cruel Habitations: a History of Working-class Housing 1780–1918*, London, Allen & Unwin, 1974, p.93. There is an excellent account of jerry building in suburban London in the second half of the nineteenth century by E. Gwynn, *Public Health*, vol.13, no.14, January 1901.

10 Before the Royal Commission on the Health of Towns in 1845. Quoted in the *Labourer's Friend,* April 1852, p.53. These were the days, too, when the removal of night soil could depend on the price of guano! See James H. Treble, 'Liverpool working-class housing, 1801–51', in Chapman, op. cit., p.185.

11 See Gauldie, op. cit., pp.110–12.

12 M.W. Flinn (ed.), *Edwin Chadwick's Report on the Sanitary Conditions of the Labouring Population of Great Britain,* Edinburg University Press, 1965.

13 J. Simon, *Public Health Reports,* vol.2, London, 1887, p.207.

14 Adam Smith, *An Inquiry into the Nature and Causes of the Wealth of Nations* (ed. E. Cannan), vol.I, London, Methuen, pp.91–2.

15 Gauldie, op. cit., pp.187–8.

16 Hobsbawm, op. cit., p.87.

17 Gauldie, op. cit., pp.106–10, 266–7.

18 *The Economist,* vol.6 (13 May 1848), p.536.

19 Gauldie, op. cit. Part 4 contains an extensive account of these movements.

20 Since the time of Aristotle it has been recognised that when a commodity is produced, be it an object or a service, a vital distinction must be drawn between two attributes, its exchange-value and its use-value. (Marx added a third attribute, the commodity's value, i.e. the labour time socially necessary to produce it.) Exchange-value is a relatively simple concept and means the quantity of another commodity for which one unit of the first commodity can be exchanged. When the exchange is between that unit and money we can simply speak of the commodity's price. Use-value is more slippery. When we reflect upon the object (or service) we can consider it from the point of view of the use to which it is put and then go on to adopt one or more measures of its usefulness so defined. Such measures include straightforward quantitative calculations of physical attributes or a notional 'score' derived from a set of such calculations, each with its own relative weight. In the specific case of a dwelling, its usefulness from the point of view of the resident reflects a number of characteristics such as the dwelling's location within the city, the character and facilities of its immediate environment, its area or volume, its effectiveness in excluding precipitation and noise, how light and dry it is, its amenities such as bathroom, sink, water closet, number of bedrooms etc., its self-containedness, whether or not it has a garden attached, its height above the ground in the case of a flat, its stability and durability and so forth and so on. In the rest of this book I shall mean by use-value the notional score of a dwelling based on these attributes. The important fact that the relative weights given to different attributes vary between individuals does not, I believe, undermine the term's usefulness as an analytic instrument.

21 Gauldie, op. cit., p.132. Also see pp.266–7.
22 Octavia Hill, *Macmillan's Magazine*, June 1874, p.135.
23 See H.J. Dyos 'Railways and housing in Victorian London', *Journal of Transport History*, vol.2, 1955–6 and 'Some social costs of railway building in London', *Journal of Transport History*, vol.3, 1957–8, also John R. Kellett, *The Impact of Railways on Victorian Cities*, London, Routledge & Kegan Paul, 1969.
24 The Earl of Shaftesbury. Quoted in Hugh Quigley and Ismay Goldie, *Housing and Slum Clearance in London*, London, Methuen, 1934, p.28.
25 Wohl, op. cit., p.19. See also John Butt, 'Working-class Housing in Glasgow, 1851–1914', in Chapman, op. cit., pp.59–63.
26 Gauldie, op. cit., ch.23, reviews the origins and results of both Acts in detail. Their full titles were the Artisans' and Labourers' Dwellings Act, 1868, and the Artisans' and Labourers' Dwellings Improvement Act, 1875.
27 Ibid., pp.282, 285.
28 Tarn says of the Metropolitan Board of Works schemes under the Act that 'in practice all the sites were offered for sale as land for house building, and only a minute proportion for commercial development.' J.N. Tarn, *Five per cent Philanthropy: An Account of Housing in Urban Areas between 1840 and 1914*, Cambridge, Cambridge University Press, 1973, p.80.
29 Paul Corrigan and Norman Ginsburg, 'Tenant Struggle and Class Struggle' in M. Edwards *et al.*, *Political Economy and the Housing Question*, London, Political Economy of Housing Workshop, 1975, pp.134–46.
30 See Gauldie, op. cit., pp.279–80.
31 Wohl, op. cit., p.20.
32 *The Builder*, vol.39 (1880, ii), p.187.
33 In Rev. A. Osborne Jay's *A Story of Shoreditch : Being a Sequel to 'Life in Darkest London'*, London, 1896, p.11. Quoted by Wohl, op. cit., p.19.
34 Hobsbawm, op. cit., p.154.
35 Quoted by Gauldie, op. cit., p.345.
36 See Wohl, op. cit., p.39.
37 Sir Sydney Waterlow in evidence to the Royal Commission on the Housing of the Working Classes, *Report*, vol.II, Minutes of Evidence, 1885, p.425.
38 See Wohl, op. cit., p.39.
39 Quoted by James Hole, *Homes of the Working Classes*, London, 1866, pp.55–6.
40 See Tarn, op. cit., p.84.
41 Ibid., p.100.
42 Ibid., p.102.
43 Quigley and Goldie, op. cit., pp.52–3.
44 The Metropolitan Association for Improving the Dwellings of

the Industrious Classes was founded in September 1841 at a meeting presided over by the Rector of Spitalfields, the Rev. Henry Taylor. See Tarn, op. cit., p.22.

45　See Gauldie, op. cit., p.234.

46　Wohl, op. cit., p.39.

47　Liverpool, then, is the first case of municipal housing using national legislation. However, this was preceded in London by the 1864 Farringdon Road Scheme of the Court of Common Council of the City of London. £37,000 was spent on six-storey blocks of two- and three-room flats for 160 families. The architect, Horace Jones, modelled his design on Waterlow's Mark Street Block. See Tarn, op. cit., p.61.

48　*Nineteenth Century*, vol.12, August 1882, p.235.

49　See Gauldie, op. cit., pp.279, 351. The most important single project was Liverpool's Victoria Buildings. Soon after it had received the Royal Assent, the Cross Act was used by the corporation to clear slums in the Nash Grove district. About 1100 people were displaced. The cleared land was offered for sale to private developers but because of the Act's rehousing requirements there were no buyers. The amending Act of 1879 led the authority to shift their position: the land could be sold and housing provided elsewhere. The initiative seems to have come to nothing. In 1883 the council agreed that it would seek permission to build its own high-density scheme on the original site. The Local Government Board agreed but refused to concede the request for continued ownership by the council beyond the 1875 Act's ten-year limit. The council then put the project out to tender nearly eight years after beginning clearance of the site. Compulsory purchase and construction were financed by a PWLC loan of £50,000. In October 1885 Sir Richard Cross opened Victoria Buildings, which provided accommodation for 271 families in one–three-room flats in five-storey blocks arranged around a central court. The sources are Tarn, op. cit., pp.89–91 and Gauldie, op. cit., pp.279, 299.

50　See Tarn, op. cit., pp.62–4 and Butt, op. cit.

51　A power first conceded by the definition of lodging houses in the 1885 Act, an Act which in retrospect we can see to have been an interim measure before 1890.

52　London's Boundary Street scheme is a major example. The London County Council first took up office in March 1889, replacing the defunct and discredited Metropolitan Board of Works, several of whose architects had been exposed for venal malpractice. There were six outstanding MBW clearance sites under the Cross Act which the new council made repeated but unsuccessful attempts to sell off in 1889–92. After the passage of the 1890 Act the council set up a Housing of the Working Classes Committee and using Part I of the Act–i.e. the amended Cross legislation–the Boundary Street Scheme in the East End was initiated. It was to be the LCC's first estate. Fifteen acres fell within the improvement scheme and 5719 people were displaced from the site. The first replacement blocks were completed in 1895 and the last in 1900. Some had been built by the LCC's own Works Department and others designed by LCC architects. The scheme provided accommodation for 4700 people in 1069 tenements, of which 88 per cent were either two- or three-room flats and 16 per cent shared either lavatory or scullery. A communal laundry was built. No attempt was made to build for the poorest fraction of the working class. The sources are Gauldie, op. cit., p.295 and Tarn, op. cit., pp.129–34.

53 The rate of interest paid by the government on consols at the end of the century was about 3 per cent. At about the same time the interest rate charged by the PWLC on their loans to local authorities was 3¾ per cent on 30-year loans and more on longer term loans. See Quigley and Goldie, op. cit., p.32 and Wohl, op. cit., p.53.

54 See Tarn, op. cit., p.130 and Wohl, op. cit., p.40.

55 Octavia Hill, 'Improvements now practicable', *Nineteenth Century*, vol.14, December 1883, p.925.

56 See Tarn, op. cit., p.113.

57 Lord Shaftesbury, *Nineteenth Century*, vol.14, December 1883, p.935.

58 John Honeyman, *The Dwellings of the Poor*, Glasgow, 1890, p.26.

59 The Marquis of Salisbury, 'Labourers' and Artisans' Dwellings', in the *National Review*, November 1883, p.312.

60 Quoted in *The Builder*, vol.47, 1884, p.746.

61 Gauldie, ibid., p.289.

62 There can be no doubt about the exclusiveness of council dwellings. See Gauldie, ibid., p.289 and Wohl, op. cit., p.41.

63 See Tarn, op. cit., pp.110–11.

64 The data on London are taken from Wohl, op. cit.

65 The number of workmen's trains running daily to London were: 1883, 106; 1897, 466; 1914, 1966. After 1871, only the outer areas of London gained population in aggregate although some of the central districts continued to grow. Ibid., pp.16, 30.

66 Ibid., p.24.

67 Quigley and Goldie, op. cit., p.64.

68 Wohl, op. cit., p.42. Also see Tarn, op. cit., Ch.8.

69 Quoted in Quigley and Goldie, op. cit., p.42.

70 See D. Englander, *The Workmen's National Housing Council, 1898–1914*, thesis submitted for the degree of MA at the University of Warwick, 1973.

71 Gauldie, op.cit., pp.298–302.

72 The 44th *Annual Report* of the Local Government Board estimated that in England and Wales in 1913–14 there existed not more than 20,000 such dwellings built under the 1890 Act. To this we can add the 160 units of the 1864 Farringdon Road scheme (see note 47); the 271 tenements in the Victoria Buildings scheme (see note 49); and the 2199 units built in Glasgow by the CIT

(see Butt, op.cit.). This gives a total of 22,630 dwellings; rounding up by a further 1370 units is probably over generous.

73 In England and Wales the average annual increase in the number of houses between 1891 and 1911 was 86,300. (The average number of council dwellings completed was about 870; see J. Parry Lewis, *Building Cycles and Britain's Growth*, 1965, p.332.)

74 The data for 1912-14 loan sanctions can be found in the Local Government Board's *Memorandum No. 4 . . . of the Housing, Town Planning, etc. Act, 1909*, London, 1915, p.7.

75 See Lewis, op.cit., p.317.

76 See London County Council, *Housing of the Working Classes 1855-1912*, 1913, p.157 and London County Council, *Housing*, 1928, p.29.

77 Wohl, op.cit., p.41.

78 Paul Wilding, 'Towards Exchequer subsidies for housing 1906-14', *Social and Economic Administration*, vol.6, no.1, 1972, p.5.

79 Ibid., p.6.

80 Ibid., pp.9-10.

81 *The History of Housing Reform*, National Unionist Association of Conservative and Liberal Unionist Organisations, 1913, p.31. Quoted by Wilding, ibid., p.10.

82 *The Land: The Report of the Land Enquiry Committee*, Hodder & Stoughton, 1914, vol.2, p.113.

83 Wilding, op.cit., p.15.

2 1914-39: housing policy and the balance of class forces

1 See Marian Bowley, *Housing and the State 1919-44*, London, Allen & Unwin, 1945, pp.10-12, 262.

2 Harry W. Richardson and Derek H. Aldcroft, *Building in the British Economy between the Wars*, London, Allen & Unwin, 1968, pp.223-4.

3 Andrew Glyn and Bob Sutcliffe, *British Capitalism, the Workers and the Profits Squeeze*, Harmondsworth, Penguin, 1972, p.25.

4 Paul Roger Wilding, *Government and Housing: a study in the Development of Social Policy 1906-39*, D.Phil. thesis of the University of Manchester, March, 1970.

5 Ibid., p.47.

6 Ibid., p.131.

7 Ibid., pp.100-1.

8 Ibid., p.107.

9 House of Commons debates, *Hansard* vol.116, 1919, c.1180.

10 Richardson and Aldcroft suggest the termination of controls brought with it a doubling of the price of some materials within months, op.cit., p.137.

11 Wilding, op.cit., p.130.

12 Ibid., p.163.

13 Ibid., p.167. There is a clear parallel here with the use of the housing-cost yardstick in the 1970s.
14 Ibid., p.158.
15 Ibid., p.175.
16 See Bowley, op. cit., pp.26–31.
17 Some Marxists argue that local authority housebuilding can be seen as the response of the state to the demands of building industry capitalists but 1920–1 is a perfect falsification of the hypothesis. The government cut came when the industry most needed a stimulus.
18 Glyn and Sutcliffe, op. cit., p.24.
19 David Ricardo, *On the Principles of Political Economy, and Taxation*, Cambridge, Cambridge University Press, 1970, p.290. (First published in 1817.)
20 The classical and neo-classical views on effective demand and public policy are sketched out in Joan Robinson and John Eatwell, *An Introduction to Modern Economics*, revised ed., London, McGraw-Hill, 1973, pp.23–5, 46–8.
21 See Bowley, op. cit., p.26.
22 See Wilding, op. cit., pp.103–4.
23 See Bowley, op. cit., p.32. Richardson and Aldcroft come to the same view, op. cit., pp.161–2.
24 Once again, Wilding's thesis provides an invaluable record of the internal debate. For a much fuller account of the death throes of the Addison subsidy, see his Chapter 8 upon which I have also drawn for the sequence of events leading up to the passage of the 1923 Act.
25 Ibid., p.184.
26 House of Commons debates, *Hansard* vol.143, 1921, c.1606.
27 Bowley, op. cit., p.271.
28 Ibid., pp.23–4.
29 Quoted by Wilding, op. cit., p.194.
30 House of Commons debates, *Hansard* vol.665, 1923, c.1543.
31 Wilding, p.209.
32 See Keith Feiling, *The Life of Neville Chamberlain*, London, Macmillan, 1946, pp.53–5, 86.
33 Wilding, op. cit., p.206.
34 Eric Hobsbawm, *Industry and Empire*, Harmondsworth, Penguin, 1969, p.209.
35 Wilding, op. cit., p.220.
36 Glyn and Sutcliffe, op. cit., pp.109–10. For an account of the return to the gold standard set within the context of international economic developments, see J.K. Galbraith, *Money: Whence it came. Where it went*, London, André Deutsch, 1975, pp.164–8.
37 Bowley, op. cit., pp.109–10.
38 Ibid., p.25.
39 Ibid., p.45.
40 Ibid., pp.97–9.

41 Ibid., p.129. Richardson and Aldcroft have pointed out that, just as with the new local authority dwellings, those houses subsidised under the Chamberlain Act but built for owner-occupation or private rental were also taken up by those strata of the population which least needed state assistance, op.cit., pp.173–4.

42 Glyn and Sutcliffe, op.cit., p.29.

43 Bowley, op.cit., p.135.

44 Ibid., pp.147–8.

45 See Henry Clay, *Lord Norman*, Macmillan, London, 1957, p.392.

46 The post-war data are drawn from Bowley, op. cit., p.271. They describe completions in England and Wales and are for the years ending 31 March. Thus, 1930, for example, means 1 April 1929–31 March 1930.

47 Ibid., p.172.

48 See, for example, Simon Clarke and Norman Ginsburg, 'The political economy of housing', in M. Edwards *et al.* (eds), *Political Economy and the Housing Question*, London, Political Economy of Housing Workshop, 1975, pp.3–33; Bowley, op. cit., Chapter 5; and Richardson and Aldcroft, op. cit., Chapter 9.

49 See Bowley, op. cit., p.279.

50 See E. Nevin, *The Mechanism of Cheap Money,* Cardiff, University of Wales Press, 1955. The shift from 75% to 95% cover was linked with the development of collateral security provided by builders. The relation of this to jerry-building was made explicit by the Borders' case. See Noreen Branson and Margot Heinemann, *Britain in the Nineteen Thirties*, St Albans, Panther, 1973, pp.206–11.

51 See Martin Boddy, 'Building and owner occupation', in M. Edwards *et al.* (eds), *Housing and Class in Britain*, London, Political Economy of Housing Workshop, 1976, p.33.

52 Bowley, op. cit., p.76.

53 See Philip Massey, 'The expenditure of 1,360 British middle-class households in 1938/9', *Journal of the Royal Statistical Society*, 1942; and Ministry of Labour Cost of Living Inquiry, *Ministry of Labour Gazette*, December 1940 and January 1941.

54 Bowley, op. cit., p.269.

55 Report on Local Expenditure, London, HMSO, 1932; Ministry of Health circulars 1311, 1334.

56 Wilding, op. cit., p.315.

57 Bowley, op. cit., p.140.

58 Wilding, op. cit., p.317.

59 Ibid., p.310.

60 Alison Ravetz, *Model Estate: Planned Housing at Quarry Hill, Leeds*, London, Croom Helm, 1974, pp.33–6.

61 Bowley, op. cit., p.148.

62 Branson and Heinemann, op. cit., p.211.

63 See Steve Schifferes, 'Council tenants and housing policy in the 1930s: the contradictions of state intervention', in Edwards *et al.*, op. cit. (1976), p.64–71.

64 Bowley, op. cit., pp.145-6.
65 Wilding, op. cit., p.354.
66 Report of the Overcrowding Survey, England and Wales, 1936.
67 Richardson and Aldcroft, op. cit., p.186.
68 Bowley, op. cit., p.167.

3 Land: site acquisition and residential densities

1 The most lucid analysis of landed property in Britain is by
D. Massey and A. Catalano, *Capital and Land: Land Ownership
by Capital in Great Britain*, London, Edward Arnold, 1978.
2 See for example Keith Davies, *Law of Compulsory Purchase and
Compensation*, London, Butterworths, 1972.
3 An alternative but similar procedure, also under Part III of the
1957 Housing Act, is by declaring a redevelopment area but these
powers are used much less frequently.
4 29 February 1976.
5 Stephen Merrett, 'A theory of the capitalist land market', unpublished paper, CES, 1978. See also Peter Ambrose, *The Land Market
and the Housing System*, Urban and Regional Studies Working
Paper no. 3, University of Sussex, 1976.
6 The concept of the degree of monopoly is discussed by Joan
Robinson and John Eatwell in *An Introduction to Modern
Economics*, London, McGraw-Hill, 1974, pp.154-5. There it is
used to explain variations in the mark-up on prime costs when
manufacturers set their product prices. The link between land
prices and the quasi-monopoly position conferred by planning is
pointed out by Max Neutze in 'Land prices and urban land market
policy', *Papers from the Urban Economics Conference 1973*, vol. 2,
London, CES, 1974, pp.441-82.
7 Roy Drewett, 'Land values and the suburban land-market', in
Peter Hall *et al., The Containment of Urban England*, vol. 2,
London, PEP, Allen & Unwin and Sage, 1973.
8 *Let us face the future*, Labour Party, 1945. On land nationalisation
see Lewis Silkin, *The Nation's Land*, Fabian Research Series,
no.70, 1943.
9 For example, J.B. Cullingworth, *Town and Country Planning in
Britain*, revised 5th ed., London, Allen & Unwin, 1974, p.147.
10 Fuller details of the Act are given in Appendix 1. Compensation
at existing use-value is not operative until after the Second
Appointed Day of the 1975 Community Land Act which will be
in 1985 at the earliest.
11 In this section I have not described the legal position with respect
to payments for well-maintained houses, special payments to
owner-occupiers, and compensation payments to owners and
leaseholders of small shops and businesses. Full details are given in
the 1936 Housing Act, the 1956 Slum Clearance (Compensation)

Act, the 1957 Housing Act, the 1965 Housing (Slum Clearance) Act, and the 1969 Housing Act.

12 Cited in National Community Development Project, *Profits against Houses: an Alternative Guide to Housing Finance*, London, NCDP, 1976, p.23.

13 H.L.I. Neuburger and B.M. Nichol, *The Recent Course of Land and Property Prices and the Factors underlying it*, Research Report no.4, London, Department of the Environment, 1976, p.16–17. The figure excludes purchases in the GLC area which are shown on p.17 of the report.

14 Ibid., p.16.

15 I have not used the data presented by Vallis in a widely quoted article since his residential land-price data are drawn overwhelmingly from the south-east region and the number of observations is very sparse—only twenty-eight for the period 1947–64. See E.A. Vallis, 'Urban land and building prices 1892–1969', *Estates Gazette*, May–June, 1972.

16 See H.W. Richardson, J. Vipond and R.A. Furbey, 'Land prices in Edinburgh 1952–67: a study of Edinburgh City Corporation land purchases', *Scottish Journal of Political Economy*, vol.21, no.1, February 1974, pp.67–75.

17 Two 'eccentric' observations are excluded. See ibid., p.72, footnote 5.

18 Chapter 1, p.17.

19 See for example Lewis Silkin, op.cit., p.20; Michael Jones and Richard Hill, 'The political economy of housing form', in M. Edwards *et al.*, *Political Economy and the Housing Question*, London, Political Economy of Housing Workshop, 1975, p.149.

20 P.A. Stone, *Urban Development in Britain:Standards, Costs and Resources, 1964-2004*, vol.1, Cambridge, Cambridge University Press, 1970, p.102.

21 Lionel Needleman, *The Economics of Housing*, London, Staples Press, 1965, p.91. Needleman was referring to his own published work of 1961, in which land cost includes the items under columns 3 and 4 in Table 3·4.

22 Peter Hall *et al.*, op. cit.; E.W. Cooney, 'High flats in local authority housing in England and Wales since 1945', in Anthony Sutcliffe (ed.), *Multi-storey Living: the British Working-Class Experience*, London, Croom Helm, 1974.

23 Peter Hall, 'The containment of urban England', *Geographical Journal*, vol.140, 1974, pp.387, 391.

24 Cooney, op.cit., pp.163–4.

25 Hall, op.cit., p.397.

26 Roy Drewett, 'The developers: decision processes', in Peter Hall *et al.*, op.cit., p.176.

27 Philip Lowe, 'The environmental lobby', *Built Environment Quarterly*, December 1975, p.238.

28 Cooney, op. cit., pp.154, 160.

29 Stone, op. cit., p.449.
30 See Peter Hall, op. cit., p.391.

4 Production: the housebuilding industry

1   Central Statistical Office, *National Income and Expenditure 1966-76*, London, HMSO, 1977, Table 1·11.
2   Donald Bishop, 'Note on some factors affecting productivity', Appendix 1 to *Report of the Committee of Inquiry under Professor E.H. Phelps Brown into Certain Matters concerning Labour and Civil Engineering*, Cmnd 3714, London, HMSO, 1968, p.170. See also C.T. Relf, 'The Building Time-table: the Significance of Duration', BERU, London, University College, 1974 (Mimeo), p.6.
3   Patricia M. Hillebrandt, *Economic Theory and the Construction Industry*, London, Macmillan, 1974, p.83.
4   P.A. Stone, *Urban Development in Britain:Standards, Costs and Resources, 1964-2004*, vol.1, *Population Trends and Housing*, Cambridge, Cambridge University Press, 1970, p.225.
5   Ibid., p.223.
6   See John Sugden, 'The place of construction in the economy', in D.A. Turin (ed.), *Aspects of the Economics of Construction*, London, George Godwin, 1976, p.5. This figure is for the construction industry as a whole.
7   *Report of the Committee of Inquiry under Professor E.H. Phelps Brown*, op. cit., p.35.
8   Stone, op. cit., p.222.
9   NEDC, *The Construction Industry*, London, HMSO, 1964, pp.16-17.
10 Stone, op. cit., p.226.
11 Bishop, op. cit., pp.177–8.
12 NBPI, *Pay and Conditions in the Building Industry*, Report no. 92, Cmnd 3837, London, HMSO, 1968, p.20. Supplementary Table II of *Housing and Construction Statistics* no. 22 shows that 22 per cent of the total value of construction output in Great Britain in 1976-7 was carried out through subcontracting.
13 See Lionel Needleman, *The Economics of Housing*, London, Staples Press, 1965, p.88. Also Ministry of Labour, *The Construction Industry*, Manpower Studies no. 3, London, HMSO, 1965, p.19.
14 Sugden, op. cit., p.10.
15 P.A. Stone and W.J. Reiners, 'Organisation and efficiency of the housebuilding industry in England and Wales', *Journal of Industrial Economics*, April 1954, p.129.
16 See Relf, op. cit., p.11.
17 Marian Bowley, *The British Building Industry: Four Studies in Response and Resistance to Change*, Cambridge University Press, 1966, pp.251–3.

18 See for example: Elizabeth Layton, *Building by Local Authorities*, London, Allen & Unwin, 1961, pp.192–4; Sir Harold Emmerson, *Survey of Problems before the Construction Industries*, London, HMSO, 1962, pp.8–10; Harry Brack, *Building for a New Society*, London, Fabian Society, 1964, p.26; Committee on the Placing and Management of Contracts, *Report*, London, 1964, pp.3–6; NBPI, Cmnd 3837, op. cit., p.19; NEDO Working Party, *The Public Client and the Construction Industries*, London, HMSO, 1975, pp.46–7.

19 Committee on the Placing and Management of Contracts, op. cit., p.7.

20 NEDO, *The Public Client and the Construction Industries*, p.38.

21 HCS, no. 18, Table XXV (a).

22 Bowley, op. cit., p.420.

23 Layton, op. cit., p.190.

24 NEDO, *The Public Client and the Construction Industries*, Chapter 3.

25 Ibid., p.29.

26 C.T. Relf, *The Building Time-table: the Public Sector*, BERU, University College, London, 1974, Fig. 3.

27 For a discussion of the rotation of capital in the private housing sector see Martin Boddy, 'Building societies and owner occupation', in M. Edwards *et al.*, *Housing and Class in Britain*, London, Political Economy of Housing Workshop, 1976.

28 NBPI Cmnd 3837, op. cit., p.19.

29 Christine Whitehead, *The U.K. Housing Market: an Econometric Model*, Farnborough, Saxon House, 1974, p.25.

30 See HCS, no. 23, Table 20.

31 NEDO, *The Public Client and the Construction Industries*, p.109.

32 HCS, no. 22, Table XXVII.

33 Layton, op. cit., p.170.

34 HCS, no. 22, Table V.

35 See, for example, North East Trade Union Studies Information Unit, *Direct Labour – the Answer to Building Chaos*, Newcastle-upon-Tyne, June 1977. The most comprehensive study of direct labour and its relationship to private contracting is to be found in Direct Labour Collective, *Building with Direct Labour*, London, 1978.

36 The graph was constructed in the following way: the price per sq. metre data in Appendix 3 were multiplied by 90 in each year so that the dwelling space was standardised at 90 sq. metres; this price series was then indexed with 1970 set at 100; this index was divided by the general index of retail prices for 1948 onwards, contained in the 1975 supplement to the Central Statistical Office's *Economic Trends* and then multiplied by 100. If the rate of increase of the standardised unit prices in tenders from 1948 to 1975 had been no different from that of the general level of retail prices, then the graph would have been a straight line at the value of 100.

37 Michael Ball, 'British housing policy and the housebuilding industry', *Capital and Class*, vol.4, Spring 1978, pp.78–99.

38 The index holds space standards constant at 90 sq. metres but not the other components of use-value.

39 Design of dwellings subcommittee of the Central Housing Advisory Committee, *Design of Dwellings*, London, HMSO, 1944.

40 Ibid., p.49.

41 *Summary Report of the Ministry of Health for the year ended 31st March, 1945*, Cmd 6710, London, HMSO, 1945, pp.34–5.

42 A useful description of the improved equipment and fittings can be found in J.B. Cullingworth's *Housing and Local Government in England and Wales*, London, Allen & Unwin, 1966, p.142.

43 *Report of the MHLG for the period 1950/51 to 1954*, London, 1955, p.14.

44 MHLG, *Homes for Today and Tomorrow*, Report of the CHAC subcommittee chaired by Sir Parker Morris, London, HMSO, 1961, pp.3–4. Several years earlier Cleeve Barr had also attacked the design weakness of the People's Home, see A.W. Cleeve Barr, *Public Authority Housing*, London, Batsford, 1958.

45 *Homes for Today and Tomorrow*, pp.21–2.

46 Vere Hole, 'Housing standards and social trends', in *Urban Studies*, November 1965, p.144.

47 MHLG, *Homes for Today and Tomorrow*, p.4.

48 Ibid., p.15.

49 Ibid., p.33.

50 Ibid., p.17.

51 Ibid., p.56. The Parker Morris report also included recommendations on play space and provision for cars. In the latter case they suggested design should provide space for a car for every dwelling and pedestrian segregation. At densities of 100–160 habitable rooms per acre the total cost per dwelling exceeded the aggregate cost of their six recommended internal improvements! The attempt to implement these proposals certainly must have played a role in the rapid increase in unit costs which we noted in Graph 4·2.

52 *Report of the MHLG 1966*, Cmnd 1725, London, HMSO, 1962, p.16.

53 MHLG, Circular 13/62, *Homes for Today and Tomorrow*, February 1962.

54 *Report of the MHLG 1965 and 1966*, Cmnd 3282, London, HMSO, 1967, p.64.

55 MHLG, *The Housing Programme 1965 to 1970*, Cmnd 2838, London, HMSO, 1965, p.14.

56 *Report for 1965 and 1966*, p.64; *Report for 1967 and 1968*, p.5.

57 MHLG, Circular 36/67, *Housing Standards, Costs and Subsidies*, April 1967.

58 See National Community Development Project, *Profits against Houses: an Alternative Guide to Housing Finance*, London, 1976, pp.26–9.

5 Production: private rehabilitation and public redevelopment

1 R.W. Kirwan and D.B. Martin, *The Economics of Urban Residential Renewal and Improvement,* CES Working Paper no.77, London, 1972.

2 The pith of Kirwan and Martin's argument is contained in pp.19–40 of their paper. For brevity's sake I have not included reference to their discussion of economic obsolescence.

3 D.L. Munby, *The Rent Problem,* London, Fabian Society, 1952; James MacColl, *Policy for Housing,* London, Fabian Society, 1954 and *Plan for Rented Houses,* Fabian Society, London, 1957; David Eversley, *Rents and Social Policy,* London, Fabian Society, 1955. Malcolm Wicks has written a useful summary of the debate within the party in his *Rented Housing and Social Ownership,* London, Fabian Society, 1973.

4 Labour Party, *Signposts for the Sixties,* London, 1961.

5 MHLG, *The Housing Programme 1965 to 1970,* Cmnd 2838, London, HMSO, 1965.

6 Allied Ironfounders, *The Stockton Test—An Experiment in British Housing,* London, 1953.

7 DoE, *Widening the Choice, the Next Steps in Housing,* Cmnd 5280, London, HMSO, 1973, p.9.

8 Chris Holmes, *Tomorrow in Upper Holloway: a Plan for Area Improvement,* London, Shelter, 1973.

9 This point is made in the separate studies of Duncan and of Kirwan and Martin. T.L.C. Duncan, *Housing Improvement Policies in England and Wales,* Birmingham, 1974, p.20 et seq.; Kirwan and Martin, op. cit., p.129 et seq.

10 Kirwan and Martin, op. cit., p.130.

11 Quoted by Simon Pepper, *Housing Improvement: Goals and Strategy,* London, Lund Humphries, 1971, p.21.

12 Stephen Merrett, 'Gentrification', in Edwards *et al*, (eds), *Housing and Class in Britain,* London, Political Economy Housing Workshop, 1976.

13 Duncan, op. cit., p.87.

14 See Duncan, op. cit., Chapter 5 and Anne Power, *David and Goliath: Barnsbury 1973,* London, Holloway Neighbourhood Law Centre, 1973.

15 Kirwan and Martin, op. cit., p.126.

16 1957 Housing Act, Sections 42 and 43. The 1957 Act definition of unfitness is identical with that in the Housing Rents and Subsidies Act, 1954.

17 Ibid., Part II.

18 Raphael Samuel, James Kincaid and Elizabeth Slater, 'But nothing happens', in *New Left Review,* January–April 1962, pp.38–69. MHLG, *Slum Clearance (England and Wales),* Cmd 9593, London, HMSO, 1955.

19 Samuel, Kincaid and Slater, op. cit., p.51.

20 *National Sample Survey of the Condition of Houses*, appendix to MHLG, *Old Houses into New Homes*, Cmnd 3602, London, HMSO, 1968.
21 MHLG, *Our Older Homes: a Call for Action*, London, HMSO, 1966, p.21. The chairperson of the sub-committee which produced the report was Mrs Evelyn Denington.
22 David Muchnik, *Urban Renewal in Liverpool*, London, Bell, 1970.
23 Pepper, op. cit., pp.25-8.
24 Ibid., p.72.
25 It is most unfortunate that after 1967 the official data do not permit this ratio to be calculated as thereafter the 'badly arranged' and 'other' houses cleared are lumped together in a single column. Was this purely for statistical brevity?
26 B.J. Parker, 'Some sociological implications of slum clearance programmes', in David Donnison and David Eversley (eds), *London: Urban Patterns, Problems and Policies*, London, Heinemann, 1973, p.268.
27 Clare Ungerson, *Moving Home*, London, Bell, 1971, p.30.
28 Ibid., p.31.
29 See C.T. Relf, *The Building Timetable: the Public Sector*, Part II, Building Economics Research Unit, London, University College, 1974.
30 But a useful report on the situation in London is given by the Action Group on London Housing, *The Public Sector Housing Pipeline in London*, 5th Report to the Minister for Housing and Construction, London, 1976.
31 One of the best studies of the interrelation of planning procedure and the design-tender-contract process is by Michael Meacher and Angela Sears, 'High flats in Finsbury', in David Donnison *et al.*, *Social Policy and Administration: Studies in the Development of Social Services at the Local Level*, London, Allen & Unwin, 1965, pp.120-51.
32 Ungerson, op. cit., pp.38-9.
33 E.W. Cooney, 'High flats in local authority housing in England and Wales since 1945', in Anthony Sutcliffe (ed.), *Multi-storey Living: the British Working Class Experience*, London, Croom Helm, 1974, pp.151-80.
34 Ibid., p.156.
35 Robert McCutcheon, 'High flats in Britain 1945 to 1971', in M. Edwards *et al.* (eds), *Political Economy and the Housing Question*, London, Political Economy of Housing Workshop, 1975, pp.93-4.
36 Ibid., p.99.
37 Joan Maizels, *Two to Five in High Flats*, London, 1961. Moreover the omission of laundries, playrooms, nurseries, community meeting centres, etc. which were part of Le Corbusier's original conception, must have made the blocks less popular with residents than they might otherwise have been.

38 Cooney, op. cit., p.173.
39 See National Community Development Project, *Profits Against Houses,* London, NCDP, 1976, p.29.
40 Lionel Needleman, *The Economics of Housing,* London, Staples Press, 1965.
41 Ibid., p.201.
42 E.M. Sigsworth and R.K. Wilkinson, 'Rebuilding or renovation?' *Urban Studies,* vol.4, no.2, 1967.
43 Ibid., p.112.
44 Lionel Needleman, 'Rebuilding or renovation? : a reply', *Urban Studies,* vol.5, no.1, 1968; E.M. Sigsworth and R.K. Wilkinson, 'Rebuilding or renovation? : a rejoinder', *Urban Studies,* vol. 7, no.1, 1970, p.93.
45 Lionel Needleman, 'The comparative economics of improvement and new building', *Urban Studies,* vol.6, no.2, 1969, pp.196-209.
46 Ibid., p.204, Already in *The Economics of Housing,* p.200, he had stated outright that redevelopment densities were below those of rehabilitation. In the final article he recognised that in principle the density advantage could go either way, ibid., p.201.
47 I have not chosen to deal with a third complication which Needleman's article introduces, i.e. the case where the unit costs of redevelopment vary inversely with the proportion of dwellings, cleared, for the case of partial clearance, partial rehabilitation.
48 Needleman never actually writes out this inequality since he runs into the analysis the unit cost variation (see note above), before moving on to the question of the supposed density shortfall.
49 MHLG, circular 65/69, *Housing Act 1969: area improvement,* p.22.
50 Ibid., p.23.
51 See for example Stephen Merrett, 'The rate of return to education: a critique', *Oxford Economic Papers,* vol.18, no.3, November 1966, pp.289-303.
52 For those interested in a critique of neo-classical economics the best source is, in my view, Joan Robinson and John Eatwell, *An Introduction to Modern Economics,* London, McGraw-Hill, 1974.
53 This paradox arises because Needleman ignores the length of redevelopment life variable.
54 *National Sample Survey of the Condition of Houses,* op. cit.
55 The number of dwellings in clearance areas in England and Wales demolished in 1967 because they were unfit or badly arranged was 47,456, HSGB, no.10, Table 33.
56 Cited by Kirwan and Martin, op. cit., p.12. See also MHLG, *Our Older Homes,* Chapter 4.
57 Cmnd 3602, April 1968.
58 Ibid., pp.1, 9.
59 MHLG, *Our Older Homes;* MHLG, *The Deeplish Study: Improvement Possibilities in a District of Rochdale,* London, 1966; Taylor

Woodrow Group, *The Fulham Study*, London, 1964; Hallmark
Securities Ltd, *Bolton: a Study for the Redevelopment of an Urban
Twilight Area*, London, 1966.

60 *The Building Societies Gazette*, vol.C, no.1198, pp.556–9. Cited
by Pepper, op.cit., p.103.

61 Duncan, op.cit., pp.43, 111, 130.

62 The high clearance rate after 1966, peaking in 1971, presumably
reflects the demand in Chapter 5 of the Denington Report for a
rapid expansion in demolition.

63 *Public Expenditure to 1977-78*, Cmnd 5519, London, HMSO,
1973, Table 2·7.

64 *Better Homes: the Next Priorities*, Cmnd 5339, London, HMSO,
1973.

65 Ibid., p.3.

66 Ibid., p.4.

67 National Community Development Project, *The Poverty of the
Improvement Programme*, London, NCDP, 1975, p.23.

68 DoE, *House Condition Survey 1971 England and Wales*, 1973,
Table 11.

69 For a description of a specific council renovation programme see
Allan Budden, 'Conversion and modernization in Birmingham',
Chartered Surveyor, September 1965, pp.146–9.

70 Joseph Swann, 'The political economy of residential redevelopment
in London', in Edwards, 1975, op.cit., pp.104–15.

71 Kirwan and Martin, op.cit., p.12.

72 In the period 1955–mid-1968 it appears 8616 properties were
improved of which total 3902 had been acquired by the authority.
Pepper, op.cit., p.72, Table III.

73 J.B. Cullingworth, *Housing and Local Government in England and
Wales*, London, Routledge & Kegan Paul, 1966, p.215. See also the
Dennington Report Appendix 4 and Pepper, op.cit., pp.67–75.

74 The story has been told in detail by Jon Gower Davies in *The
Evangelistic Bureaucrat*, London, Tavistock, 1972. Also see Pepper,
op.cit., pp.75–90.

75 Davies, op.cit., p.149.

76 *Better Homes: the Next Priorities*, op.cit., p.7.

77 Based on the constant price expenditure estimate of annex A of
the study group on programmes of social ownership and renovation
of council dwellings, *First Report*, London, 1976.

78 See J.F. Wright, 'Municipalization: an examination of local authority
policies for buying private housing for continued use', unpublished
M.Phil. thesis, University of London, 1975; D.A. Gordon, 'Municipalization: a case study of policy and practice in Newham',
unpublished M.Phil. thesis, University of London, 1977; Evelyn
Shaw *et al.*, 'Municipalization: a study in Islington', unpublished
project report, London, University College, 1977.

79 Shaw *et al.*, op.cit., Section 1·2.

80 *The Government's Expenditure Plans*, vol.II, Cmnd 7049–II,
London, HMSO, 1978, Table 2·7.

6 Finance: the capital market

1 N.P. Hepworth, *The Finance of Local Government*, London, Allen & Unwin, 1976, p.24. This book is the standard introduction to the subject.
2 Ibid., Ch. 6.
3 PWLB, *100th Annual Report of the Public Works Loan Board 1974–75*, London, 1975, p.3.
4 Ministry of Health, *Summary Report for the Year ended 31st March 1945*, p.71. All further references in this chapter to the absolute or proportional scale of reliance on PWLB finance are derived from Appendix 4.
5 Ministry of Health, *Report for the Year ended 31st March 1947*, p.195; Ministry of Health, *Report for the Year ended 31st March 1948*, p.259. The figures are for England and Wales.
6 MHLG, *Report for the Period 1950/51 to 1954*, p.109.
7 Ibid., p.110.
8 Appendix 5 shows there is an unfortunate break in the data series in the two years 1960–2 as well as a redefinition of the statistic, so that the nadir of reliance on the board is not known. Certainly in 1962–4 net borrowing was negative.
9 MHLG, *Report for the Year 1955*, p.87.
10 MHLG, *Report of the MHLG 1957*, p.118.
11 *Committee on the Working of the Monetary System: Report*, Cmnd 827, London, HMSO, 1959.
12 MHLG, *Report of the MHLG 1961*, p.8.
13 H.M. Treasury, *Local Authority Borrowing*, Cmnd 2162, London, HMSO, 1963.
14 MHLG, *Report of the MHLG 1964*, pp.10–11.
15 MHLG, *Report of the MHLG 1965 and 1966*, p.25.
16 PWLB, *102nd Annual Report of the PWLB 1976–7*, London, 1977, pp.6–8.
17 DoE, *Housing Policy: a Consultative Document*, Technical Volume Part I, 1977, p.169.
18 The indexed value of a figure in year t in terms of year o values is equal to the money value divided by $(1 + r)^t$ where r is the rate of inflation.
19 I assume the real rate of interest is 1·08 per cent per annum, the redemption period is sixty years and the rate of accumulation is 3 per cent per annum.
20 DoE, op. cit., Technical Volume III, Table VIII.12.
21 Ibid., Technical Volume I, Table IV.17. The increase in debt charges due to higher pool rate is £385 million in 1971–2 to 1975–6. The increase in the charge on account of additions and acquisitions is £288 million. Unfortunately the table does not distinguish between interest rate increases due to refinancing old debt and increases due to new capital expenditure at higher marginal rates.

22 This 'bunching' of heavily front-loaded schemes was first perceived as such in an article of great originality written by David Webster. See 'Council house costs: why we should all calm down', *Roof*, October 1975, pp.7–10. It should be borne in mind that front-loading as a concept applies to individual schemes, where the appropriate real and money interest rates are those on new advances, i.e. the marginal rates.

7 Consumption: rents and subsidies

1 DoE, *Housing Policy*, Technical Volume, Part I, London, HMSO, 1977, p.178.
2 Strictly speaking this pattern of gross rents has existed only since 1975. Between 1972 and 1975 the Housing Finance Act was in force with its 'fair rents' (see Section 7). Before 1972 the most common practice was to adopt 'standard rents' which were calculated in broadly the same way as gross rents except that before 1972 no mandatory rent rebate system existed so that the concept of an 'unrebated rent' might not have much meaning. Charges for amenities and for lodgers or additional earners were added to the 'standard rent'.
3 See Chapter 2, p.58.
4 NBPI, *Increases in Rents of Local Authority Housing*, London, HMSO, 1968, p.8.
5 In a rebate scheme the standard or gross rent is known and a specific sum is calculated, the rebate, which brings the rent down to a level the tenant is presumed to be able to afford. The sum of these rebates was easily calculated. In the case of differential rents the rent set on the dwelling was itself based, in part, on the tenant's economic circumstances so that there was no distinction between rebated and unrebated rent from which it followed that the scale of rebates received was logically impossible to calculate, although differential rents and rebated rents served the same purpose.
6 See note 2.
7 R.A. Parker, *The Rents of Council Houses*, London, Bell, 1967, p.46.
8 NBPI, *Increases in Rents of Local Authority Housing*, Statistical Supplement, p.24.
9 Parker, op. cit., pp.75–8.
10 NBPI, *Increases in Rents of Local Authority Housing*, p.19.
11 DoE, *Housing Policy*, Table I.27.
12 MoH, *Report for the year ended 31st March 1948*, 1949, p.244.
13 MoH, *Report for the year ended 31st March 1949*, 1950, p.323, and *Report for the year ended 31st March 1950*, 1951, p.126.
14 All further references in this chapter to the absolute level of government subsidies are drawn from Appendix 5.
15 CHAC, *Transfers, Exchanges and Rents*, 1953.

16 Whilst the accounts of the separate estates had been consolidated in 1935, systematic rent pooling was probably not widespread until the late 1950s. Although the pooling of rents and the rebating of rents are quite distinct, rebated or differential rents only make much sense when the gross or standard rent is not set equal to its historically specific level. This was why pooling and rebating were often spoken of in the same breath, often confusing one with the other.

17 *Hansard*, 27 October 1955.

18 NBPI, *Increases in Rents of Local Authority Housing*, pp.10–12.

19 The account which follows is taken from Dave Burn's *Rent Strike: St Pancras 1960*, London, Pluto Press, 1972.

20 The pamphlet's author was Arthur A. Jones and is quoted in Parker, op. cit., p.17.

21 DoE, op. cit., Technical Volume III, pp.47–8.

22 MHLG, *Housing*, Cmnd 2050, London, HMSO, 1963.

23 MHLG, *The Housing Programme 1965 to 1970*, Cmnd 2838, London, HMSO, 1965, p.15.

24 NBPI, *Increases in Rents of Local Authority Housing*, pp.25–8.

25 DoE, *Housing Policy*, Technical Volume I, pp.42–3.

26 Parker, op. cit., p.42 and NBPI, *Increases in Rents of Local Authority Housing*, Statistical Supplement, p.16.

27 Ibid., Table II.

28 Under the 1956 Act the extra subsidy per flat in blocks of four, five and six storeys were approximately £10, £16 and £28 respectively with an extra £1 15s per flat for each storey in excess of six. Under the 1967 Act the extra subsidies for 4-, 5- and 6-storey blocks were £8, £14 and £26 respectively with no additions above 6 storeys. The real value of each £1 of money subsidy had fallen considerably between 1956 and 1967.

29 DoE, op. cit., Technical Volume III, pp.48–9. Note that whilst the new Act marked a clear break with the post-1923 system because the subsidy on each dwelling became a function of its approved cost, it still remained true that once the money subsidy was determined for an individual dwelling it was scheduled to remain unchanged for sixty years.

30 DoE, *Housing Policy*, Technical Volume I, pp.190–1.

31 MHLG, *Report 1965 and 1966*, 1967, p.72.

32 MHLG, *Report 1967 and 1968*, 1969, p.15.

33 See James Goudie, *Councils and the Housing Finance Act*, 1972, pp.22–6 and Stephen Merrett, 'Council rents and British capitalism', in Edwards *et al.* (eds), *Political Economy and the Housing Question*, London, Political Economy of Housing Workshop, 1975, pp.85–9.

34 *Fair Deal for Housing*, Cmnd 4728, London, HMSO, 1971, p.1.

35 DoE, *Housing Policy*, Technical Volume III, p.45.

36 See David Skinner and Julia Langdon, *The Story of Clay Cross*, Nottingham, Spokesman Books, 1974.

37 DoE, *Housing Policy*, Technical Volume I, p.184. Because the rents

of tenants receiving supplementary benefit were paid in part by
the SBC before October 1972 and any subsidy was met entirely
thereafter by the local housing authority, the statistical series on
Exchequer subsidies of Appendix 6 has a break between the years
1971–2 and 1972–3.

38 DoE, *Housing Policy*, Technical Volume III, p.40.
39 The major work, of which the first volume was published in 1867,
is: *Capital: A Critique of Political Economy*, New York, International Publishers, 1967. A brief outline of his political economy
can be found in Marx's *Wages, Price and Profit* of which innumerable
editions exist.

8 Consumption: council house management

1 Quoted in *Roof*, 1977, vol.2, no.6, p.168.
2 Compare with A. Murie, P. Niner and C. Watson, *Housing Policy
and the Housing System*, London, Allen & Unwin, 1976.
3 Unless otherwise stated, the data used in this section have been
extracted and compiled from DoE, *Housing Policy Consultative
Document*, Technical Volume Parts I and III, London, HMSO,
1977.
4 C. Holmes, 'Housing', in F. Williams (ed.), *Why the Poor Pay More*,
London, Macmillan, 1977, p.36.
5 Figures extracted from The Chartered Institute of Public Finance
and Accountancy, *Housing Statistics (England and Wales) Part 1*,
CIPFA, London, 1977, p.5.
6 See Murie *et al.*, op. cit., p.114.
7 CDP, *Whatever Happened to Council Housing?*, London, CDP,
1976(a), p.11.
8 DoE, *Housing Policy*, Part III, p.11.
9 A. Murie, 'Council house sales mean poor law housing', *Roof*,
vol.2, no.2, 1977, pp.46–9. Quote p.48. Original emphasis.
10 Ibid.
11 See CDP, *Profits Against Houses*, London, CDP, 1976(b), pp.32–4.
12 NUPE/SCAT, *Up Against a Brickwall: The Dead-end in Housing
Policy*, London, NUPE/SCAT, 1978.
13 National Consumer Council, *Do Council Tenants Get a Fair Deal on
Repairs?*, London, National Consumer Council, 1978.
14 In the case of London, the Greater London Council and the
London Boroughs.
15 M. Grant, *Local Authority Housing: Law, Policy and Practice in
Hampshire*, Southampton, Hampshire Legal Action Group, 1976,
p.1.
16 The most important being the nine reports on council housing of
the now abolished Central Housing Advisory Committee (CHAC).
17 See, for example, the views on this topic expressed in Scottish
Housing Advisory Committee, *Choosing Council Tenants*,
Edinburgh, HMSO, 1950.

18 For example, CDP, *Limits of the Law*, London, CDP, 1977, and
    D.S. Byrne, *Problem Families: a Housing Lumpen-proletariat*,
    University of Durham Department of Sociology and Social
    Administration Working Paper 5, 1974.
19 Although merit systems are still dominant in particular areas. See,
    for example, Welsh Consumer Council, *Council Housing: a Survey
    of Allocation Policies in Wales*, Cardiff, Welsh Consumer Council,
    1976.
20 CDP, op. cit., 1977, p.30.
21 See, for example, National Consumer Council, *Tenancy Agreements
    Between Councils and their Tenants*, London, National Consumer
    Council, 1976.
22 For evidence of this see, for example, 'Good behaviour no guarantee
    of security for council tenants', *Roof*, vol.2, no.5, 1977, p.156.
23 See R.D. Cramond, *Allocation of Council Houses,* University of
    Glasgow Social and Economic Studies, Occasional Paper 1.
24 Southwark CDP, *Housing For the Poor?*, London, Southwark
    CDP, 1975.
25 D.S. Byrne, op. cit., and P. Griffiths, *Homes Fit for Heroes*,
    London, Shelter, 1975.
26 See, for example, the management tasks discussed in texts such
    as J.P. Macey and C.V. Baker, *Housing Management*, London,
    The Estates Gazette, 1965.
27 J. Tucker, *Honourable Estates*, London, Gollancz, 1966, p.11.
28 In recent years increasing concern has been expressed about the
    lack of training. See, for example, M. Brion, M. Bieber and
    C. Legg, 'How do you train your staff?', *Housing,* vol.14, no.4,
    1978, pp.7–9.
29 S. Damer, 'A note on housing allocation', in M. Edwards *et al.*
    (eds), *Housing and Class in Britain*, London, Political Economy
    of Housing Workshop, 1976, pp.72–4.
30 Quoted in C. Ward, *Tenants Take Over*, London, Architectural
    Press, 1974, p.12.
31 F. Gray (1976a), 'The management of local authority housing',
    in M. Edwards *et al.*, op. cit., pp.75–86, quote p.83.
32 See, for example, the evidence provided by P. Griffiths, op. cit.,
    and CHAC, *Council Housing Purposes, Procedures and Priorities*,
    London, HMSO, 1969.
33. S. Damer, op. cit.,
34 *Housing*, 19 January 1920, p.189.
35 *Housing* 16 August 1919, p.44.
36 *Housing*, 19 January 1920, p.189.
37 *Housing*, 5 January 1920, p.174.
38 *Housing*, 19 January 1920, p.189.
39 *Housing*, 19 July 1920, p.2.
40 Scottish Housing Advisory Committee, *Housing Management in
    Scotland*, Edinburgh, HMSO, 1967a, p.14.
41 Ministry of Health, *Circular 13/49*, 1949, p.1.

42 *Housing Policy*, Cmnd 6851, 1977, p.79.
43 CHAC, *Council Housing: Purposes, Procedures and Priorities*, 1969.
44 CHAC, *The Management of Municipal Housing Estates*, London, HMSO, 1939, p.19.
45 Scottish Housing Advisory Committee, 1967a, op. cit., p.46.
46 CHAC, op. cit., 1939, p.19.
47 Quoted in J. O'Brien, 'Problem families to live in council ghetto', *Daily Telegraph*, 26 November 1977. See also *Roof*, vol.3, no. 1, 1978, p.8.
48 See, for example, J.P. Macey and C.V. Baker, op. cit.
49 CHAC, *Council Housing: Purposes, Procedures and Priorities*, 1969, p.31.
50 CHAC, *The Management of Municipal Housing Estates*, 1939, p.1.
51 Ibid., p.6.
52 Ibid.
53 Ibid., p.7.
54 CDP, op. cit., 1976 (a), p.28. See also Southwark CDP, op. cit.
55 A. Murie *et al.*, op. cit., p.126.
56 F. Gray (1976b), 'Selection and allocation in council housing', *Transactions of the Institute of British Geographers*, vol.1, no.1, 1976, pp.34–46, and Southwark CDP, *Housing For the Poor?*
57 Central Statistical Office, *Social Trends No.8*, London, HMSO, 1977.
58 See, however, C. Ungerson, *Moving Home*, Occasional Papers on Social Administration, 44, London, Bell, 1971; C. Duke, *Colour and Rehousing: a Study of Redevelopment in Leeds*, London, Institute of Race Relations, 1970; C. Paris, 'Urban renewal in Birmingham, England—an institutional approach', *Antipode*, vol.6, no.1, 1974, pp.7–15; J.G. Davies, *The Evangelistic Bureaucrat*, London, Tavistock, 1972; J. English, R. Madigan and P. Norman, *Slum Clearance*, London, Croom Helm, 1976; D. Haworth, 'The corporation and the people', *Listener*, 20 May 1974, pp.794–6; and, D.M. Muchnik, *Urban Renewal in Liverpool*, Occasional Papers on Social Administration, 33, London, Bell, 1970.
59 *Report of the Committee on One-Parent Families*, Cmnd 5629, London, HMSO, 1974.
60 See, for example, F. Gray, op. cit., 1976a; S. Damer and R. Madigan, 'The housing investigator', *New Society*, 25 July 1974, pp.226–7; and CHAC, *Council Housing: Purposes, Procedures and Priorities*, 1969.
61 Ibid., p.32.
62 J.P. Macey and C.V. Baker, op. cit., p.214. For a discussion of local authority attitudes and actions towards homelessness before the implementation of the 1977 Housing (Homeless Persons) Act, see B. Widdowson, *Blunt Powers—Sharp Practices*, London, Shelter, 1976.

63 DoE, Housing (Homeless Persons) Act 1977. *Code of Guidance (England and Wales)*, London, HMSO, 1977.

64 B. Widdowson, 'Homeless Persons Act—present indicative in England', *Roof*, vol.3, no.1, 1978, p.3.

65 Housing Act 1957, Section 113.

66 Scottish Housing Advisory Committee, *Allocating Council Houses*, Edinburgh, HMSO, 1967(b), p.12.

67 P.C. Brown, *Smallcreep's Day*, London, Gollancz, 1965, p.85.

68 For discussion of waiting lists see, for example, R.D. Cramond, op. cit.; CDP, op. cit., 1977; P. Niner, *Local Authority Housing Policy and Practice–a Case Study Approach*, University of Birmingham Centre for Urban and Regional Studies, Occasional Paper, 31, 1975; N. Lewis, 'Council housing allocation: problems of discretion and control', *Public Administration*, summer, 1976, pp.147–60; Welsh Consumer Council, op. cit.; J. Lambert, B. Blackaby and C. Paris, 'Neighbourhood politics and housing opportunities', in M. Harloe (ed.), *Centre for Environmental Studies, Conference Paper*, 14, 1975; and P. Gregory, 'Waiting lists and the demand for public housing', *Policy and Politics*, vol.3, no.4, 1975, pp.71–87.

69 P. Gregory, ibid., p.72.

70 N. Lewis, op. cit., p.159.

71 CDP, op. cit., 1977, p.31. See also J. Lambert *et al.*, op. cit.

72 CDP, op. cit., 1977, p.31.

73 Quoted in C. Duke, op. cit., p.8. The authority was Slough.

74 Discussed in CDP, op. cit., 1977.

75 P. Niner, op. cit.

76 J. Hillman, 'Dial yourself a home—your points add up', *Guardian*, 31 October 1977.

77 H. Bird and M. Whitbread, 'Council house transfers and exchanges', *New Society*, 14 August 1975, pp.356–61.

78 N. Lewis, op. cit.,

79 For discussions of allocation see F. Gray, op. cit., 1976a and 1976b; S. Damer and R. Madigan, op. cit., 1969; J. Tucker, op. cit.; and DoE, *Inner London: Policies for Dispersal and Balance. Final Report of the Lambeth Inner Area Study*, London, HMSO, 1977.

80 E. Gittus, *Flats, Families and the Under-fives*, London, Routledge & Kegan Paul, 1976, and R. Franey, 'High rise hiatus', *Roof*, vol.3, no.6, 1977, p.163.

81 DoE, *Housing Policy*, Part III, p.15.

82 L. Corina, *Housing Allocation Policy and its Effects*, University of York, Department of Social Administrative and Social Work, Papers in Community Studies, no.7, 1976, p.13.

83 Quoted in F. Gray, 1976a, op. cit.

84 Macey and Baker, op. cit., p.215.

85 L. Corina, op. cit.; P. Griffiths, op. cit.; O. Gill, *Luke Street*, London, Macmillan, 1977; S. Damer, 'Wine-Alley—the sociology of a dreadful enclosure', *Sociological Review*, vol.22, 1974,

pp.221–48; D.S. Byrne, op. cit.; and, Benwell CDP, *Noble Street and Norwich Place Report,* Benwell CDP, Newcastle, 1974.

86 S. Damer, op. cit., 1976.
87 D.S. Byrne, op. cit.
88 See Southwark CDP, *Housing for the Poor?*
89 *Report of the Committee on One-Parent Families,* and H. Simpson, *One-Parent Families – The Role of Housing Authorities,* National Council for One-Parent Families, London, 1977.
90 Runnymede Trust, *Race and Council Housing in London,* London, Runnymede Trust, 1975; C. Duke, op. cit.; D. Smith and A. Whalley, *Racial Minorities and Public Housing,* PEP Broadsheet, 556, 1975; J. Parker and K. Dugmore, *Colour and the Allocation of GLC Housing,* Greater London Council Research Report, 21, 1976; H. Fleet, *Council Housing and the Location of Ethnic Minorities,* University of Bristol, SSRC Research Unit on Ethnic Relations, Working Papers in Ethnic Relations, 5, 1977; and, R. Ward, *Coloured Families in Council Housing,* Manchester Council for Community Relations, Manchester, 1971.
91 See, for example, the reports of the actions of tenant groups in *Community Action,* particularly nos 24–6, 1976. Interestingly, the available evidence indicates that tenants' struggles over rent, and to a lesser extent repairs, are more frequent and intense than over the management activities detailed in this chapter. For example, evidence for the inter-war period is provided by S. Schifferes, 'Council tenants and housing policy in the 1930s: the contradictions of state intervention', in M. Edwards *et al.,* op. cit., pp.64–71.
92 C. Duke, op. cit., p.76. Also compare with D.S. Byrne, op. cit.
93 National Consumer Council, op. cit., 1976.
94 See, for example, 'The irresistible rise of building societies', and 'Red line districts', *Roof,* vol.1, no.4, 1976.
95 A. Murie, *The Sale of Council Houses,* University of Birmingham Centre for Urban and Regional Studies, Occasional Paper, 35, Birmingham, 1975, and A. Murie, op. cit., 1977.
96 V. Karn, 'The newest profession', *Roof,* vol.2, no.6, 1977, pp.177–9, quote p.177.
97 J. Hillman, 'New Deal for council tenants as empty houses threat grows', *Guardian,* 25 June 1977.
98 DoE, *Housing Policy,* p.79.

9 Housing policy since the war

1 Ralph Miliband, *The State in Capitalist Society: the Analysis of the Western System of Power,* London, Quartet Books, 1973, p.96; see also Ralph Miliband, *Parliamentary Socialism: a study in the Politics of Labour,* London, Merlin Press, 1975, Ch. 9.
2 Ibid., pp.276–7.

3   A.A. Rogow and P. Shore, *The Labour Government and British Industry 1945–51*, Oxford, Blackwell, 1956, p.25.
4   J.C.R. Dow, *The Management of the British Economy 1945–60*, Cambridge, Cambridge University Press, 1965, p.12.
5   Most of the data on war-time building and destruction are taken from the annual reports of the Ministry of Health although I have had to add a little guesswork.
6   Ministry of Reconstruction, *Housing*, Cmd 6609, London, HMSO, 1945.
7   MoH, *Report for the Year ended 31st March 1949*, 1950, p.324.
8   MoH, *Report for the Year ended 31st March 1950*, 1951, p.130.
9   Ibid., p.130.
10 MoH, *Report for the Year ended 31st March 1949*, p.328.
11 MoH, *Report for the Year ended 31st March 1950*, p.130.
12 MoH, *Report for the Year ended 31st March 1948*, p.248.
13 The only reference to it in the annual reports is a single sentence when it is said to be 'under consideration', MoH, *Report for the Year ended 31st March 1946*, p.166.
14 See Ron Bailey, *The Squatters*, Harmondsworth, Penguin, 1973, Chapter 2.
15 MoH, op. cit., pp.159–60.
16 Quoted in Michael Foot, *Aneurin Bevan 1945–1960*, St Albans, Paladin, 1975, p.71.
17 Ibid., p.71.
18 MoH, *Report for the Year ended 31st March 1947*, 1948, p.170.
19 MoH, *Report for the Year ended 31st March 1946*, p.170.
20 Marian Bowley, *Britain's Housing Shortage*, London, Oxford University Press, 1944, p.7.
21 MHLG, *Housing*, Cmd 6609, p.3.
22 Foot, op. cit., pp.63–4, 80.
23 Dow, op. cit., p.144.
24 Ibid., pp.158–62.
25 MoH, *Report for the Year ended 31st March 1947*, p.168.
26 Ibid., p.169.
27 See Bowley, op. cit., pp.8–9.
28 Communist Party of Great Britain, *A Memorandum on Housing*, 1944, p.19.
29 Ibid., p.16.
30 See Dow, op. cit., pp.223–7.
31 MoH, *Summary Report for the Year ended 31st March 1943*, 1943, p.38.
32 MHLG, *Housing*, Cmd 6609, p.6.
33 MoH, *Report for the Year ended 31st March 1946*, p.160.
34 Dow, op. cit., pp.13–18.
35 Quoted by Foot, op. cit., p.92.
36 MoH, *Report for the Year ended March 31st 1948*, pp.239–40.
37 Ibid., p.239.
38 Foot, op. cit., p.95.

39 Dow, op. cit., p.31.

40 Ibid., pp.34–5.

41 MoH, *Report for the Year ended March 31st 1949*, p.319.

42 Foot, op. cit., p.94.

43 D.L. Munby, *The Rent Problem*, London, Fabian Society, 1952.

44 Foot, op. cit., pp.304–5.

45 MHLG, *Houses: the next step,* Cmd 8996, 1953.

46 Ibid., pp.3–4.

47 Ibid., p.17.

48 This deserves a brief comment. The procedure is that the Inland Revenue, in computing a person's tax liability, deducts mortgage interest from the gross wage or salary. The result is that income tax is reduced by the product of the interest and the marginal rate of taxation. Precisely the same economic effect would be achieved by raising the full amount of taxation and sending the owner-occupier a cheque for his subsidy entitlement, which few would dispute to be a state expenditure. This is *not* done because it would be administratively more cumbersome. Thus in an economic sense, but not in a narrow administrative sense, subsidies to owner-occupiers are a state expenditure.

49 MHLG, *Report for the Year 1955*, 1956, p.3.

50 Dow, op. cit., p.235.

51 When comparing Table 9·1 with Graph 9·1 it should be remembered that 'public sector', in addition to council production, includes the New Towns, housing associations and government departments.

52 Dow, op. cit., pp.79–80, 90–103.

53 Ibid., p.96.

54 MHLG, *Report 1957*, 1958, p.2.

55 MHLG, *Report 1958*, 1959, p.33.

56 MHLG, *Report 1957*, 1958, p.17.

57 MHLG, *Housing in England and Wales*, Cmnd 1290, 1961, p.3.

58 *National Institute Economic Review*, February 1962, pp.4–18.

59 *National Institute Economic Review*, February 1963, pp.4–19.

60 *National Institute Economic Review*, February 1964, pp.4–12.

61 MHLG, *Housing*, Cmnd 2050, London, HMSO, 1963.

62 MHLG, *Report 1963*, 1964, p.14. Command 2050 stated: 'But it is not realistic to envisage a higher rate than 350,000 at present. It is no use loading the industry with more than it can digest', MHLG, *Housing*, op. cit., p.4.

63 MHLG, *The Housing Programme 1965 to 1970*, Cmnd 2838, London, HMSO, 1965, p.8. Richard Crossman, who was the Minister from 1964 to 1966, records that the Cabinet spent eight minutes discussing the entire White Paper. See *The Diaries of a Cabinet Minister*, Volume 1, London, Hamish Hamilton and Jonathan Cape, 1975, p.383. Crossman's own attitude is set out on the same page and on page 325.

64 See Crossman, op. cit., p.230.

65 The close relationship between the fall in private housebuilding

starts and the argument for an increase in municipal approvals is made crystal clear by Crossman, op. cit., pp.295, 501, 514, 535.

66 MHLG, *Report 1965 and 1966*, 1967, p.62.
67 *National Institute Economic Review*, February 1968, p.10.
68 MHLG, *Report 1967 and 1968*, 1969, p.2.
69 Ibid., p.3.
70 MHLG, *Old Houses into New Homes*, Cmnd 3602, London, HMSO, 1968.
71 *National Institute Economic Review*, February 1971, pp.4–20.
72 Ibid., February 1973, pp.9–25.
73 DoE, *Housing Policy: a Consultative Document*, Cmnd 6851, London, HMSO, June 1977, p.42.
74 Ibid., p.7.
75 Ibid., p.35.
76 Ibid., p.50.
77 Ibid., p.52.
78 Ibid., p.44. See also p.75.
79 Ibid., p.42.
80 Ibid., p.44.
81 Ibid., p.128.
82 Ibid., p.32.
83 Ibid., pp.36–7.
84 Ibid., pp.86–7.
85 Ibid., p.30.
86 Ibid., p.84.
87 Ibid., p.86.
88 Ibid., pp.47–8, 79, 101–2.

10 State housing and state policy in historical retrospect

1 The main influence on my thinking has come from the preparation of the two historical chapters of the book, particularly the inter-war period. I am also indebted to Ralph Miliband's *The State in Capitalist Society: the Analysis of the Western System of Power*, London, Quartet Books, 1973; and to James O'Connor's *The Fiscal Crisis of the State*, New York, St Martin's Press, 1973; and even to Nicos Poulantzas's extremely obscure *Political Power and Social Classes*, London, New Left Books, 1975, particularly Part IV.
2 Karl Marx and Friedrich Engels, *The Communist Manifesto*, Peking, Foreign Languages Press, 1965, p.33.
3 Poulantzas, op. cit., pp.284–5.

11 A strategy for the future

1 This problem is a familiar one to the DoE's forecasting experts. See, for example, A.E. Holmans, 'A forecast of effective demand

for housing in Great Britain in the 1970s', *Social Trends,* no.1, 1970, pp.33–42. See also DoE, *Housing Policy, a Consultative Document,* Technical Volume I, Cmnd 6851, London, HMSO, 1977, Chapter 3.

2   Of course the case for land nationalisation rests on a wider basis than the abolition of notional ground rent in the state housing sector. See for example Richard Barras, Andrew Broadbent and Doreen Massey, 'Planning and the public ownership of land', *New Society,* 21 June 1973, pp.676–9; and Jack Brocklebank *et al., The Case for Nationalising Land,* London, Campaign for Nationalising Land, 1973.

3   The Labour Party, *Building Britain's Future: Labour's Policy on Construction,* London, 1977. Two much earlier reports covering some of the same ground are: Kenneth Albert, *Policy for the Building Industry,* Fabian Research Series 170, London, Fabian Society, 1955, and Harry Brack, *Building for a New Society,* Fabian Research Series, 239, London, Fabian Society, 1964. It is worth noting that no policy document on the construction industry, one of the country's largest economic sectors, has been produced by the Communist Party of Great Britain or the Trotskyist groups and parties. However, the Political Economy of Housing Workshop has published a detailed study of DLOs, which contains a number of policy recommendations. See Direct Labour Collective, *Building with Direct Labour,* London, 1978.

4   The Labour Party, op. cit., p.28. It is worth noting that the document conceives demand stabilisation in terms of the maximum permissible cut below future *scheduled* work, i.e. if the Public Expenditure Survey Committee schedules expenditure to fall because of a 'public expenditure crisis', the document accepts this as a *fait accompli.*

5   See, for example, N. Rosenberg, *Economic Planning in the British Building Industry 1945–49,* Philadelphia, University of Pennsylvania Press, 1960.

6   These proposals on development finance are worth comparing with those of Frank Allaun. (See *No Place Like Home,* London, André Deutsch, 1972, pp.190–1.) He argues that in the long run all local authority capital expenditure on housing should be financed out of interest-free loans on the grounds that 'when the Government builds a motorway or a battleship it does not pay one penny in interest. It builds it out of revenue—for cash payment.' My differences with Allaun are that he forgets that an important part of total central government expenditure *is* financed out of borrowing, although these loans are not tied to specific outlays; and also he is willing to forget that inflation would mean that in real terms the original value of interest-free loans would never be paid. At a zero rate of inflation our proposals coincide.

7   The effect of this will be to raise net mortgage payments by the end of the transitional period when relief has been completely

eliminated. Owner-occupiers will, however, benefit from increased efficiency in the housebuilding industry and, if land prices have played a part in high home prices, from CLB purchase of new housing land for speculative building at existing use-value. In addition the state should set up a National Conveyancing Service with the fee on each transaction set at a nominal level to bring to an end the conveyancing fraud.

8 DoE, *Tenancy Agreements*, Report by the Housing Services Advisory Group, 1977; National Consumer Council Social Policy Unit, *Housing Management : a Tenants' Charter*, 1977.

Select bibliography

Books, research papers, pamphlets and articles

Allaun, F., *No Place Like Home*, London, André Deutsch, 1972.

Ambrose, P., *The Land Market and the Housing System*, University of Sussex Urban and Regional Studies Working Paper no. 3, 1976.

Ambrose, P., *Who Plans Brighton's Housing Crisis?*, London, Shelter, 1976.

Bailey, R., *The Squatters*, Harmondsworth, Penguin, 1973.

Ball, M., 'British housing policy and the housebuilding industry', *Capital and Class*, vol.4, Spring 1978, pp.78–99.

Barr, Cleeve A.W., *Public Authority Housing*, Batsford, 1958.

Barras, R., Broadbent, A., and Massey, D., 'Planning and the public ownership of land', *New Society*, 21 June 1973, pp.676–9.

Bassett, K., *Public Housing in Britain 1918–39 : a Study of National Policies and Local Response*, Bristol Housing Studies no. 1, University of Bristol, Department of Geography, 1976.

Benwell CDP, *Noble Street and Norwich Place Report*, Newcastle-upon-Tyne, Benwell CDP, 1974.

Berry, F., *Housing : the Great British Failure*, London, Charles Knight, 1974.

Bowley, M., *Britain's Housing Shortage*, London, Oxford University Press, 1944.

Bowley, M., *Housing and the State 1919–44*, London, Allen & Unwin, 1945.

Bowley, M., *The British Building Industry : Four Studies in Response and Resistance to Change*, Cambridge, Cambridge University Press, 1966.

Brack, H., *Building for a New Society*, London, Fabian Society, 1964.

Branson, N., and Heinemann, M., *Britain in the Nineteen Thirties*, St Albans, Panther, 1973.

Brocklebank, J., *et al.*, *The Case for Nationalising Land*, London, Campaign for Nationalising Land, 1973.

Budden, A., 'Conversion and modernization in Birmingham', *Chartered Surveyor*, vol.98, no.3, September 1965, pp.146–9.

Burn, D., *Rent Strike : St Pancras 1960*, London, Pluto Press, 1972.

Byrne, D.S., *Problem Families : a Housing Lumpen-proletariat*, University of Durham Department of Sociology and Social Administration, Working Paper 5, 1974.

Select bibliography

Chapman, S.D. (ed.), *The History of Working-class Housing: a Symposium*, Newton Abbot, David & Charles, 1971.

Collison, P., *The Cutteslowe Walls : a Study in Social Class*, London, Faber & Faber, 1963.

Communist Party of Great Britain, *A Memorandum on Housing*, London, CPGB, 1944.

Corina, L., *Housing Allocation Policy and its Effects*, University of York Department of Social Administration and Social Work, Papers in Community Studies no. 7, 1976.

Craddock, J., *Council Tenants Participation in Housing Management : a Study of Four Schemes*, London, Association of London Housing Estates, 1975.

Cramond, R.D., *Allocation of Council Houses*, University of Glasgow Social and Economic Studies, Occasional Paper no. 1, Edinburgh, Oliver & Boyd, 1964.

Crossman, R.H.S., *The Diaries of a Cabinet Minister. Vol. 1 : Minister of Housing 1964--66*, London, Hamish Hamilton and Jonathan Cape, 1975.

Cullingworth, J.B., *Housing Needs and Planning Policy*, London, Routledge & Kegan Paul, 1960.

Cullingworth, J.B., *Housing and Local Government in England and Wales*, London, Allen & Unwin, 1966.

Damer, S., 'Wine Alley—the sociology of a dreadful enclosure', *Sociological Review*, vol. 22, no. 2, May 1974, pp. 221–48.

Davies, J.G., *The Evangelistic Bureaucrat : a Study of a Planning Exercise in Newcastle upon Tyne*, London, Tavistock, 1972.

Dennis, N., *People and Planning : the Sociology of Housing in Sunderland*, London, Faber & Faber, 1970.

Dewsnup, E.R., *The Housing Problem in England: its Statistics, Legislation and Policy*, Manchester, Manchester University Press, 1907.

Direct Labour Collective, *Building with Direct Labour : Local Authority Building and the Crisis in the Construction Industry*, London, Political Economy of Housing Workshop, 1978.

Donnison, D.V., *The Government of Housing*, Harmondsworth, Penguin, 1967.

Donnison, D.V., Chapman, V. *et al.*, *Social Policy and Administration: Studies in the Development of Social Services at the Local Level*, London, Allen & Unwin, 1965.

Donnison, D.V., and Eversley, D.E.C., *London : Urban Patterns, Problems and Policies*, London, Heinemann, 1973.

Duke, C., *Colour and Rehousing: a Study of Redevelopment in Leeds*, London, Institute of Race Relations, 1970.

Duncan, T.L.C., *Housing Improvement Policies in England and Wales*, Birmingham, CURS Research Memorandum no. 28, 1974.

Edwards, M., Merrett, S., and Swann, J. (eds), *Political Economy and the Housing Question*, London, Political Economy of Housing Workshop, 1975.

Edwards, M., Gray, F., Merrett, S., and Swann, J. (eds), *Housing and Class in Britain*, London, Political Economy of Housing Workshop, 1976.

Emmerson, Sir H., *Survey of Problems before the Construction Industries*, London, HMSO, 1962.

English, J., Madigan, R., and Norman, P., *Slum Clearance: the Social and Administrative Context*, London, Croom Helm, 1976.

Eversley, D.E.C., *Rents and Social Policy*, London, Fabian Society, 1955.

Flett, H., *Council Housing and the Location of Ethnic Minorities*, University of Bristol SSRC Research Unit on Ethnic Relations, Working Papers in Ethnic Relations no.5, 1977.

Gauldie, E., *Cruel Habitations: a History of Working-class Housing 1780-1918*, London, Allen & Unwin, 1974.

Gill, O., *Luke Street: Housing Policy, Conflict and the Creation of the Delinquent Area*, London, Macmillan, 1977.

Gittus, E.G., *Flats, Families and the Under-fives*, London, Routledge & Kegan Paul, 1976.

Goudie, J., *Councils and the Housing Finance Act*, London, Fabian Society, 1972.

Grant, M., *Local Authority Housing: Law, Policy and Practice in Hampshire*, Southampton, Hampshire Legal Action Group, 1976.

Gray, F., 'Selection and allocation in council housing', *Transactions of the Institute of British Geographers*, vol.1, no.1, 1976, pp.36-46.

Gray, H., *The Cost of Council Housing*, London, Institute for Economic Affairs, 1968.

Gregory, P., 'Waiting lists and the demand for public housing', *Policy and Politics*, vol.3, no.4, June 1975, pp.71-87.

Griffiths, P., *Homes Fit for Heroes: a Shelter Report on Council Housing*, London, Shelter, 1975.

Hall, P., Gracey, H., Drewett, R., and Thomas, R., *The Containment of Urban England. Volume 1: Urban and Metropolitan Growth Processes: Volume 2: The Planning System*, London, PEP, Allen & Unwin and Sage Publications, 1973.

Hall, P., 'The containment of urban England', *Geographical Journal*, vol.140, January-December 1974, pp.386-407.

Hallmark Securities Limited, *Bolton: a Study for the Redevelopment of an Urban Twilight Area*, London, 1966.

Harloe, M. (ed.), *Proceedings of the Conference on Urban Change and Conflict*, London, CES, 1975.

Harloe, M., Issacharoff, R., and Minns, R., *The Organization of Housing: Public and Private Enterprise in London*, London, Heinemann, 1974.

Hepworth, N.P., *The Finance of Local Government*, London, Allen & Unwin, 1976.

Hill, O., *Homes of the London Poor*, London, Macmillan, 1883.

Hillebrandt, P.M., *Economic Theory and the Construction Industry*, London, Macmillan, 1974.

Select bibliography

Hole, J., *The Homes of the Working Classes with Suggestions for their Improvement*, London, 1866.

Hole, V., 'Housing standards and social trends', *Urban Studies*, vol.2, no.2, November 1965, pp.137–46.

Holmans, A.E., 'A forecast of effective demand for housing in Great Britain in the 1970s', *Social Trends*, no.1, 1970, pp.33–42.

Holmes, C., *Tomorrow in Upper Holloway: a Plan for Area Improvement*, London, Shelter, 1973.

Honeyman, J., *Dwellings of the Poor*, Glasgow, 1890.

Jarmain, J.R., *Housing Subsidies and Rents: a Study of Local Authorities' Problems*, London, Stevens, 1948.

Jephcott, P., *Homes in High Flats*, Edinburgh, Oliver & Boyd, 1971.

Jevons, R., and Madge, J., *Housing Estates: a Study of Bristol Corporation Policy and Practice between the Wars*, Bristol, Arrowsmith, 1946.

Karn, V., 'The newest profession', *Roof*, vol.2, no.6, November 1977, pp.177–9.

Kellett, J.R., *The Impact of Railways on Victorian Cities*, London, Routledge & Kegan Paul, 1969.

Killick, A., *Council House Blues*, London, Bow Publications, 1977.

Kirwan, R.W., and Martin, D.B., *The Economics of Urban Residential Renewal and Improvement*, London, CES, 1972.

The Labour Party, *Building Britain's Future: Labour's Policy on Construction*, London, The Labour Party, 1977.

Labour Publications Department, *Labour Solves the Housing Problem: an Exposition of the Wheatley Scheme*, London, LPD, 1924.

Lamb, D., *The Lump: an Heretical Analysis*, London, Solidarity, 1974.

Lansley, S., and Fiegehen, G., *Housing Allowances and Inequality*, London, Fabian Society, 1973.

Layton, E., *Building by Local Authorities*, London, Allen & Unwin, 1961.

Lewis, J.P., *Building Cycles and Britain's Growth*, London, Macmillan, 1965.

Lewis, N., 'Council housing allocation: problems of discretion and control', *Public Administration*, vol.54, summer 1976, pp.147–60.

MacColl, J., *Policy for Housing*, London, Fabian Society, 1954.

MacColl, J., *Plan for Rented Houses*, London, Fabian Society, 1957.

Macey, J.P., and Baker, C.V., *Housing Management*, London, Estates Gazette, 1965.

Maizels, J., *Two to Five in High Flats*, London, 1961.

Mason, T., *Inner City Housing and Urban Renewal Policy: a Housing Profile of Cheetham Hill, Manchester and Salford*, London, CES, 1977.

Morrison, A., *A Child of the Jago*, London, MacGibbon & Kee, 1969.

Muchnik, D., *Urban Renewal in Liverpool: a Study of the Politics of Redevelopment*, London, Bell, 1970.

Munby, D.L., *The Rent Problem*, London, Fabian Society, 1952.

Murie, A., *The Sale of Council Houses*, Birmingham, CURS, 1976.

Murie, A., 'Council house sales mean poor law housing,' *Roof*, vol. 2, no. 2, March 1977, pp.46–9.

Murie, A., Niner, P., and Watson, C., *Housing Policy and the Housing System*, London, Allen & Unwin, 1976.

National Community Development Project, *The Poverty of the Improvement Programme*, London, CDP Information and Intelligence Unit, 1975.

National Community Development Project, *Profits against Houses: an Alternative Guide to Housing Finance,* London, CDP Information and Intelligence Unit. 1976.

National Community Development Project, *Whatever Happened to Council Housing?*, London, CDP Information and Intelligence Unit, 1976.

Needleman, L., *The Economics of Housing*, London, Staples Press, 1965.

Needleman, L., 'Rebuilding or renovation?: a reply', *Urban Studies*, vol. 5, no. 1, February 1968, pp.86–90.

Needleman, L., 'The comparative economics of improvement and new building', *Urban Studies*, vol. 6, no. 2, June 1969, pp.196–209.

Neuburger, H.L.I., and Nichol, B.M., *The Recent Course of Land and Property Prices and the Factors underlying it*, Research Report no. 4, Department of the Environment, 1976.

Nevitt, D.A., *Housing, Taxation and Subsidies: a Study of Housing in the United Kingdom*, London, Nelson, 1966.

Nevitt, D.A., *Fair Deal for Householders*, London, Fabian Society, 1971.

Niner, P., *Local Authority Housing Policy and Practice--a Case Study Approach*, Birmingham, CURS Occasional Paper no. 31, 1975.

North East Trade Union Studies Information Unit, *Direct Labour--the Answer to Building Chaos*, Newcastle-upon-Tyne, 1977.

Nutt, B. *et al., Obsolescence in Housing: theory and applications,* Farnborough, Saxon House, 1976.

Paris, C., 'Urban renewal in Birmingham, England—an institutional approach', *Antipode*, vol. 6, no. 1, April 1974, pp.7–15.

Parker, J., and Dugmore, K., *Colour and the Allocation of GLC Housing*, London, GLC Research Report no. 21, 1976.

Parker, R.A., *The Rents of Council Houses*, London, Bell, 1967.

Pepper, S., *Housing Improvement: Goals and Strategy*, London, Lund Humphries, 1971.

Quigley, H., and Goldie, I., *Housing and Slum Clearance in London*, London, Methuen, 1934.

Ravetz, A., *Model Estate:Planned Housing at Quarry Hill, Leeds*, London, Croom Helm, 1974.

Richardson, H.W., and Aldcroft, D.H., *Building in the British Economy between the Wars*, London, Allen & Unwin, 1968.

Richardson, H.W., Vipond, J., and Furbey, R.A., 'Land prices in Edinburgh 1952–67: a study of Edinburgh City Corporation land purchases', *Scottish Journal of Political Economy*, vol. 21, no. 1, February 1974, pp.67–75.

Roberts, R., *The Classic Slum: Salford Life in the First Quarter of the Century*, Harmondsworth, Penguin, 1973.

Rosenberg, N., *Economic Planning in the British Building Industry 1945–49*, Philadelphia, University of Pennsylvania Press, 1960.

Runnymede Trust, *Race and Council Housing in London*, London, Runnymede Trust, 1975.

Sabatino, R.A., *Housing in Great Britain 1945–49*, Dallas, Southern Methodist University Press, 1956.

Samuel, R., Kincaid, J., and Slater, E., 'But nothing happens', *New Left Review*, nos.13–14, January–April 1962, pp.38–69.

Saul, S.B., 'House building in England 1890–1914', *Economic History Review*, vol.15, no.1, 1962, pp.119–37.

Sharp, E., *The Ministry of Housing and Local Government*, London, Allen & Unwin, 1969.

Shelter, *A Better Place: the Story of the Holloway Tenant Co-operative*, London, Shelter, 1974.

Sigsworth, E.M., and Wilkinson, R.K., 'Rebuilding or renovation?' *Urban Studies*, vol.4, no.2, June 1967, pp.109–21.

Sigsworth, E.M., and Wilkinson, R.K., 'Rebuilding or renovation?: a rejoinder', *Urban Studies*, vol.7, no.1, February 1970, pp.92–4.

Silkin, L., *The Nation's Land*, London, Fabian Society, 1943.

Skinner, D., and Langdon, J., *The Story of Clay Cross*, Nottingham, Spokesman Books, 1974.

Smith, M.E.H., *Guide to Housing*, London, Housing Centre Trust, 1977.

Southwark CDP, *Housing for the Poor? Council Housing in Southwark*, London, Southwark CDP, 1975.

Stafford, D.C., *The Economics of Housing Policy*, London, Croom Helm, 1978.

Stedman Jones, G., *Outcast London: a Study in the Relationship between Classes in Victorian Society*, Oxford, Clarendon Press, 1971.

Stone, P.A., 'The economics of housing and urban development', *Journal of the Royal Statistical Society*, series A, vol.122, part 4, 1959.

Stone, P.A., *Urban Development in Britain: Standards, Costs and Resources, 1964–2004*, Cambridge, Cambridge University Press, 1970.

Stone, P.A., and Reiners, W.J., 'Organisation and efficiency of the housebuilding industry in England and Wales', *Journal of Industrial Economics*, vol.2, no.2, April 1954, pp.118–34.

Sutcliffe, A. (ed.), *Multi-storey Living: the British Working Class Experience*, London, Croom Helm, 1974.

Tarn, J.N., *Working Class Housing in 19th Century Britain*, London, Lund Humphries, 1971.

Tarn, J.N., *Five per cent Philanthropy: an Account of Housing in Urban Areas between 1840 and 1914*, Cambridge, Cambridge University Press, 1973.

Tilley, J., *Changing Prospects for Direct Labour*, London, Fabian Society, 1976.

Townroe, B.S., *Britain Rebuilding: the Slum and Overcrowding Campaigns*, London, Muller, 1936.

Tucker, J., *Honourable Estates*, London, Gollancz, 1966.

Turin, D.A. (ed.), *Aspects of the Economics of Construction*, London, Godwin, 1976.

Ungerson, C., *Moving Home: a Study of the Redevelopment Process in two London Boroughs*, London, Bell, 1971.

Ward, C. (ed.), *Vandalism*, London, Architectural Press, 1973.

Ward, C., *Tenants Take Over*, London, Architectural Press, 1974.

Ward, R., *Coloured Families in Council Housing*, Manchester, Manchester Council for Community Relations, 1971.

Webster, D., 'Council house costs: why we should all calm down', *Roof*, October 1975, pp.7–10.

Whitehead, C., *The U.K. Housing Market: an Econometric Model*, Farnborough, Saxon House, 1974.

Wicks, M., *Rented Housing and Social Ownership*, London, Fabian Society, 1973.

Widdowson, B., *Blunt Powers–Sharp Practices: Local Authorities' Policy on Homelessness*, London, Shelter, 1976.

Widdowson, B., 'Homeless Persons Act–present indicative in England', *Roof*, vol.3, no.1, January 1978, p.3.

Wilding, P., 'Towards Exchequer subsidies for housing 1906–14', *Social and Economic Administration*, vol.6, no.1, January 1972, pp.3–18.

Wilding, P., 'The Housing and Town Planning Act 1919: a study in the making of policy', *Journal of Social Policy*, vol.2, part 4, October 1973, pp.317–34.

Williams, F. (ed.), *Why the Poor Pay More*, London, Macmillan, 1977.

Willmott, P., *Evolution of a Community–a Study of Dagenham after Forty Years*, London, Routledge & Kegan Paul, 1963.

Wilson, R., *Difficult Housing Estates*, London, Tavistock, 1963.

Wohl, A.S., *The Eternal Slum: Housing and Social Policy in Victorian London*, London, Edward Arnold, 1977.

Wood End Tenants *et al.*, *Coventry Council Houses: the New Slums*, London, Shelter, 1974.

State papers

CHAC, *The Management of Municipal Housing Estates*, 1939.

CHAC, *Design of Dwellings*, 1944 (the Dudley Report).

CHAC, *Living in Flats*, 1952.

CHAC, *Transfers, Exchanges and Rents*, 1953.

CHAC, *Our Older Houses: a Call for Action*, 1966.

CHAC, *Council Housing: Purposes, Procedures and Priorities*, 1969.

Committee appointed by the President of the LGB etc., *Report*, Cd 9191, 1918 (the Tudor-Walters Report).

Committee on the Cost of House-building, *The Cost of Housebuilding*,
Reports in 1948, 1950 and 1952 (the Girdwood Reports).

Committee on the Placing and Management of Contracts for Building
and Civil Engineering Works, *Report*, 1964.

Committee on the Working of the Monetary System, *Report*,
Cmnd 827, 1959 (the Radcliffe Report).

DoE, *Fair Deal for Housing*, Cmnd 4728, 1971.

DoE, *The Estate outside the Dwelling: Reactions of Residents to
Aspects of Housing Layout*, 1972.

DoE, *Housing Condition Survey 1971 England and Wales*, 1973.

DoE, *Widening the Choice: the Next Steps in Housing*, Cmnd 5280,
1973.

DoE, *Better Homes: the Next Priorities*, Cmnd 5339, 1973.

DoE, Action Group on London Housing, *The Public Sector Housing
Pipeline in London*, 1976.

DoE, Study Group on Programmes of Social Ownership and
Renovation of Council Dwellings, *First Report*, 1976.

DoE, *Tenancy Agreements*, Report by the Housing Services Advisory
Group, 1977.

DoE, *Housing Policy: a Consultative Document*, Cmnd 6851, 1977
(with an accompanying technical volume in three parts).

DoE, The Development Management Working Group, *The Management
of Local Authority Housebuilding Programmes*, 1977.

HM Treasury, *Local Authority Borrowing*, Cmnd 2162, 1963.

House of Commons Select Committee on Estimates, *Housing Subsidies*,
Fourth Report for the Session 1968-69, 1969.

Local Government Board, *Memorandum No. 4 . . . of the Housing,
Town Planning, etc. Act, 1909*, 1915.

LCC, *Housing of the Working Classes in London 1855-1912*, 1913.

LCC, *Housing: with Particular Reference to Post-War Housing
Schemes*, 1928.

LCC, *Housing: a Survey of the Post-War Housing Work of the LCC
1945-49*, 1949.

MHLG, *The Density of Residential Areas*, 1952.

MHLG, *Houses: the Next Step*, Cmd 8996, 1953.

MHLG, *Slum Clearance (England and Wales)*, Cmd 9593, 1955.

MHLG, *Flatlets for Old People*, 1958.

MHLG, *Flats and Houses 1958: Design and Economy*, 1958.

MHLG, *Homes for Today and Tomorrow*, 1961 (the Parker Morris
Report).

MHLG, *Housing in England and Wales*, Cmnd 1290, 1961.

MHLG, *Housing Cost Yardstick for Schemes at Medium and High
Densities*, 1963.

MHLG, *Housing*, Cmnd 2050, 1963.

MHLG, *The Housing Programme 1965 to 1970*, Cmnd 2838, 1965.

MHLG, *The Deeplish Study: Improvement Possibilities in a District
of Rochdale*, 1966.

MHLG, *Housing Subsidies Manual: Housing Subsidies Act 1967*, 1967.

MHLG, *Old Houses into New Homes*, Cmnd 3602, 1968.

Ministry of Labour, *The Construction Industry*, Manpower Studies no.3, 1965.

Ministry of Public Building and Works, *A National Building Agency*, Cmnd 2228, 1963.

Ministry of Reconstruction, *Housing,* Cmd 6609, 1945.

NBPI, *Increases in Rents of Local Authority Housing,* Cmnd 3604, 1968 (accompanied by a Statistical Supplement, Cmnd 3604 I).

NBPI, *Pay and Conditions in the Building Industry*, Report no.92, Cmnd 3837, 1968.

National Consumer Council, *Behind with the Rent: a Study of Council Tenants in Rent Arrears*, London, NCC, 1976.

National Consumer Council, *Tenancy Agreements between Councils and their Tenants*, London, NCC, 1976.

National Economic Development Council, *The Construction Industry*, 1964.

National Economic Development Office Working Party, *The Public Client and the Construction Industries*, 1975.

National Economic Development Office, *Housing for All: a Document for Discussion*, 1977.

Poor Law Commissioners, *Report on an Inquiry into the Sanitary Condition of the Labouring Population of Great Britain*, 1842.

Report of the Committee of Inquiry under Professor E.H. Phelps Brown into Certain Matters concerning Labour in Building and Civil Engineering, Cmnd 3714, 1968.

Royal Commission on the Housing of the Industrial Population of Scotland, *Report,* Cd 8731, 1918.

Royal Commission on the Housing of the Working Classes, *Report*, 1885.

Royal Commission on the State of Large Towns and Populous Districts, *First Report*, 1844; *Second Report*, 1844–5.

Scottish Housing Advisory Committee, *Choosing Council Tenants*, 1950.

Scottish Housing Advisory Committee, *Allocating Council Houses*, 1967.

Scottish Housing Advisory Committee, *Housing Management in Scotland*, 1967.

Select Committee on the Health of Towns, *Report*, 1840.

Welsh Consumer Council, *Council Housing: a Survey of Allocation Policies in Wales*, Cardiff, Welsh Consumer Council, 1976.

Journals and series

Annual Bulletin of Construction Statistics.
CES Review.
CIPFA *Housing Management and Maintenance Statistics.*
CIPFA *Housing Statistics (England and Wales).*

Select bibliography

CIPFA *Return of Outstanding Debt.*
Community Action.
The Government's Expenditure Plans.
Handbook of Statistics.
Housing and Construction Statistics.
Housing Return for England and Wales.
Housing Return for Scotland.
Housing Review.
Housing Statistics Great Britain.
Local Government Board : Annual Reports.
Local Government Financial Statistics.
Local Housing Statistics England and Wales.
MoH Annual Reports.
MHLG Reports.
PWLB *Annual Reports.*
Roof.

Name index

General index

369